Sebastián Lerdo de Tejada, 1823–1889.

The Life of Sebastián Lerdo de Tejada
1823-1889

A Study of Influence and Obscurity

BY

FRANK AVERILL KNAPP, JR.

GREENWOOD PRESS, PUBLISHERS
NEW YORK   1968

Reprinted with the permission of
The University of Texas Press.

Reprint edition, 1968

LIBRARY OF CONGRESS catalogue card number: 68-23305

Printed in the United States of America

Table of Contents

PREFACE

There are some men who play long, vivid, and crucial rôles in history whose names are forgotten by the historians after them. Such a man was Sebastián Lerdo de Tejada. Not only is he unknown to the world at large, but his significance has been lost even to the vast majority of the Mexican people; yet Lerdo undoubtedly ranks among the foremost political figures of his nation during the turbulent nineteenth century. The intelligence behind Juárez's stubborn courage during the epoch of the French intervention, a leading proponent of liberalism, a proud nationalist in both domestic and international affairs, the holder of every political honor which his country could have conferred upon him—from congressional deputy to president—Lerdo, oddly enough, remains one of Mexico's forgotten patriots and statesmen.

The fundamental purpose of this monograph has been to present a complete and detailed study of the life of Lerdo, a task which was complicated because of gaps in essential source material. Unfortunately, the delicate balance between career and personality was virtually impossible: the more intimate keys to Lerdo the man, his habits, ambitions, ideals, and all those elements which motivate external actions were unreliable or missing altogether. Much of the personal aspect of his life has been reconstructed by necessarily indirect evidence and frequently by implication. But the dearth of information of this type was more than compensated by the fascinating relationships which connected him with practically every prominent Mexican of his day, from Santa Anna to Juárez and Díaz. Therefore, the story of Lerdo's life, while revealing a great deal of interesting and enlightening data concerning those with whom he associated, became a biography, to a large extent at any rate, through the study of others.

In contrast to his personal life, the political career of Lerdo for the years 1861 through 1876 could be drawn in detail from a storehouse of valuable material representing the remarkable development of journalism and historical interest during that period. It is interesting to note that many of the contemporary authors and publishers knew Lerdo personally and most of them were or became his political enemies.

In addition to the detailed factual reconstruction of Lerdo's life, a second objective of equal importance was an impartial analysis of his influence on the outstanding events and trends of the historical era which his life spanned: the Reform; the French intervention; reconstruction under the presidency of Juárez; and his own term as chief executive. Perhaps no nation has unfolded a more congested, complex, and colorful chronicle in the span of so few decades than Mexico, and a large part of the epoch corresponded to the political life of Lerdo. As a result, the biographical problem was compounded; but without losing perspective or omitting background explanation, it has been essential to remember that the emphasis rested upon Lerdo's part, not upon the general narrative of history. Although every aspect of his life has been neglected to date, there was a particular need for an unbiased interpretation of his presidency, since hostile writers under the influence of the Díaz régime have bequeathed a distorted heritage of that period to later historians. While the perspective was oriented consciously to bring out an understanding of Lerdo's position, there was no attempt to deify the subject, magnify his contributions, or mitigate his errors—and he made many.

Finally, there remained one question which the present study sought to answer: If a man is outstanding to the point of meriting a detailed investigation, in what manner could his life have become obscured and forgotten in little more than half a century after his death? The chronological development of his career will serve to explain the enigma, but from the outset certain basic factors which are responsible should be kept in mind.

First, Lerdo's departure from the Mexican political scene was in the rôle of defeat; and, from the Latin standpoint, that was an almost unpardonable manner of making an exit for one who desired to be remembered historically. Secondly, Lerdo's true influence was concealed between two more brilliant and durable personalities, Benito Juárez and Porfirio Díaz; and for more than one-third of a century of dictatorship under Díaz, the government directly or indirectly discouraged any favorable publications on his career. In addition, Lerdo spent the last thirteen years of his life in exile, a recluse with few visitors and friendship connections which waned as his years increased. A bachelor, without descendants to retain any kind of record of his personal life, polished, gracious, reserved, and proud, he was without military glory or any sensational qualities which appeal to Mexican biographers. Always a man in the background of political scenes, always exerting an almost imperceptible influence, Lerdo and his present historical obscurity can be understood only in the light of the above interlocking factors.

The investigation of the life of Sebastián Lerdo de Tejada was initiated in the fall of 1946 and has progressed more or less continuously since that date. For the completion of the undertaking the writer wishes to express his gratitude to Dr. Charles W. Hackett, the supervisor, for his constant and sustaining interest, for his helpful suggestions at all stages, and especially for the freedom which he has allowed in style and organization and selection of materials; to Dr. Carlos E. Castañeda, for first suggesting the topic and for his patient listening to the writer's problems over the course of many months; to Dr. Nettie Lee Benson, librarian of the Latin-American Collection, The University of Texas, for a multitude of helpful suggestions, for her unlimited courtesy and co-operation, for reading portions of the manuscript, and for her invaluable words of encouragement; to Dr. Wilbert H. Timmons of Texas Western University, who heard with patience and interest the writer's interminable discussions of the major and minor problems which he encountered at virtually every phase of the development of the subject; to Miss Edith Parker, who gave her limited time to read every page of the manuscript and who convinced the writer that it was not totally incoherent to one outside the field of Mexican history; to Dr. Gifford P. Orwen of Washington, D.C., for checking references not readily accessible to the writer; and to Miss Florence Escott, whose varied assistance defies all attempts at summarization. The writer also wishes to express a deep appreciation to all members of the supervisory committee, not simply for reading the finished product, but because their instruction, ideas, and example have contributed substantially, though indirectly perhaps, to whatever value the work may have.

Among other persons who should be mentioned here, without whom the listing would be even less complete, are: Licenciado Ernesto de la Torre Villar, formerly an assistant in the Archivo General de la Nación, Mexico, D.F.; all the living descendants of the family Lerdo de Tejada in Mexico who graciously made available to the writer what little they knew of their obscure relative; and to many other persons in Mexico who gave so freely of their time to aid a foreign student in every way possible.

In regard to certain members of his family, who can identify themselves without being mentioned specifically, the writer is conscious that their moral support and confidence in him provided the subjective impetus and necessary determination, not only to start a task but also to see it through to completion, despite the discouraging obstacles which arose along the way.

Finally, the writer is deeply grateful to Mrs. Martha Ann Zivley, who typed the excellent final copy and whose scrutiny uncovered various mechanical errors and inconsistencies which are bound to escape the closeness of a composer's perspective.

FRANK A. KNAPP, JR.

The University of Texas
Austin, Texas

Chapter I

Childhood and Early Education

Sebastián Lerdo de Tejada y Corral was born on April 24, 1823, in the provincial city of Jalapa, which lies among the mountains a few miles northwest of the port of Vera Cruz.[1] The event was no novelty in the Lerdo household, several other children having already blessed the productive marriage of Don Juan Antonio Lerdo de Tejada and Doña Concepción Corral y Bustillos. According to the baptismal record, which indicated that the parents were conscientious in complying with their religious obligations, Sebastián was taken to the Church of San José, duly baptized, christened, annointed, and provided with godparents one day after his birth.[2]

Unfortunately, it is possible to reconstruct only the most fragmentary outline of the family background. The father, Juan Antonio, was of pure Spanish descent, born in the village of Muro de Cameros in the province of Valladolid, Spain,[3] and hence he belonged to the privileged socio-political class known in the Indies as *gachupín*. Exactly why or when he came to New Spain are matters of conjecture: fortune, adventure, or any of a number of stimuli which had lured so many Europeans to the distant shores of the American Continent are possible reasons. At any rate, he settled in the bustling port of Vera Cruz (probably at the beginning of the nineteenth century), where he engaged in commerce and functioned in the capacity of a minor administrative official in the

---

[1]Both contemporary and secondary historians have been consistently inaccurate on the date of Lerdo's birth. A listing of the errors would form a bibliography in itself, but for a few examples, see Juan E. Pérez, *Almanaque de las Oficinas*, 223; Gustavo Baz, *Vida de Benito Juárez*, 256; H. H. Bancroft, *History of Mexico*, VI, 391.

[2]*Boletín Oficial del Consejo Superior de Gobierno del Distrito Federal*, III (September 27, 1904), 409. The baptismal record has also been published in Vicente de P. Andrade, *Partidas de Bautismo de Gobernantes de México*, No. XXII, 14; and *Diario del Hogar* (Mexico), May 11, 1889.

[3]Nicolás Paradinas, *Relación de Méritos y Exercicios Literarios del Doctor Don Ignacio Lerdo de Tejada y Matute . . .* , no page; P. Gerardo Decorme, S. J., *Historia de la Compañia de Jesús en la República Mexicana durante el Siglo XIX*, I, 122–123; César Sepúlveda, *Breves Notas Biográficas sobre D. Sebastián Lerdo de Tejada* (Typescript), 3. Ignacio Lerdo de Tejada, a famous cleric and scholar, was a younger brother of Juan Antonio.

R. B. Valenciano de Rhodo, who claimed to have been a frequent visitor of Sebastián Lerdo during his exile in New York, quoted him as saying: "I think and feel in the style of Old Castile, my descendancy being not very distant, my father being a son of Valladolid . . . ."—*D. Sebastián Lerdo de Tejada y la Misión de la América Española*, no page.

municipal government.[4] There he met and married Señorita Concepción Corral, also of pure Spanish blood, but of the *criollo* class, being a native of Vera Cruz.[5] Within the next few years, while Juan Antonio was a resident of the coastal city, the Lerdos had four or five children, among them Miguel, born July 6, 1812, and destined to precede his brother in a brilliant, yet brief political career.[6] Ultimately there were seven brothers and one sister, believed to rank in order of age as follows: Francisco, Ignacio, Pablo, Miguel, Juan, Sebastián, Angel, and Soledad.[7]

Around 1821, the year of Mexican independence, Juan Antonio moved to Jalapa,[8] long important strategically and commercially because of its position along the vital connecting route between the capital and the Atlantic coast. He abandoned his administrative post, possibly from necessity after the collapse of Spanish authority, to devote his full efforts to commerce, a change which apparently was accompanied by an improved financial status.[9]

The friendship alleged to have existed some years later between the Lerdo family and Antonio López de Santa Anna, the unique and notorious figure in Mexican history, may have had some basis in fact.[10] According to Manuel Rivera, Santa Anna was born in the

---

[4]Ernesto Alconedo, "Miguel Lerdo de Tejada," *Diez Civiles Notables de la Historia Patria*, 118. Ignacio Lerdo de Tejada passed through Vera Cruz in 1811 on his way to Mexico City and "spent some days in the house of his brother, a merchant in that city. . . ."—Decorme, *Historia de la Compañia de Jesús*, I, 123. At least, as late as 1821, Juan Antonio was a member of the *ayuntamiento* of Vera Cruz.—*Gaceta del Gobierno de México*, XII (March 29, 1821), 316–317.

[5]Ireneo Paz (ed.), "Angel Lerdo de Tejada," *Los Hombres Prominentes de México*, 159. Angel Lerdo, a younger brother of Sebastián, was a resident of Mexico City at the time this work was published and probably furnished the above information about his mother to the editor. Descendants of the Lerdo family whom this writer has visited confirm the above data regarding the parents.

[6]Unlike Sebastián, there is consistent agreement among authorities on the date of Miguel's birth; however, no complete biographies or even adequate sketches have been published on his life. For a brief outline, see Alconedo, *Diez Civiles Notables*, 117–126; Margarita Olivo Lara, "Biografías de Veracruzanos Distinguidos," *Anales del Museo Nacional de Arqueología, Historia y Etnografía*, VI (Cuarta Época, 1929), 159–161.

[7]This information was given to the writer by Sr. Juan Antonio Lerdo de Tejada y Sanz, grandson of Francisco, who is known to have been the eldest child.—Interview, Mexico, July 11, 1947. Angel was born in Jalapa, October 2, 1828.—Paz (ed.), *Los Hombres Prominentes de México*, 159. See also Ricardo Ortega y Pérez Gallardo, "Familia Sanz," in *Historia Geneológica de las Familias Más Antiguas de México*, III, 31, 32.

[8]Sepúlveda, *Breves Notas*, 3.

[9]*Ibid*. Miguel Trejo y Lerdo de Tejada, great-grandson of Miguel Lerdo, stated that the father, Juan Antonio, was moderately successful as a merchant in Jalapa.—Interview, Mexico, July 23, 1947.

[10]Blas José Gutiérrez and Flores Alatorre (eds.), *Leyes de Reforma, Colección de las Disposiciones Que se Conocen con Este Nombre, Publicados desde el Año de 1855 al de 1868*, II, 508 n.

house adjacent to the one which the Lerdos occupied in Jalapa for many years;[11] and there easily could have been an acquaintance between the two fathers, considering their common racial backgrounds and similar occupations.[12]

Obscurity surrounds not only the parentage but also the early years of Sebastián's childhood, important years which often leave an indelible stamp upon the pattern of a personality. Indeed, it is not until he emerges into manhood that his character can be drawn with any degree of completeness. He must have been witness to a number of interesting sights, however, for Jalapa was frequently a center of political intrigue during the sinuous early period of the Mexican nation. There, Anastasio Bustamante proclaimed the Plan of Jalapa in 1829, which was to lead to his presidency; and before Lerdo departed in 1836, Santa Anna had learned the valuable device of retiring to his nearby estate of Manga de Clavo to watch the current of popular opinion. Perhaps Lerdo as a child had gaped at the dashing hero as he rode through the streets of the city.[13] Although there was a local newspaper, a theater, and other forms of diversion, occasions such as these no doubt could set the townspeople buzzing for days. In addition, the regular passage of travelers, merchants, and foreign emissaries through Jalapa, coming or going between Mexico and Vera Cruz, would have been exciting events in the eyes of any small boy, lending something of a cosmopolitan aspect to the drabness and simplicity of routine provincial life. Rustic as it may appear by modern standards, Jalapa was one of the chief urban communities of early nineteenth-century Mexico.

There was no evidence of strong parental sway or in fact any intimate tie connecting Lerdo with other members of the family. Although Alconedo commented that the father's civic spirit was "vigorously influential" over Miguel, he did not elaborate,[14] nor was there reason to believe the same applied to Sebastián. That he was loyal to his family is indicated by a letter written several years later to the Minister of Justice in which he spoke of an ambition

---

[11]Rivera, *Historia Antigua y Moderna de Jalapa y de las Revoluciones del Estado de Veracruz*, I, 308.

[12]See Wilfrid Hardy Callcott, *Santa Anna, the Story of an Enigma Who Once Was Mexico*, 4.

[13]There appears to be but one anecdote extant on Lerdo's childhood in Jalapa and it is a fabrication, related in the apocryphal *Memorias Inéditas del Lic. Don Sebastián Lerdo de Tejada* (Novísima Edición, 1912), Segunda Parte, 69. The incident concerns the procession of President Guadalupe Victoria through Jalapa in April, 1829, a sight which Lerdo purportedly witnessed (at the age of four) supported on the shoulders of his brother Miguel, so that he could see above the crowd. Sebastián was six years old in April, 1829.

[14]Alconedo, *Diez Civiles Notables*, 118.

"to be useful to my family for whose service I have a saintly and imperious obligation to devote myself."[15]

On the other hand, the early home environment and training must have left a lasting impression in forming his standards of personal conduct. Soon after arriving at the seminary in Puebla, he distinguished himself, as will be shown, by unusual poise, courtesy, and manners. Furthermore, Don Juan Antonio and his wife may have encouraged Sebastián to enter the priesthood, a natural and customary thing at the time, especially since there were many sons in the family and since one of his uncles was an outstanding Jesuit of Mexico.[16] Certainly Sebastián's early study of Latin and theology pointed toward service in the church—a study which no doubt was promoted by his parents, possibly on the basis of his childhood aptitudes.

Under the private instruction of the parish priest, Francisco Ortíz de Loza, he began the study of Latin grammar while still very young, laying the cornerstone of an education which ultimately was to be the finest his country could offer. His natural ability for scholarship, one of his most valuable talents, was soon revealed, for he obtained a fellowship to the old and renowned Seminario Palafoxiano in Puebla.[17]

In the year 1836, he left Jalapa and the modest home on Royal Street[18] to begin his formal education, ending the period of close family supervision and relationship at the age of thirteen. A long unbroken path of study lay ahead under strict discipline and regimentation in the halls of theological colleges. Somber and colorless was all the youth of Sebastián Lerdo, and the effect upon his personality was enduring; but the reward was to be a vast knowledge, a

---

[15]Lerdo to the Minister of Justice, August 8, 1844, *Ynstrucción Pública* (MS.), LI, Archivo General de la Nación, Mexico (hereafter cited A.G.N.). The father died in late 1844 or early 1845, a fact revealed in a letter written from Rome by Lerdo's Jesuit uncle, Ignacio Lerdo (quoted by Decorme, *Historia de la Compañía de Jesús*, I, 405).

Sebastián once suggested that a great nephew, a descendant of the line of his oldest brother Francisco, be named Juan Antonio, after his (Sebastián's) own father.—Sebastián Lerdo to Francisco A. Lerdo, April 19, 1884. The letter is in possession of Juan Antonio Lerdo de Tejada y Sanz (Mexico, D.F.), whose name proves that Sebastián's request was fulfilled.

[16]Decorme, *Historia de la Compañía de Jesús*, I, 252, 296. Lerdo once mentioned his relative as "my uncle the Jesuit."—Lerdo to Mariano Riva Palacio, January 8, 1868, Mariano Riva Palacio Papers, Folder 170, University of Texas Archives (hereafter cited UT).

[17]Eduardo Ruíz, *Biografía del Ciudadano Melchor Ocampo*, 273. Lerdo himself spoke of that initial primary education as under a private tutor, without mentioning the priest's name.—Lerdo to the Minister of Interior and Exterior Relations, August 19, 1848, *Ynstrucción Pública*, XLIII, A.G.N.

[18]A diagram of the house was printed in *El Nacional* (Mexico), April 25, 1889, shortly after Lerdo's death.

discriminating taste, and, most important of all, a cultivated, incisive mind.

Of the fifteen years Lerdo devoted to formal education, five were spent at the seminary in Puebla, from September, 1836, until the close of 1841. An educational appendage of the church founded in 1604, the school had an ancient tradition. Under the guidance of zealous prelates, particularly Bishop Juan de Palafox y Mendoza, for whom the school was named, it had expanded rapidly in size and scope of instruction.[19] Primarily intended for the training of priests, the seminary was medieval in its educational concepts and its curriculum centered around a nucleus of theological exercises. Nevertheless, it must be remembered that the church, which held a virtual monopoly of education in Mexico during that period, offered the only educational opportunities worthy of the name.

Through strange coincidence, the archives of the three schools which Lerdo attended, including the seminary, have been lost or destroyed for the years when he was enrolled, but fortunately he left a detailed account of his literary career and achievements: an official letter which was a transcript of his complete school record, except for the final stage before he obtained his law degree. Upon this one invaluable document rests the reconstruction of much of his academic career.[20]

Soon after arriving at Puebla, he took entrance examinations over the entire field of Latin grammar and, in addition, over materials not required. The examining professors, duly impressed, qualified him "very well advanced, with very good extension; he spoke very well from memory. . . ." With this excellent beginning, Lerdo quickly became outstanding among his fellow students, amassing an impressive list of prizes and awards. During the five-year period, corresponding to the modern high school, through a sequence of courses including philosophy, physics, logic, ethics, metaphysics, arts, and theology, he never relaxed his diligence or application. Each year brought additional honors: in 1837, he passed philosophy "first in order and in honor"; in 1838, he shared a prize of books with two other students for the competition in logic, metaphysics, and ethics; and in the following year he and one

---

[19]Nicanor Quiroz y Gutiérrez, *Historia del Seminario Palafoxiano de Puebla, 1644–1944*, 10–73, *passim*.

[20]Lerdo to the Minister of Interior and Exterior Relations, August 19, 1848, *Ynstrucción Pública*, XLIII, A.G.N. Since Lerdo presented the data in application for one of the vacant professorships, it can be assumed that he omitted nothing which would have reflected to his credit. Of the absolute validity of the record, there can be no doubt, since it was certified by the secretary of the college as conforming to the official college record of examinations and other documents given to him by Lerdo.

other student gained the prize in physics. Thus the record runs for every year and every course without exception; and perhaps the highest honor came at the close of his preparation in Puebla when he composed and recited the Latin panegyric for a celebration held in the Convent of Santo Domingo. Soon afterwards, on completion of his final public examination at the seminary, he was named the "best student" by the general council of professors.[21]

A mere catalogue of courses and awards is insufficient to present a complete picture of Lerdo at Puebla. What sort of youth was he? What had been the effects of his home environment in the early years at Jalapa? As seen through the eyes of a fellow student, José María Bautista, he was a small boy of "the most privileged genius, the sparkle of knowledge ,the admiration of scientific notables . . . flattered by Bishop Vázquez and by Rector Gallo and all the superiors, the best liked of all the students."[22]

After the lapse of some forty years, Bautista still retained a vivid impression of one of the schoolboy incidents in which Lerdo played the leading rôle. It was the custom of the college to hold thirty-minute discussions each day in the patio to review various academic topics and to develop the students' abilities in philosophical argumentation and extemporaneous speaking.[23] Lerdo's subsequent renown for effective oratory undoubtedly sprang from this early practical experience at the seminary. Presumably during one of the sessions, the following incident, related by Bautista, developed:

. . . the professor who was a notable in science, was routed by you [Lerdo] in an address on a scientific question, to the point of not letting you leave, and, offended in his pride, he molested you unjustly, and this circumstance divided the group into two bands, one in favor of the master, directed by Manuel Zamacona; and the other supporting you: then I was on your side.

Without giving the dénouement of the episode, Bautista continued to elaborate upon the character of his friend:

. . . your grand talent, your manners, your education and delicacy elevated you to the first place in the consideration of all the college, and you knew how to preserve this preëminence with decorum and dignity: . . . [you were] a youth of order and morality, and honored to the point of escaping the jokes of the students . . . and in all your actions gleamed your discrimination, your gentlemanliness, your frankness.[24]

[21]Ibid.

[22]José María Bautista to Sebastían Lerdo, September 8, 1876, Memoria de la Academia Nacional de Historia y Geografía (No. 2, 1946), 47.

[23]See Quiroz y Guitérrez, Historia del Seminario Palafoxiano de Puebla, 72.

[24]José María Bautista to Lerdo, September 8, 1876, Memoria de la Academia Nacional de Historia y Geografía (No. 2, 1946), 47. It is interesting to note that Manuel María de Zamacona, one of the first in a long list of prominent figures whom Lerdo was to meet during his college career, eventually came to be his bitter political enemy. See below, p. 70ff.

Lerdo's close friendship with Bishop Pablo Vázquez, mentioned in Bautista's letter, was a rare exception in a life almost shorn of strong personal influences. The direct result was his acceptance of the minor orders and the donning of clerical vestments.[25] Perhaps the effects of the association were more lasting on his character traits and habits, or as an incentive to high standards of scholarship, than on his choice of profession. As early as 1841, he had rejected the idea of entering the priesthood, if such had ever been his intention, and in that year he departed for Mexico City to enter the College of San Ildefonso with the specific purpose of studying jurisprudence.[26]

---

[25]Enrique Gómez Haro, "Qué Frutas Ha Dado el Seminario Palafoxiano de Puebla?" *Palafoxianum* (Puebla, February–March, 1944), 28; [Salvador Quevedo y Zubieta], *Porfirio Díaz (Septiembre 1830–Septiembre 1865), Ensayo de Psicología Histórica*, I, 10. Bancroft mentioned that Lerdo studied theology under Bishop Vázquez, but did not comment on any personal association.— *History of Mexico,* VI, 391.

[26]Lerdo to the Minister of Interior and Exterior Relations, August 19, 1848, *Ynstrucción Pública*, XLIII, A.G.N. Bautista stated that Lerdo departed from Puebla because he did not want to enter the priesthood.—Bautista to Lerdo, September 8, 1876, *Memoria de la Academia Nacional de Historia y Geografía* (No. 2, 1946), 47. Presumably, the close connection with the Bishop and the consequent personal indebtedness became rather embarrassing under those circumstances.

Chapter II

Student and Professor:
The Early Years at San Ildefonso, 1841-1852

For twenty-two years, from 1841 until his flight from the capital in 1863, Lerdo was closely connected with the National College of San Ildefonso of Mexico, as a student, a professor, and finally, as rector. Thus, he reached the highest office, in a nonpolitical sense, during a rather remarkable educational career. The vital significance of this period should not be judged by the brief space allotted to it here, due to the lack of adequate source material; for the institution of San Ildefonso appeared to have been one of the greatest influences on his life. There he developed the good and bad aspects of a personality which crystallized early and was to react visibly on his political fortunes: the vast knowledge, the cultivated mind and taste, the cautious, legal approach; but also, the reserve, hauteur, subtle arrogance and pride—the natural offspring of scholastic brilliance—which later wounded or alienated important associates. There, too, he gained an unusually broad experience in administration, for the problems and duties of a rector were varied, a training in leadership, and invaluable associations which drew him toward the fascinating and precarious path of nineteenth-century Mexican politics.

Although Lerdo held high political offices prior to 1863, his connection with the college was continuous; and it is reasonable to assume that his primary interest was directed toward education, at least until as late as 1861. There was, however, a blending of politics in the later years of this phase of his life after he had assumed the rectorship, and that aspect will be presented in a later chapter. With this exception, Lerdo was completely divorced from the turbulent historical events commonly styled the "Epoch of Santa Anna" after the opportunist who dominated the myriad executive changes for more than two decades. Probably like the great majority of the Mexican populace, Lerdo seems to have been unconcerned with (and not directly affected by) the low level of personalized politics reflected in countless *cuartelazos,* most of which saw the periodic return of Santa Anna to the presidency. Since the final departure of Santa Anna from the Mexican political scene was almost coincident with Lerdo's first appearance, it is possible to turn an undivided attention toward the formation of a personality in the secluded atmosphere of a nineteenth-century Mexican college.

Out of this obscurity was to emerge one of Mexico's prominent liberal leaders.

The attainment of Mexican independence had not altered noticeably the rigid social concepts inherited from more than three hundred years of Spanish domination. Business pursuits remained somewhat stigmatized with a medieval disdain, or at best were generally not the means to prestige and power. For the man of ambition the choice was limited: the bureaucracy, the church, the army, and, to a lesser extent, the professions retained the loftiest social distinction and privileges. Any of these pursuits might be stepping stones to high political office. Perhaps conscious of the class system and having rejected an ecclesiastical career for unknown reasons, Lerdo arrived in Mexico in December, 1841, to begin a four-year course in jurisprudence at the National College of San Ildefonso.

He could not have made a better choice of schools, for San Ildefonso was the equal if not the best of all universities in Mexico at the time for the study of law and theology. Founded in 1573 and enlarged by the incorporation of minor colleges at various stages, it possessed an ancient tradition and a reputation for producing outstanding leaders in many fields.[1] Although the college had been nationalized shortly after independence, apparently this had little if any effect on the routine of student life or the general plan of studies. Embracing Jesuit traditions of discipline and strict regulation throughout its long history, San Ildefonso, during the years Lerdo attended, still emphasized theology as its principal course and subjected the students to an inflexible routine which included frequent religious exercises.

A detailed and comprehensive report submitted by the rector to the minister of Justice and Public Instruction in 1845 presented not only an interesting insight into higher education in the early days of the Mexican republic, but a view of the life Lerdo followed for so many years. The students entered either the major or minor faculty, depending upon age and previous education;[2] each lived in distinct parts of the solemn old building which housed the college; and each wore distinctive uniforms and followed a progressive plan

---

[1] For brief sketches of the founding and development of San Ildefonso, see Artemio de Valle-Arizpe, *Historia de la Ciudad de México según los Relatos de Sus Cronistas*, 402–410; Dr. Félix Osores, *Noticias Bio Bibliográficas de Alumnos Distinguidos del Colegio de San Pedro, San Pablo y San Ildefonso de México* [Genaro García (ed.), *Documentos Inéditos ó Muy Raros para la Historia de México*, XIX], pp. x–xi.

[2] Lerdo's schooling in Puebla corresponded to the *Colegio Chico o del Rosario* (minor faculty), and therefore he was entitled to begin with the work in the major faculty upon entrance.

of courses. The enrollment varied from time to time, but was generally around two hundred students of all classifications.

None escaped the hourly regimentation, although the younger group was even more closely supervised than the older. In the *Colegio Grande* (major faculty), in which Lerdo was enrolled from 1841 to 1845, the bell for rising rang at 6:30 A.M. and at 10:00 P.M. "no one may have light in his room." The hours between were distributed as follows: 7:00 A.M., mass; 8:00 to 8:30, study; 9:00 to 10:00, classes; 12:30 P.M., refectory; 3:00 to 3:30, study; 4:00 to 5:00, classes; 5:30 to 6:30, "study is permitted"; and at 7:30, rosary. Except for academy meetings, semi-formal instruction and discussion conducted in the evenings on Tuesday and Friday of each week, there was little variation of the routine.[3] One can readily perceive that spiritual exercises did not suffer neglect from over-emphasis on classroom work. But this was natural, since San Ildefonso had long been a Jesuit organ, and the rector, even in Lerdo's student days, was a priest.[4]

Despite the outward appearance, the regimen of the college was not reactionary or confining in scholastic rules and principles of instruction. In fact, José María Iglesias, a fellow student of Lerdo's at San Ildefonso, commented on the progressive spirit of the institution as evidenced by the adoption of reforms of various kinds, such as the substitution of modern for classical authors. Iglesias recognized that this educational environment was one of the main sources of his liberal ideas, and the same may have been true of Lerdo.[5]

The early scholastic habits formed at Puebla served Lerdo well in his four years of study of jurisprudence at San Ildefonso. Although he did not list all his courses individually in the letter containing his educational record,[6] the plan of studies for the course of jurisprudence included international, public, and natural law and the elements of Roman law during the initial two years; while civil, criminal, and canon law comprised the fields for the final two years. In addition, since 1843, all students in either of the major faculties (law or theology) were required to study French.[7]

---

[3]"Colegio Nacional de S. Yldefonso, Documentos," March 4, 1845, *Ynstrucción Pública*, XLII; "Presente Distribución de Horas de los Estudiantes," Rector de San Ildefonso, July 30, 1849, *ibid.*, XLIII, A.G.N.

[4][Quevedo y Zubieta], *Porfirio Díaz*, I, 10.

[5]José María Iglesias, *Autobiografía del Sr. Lic. D. José M. Iglesias*, 11. The alumni of San Ildefonso often referred to themselves as *gregorianos;* and later an organization of that name was formed. See "Algunos Gregorianos Ilustres," *Boletín Oficial* (April 29, 1910) in which both Iglesias and Lerdo were listed.

[6]Lerdo to the Minister of Interior and Exterior Relations, August 19, 1848, *Ynstrucción Pública*, XLIII, A.G.N.

[7]"Colegio Nacional de San Ildefonso, Documentos," March 4, 1845, *ibid.*, XLII, A.G.N.

To excel at jurisprudence one must have not only a natural bent toward analysis but also a sincere fascination for the subject. It is tedious, meticulous, often incomparably dull, and exacting to the point of exasperation; yet perhaps no other field provides a more thorough mental discipline or greater training in the exercise of careful evaluation. The admirable record which Lerdo left in his legal courses attested to both the inherent qualifications he possessed and the genuine liking for his choice of profession. As at Puebla, he managed to monopolize the highest awards and ratings, setting a precedent in 1843 by winning the prize of law conferred by the junta of professors, an unusual distinction which had not been granted previously to students in the second year of legal study. The final two years, in which Lerdo led his class, were merely the continuance of the outstanding position he had retained among his classmates with a consistency which no doubt was galling to some of the less zealous among them.

Nor were these all his claims to superiority. Frequently the faculty selected him for debating in the college conferences, after which he was often rated "excellent" by a unanimous vote of the professors.[8] Years later Lerdo was to realize the practical benefit of his oratorical ability as applied to politics, an ability which probably stemmed from the classes in rhetoric at Puebla and the periodic experience in public speaking and argumentation at San Ildefonso.

Again, the enumeration of honors which Lerdo related was less impressive than the description of his old classmate, José María Bautista, who also attended San Ildefonso for a brief period. Recalling those distant school days, he wrote Lerdo:

. . . and not wanting to become a cleric you abandoned Puebla [i.e., the seminary], and passed to the college of San Ildefonso, in the capital, where just as at the seminary, but with keener competition, you sparkled to advantage at the side of men of science: I followed you there, and again we came to be fellow students in the study of law, under the noted professors D. Juan B. Morales and D. Miguel Atristain, and Lerdo [was] always the same, that is, the first of all the students. You progressed as a model of virtues. . . .[9]

But outstanding scholastic achievement frequently exacts a high penalty in the deep stamps it leaves on a personality. While all authorities, including those prejudiced against him, concede to Lerdo an exceptionally keen intelligence, none has marked him a genius. Consequently, the attempt to achieve a first place in all the classes—and he seemed to have approached the goal—must have demanded an almost monkish devotion to books. Lerdo himself,

---

[8]Lerdo to the Minister of Interior and Exterior Relations, August 19, 1848, *ibid.*, XLIII, A.G.N.

[9]Bautista to Lerdo, September 8, 1876, *Memoria de la Academia Nacional de Historia y Geografía* (No. 2, 1946), 47.

in mentioning his "incessant application" to studies, tacitly admitted that the maintenance of his academic standing had been something of an ordeal.[10] When the picture of Lerdo the man assumes a more positive form in a later period, it is difficult not to believe that the sober and reserved lines in which it is revealed can be traced to those years of theological discipline and countless hours poring over books, to the neglect of lighter diversions which normally accompany youth. Sepúlveda is probably accurate in stating that Lerdo made few close friends at the college, excepting Romero Rubio, because of his isolation in a dismal room on the Calle Seminario and his inherent aloofness of character.[11]

Nor were these years free of financial worries, possibly another factor which, by touching his sensitive pride, forced Lerdo to retire from companionship to the more solitary path of scholarship. This trait of self-sufficiency was later to be the foundation for sustaining his pride during thirteen bitter years of exile outside a Mexico which was all he had ever known or ever cared to know. Although the evidence regarding monetary worries is indirect, it is nevertheless convincing. The importunity of earning a living is about the only logical reason for his long delay in completing the requirements for the degree of *licenciado*. In August, 1844, Lerdo filed a plea for exemption from a portion of the regular training in legal theory, since he had already faced innumerable obstacles—almost enough to force him to abandon his studies and thus endanger his entire career. If that should occur, he commented, "the many and best years of my youth [would be] absolutely lost. . . ." Not failing to remind the minister of Public Instruction of his fine academic record, he further explained that the reason for his request was the cost of an extended education, complicated by "so long a period of time, changes so diverse and unexpected, which could not be obviated by even the most penetrating foresight."[12] Lack of funds was probably responsible for postponement of his public examination at the conclusion of his fourth year of law, which he should have upheld in November, 1845, but postponed "because of some private circumstances which prevented it."[13]

---

[10]Lerdo to the Minister of Justice and Public Instruction, August 8, 1844, *Ynstrucción Pública*, XLI, A.G.N.

[11]Sepúlveda, *Breves Notas*, 3–4. The Calle Seminario is within four blocks of the National Preparatory School which today occupies the building of the old College of San Ildefonso. It is possible Sepúlveda obtained the location of Lerdo's student address from the *Memorias Inéditas del Lic. D. Sebastián Lerdo de Tejada*, Primera Parte, 33. Sometime after 1845, Lerdo terminated his rooming arrangements at the college and moved to a private residence, probably in the vicinity of the school.—Lerdo to the Minister of Interior and Exterior Relations, March 9, 1848, *Ynstrucción Pública*, XLIII, A.G.N.

[12]Lerdo to the Minister of Justice and Public Instruction, August 8, 1844, *Ynstrucción Pública*, XLI, A.G.N.

[13]Lerdo to the Minister of Interior and Exterior Relations, August 19, 1848, *ibid.*, XLIII, A.G.N.

Judging by his frequent applications for a position, Lerdo, as early as 1845, had determined to be a college professor as well as a lawyer, and the former pursuit seemed to hold his primary interest. Immediately after receipt of the bachelor's degree in late 1845, he filed for a vacant professorial chair, although he had to console himself with a second place.[14] Still, the junta of professors, which selected the men to fill vacancies after due consideration of applicants,[15] had acknowledged Lerdo's aptitudes by rating him second among the candidates, since he was only twenty-two years of age at the time.

Meanwhile, Lerdo began the two-year course in the *Academia de Teórica Práctica*,[16] required of all students intending to take the degree of *licenciado*, and he completed this prerequisite by 1848. His list of honors, which had reached the point of monotony, was further inflated by his work at the *Academia*. At the close of his first year of study he was named to deliver the annual discourse at the opening of the new sessions in January, 1847. In a training school where much of the time was devoted to public speaking and judicial argumentation, that was no small recognition of his ability in the practice of rhetoric; and, as Lerdo observed, it proved he could win distinction not only at San Ildefonso but in competition with the young legal aspirants from all parts of the city as well.[17]

The years after he received his bachelor's degree were indeed crowded ones. Having been unsuccessful in his original application for a professorship, he obtained an appointment (September, 1846) as substitute to *Licenciado* Guillermo Valle, who held the chair of Latin grammar at San Ildefonso. In early 1848, he became the substitute in the course of canon law for his old professor Juan B. Morales, then a magistrate of the Supreme Court of Justice. Since this was a class of the major faculty, it represented a definite advancement, corresponding to the university level of studies.[18]

Those positions were honorific, and, in fact, an expense to the holder which Lerdo could ill afford. Being officially connected with

[14]Rector to the Minister of Justice and Public Instruction, December 21, 1845, *ibid.*, XLII, A.G.N.

[15]Approval of the president through the office of the Minister of Justice was a mere formality, the government never tampering with the recommendations for appointment made by the junta. The freedom from political influence in that regard is worthy of note.

[16]In addition to the classroom work of the academy, the law required students of jurisprudence, at this stage of training, to become apprentices or assistants of recognized lawyers.—"Plan General de Estudios," August 18, 1843, *Colección de los Decretos y Órdenes de Interés Común, 1839–1848*, III, 100.

[17]Lerdo to the Minister of Interior and Exterior Relations, August 19, 1848, *Ynstrucción Pública*, XLIII, A.G.N.

[18]Lerdo to the Minister of Interior and Exterior Relations, August 19, 1848, *ibid.*, XLIII, A.G.N.

the college, although he had completed his studies and was living elsewhere, he had to meet regular pension payments. In early 1848, he requested release from all his back payments and exemption from those in the future while he continued to teach, since, as he explained, only "in the character of an individual of the establishment can I contribute my small services." He remarked, too, that he had no pecuniary interest and realized that the honor attached to the position of substitute teacher was far above his own merits.[19] If the tone was affectedly modest, it could not be doubted that his ambition to become a professor was a determined one.

Whenever there was a vacant chair between 1845 and 1848, Lerdo missed no opportunity to file his own application—for the courses of arts, philosophy, Latin grammar, and civil law; but he never advanced beyond the second choice among the candidates. Perhaps in sympathy or in admiration of his dogged perseverance, the rector filed a statement with the secretary of the junta of professors so that the distinguished career of the young alumnus might be kept on record and his talents utilized at the earliest opportunity.[20] Either the junta became embarrassed by the frequent rejections of one of the outstanding ex-students or the letter of recommendation was effective, for within three and one-half months after Lerdo's last unsuccessful application, he was officially confirmed in the chair of Arts and was scheduled to assume his duties as a full professor for the session beginning January 1, 1849. Considering his persistent efforts to win a spot on the faculty, that there were only two competitors, including himself, should not have rendered the prize less valuable.[21] It will be remembered that he was but twenty-five at that time, which may have been responsible for the reluctance of the junta to concede him the honor on past occasions. From the practical standpoint, the annual salary of 650 pesos probably meant a degree of security which he had not hitherto known.[22]

In striking contrast to the delayed opening of his educational career, once launched, Lerdo's rise in the college was spectacular. Before he was twenty-seven years of age and before he had received the degree of *licenciado*, he was promoted to the major faculty to

[19]Lerdo to the Minister of Interior and Exterior Relations, March 9, 1848, *ibid.*, XLIII, A.G.N.

[20]Rector to the Minister of Interior and Exterior Relations, September 2, 1848, *ibid.*, XLIII, A.G.N.

[21]Rector to the Minister of Interior and Exterior Relations, November 22, 1848, *ibid.*, XLIII, A.G.N.; Minister of Interior and Exterior Relations to Rector of San Ildefonso, November 25, 1848, *ibid.*, XLIII, A.G.N.

[22]By the rates effective in 1845, a professor holding a chair of the major faculty received 850 pesos annually, while those of the minor faculty received 650 annually. The highest remuneration—1,300 pesos—was attached to the rectorship.—"Colegio Nacional de San Ildefonso, Documentos," March 4, 1845, *ibid.*, XLII, A.G.N.

teach the first year of jurisprudence. Although there were no other applicants for the chair at the time the vacancy occurred, the rector, in submitting Lerdo's name for official confirmation, hastened to add that the professors had "qualified him very worthy of discharging the professorship."[23]

The courses included in the first two years of jurisprudence were natural law, international and public law, principles of legislation, and the elements of Roman law.[24] Undoubtedly, those years as a professor, during which Lerdo taught in diverse fields, vastly augmented a long formal education under highest contemporary standards. No broader groundwork could have been laid for the political career which was to follow. When later he was described as a man of vast intelligence, of a trained and cultivated mind, or cultured taste; when he was admired for his parliamentary skill, his diplomatic finesse, or his logic in debate, it was probable that the roots of those qualities lay in the obscure period of his life as a teacher and a student.

While Lerdo had long since completed the required residence work for the law degree, it was not until October 14, 1851, at the age of twenty-eight, that he passed the bar examinations.[25] He must have reflected with satisfaction over the last achievement of his formal education, for the years since Jalapa and the childhood study of Latin had been many and arduous. He was no longer a youth but a mature man filling a responsible position.

In addition to his teaching duties, Lerdo assumed another important office at the College of San Ildefonso. Sometime in the latter part of 1850, although the exact date is unknown,[26] he became the secretary. It was a valuable function for the intimate knowledge

---

[23]Rector to the Minister of Relations, April 3, 1850, *ibid.*, LX, A.G.N. The draft manuscript of the confirmed appointment, issued in the name of the President of Mexico, General José Joaquín Herrera, is dated April 10, 1850.— *Ibid.*, LX, A.G.N.

[24]Lerdo's appointment did not state specifically which chair of jurisprudence he was to hold; however, an official report of an inspection of the college held in December, 1851, listed his position as "First Year of Jurisprudence."— "Colegio Nacional de San Ildefonso. Lista de los Sres. Empleados y Catedráticos," February 16, 1852, *ibid.*, LX, A.G.N.

[25]*Libro Donde se Asientan las Matrículas de los Individuos de Este Ilustre Nacional Colegio de Abogados* (MS.), 18, Archivo del Nacional e Ilustre Colegio de Abogados, Mexico. The entry was signed by Lic. M. Buenrostro with a reference to the "book 39" for the examination paper. That record is missing. A series of account books showed Lerdo's signature and his regular payments of monthly dues, indicating continuous attendance at the meetings where lawyers from all parts of the city gathered. A large portrait of Lerdo hangs in the building which now houses the organization.

[26]On November 20, 1850, Lerdo certified, as secretary, an application written by one Ysidoro Guerrero to the Minister of Interior and Exterior Relations.— *Ynstrucción Pública*, LX, A.G.N. That was the first correspondence discovered by the writer in which Lerdo signed with the title "secretary."

which the holder gained of the varied details and problems connected with the administration of the college. Actually, the secretary was the first assistant of the rector. Perhaps the experience
qualified him, despite his youth, for consideration when the rectorship was left vacant in June, 1852, by the death of the elderly José
María Guzmán. Thus, in the brief period of three and one-half
years—almost as long as he had waited for his first professorial
appointment—Lerdo attained the highest position in the college.

Chapter III

The Rectorship of San Ildefonso, 1852-1863

It is difficult to dispense, in a few terse sentences, with the Mexican political maze during the years 1852 to 1863, when Lerdo was rector of San Ildefonso. The resignation of Mariano Arista from the presidency was followed by the last of Santa Anna's dictatorships; then came the Revolution of Ayutla and the launching of a drastic set of reforms, cutting deep into the traditional economic, political, and religious foundations of Mexican life. To Ignacio Comonfort fell the responsibility of guiding the nation through that hurricane of transition, perhaps an assignment too unbounded for any man. In the tragedy of Comonfort's vacillation and fall in 1858 was discovered the occasion for the outbreak of the embittered era of internecine strife known as the War of the Reform, when the conservative and liberal elements fought another but still not decisive round in their ancient struggle over concepts of church, state, and society, and for control of the machinery of government.

Those were the times which made great men, when those with convictions, conscience, or personal interests found compromise impossible. Among such men, none was more acrimoniously condemned nor more fulsomely praised, by the extremists of the conservative and liberal groups, than Miguel Lerdo de Tejada, one of Sebastián's older brothers. In his fertile brain was conceived the law which struck the root of the church's power over the state—its stranglehold on the nation's economic wealth—and in part roused the conservatives to make their final effort to maintain a régime of privilege and caste. More will be said of Miguel's brilliance in a later portion of this work. What of Sebastián? What part did he play during the time of troubles, while his brother rose to a deserved fame as one of the idols of the reform element? In general, his was the quiet rôle of rector of San Ildefonso, an obscure, undramatic routine which seemed to hold his interest and absorb his chief energies. As already pointed out, that office was not political, but the occupant inevitably came into constant contact with the central government for the obvious reason that San Ildefonso was a national college under the supervision of one of the secretaries of State, usually that of Justice.

What a valuable history Sebastián might have written as a contemporary observer during that chaotic period, watching the confusing changes in cabinets, the rise and fall of many governments.

As rector, he was a subordinate of the administrations of Mariano
Arista, Santa Anna, Juan Álvarez, Ignacio Comonfort, Félix
Zuloaga, Miguel Miramón, and Benito Juárez; he had seen old professors, friends, and students leave the college for a plunge into
the swirling current of politics. He himself had tested the water,
but no more than to dampen his feet. His political activities, at
least until 1861 when Juárez returned in triumph to Mexico City,
were ancillary and even insignificant when compared to those of
his brother Miguel. But it is not to be forgotten that he was "testing
the waters," occasionally functioning in a dual rôle as a government
official and a college rector. Nevertheless, he always found the
rectorship a neutral bastion in which he might retire behind a protective shield of political anomaly; and he retained the post until
he fled from Mexico City with the Juárez government at the approach of the French intervention troops in May, 1863.

To understand the nature and scope of the rectorship of San
Ildefonso in 1852, one must relieve his mind of almost a century of
educational advances. In the college which Lerdo supervised, there
was no multitude of students in pursuit of varied professional,
scientific, and liberal arts careers; no bulky catalogue containing
numerous courses to confuse the student; and no elaborate physical
plant or complex administrative machinery. San Ildefonso averaged
about 250 students during the last period of its existence,[1] ranging
from children in their early teens to young men in their twenties.
It was possible to enter at about age twelve and continue through
the degree of doctor of theology or law.

The rector was no specialist. His office held much prestige, but
procured for him a low income of 1,350 pesos annually,[2] a characteristic of the educational field which is not peculiar to any age or
country. Yet he was relatively free from outside controls, except
for what was in fact a nominal supervision of the central government. Indeed, so wide was his range of responsibility that he might
be depicted as operating a sort of benevolent despotism within a
limited sphere, with the characteristic paternalism revealing itself

---

[1]In a report to the Minister of Justice, dated January 30, 1854, Lerdo (Sebastián) listed 249 students in all branches of study.—*Ynstrucción Pública,*
LXII, A.G.N. For a comparison of the enrollment of all nine national colleges
in Mexico City in 1856, see Miguel Lerdo de Tejada, *Cuadro Sinóptico de la
República Mexicana en 1856* . . . , 71.

[2]This figure may be found in any of the monthly budget reports of the college in *Ynstrucción Pública,* A.G.N., and is also included in the official certificates of Lerdo's appointments to the rectorship. One of these is signed by
Mariano Arista, June 1, 1852, and the other by Santa Anna, December 30,
1854, the second being a perfunctory confirmation of the office. Both originals
are in the possession of Sr. Angel Lerdo de Tejada, Mexico, D.F.

through the authority he held over the private lives of the students. By way of compensation for the modest salary, the rector seemed to have a security of tenure which, in Lerdo's case, was completely unaffected by political changes. His predecessor, José María Guzmán, had also served an extended term, from 1829 until his death in 1852.[3]

In retrospect Lerdo's succession to the vacant office seems remarkable, since he had just passed his bar examinations the previous year. A closer view will show, however, that it was not so facile a matter as stepping from a student's shoes into those of a college rector, although some writers have left that impression.[4] While Lerdo's final educational step had long been deferred—the bar examination for the degree of *licenciado*—meanwhile he had gained much practical educational and administrative experience through his teaching positions and as secretary to Rector Guzmán. Thus he was a qualified and logical candidate for the office left vacant by the death of the elderly incumbent on May 18, 1852.[5] Furthermore, when the junta of professors met to select three candidates for the perfunctory approval of the government, as was the custom in filling vacant offices, Lerdo was not the first but the second choice on the panel.[6] After the preferred nominee declined, the Minister of Relations ordered a second convocation of the junta, and on that occasion Lerdo moved into first place among the three candidates proposed.[7]

Within a few days, President Mariano Arista confirmed the appointment,[8] and Lerdo accepted "so honorable a distinction" with a humility which revealed the depth of his satisfaction in obtaining the position. He promised to procure, to the extent of his meager

[3]Vice-Rector of San Ildefonso to the Minister of Relations, May 18, 1852; June 3, 1852, *Ynstrucción Pública*, LX, A.G.N.

[4]Pérez, *Almanaque de las Oficinas*, 223; *Sebastián Lerdo de Tejada (1823–1889), In Memoriam*, 27–28; *El Nacional*, April 22, 1889.

[5]Vice-Rector to the Minister of Relations, May 18, 1852, *Ynstrucción Pública*, LX, A.G.N. Francisco Guerrero Moctezuma, a student under Lerdo at San Ildefonso, indicated that he (Lerdo) was the real supervisor in the period prior to the actual appointment: "D. Sebastián Lerdo de Tejada, cuando se recibió de abogado, fué ya definitivamente Rector de San Ildefonso. . . ."— "El Colegio de San Ildefonso en 1847, según un Colegial de Entonces," *Boletín de la Escuela N. Preparatoria* (Número Extraordinario, 1909), 24.

[6]Vice-Rector to the Minister of Relations, May 12, 1852, *Ynstrucción Pública*, LX, A.G.N. The junta met in anticipation of Guzmán's death.

[7]José Urbano Fonseca to the Minister of Relations, May 26, 1862; Minister of Relations to the Vice-Rector of San Ildefonso, May 26, 1852; Vice-Rector of San Ildefonso to the Minister of Relations, May 27, 1852, *ibid.*, LX, A.G.N.

[8]Minister of Relations to the Vice-Rector of San Ildefonso, June 1, 1852, *ibid.*, LX, A.G.N. A draft copy of the appointment, entitled "Nombramiento de Rector del Colegio de San Ildefonso á Favor del Lic. D. Sebastián Lerdo de Tejada," may be found in *ibid.*, LX. The original has been cited previously (p. 18n).

ability, the major well-being of the establishment and hoped that his additional efforts might "in some manner compensate for [his] lack of merit."[9] Perhaps it was of little consequence that the press grumbled about the victory of youth over age and seniority in filling the rectorship,[10] yet it should be remembered that there was an admixture of chance and good fortune along with merit and unquestioned ability which made possible the promotion of a man scarcely twenty-nine years old.

The study of Lerdo as rector of San Ildefonso offers an enticing bypath along which one might pause to view the interesting conditions of Mexican education in the middle nineteenth century; but the primary object is to see the character and ability of Lerdo in his performance of a variety of routine duties. None is perhaps more important nor more enlightening than the continuous problem of discipline which involved not only the students but the compact staff of professors and assistants as well.

Lerdo was not to wait long before he faced his first and probably most serious crisis in maintaining the order and reputation of San Ildefonso. Between the dates of his appointment and formal assumption of duties,[11] two serious outbreaks occurred in the college, unprecedented eruptions involving three professors and a student. When the smoke had cleared from the clash of four hasty tempers, there had been two scandalous incidents of open fisticuffs! The causes of those undignified happenings were trivial and not without a touch of humor: in the first case, one teacher allegedly had cast aspersions during his lecture upon the abilities of a colleague, and, in the second, a student had removed a chair from the classroom without permission. Lerdo was quick to sense, in his initial rôle as dispenser of justice, that the keystone of order in the school and his future reputation were at stake. Without the prestige of age and just entering upon his new duties, he resolved a delicate and tense situation with admirable firmness.

He convened the junta of professors and one by one the guilty parties were summoned to appear before that body. After a solemn discussion and a secret ballot on the matter, the junta suspended the three professors for brief periods and pronounced the maximum penalty of permanent expulsion for the student, one Jiménez by name.

But the end of the affair was not yet. After the decisions were announced to the student body, "united in the general hall," several

---

[9]Lerdo to the Minister of Relations, June 2, 1852, *ibid.*, LX, A.G.N.

[10]*El Omnibus* (Mexico), June 2, 1852. Reprint of an article in *El Universal* (Mexico).

[11]The ceremony giving formal possession of the rectorship took place on June 19.—Lerdo to the Minister of Relations, June 19, 1852, *Ynstrucción Pública*, LX, A.G.N.

of the older members organized a movement of passive resistance, remaining in their rooms in protest, and drafted a petition to the government requesting revocation of the student's punishment, by-passing the rector's authority.

Lerdo's hand was now forced, but he proved that he would brook no such open insurrection. Having imposed "severe yet prudent penalties" upon those responsible for the final outburst, he called upon the Minister of Relations to support him in those measures, since the scandal demanded "a healthful example to reëstablish discipline in the college." In his lengthy report on the sequence of events, he pointed out that the combined sentences had already produced "results which are noted in the courteous and respectful manners of the students and the regular exactitude with which they already comply with their duties." No one was more cognizant than Lerdo of the seriousness of a sentence of expulsion to a law student who was approaching the close of his academic requirements; "nevertheless," he insisted, "I do not hesitate to ask you [the Minister of Relations] to be kind enough not to accede to the solicitude of the student Don Manuel Jiménez, in the interest of the superiors of the establishment and of the efficiency and good effect of their resolutions."[12] Reeking with importunity, his report displayed a quality of will and decision characteristic of the man, unswerving and often brittle. His sense of justice was imbedded in a mould which allowed for little flexibility. One should not encroach upon a future episode far removed in time and far different from the above incidents, but there remains a striking similarity between Lerdo's stance here and his attitude many years later when a life was at stake—that of an idealistic adventurer who was wont to style himself the Emperor Maximilian of Mexico.

The dramatic situation which Lerdo encountered at the outset of his administration was not typical of the ordinary problem of discipline. While he demanded obedience, he was neither harsh nor did he invariably impose the most severe penalty for a breach of regulations. For example, a student was suspended one month for absenting himself without permission, yet Lerdo might have applied a doubly severe penalty for that violation.[13] Still, he was a firm believer in subordination and ever on the lookout for misconduct which might serve as a precedent for future difficulties.

One thing he refused to tolerate in any form was the violation of rules, which probably revealed the influence of his legal training. Inured to many years of strict educational discipline and having a perfect record of conduct himself, he was, in a sense, justified in demanding conformity and obedience from his charges. The college had a set of by-laws governing the various phases of student life

---

[12]Lerdo to the Minister of Relations, June 20, 1852, *ibid.*, LX, A.G.N.
[13]Lerdo to the Minister of Justice, October 21, 1854, *ibid.*, LXII, A.G.N.

and internal administration, and Lerdo cited them constantly in his official correspondence. The laws were not sacred nor inalterable, but until amended or abrogated they must be obeyed to the letter without exception.

On taking possession of the rectorship, Lerdo discovered that there had been some laxness in enforcing the rules governing the curfew hour for the honor students who held special privileges in regard to entry and departure. While ordering a strict conformity, he also entertained a request of those students to extend the time of the curfew, discussed the subject with the junta of professors, and, when they "justly" agreed that no undue harm would result, he modified the older regulations. This change was effected, however, in a strictly "constitutional" way and with a due saving of the rector's prerogative to give the final assent.[14]

In handling requests and solicitations, Lerdo showed a familiarity with particular cases; and the college enrollment was not so large that he would have been precluded from maintaining a fairly close scrutiny over individual students. A Javert in following the letter of the law, he was human enough to discern mitigating circumstances and to reward attitude when ability seemed to be lacking. Once an unhappy father petitioned for reëntry of his habitually failing son, José M. Vargas.[15] Lerdo replied that "by Article 73" of the regulations, a student who had failed the examinations for a course twice in the same year could not be readmitted without special dispensation of the government. "Nevertheless, that young man has always observed very good conduct, has manifested some application recently, and is of tender age, which circumstances may be considered by Your Excellency, if you so desire, in resolving his solicitude."[16]

But when a student sought equity from Lerdo, it was almost certain he had to appear with clean hands in order to hope for a chance of success. Lack of industry was for him sufficient grounds to reject a scholarship application, even though the continuation of the student's education depended upon obtaining a subsidy.[17]

Occasionally there were young men whose personalities could not be moulded by the orthodox methods of discipline. If one can trust an anecdote related by Salvador Quevedo y Zubieta, Lerdo possessed

[14]Lerdo to the Minister of Relations, July 5, 1852, *ibid.*, LXI, A.G.N.

[15]The father's petition was filed with the government and forwarded to Lerdo for action.—Minister of Justice to the Rector of San Ildefonso, February 13, 1858, *ibid.*, LXXV, A.G.N.

[16]Lerdo to the Minister of Justice, February 13, 1858, *ibid.*, LXXV, A.G.N.

[17]Antonio Tapia to Mariano Riva Palacio, April 12, 1860, Mariano Riva Palacio Papers, Folder 169, UT. Tapa requested that Riva Palacio interpose his influence with Lerdo and others in behalf of his son's application: "It appears to me that the first-mentioned person [*i.e.*, Lerdo] has denied the grant which I am requesting, because of the lack of application of my son. . . ."

a subtle sarcasm and a keen perception of human nature which equipped him for dealing with the unique. As the story goes, a wealthy young man, dressed like a dandy and with a manner as blatant as his taste, arrived to enroll in the college. The second time he passed the Rector in the halls and failed to observe the proper courtesies, Lerdo casually withdrew a coin from his pocket and ordered the newcomer to dash off to a nearby shop and purchase a few cigars for him. Then, in a feigned recovery from his premeditated contretempts, he added quickly, "Oh, please excuse me, I thought you were a servant!" The gaudy clothing and noisy mannerisms vanished with an inexplicable suddenness.[18]

In managing the younger students, especially in maintaining classroom discipline, the problem was quite different. Some sort of physical punishment was indispensable, and it usually was in the form of the *palmeta*, a perforated wooden disc for slapping the hands.

Lerdo's personal opinions on the matter and the policy he enforced at the college probably would have remained a moot point, but, fortunately, one day he received a provocative letter from an administrative official of one of the local departments denouncing the cruelty with which the professors of his school administered the *palmeta*, a practice "which condemns the cultured society of the century in which we live and which is highly repugnant to civilization." Not content with tactless language, the official ordered Lerdo "to be kind enough to repress such abuses . . . substituting only those [punishments] which are permitted."[19]

The letter was a complete violation of ethics, being outside the chain of administrative command, and, in addition, the brusque phraseology served to rouse Lerdo's wrath, for he was sensitive about his prerogative. Furthermore, he was not the man to be accosted on the question of what was and what was not "permitted" according to the regulations. His piercing retort is something more than the story of the use of the *palmeta* at San Ildefonso; something more than Lerdo, the indignant rector; it is also Lerdo the defense lawyer as he must have appeared before the bar—logical, cold, and fortified with an excess of precedents.

First, he related the historical background of the *palmeta*, used since "time immemorial" in San Ildefonso as in other establishments of higher education in Mexico City, but used only with moderation

---

[18] [Quevedo y Zubieta], *Porfirio Díaz*, I, 12n. Although this incident may have been only oral tradition, the author included additional information about Lerdo as rector which is both rare and unusually accurate, indicating a firsthand knowledge.

[19] Secretary of the Governor of the Department of the Valley of Mexico to the Rector of San Ildefonso, May 12, 1860, *Ynstrucción Pública*, LXXVI, A.G.N.

and in the beginning classes for younger students. Then followed an avalanche of rules and regulations, proving beyond the shadow of a doubt that the *palmeta* was still a legal method of discipline. What was a feasible substitute, he asked, for a quick, non-distracting punishment, when professors had to handle large classes of young students "who arrive well or poorly trained by their parents?" Finally, he turned the full force of his attack upon the complainant: ". . . for more than two and one-half centuries, on the date of the royal *cédula* which I cited and which is the law 13, title 23, book one of the *Recopilación de Yndias,* this college has been, without any variation to the present time, directly and exclusively subject to the patronage of the Supreme Government." For emphasis, he repeated that there was no precedent for such unwarranted meddling in the concerns of the college: "I can guarantee this in respect to the eight years I have been rector and I am also certain in regard to former times."[20]

Within a few days the complaining official received formal instructions from the Minister of Justice in regard to the proper procedure for lodging complaints about administration in the national colleges.[21]

It would be misleading to leave the impression that Lerdo confined his paternalism to the students: the professorial staff received its share of his surveillance, too. The instance of the three professors suspended at the outset of his rectorship has been noted; and there was a clear implication in his report on that occasion that he believed the sentence far too mild, for he called the Minister's attention to the fact that a minority of the junta desired the imposition of the maximum penalty, not only for the student but also for all principals involved.[22]

Nor was Lerdo pleased with the cumbersome method of enforcing a regular and prompt attendance of instructors at their lectures. When Guzmán had been rector, a detailed record of punctuality was required for each teaching member of the staff, monthly salaries being discounted in proportion to the amount of lecture time missed. No doubt, as a professor himself, Lerdo had found

[20]Lerdo to the Minister of Justice, May 25, 1860, *ibid.,* LXXVI, A.G.N.

[21]Minister of Justice to the Governor of the Department of the Valley of Mexico, May 29, 1860, *ibid.,* LXXVI, A.G.N. Lerdo is reported to have suspended the use of the *palmeta* on one occasion, because of harsh usage on the part of certain professors. See [Quevedo y Zubieta], *Porfirio Díaz,* I, 11, 11n; Enrique Fernández Ledesma, *Galería de Fantasmas, Años y Sombras del Siglo XIX,* 121–122.

[22]Lerdo to the Minister of Relations, June 20, 1852, *Ynstrucción Pública,* LX, A.G.N.

that system onerous and degrading.[23] At any rate, once in a position to institute a reform, he decided to have no more of that practice which "embarrassed" professors without obtaining any results. Therefore, on his own initiative, he drafted a statute of ten articles governing the punctuality of professors, not only at lectures but also at the staff meetings. After almost a year's trial, Lerdo could report his success, for the new system had been completely "effective."[24]

Although there was reason and composure in most of those measures, beneath Lerdo's exterior of "habitual courtesy,"[25] rested the ability to act sharply, if and when circumstances demanded. There was no lack of firmness, decision, or energy in his makeup, whether dealing with professors or students, stated Miranda y Marrón, who learned much about the Rector through his friendship with a former member of the college staff. He illustrated his description with the following anecdote:

One year the three instructors presiding at the final oral examinations were so unreasonable that even the outstanding students were failing. In the midst of the proceedings and while the questioning continued, Lerdo consulted with the nonparticipating professors. Suddenly—at ten o'clock at night—he ordered the examiners to report to his office and discharged them without any forewarning. They departed the next day amid the rejoicings of the students who had been their victims a few hours previously.[26]

In retrospect it is easy to see a touch of severity and even harshness at times in the obedience which Lerdo demanded of the members of the college. But if the lugubrious sound of the bell was heard not a few times from 1852 to 1863, indicating in solemn tones that a classmate had been expelled,[27] those who received the warning could find compensation in the fact that justice had been rendered upon careful reasoning. The continuity of order at San Ildefonso spoke well for the methods adopted to obtain it. There were no out-

---

[23]It is not clear how this check on individual professors was administered, but obviously snooping and interference were requisite. One of the monthly reports, dated January 31, 1852, which includes Lerdo's record, will illustrate the point. It is entitled "Apunte de la Asistencia de los SS. Catedráticos de Facultad Mayor a Sus Respectivas Cátedras el Mes de Enero de 1852." In the column beside Lerdo's name is an entry to the effect that he missed a total of five and one-half hours of his lecture time during the month, "247 minutes" of which were exempted from the monetary fine since he offered a satisfactory excuse.—*Ibid.*, LXI, A.G.N.

[24]Lerdo to the Minister of Justice, July 6, 1853, *ibid.*, LXI, A.G.N.

[25][Quevedo y Zubieta], *Porfirio Díaz*, I, 12n.

[26]M. Miranda y Marrón, "El Colegio de San Ildefonso de 1848 á 1867," *Boletín de la Escuela Nacional Preparatoria*, II (December, 1909–January, 1910), 119–120.

[27]Miranda y Marrón, "El Colegio de San Ildefonso de 1848 á 1867," *ibid.*, II, 118.

breaks; there was no need for governmental interference; and no closing of the college doors, as occurred at times in other schools in the city.[28] With much of San Ildefonso's fine reputation resting upon Lerdo personally and considering that education and discipline were elements inseparable, it is a compliment to say that, as a rector, he was "scrupulous but fair, energetic, but one who rigorously observes justice."[29]

In turning to the less colorful aspects of the rectorship, one can discern in the variety of business, a balanced and thorough training in administration.[30] Little wonder that Lerdo could assume governmental duties with ease when fortune favored a political career. In addition to general supervision of the establishment, he handled the bulky correspondence which formed the main link with the central government; advised the Minister of Justice (or Relations) on all outstanding occurrences in the institution as well as on any changes of rules or personnel; and complied with all decrees and directives which applied to public instruction in general or San Ildefonso in particular.[31]

Personnel matters alone, in addition to discipline, required no small expenditure of time. Appointments, promotions, and resignations, applications for admittance, requests for scholarship grants, leaves of absence, and attendance reports are a few examples of the routine business which found its place on Lerdo's desk. And he had to be well versed on the financial problems of the college, such as salaries, tuition and pension payments, and maintenance and extraordinary expenditures; for each monthly budget carried his signature of approval before it was forwarded to the government. One item alone, the investment representing various scholarship endowments, aggregated several hundred thousands of pesos, and, if he delegated the supervision and upkeep of those sums to

---

[28]See, for example, the scandals in which the colleges of Mining, Medicine, and Agriculture were involved in 1858.—*La Sociedad*, July 23, 24, 26; August 3, 4, 1858.

[29]Enrique M. de los Ríos, *Liberales Ilustres Mexicanos de la Reforma y la Intervención*, 227.

[30]The following summary is a synthesis of the broad scope of the rectorship, based on the ponderous MSS. correspondence between Lerdo and the Minister of Justice (or Relations) in the volumes entitled *Ynstrucción Pública*, A.G.N. To understand the standards the government was attempting to maintain, see the various *reglamentos* on public instruction issued during th s period in Manuel Dublán y José María Lozano, *Legislación Mexicana*. . . .

[31]There was, of course, a small staff of assistants who aided with the different phases of routine, the vice-rector, secretary, mayordomo, and chaplain being the most important. Besides those officials, Lerdo's résumé in 1858 included twelve professors, a doctor, and a lawyer.—"Lista de los Superiores, Catedráticos, y Empleados Que Actualmente S rven en Este Colegio," January 25, 1858, *Ynstrucción Pública*, LXXIV, A.G.N.

others,[32] he could not escape the ultimate responsibility of his fiduciary capacity.

The rectorship also entailed ceremonial functions. Occasionally Lerdo was called upon to represent the school in general celebrations, as in 1856, when a *junta popular* was being formed to celebrate the first anniversary of Ignacio Comonfort's interim presidency.[33] Within the college itself there were regular matriculations, the annual award of prizes, and other fêtes at which the rector must be on hand to preside.[34] It was at one of those graduation exercises in 1855, when the principal patio of the school was "decorously adorned and illuminated," that one Benito Juárez, minister of Justice for the interim government of Juan Álvarez, was present as guest of honor.[35] Little could the Zapotec Indian and Rector Lerdo have realized, in what may have been their first personal meeting, how closely their lives would be associated through the important political rôles each was to play in the years to follow.

Notwithstanding those many other duties, the rector had to be an educator, familiar with the standards of the times and observant of the manner in which they were being fulfilled in his own bailiwick. How else could one enforce discipline, determine eligibility for matriculation, or even prescribe the textbooks to be used in the different courses? Nor was the last-named function an insignificant one: Lerdo's review of a Castilian grammar, from the standpoint of teaching merit, was once reprinted as a front page item in a leading newspaper of Mexico City.[36]

Had he remained in the educational field permanently, it is highly improbable that he ever would have conceived or promoted drastic changes in the basic concepts and patterns of the training methods of his day. He was perhaps too egotistical and self-satisfied with his own exceptional culture and respected the system through which it had been acquired. Yet within the existing framework he operated with energy, care for detail, and a spirit of reform which makes

---

[32]Miranda y Marrón, "El Colegio de San Ildefonso de 1848 á 1867," *Boletín de la Escuela Nacional Preparatoria*, II, 118–119, 128.

[33]*Diario de Avisos* (Mexico), December 8, 1856. At the special request of the President, this particular festivity was cancelled.—*Ibid.*, December 9, 1856.

[34]At San Ildefonso, in 1858, the outstanding student in "Idioma Inglés" was given Prescott's *History of the Conquest of Mexico.*—*La Sociedad*, November 19, 1858. Is is amusing to note that Lerdo awarded the same volume as a prize for good conduct in the celebration of 1861.—*El Siglo*, November 24, 1861.

[35]*Distribución Anual de Premios en el Colegio Nacional y Más Antiguo de San Ildefonso el 16 de Noviembre de 1855*, 1. This pamphlet of 31 pages, located in the Biblioteca Lafragua, Puebla, gives an interesting picture of the programs on such occasions.

[36]Lerdo to the Minister of Public Instruction, January 27, 1862, *El Siglo*, March 11, 1862. His recommendations on textbooks for all courses in 1854 may be found in a letter to the Minister of Justice, January 5, 1854, *Ynstrucción Pública*, LXII, A.G.N.

a striking contrast with the régime of old Guzmán, who seems to have atrophied in office.[37]

Lerdo's letters to the government contain many new ideas and suggestions for improving San Ildefonso, a few of which have been indicated already. But they covered many subjects, nothing being too trivial to escape his scrutiny. Once he complained about the bill of fare served at the college, which for years had included only drab, staple foods; and there was, he believed, a simple solution for that "notorious defect." Certainly the students would be much happier if the government would approve of the addition of two chocolates to the daily diet. Official approval was forthcoming almost immediately.[38]

On another occasion he displayed indignation at the dearth of scientific equipment at San Ildefonso, while all other colleges, so he claimed, were richly endowed in that regard. Such a condition could only result in a "grave prejudice to teaching" in the courses of natural science. Lacking the necessary instruments and mechanisms, the unfortunate professors had to rely solely on diagrams and their own verbal explanations, the students thus missing "all the extension of the theories [and] all the uses which the doctrines naturally suggest when they are practiced with equipment in some manner." That state of affairs, Lerdo insisted, was "unworthy of our society, and not very profitable for youth."[39] The proposed remedy for the critical condition was a grant of 10,000 pesos for the purchase of laboratory cabinets to be used in physics and chemistry, a sum which Lerdo maintained was not excessive considering the purpose. Although there appears to be no record of an answer from the Minister, the government probably had far more urgent demands upon the meager public funds.

One other incident might be related here to illustrate Lerdo's promotion of the welfare at San Ildefonso. When the General Inspector of Public Instruction made his visitation in 1856,[40] Lerdo met him with a volley of requests for the renovation of the buildings. Not only the altars and objects in the chapel needed repairs,

---

[37]Of course, no specific citations can be given for this conclusion, which is founded upon a comparison of the correspondence of the two men as successive rectors of the same institution.

[38]Lerdo to the Minister of Justice, December 27, 1855; Inspector of Public Instruction to the Rector of San Ildefonso, December 29, 1855, *Ynstrucción Pública*, LXXIII, A.G.N.

[39]Lerdo to the Minister of Justice, March 22, 1853, *ibid.*, LXI, A.G.N.

[40]The *reglamento* of December 19, 1851, setting forth in minute detail the duties of the college *visitador*, is invaluable not only for showing the standards established by the government, but for the insight it gives into the actual operation of the institutions of higher learning of the day. By these instructions, not a nook or cranny of the buildings or any phase of the college administration was to escape the inspector's examination.—Dublán y Lozano, *Legislación Mexicana*, VI, 134–136.

but also it was "indispensable" that action be taken to restore the shelves in the library and increase their storage capacity, since many books were jammed together in double rows while others had to be stacked on top of cabinets.[41] Thus, in many ways he injected his pride, industry, and meticulousness into the operation of San Ildefonso, so that its reputation was perhaps enhanced by him.

Although Lerdo's rectorship has been considered primarily from the standpoint of the internal administration of the school, he also served in educational positions of a more general nature. While the data on that activity are scarce, it was no doubt significant as a channel for meeting important political figures, displaying his abilities, and broadening his experience. During 1853, he was a member of a governmental commission appointed to draft a broad revision of public instruction.[42] Associated in the project was Blas Balcárcel, director of the College of Mining, who scarcely could have surmised that twenty years later he would be serving again with the serious young Rector of San Ildefonso, but in a different capacity: that of a cabinet minister to a president of the republic.

The following year Lerdo was called upon to substitute temporarily for one of the three members of the Commission of Funds for Public Instruction, a board under the supervision of the Inspector General and within the Ministry of Justice.[43] When the regular official resumed his place, the Inspector General requested that Lerdo be permitted to continue: "I feel his services on the Commission are very useful, since he has comprehended many affairs on which I have consulted with him."[44] To that petition "His Most Serene Highness" had the graciousness to consent.[45] Again, it is interesting to note that the man for whom Lerdo had substituted— Marcelino Castañeda—was associated with him in the cabinet which President Comonfort formed in June, 1857. The rectorship of San Ildefonso was certainly a medium for meeting influential and promi-

---

[41]Inspector General of Public Instruction to the Minister of Justice, November 25, 1856, *Ynstrucción Pública*, LXXXI, A.G.N. The Inspector quoted the remarks Lerdo had made during their conference of November 20.

The library of San Ildefonso was one of the outstanding collections in Mexico, containing, in 1856, some 8,361 volumes of printed works and manuscripts.—Miguel Lerdo de Tejada, *Cuadro Sinóptico de la República Mexicana en 1856*, 73.

[42]Secretary for the Direction of Studies to the Minister of Justice, May 20, 1853, *Ynstrucción Pública*, LXIII, A.G.N.

[43]Inspector General of Public Instruction to the Minister of Justice, May 6, 1854, *ibid.*, LXIV, A.G.N.

[44]Inspector General of Public Instruction to the Minister of Justice, August 22, 1854, *ibid.*, LXV, A.G.N.

[45]Minister of Justice to the Inspector General of Public Instruction, August 25, 1854, *ibid.*, LXV, A.G.N.

nent persons and a rung on the ladder leading to other duties or honors, official and otherwise.[46]

But what can be said of Lerdo the man, his character and personality, for surely the ingredients crystallized during that period of over a decade as rector of San Ildefonso? Just as during all his life, those more intimate facets remain elusive, dim, and puzzling. Beneath his veneer of graciousness and correctness in all the social amenities, lay an impenetrable surface, an almost Oriental stoicism; and the investigator must do his prying without the aid of the specialized documentary tools. Perhaps there must always remain about Lerdo a patina of mystery and enigma.

Yet treacherous as the terrain may be at this point, it is not altogether impossible. His acts spoke rather clearly for what he was: a tendency to sternness tempered by a strong sense of justice; industry and conscientiousness with no small belief in his own capacities; and a certain unwillingness to delegate authority to others. Perhaps this last characteristic should not be overemphasized simply because it was one of his chief deficiencies at a later period. But might it not be inferred that Lerdo acquired that trait at San Ildefonso, since the very essence of the rectorship was paternalism? Furthermore, Miranda y Marrón pointed out, on the basis of information obtained from one of Lerdo's favorites at the college, that there were very few to whom he would entrust real responsibility.[47] The conviction that he was the keystone of the proper functioning of the school was also revealed indirectly in one of his letters to the Minister of Justice in which he requested a license to reside outside the college for a brief period in order to improve his health: "I shall be able to come daily during the major part of the day, in such manner as to attend to the reëstablishment of my health without neglecting the duties of the rectorship and without prejudicing in the least the discipline of the college."[48]

To penetrate Lerdo's religious convictions at that period poses another difficult problem. As has been pointed out, his youth was spent in institutions with a strong religious atmosphere and probably he was destined to serve the church at one stage of his life. It has been shown, too, that a substantial part of the routine

[46]No doubt Lerdo's position as rector of San Ildefonso was an influencing factor in his election (January, 1862) to the presidency of the Sociedad Lancasteriana, an organization promoting the advancement of primary education, especially for children of the poor. For the minutes of the meeting in which Lerdo was elected, see El Siglo, January 28, 1862.

[47]Miranda y Marrón, "El Colegio de San Ildefonso de 1848 á 1867," Boletín de la Escuela Nacional Preparatoria, II, 119.

[48]Lerdo to the Minister of Justice, March 8, 1856, Ynstrucción Pública, LXXIV, A.G.N. He also stated that in four years as rector he had never solicited a leave of absence.

of San Ildefonso was concerned with religious devotions and exercises. As rector, Lerdo was expected to be an example of devoutness and morality; and legend holds that he fulfilled the obligation with zeal. According to the story, the secular path was first opened to Lerdo, after ten years of personified piety, when reading passages of the letters of Lord Chesterfield to the students at the refectory in substitution for the standard "Aristotelian" works.[49] Although that evidence cannot be discounted altogether,[50] it seems much too flimsy an explanation for one with Lerdo's stolid habits and background. Whatever may have been the true forces affecting his outlook on religion—his intellectual pursuits, his political associations, his brother's fame as a leader of the radical party, or the onrushing spirit of secularism—one thing can be assumed with relative certainty: At some stage during those years, probably toward the latter part of the period, a pronounced change must have occurred in his views. Again, one must rely on his acts rather than on any insight into his mental processes to demonstrate the point in its proper place.

If Lerdo's personal convictions must be sketched with hesitancy, his outward appearance and demeanor struck his contemporaries with a notable sameness.[51] Poised and gracious, on occasion austere and aloof, the thickset little man of less than average height fitted his somber black suit as well as he fitted the part he played as rector. He always was impeccably groomed, in the same mournful attire—black suit, waistcoat, and tie, and a spotless white shirt with high collar. With prominent and penetrating eyes and a fringe of chestnut-colored hair framing an oval face and a spacious bald pate, he well might have passed for a village parson.[52] Although his

---

[49][Quevedo y Zubieta], *Porfirio Díaz*, I, 10–11; Fernández Ledesma, *Galería de Fantasmas*, 123–124.

The late Father Mariano Cuevas, well-known Mexican church historian, informed the present writer that his father, a student at San Ildefonso when Lerdo was rector, recalled the latter's piety and the personal interest he took in arranging the religious ceremonies held in the college.—Interview, Mexico, D.F., June 16, 1947.

[50]In the library of the Escuela Nacional Preparatoria, which absorbed the old College of San Ildefonso in 1868, there were several volumes of Lord Chesterfield's letters, most of which were in Spanish translation.—*Catálogo de las Obras que Forman la Biblioteca Pública de la Escuela N. Preparatoria, Fundado el Año de 1879*, 69. It is easy to discern much of Lord Chesterfield's advice in Lerdo's habits and dress, although such influences must be conjectured.

[51]This brief physical description, which will be elaborated from time to time, is based upon a variety of sources. For a few examples of accurate, concise characterizations, see *Sebastián Lerdo de Tejada (1823–1889), In Memoriam*, 33–35; Enrique M. de los Ríos, *Liberales Ilustres*, 229; [Quevedo y Zubieta], *Porfirio Díaz*, I, 10.

[52]The best portraits of Lerdo may be found in José M. Vigil, *La Reforma* [Vicente Riva Palacio (ed.), *México á Través de los Siglos*, V], 224 (here-

appearance was easily adapted to caricature,[53] in person he was dignity incarnate. Often, too, there was a cynical twist to his thin mouth which might be transformed into an expression of inflexible determination. When the sketch is completed with his pale complexion, it was certain that his makeup was more Anglo-Saxon than Latin,[54] although he would not have been flattered by the comment.

While the years of the rectorship were not of any great historical importance, their influence on Lerdo personally and on his later fortunes cannot be exaggerated. The threads of a political career were already being interwoven into his life of which he had made a substantial success, limited as the sphere may have been; and eventually they were to extract him from it altogether. Yet he left his name and his stamp upon San Ildefonso, becoming as much a part of the institution as the flagstones of the patio. That its welfare was uppermost in his mind was shown by the fact that one of his last acts on the night he departed from Mexico City with the Juárez government (May 31, 1863) was to leave minute verbal instructions for the operation of the college with one of his old friends and protegés, Francisco Artigas, then vice-rector.[55] Nor did the older members of the college forget him in the years when Maximilian's Empire was supported by the French troops in Mexico. One day in 1865 an imperial official appeared at the rectory and discovered Lerdo's portrait in the place of honor instead of that of the Emperor. Upon demanding an explanation from one of the older professors about this error, he received the following answer: ". . . everything which the College of San Ildefonso was, it owed physically and morally to Sr. Lerdo de Tejada, and for the same reason he should continue to preside over it, though only in effigy."[56] Could a finer tribute have been paid for a job well done?

---

after cited by the general title) ; Justo Sierra, *Juárez Su Obra y Su Tiempo*, opposite p. 482; Ireneo Paz (ed.), *Hombres Prominentes*, opposite p. 51.

There are two large oil portraits of Lerdo, one in the Ministry of Foreign Relations and the other in the archive of the National College of Lawyers, Mexico, D.F., both of which are formal and probably exaggerate his severity. The best likeness of which the writer is aware is a small photograph about five by seven inches in size, located in the office of Sr. José Romero, Mexico, D.F. It is inscribed by Lerdo to the owner's uncle, Matías Romero, as follows: "Al Sr. D. Matías Romero en testimonio de sincera amistad. Marzo 1° de 1868." S. Lerdo de Tejada (rubric).

[53]See the cartoons in *El Ahuizote* (Mexico) during the years of Lerdo's presidency.

[54]See Philip de Toulza, *La Princesse Agnes de Salm-Salm au Mexique en 1867, Ses Souvenirs sur la Chute et la Fin de Maximilien 1er*, 167–168.

[55]Miranda y Marrón, "El Colegio de San Ildefonso de 1848 á 1867," *Boletín de la Escuela Nacional Preparatoria*, II, 120–121.

[56]Quoted by Miranda y Marrón, *ibid.*, II, 130.

Chapter IV

The Genesis of a Political Career, 1855-1861

The years of the Mexican chronicle from 1855 to 1861 present but one feature of simplicity: they form a convenient period which is delimited by relatively marked changes in historical trends. At the outset, there is the end of something old and consequently the beginning of something new. The old was Santa Anna, whose departure from Mexico in August, 1855, was the final occasion when the bizarre political chameleon would influence the destiny of his country. The new was a revolution, the adapted and delayed reverberation of its grander prototype in France in the late eighteenth century, carrying with it much of the same ideology and many of the specific reforms of the famous progenitor. The first six years of the Mexican upheaval resulted in the firm implanting of the ideals, but the effort to bridge what then appeared to be a hopeless gap between theory and practice continues today in more tranquil, evolutionary stages.

When Juárez returned to the capital in 1861, as the representative of reform, legality, and the Constitution of 1857, Mexico once again was united, though superficially, after three years of divided allegiance, dual governments, and devastating civil war. The forces of reaction, momentarily victorious in 1858, were stunned but not defeated; still, one can say that the first phase of the violent aspect of revolution had ended.

Although the outline of this brief era stands forth clearly, it is choked with numberless events, personalities, and issues of a highly confusing and controversial nature. To insert Lerdo into this chaos is not an easy task, especially since he was a minor detail. Historians allot his name a few casual references, and justly so, for his activities were short-lived and left no impression of any depth upon the current of events. His prominence must await a later period. There were too many brilliant figures willing to devote their full efforts and even their lives to the first phase of revolution.

Even in regard to his own life, those sporadic entrances in politics from 1855 to 1857 are of no great significance, except that they may have whetted his ambition. If so, he fortunately held the impulse in check during the three years when the conservative faction controlled Mexico City and the great central arena of the country. No doubt there were opportunities for him to join the reaction and satiate any such appetite; yet his resumption of political obscurity as rector of San Ildefonso after 1857 and his refusal to participate in conservative governmental experiments indicated his acceptance of the principles of the revolution. If he held personal convictions on the specific method and pace to be adopted in accomplishing the reforms, he was like many other members of that vague and fluid faction which is poorly defined as the moderate element of the liberal party.

When General Juan Álvarez and the victorious promoters of the Revolution of Ayutla entered Mexico City in late 1855, it might have been expected that all those connected with the anathematized régime of Santa Anna must seek political oblivion; that, at the very least, there would be a thorough housecleaning in the central administrative offices. In fact this was far from the actual practice, Miguel Lerdo being one notable example. Although thoroughly soiled by his official connection with the dictatorship, he continued to serve as undersecretary of Fomento until he became minister of Finance in May, 1856.[1]

Sebastián himself was mildly tainted by having accepted an appointment from Santa Anna as *fiscal* (prosecuting attorney) of a special tribunal which heard only cases involving the personnel of the highest court in the land, the Supreme Court of Justice. This occurred just a few weeks before "His Most Serene Highness" embarked at Vera Cruz for an extended period of exile.[2] Even when combined with his activities on various commissions of public instruction, the sum did not amount to an impressive debut into the political world. Actually those modest beginnings were quasi-political, offshoots of technical skills either from educational experience or legal ability; and eventually it was the judicial branch of government which served as a medium to attract him toward public life during the period of transition following the triumph of the Revolution of Ayutla.

---

[1] *El Siglo*, January 26, May 21, 1856; Rivera, *Historia de Jalapa*, IV, 405, 583–584, 662–663.

Edward Lee Plumb, the resident agent of an American corporation, was seeking in 1855 the confirmation of a mining concession (granted by the government of Santa Anna) from the new revolutionary régime. He commented as follows, after an interview with Miguel Lerdo: "I found the Bureau [the ministry of Fomento], in charge of Mr. Lerdo, Oficial Mayor, holding over from Santa Anna's Administration on a/c of his standing as a gentleman of great administrative ability and high character."—Plumb to T. Olcott, Mexico, November 25, 1855, *The Papers of Edward L. Plumb*, II (MSS.), Division of Manuscripts, The Library of Congress, Washington, D.C. (hereafter cited *Plumb Papers*).

[2] Decree of June 27, 1855, *Colección de las Leyes, Decretos y Órdenes Espedidas por S.A.S. el Presidente de la República D. Antonio López de Santa Anna . . .*, VIII, 299. The decree is also printed in *El Universal* (Mexico), July 7, 1855, along with a notice that Lerdo took the oath of office on July 5.

Although the exact date is not known, Lerdo obtained an appointment as *fiscal* of the Supreme Court, probably in December, 1855, about the time he also was named alternate magistrate for that body when Benito Juárez was minister of Justice for Interim President Juan Álvarez.[3] He continued in the dual rôle until June, 1857, when he entered the cabinet of the second revolutionary executive, Ignacio Comonfort.[4]

To accept the court position—to serve the new régime—was *prima facie* to adopt the principles of the revolution; and it was made binding by an oath required of all officials serving the judiciary during the period of transition.[5] Sebastián had thus connected himself with the liberal group, although it is impossible to define his convictions any further at that time.

There are two questions which seem to justify a pause for clarification: Who was the Benito Juárez of 1855 and why had he recommended Sebastián Lerdo for a court position? In regard to the full-blooded Zapotec Indian, who had risen to a place in the cabinet, he had been important primarily in the government of his native state of Oaxaca, had been imprisoned briefly and subsequently exiled by Santa Anna, only to return from New Orleans to play a prominent part close to Álvarez in support of the revolution, thus balancing the score with his former persecutor. A lawyer who visited Juárez shortly after his arrival in Mexico City described him as a man reserved and circumspect who would issue no decrees except those which were necessary.[6] Almost exactly one month later the first great reform law was promulgated, proving beyond a doubt that the Revolution of Ayutla was in essence strikingly different from its countless, stereotyped predecessors. Styled after its author, the Ley Juárez suppressed all special tribunals except the military and ecclesiastical, and from those it removed all civil jurisdiction, which was indeed a substantial bite of privilege. Although a moderate measure with a promise of more drastic action in the future, it was, nevertheless, a significant advance in the direction of equality before the law.[7]

---

[3]In accordance with a decree of November 26, 1855, the regular and substitute magistracies were filled, Lerdo being one of five named for the second group.—*El Siglo*, December 3, 1855.

[4]Parada Gay gave the general dates of 1856 through a part of 1857 as the period during which Lerdo acted as *fiscal*.—*Breve Reseña de la Suprema Corte de Justicia de la Nación*, 50.

[5]Dublán y Lozano, *Legislación Mexicana*, VII, 605.

[6]R[afael] M[artínez] de la Torre to Manuel Doblado, October 24, 1855, Genaro García (ed.), *La Revolución de Ayutla según el Archivo del General Doblado* (*Documentos Inéditos ó Muy Raros para la Historia de México*, XXVI), 251.

[7]For the law, see Dublán y Lozano, *Legislación Mexicana*, VII, 598–606. The Ley Juárez, which also set forth provisional regulations to govern the court system, frequently is misinterpreted as abolishing the military and ecclesiastical *fueros*.

Returning to the explanation of Lerdo's appointment, Juárez wrote that the administration of justice was "paralyzed" just prior to the publication of his famous law, because of the lack of justices legally approved,[8] and hence he probably was grateful to locate competent persons willing to serve. Perhaps he had posed the offer to Rector Lerdo the night in mid-November when he had been guest of honor for the matriculation festivities at San Ildefonso. On the other hand, Juan B. Morales, named president of the court, was a man under whom Lerdo had studied law and for whom he also had acted as a substitute teacher; and he may have made the recommendation.[9]

Certainly the months from late 1855 to June, 1857, formed a rugged schooling for a novice in the public service. Governmental affairs were in a state of great disquiet, caused by countless revolts, fomented by the forces of reaction, and by the necessity of carrying on routine business with a barren treasury and under temporary regulations while the new organic law was being drafted. Other factors existed to compound the havoc, especially the hopeless disunity among the liberal elements on the specific methods to be followed in revamping a society which largely retained its ancient mould of privilege. Unwilling to await the finished product of the constituent assembly, in session during most of the period, the interim governments of Álvarez and Comonfort proceeded to decree transcendental reforms, simultaneously ripping out the fabric established under the late dictatorship of Santa Anna. Thus, to the prosecutor of the court, the interpretation of the law must have been at best highly confusing.

Although it seems unnecessary to describe the nature of a magistrate's duties, those of the *fiscal* require some explanation. Under the provisional regulation for the Supreme Court, there were two such officials, and, in the absence of a regular justice, one of them sat to complete the bench for judicial hearings, taking precedence over the alternate magistrates. Such a function was secondary, however, the principal one being responsibility for prosecution: filing indictments; studying the briefs of cases on appeal from the lower courts for recommendations to the bench; representing the interest of the state in all private, civil litigation; and giving the best technical interpretation of the law either to the executive branch of the government or to the court whenever called upon to do so. Moreover, the *fiscal* was burdened with administrative obli-

---

[8]Matías Romero, *Biografía del Ciudadano Benito Juárez*, 36.

[9]Morales was a strong liberal whose career dated back to the early epoch of Mexican independence. His death in July, 1856, was considered a great loss by the liberals. See *El Siglo*, January 3, February 13, July 29, 1856; *Los Padres del Agua Fría* (Mexico), July 30, 1856.

gations, involving the personnel problems of the members of the federal courts.[10]

To pursue Lerdo's activities as a court official would be impossible and relatively fruitless. Suffice it to say that the business was varied. Whether drafting the indictment against Santa Anna and his ex-ministers,[11] sitting on the bench at court martial proceedings,[12] reviewing the briefs on a revenue case from a circuit court, or recommending leave of absence for a justice of a lower tribunal,[13] he was accumulating the practical experience which was the source of his reputation as a skilled lawyer.

During the same period which found Lerdo connected with the court, a law was issued from the office of the minister of Finance which has just claim to being one of the most penetrating reforms in Mexican history. Later elevated to the height of an organic provision by being incorporated in the Constitution of 1857, the decree became legislation only in an *ex post facto* sense. The minister who authored the measure was Sebastián's brother Miguel, and he has come to be remembered more as a law—the Ley Lerdo—than as a personality. The unbounded socio-economic effects of the Ley Lerdo amounted to a complete and inalterable overthrow of the ancient balance of political power inherited from the days of the Spanish Empire. By its provisions, "no corporation—meaning the clergy, as the church was the only corporation existing in Mexico—" could hold real estate not in immediate use for religious purposes. Real property, urban and rural, which fitted this definition, was to be sold to the tenants then in occupancy at a figure determined by calculating the annual rental charge as six per cent of the capital investment.[14] The procedure for evaluation and conveyance was called *desamortización*.

The study of this law and its significance forms a separate chapter in Mexican history, but what its implementation meant to a contemporary society, already seething with unrest, can well be

---

[10]See the decree of November 23, 1855, in Dublán y Lozano, *Legislación Mexicana*, VII, 598–606, especially Articles 2, 5, and 8. The interim governments of Álvarez and Comonfort never clearly defined the *fiscal's* duties, and consequently most of the above details have been drawn from the rules enforced under Santa Anna.—*Ibid.*, VI, 842–843.

[11]Dublán y Lozano, *Legislación Mexicana*, VIII, 122–124.

[12]*El Omnibus*, September 24, 1856.

[13]"Decretos de la Suprema Corte de Justicia, Año de 1856," September 30, 1856, Legajo 1, Archivo 40; January 9, 1856, Legajo 1, Archivo 3, Archivo General de la Suprema Corte de Justicia, Mexico, D.F. (MSS.).

[14]M. Romero, "The Philosophy of the Mexican Revolution," *The North American Review*, CLXII, 42. The quoted part of the statement is not strictly accurate, since the law applied to both civil and ecclesiastical corporations; but the real intent was to disengage property held by the church in mortmain.

For the decree, see Dublán y Lozano, *Legislación Mexicana*, VIII, 197–200.

imagined.[15] It has been claimed that Sebastián contributed substantially to the enforcement of the law in those difficult months after its promulgation in June, 1856, by collaborating with his famous brother as a legal adviser.[16] While the possibility exists that he was called upon for technical advice because of his position on the court, if so, no written record appears to be available of those consultations, nor is it logical to assume that his alleged counsel affected policy as opposed to administration. Moreover, for various reasons which will be discussed in the following chapter, the brothers seem not to have been closely associated at any time, and their political opinions were probably widely divergent in 1856. At any rate, Sebastián has little if any right to encroach upon his brother's fame arising from the vital reform.

Without exaggeration, the Ley Lerdo became the fulcrum of a desperate society: on one end of the balance rested the enraged opponents whose interests were being attacked, the church and its conservative backers; on the other side stood the radicals, the *puros*, or "progressives," who demanded an uncompromising advance of the reform; and in the center milled the variegated shades of moderates, wavering and undecided. "Such was the state of society in which our constituents found themselves in the year 1856," wrote Ricardo García Granados, "that the solution of the problem was not only difficult but absolutely impossible."[17]

Since the law defined the issue severing the hostile groups, its author became the symbol which guaranteed the continuance of the aims of the revolution. So far had he catapulted to fame above all other leaders of the *puro* faction that his resignation from the cabinet in January, 1857, struck consternation in their ranks.[18] Miguel Lerdo appeared to be in disagreement with the ideas of Interim President Ignacio Comonfort. Did this signify a change

---

[15]Helen Phipps, *Some Aspects of the Agrarian Question in Mexico: A Historical Study*, 77–81. See also the excellent summary of Manuel Payno on the Ley Lerdo, the clerical opposition, and the importance of the reform to the three-year civil war which was soon to follow.—*Colección de las Leyes, Decretos, Circulares y Providencias Relativas á la Desamortización Eclesiástica* . . . , I, Introduction, especially pp. lxxxvii–cii. For the typical protest of the clergy, see Clemente de Jesús Munguía, *Defensa Eclesiástica en el Obispado de Michoacán desde Fines de 1855 hasta Principios de 1858* . . . , I, 470–473, 478.

[16]Pérez, *Almanaque de las Oficinas*, 223; Enrique M. de los Ríos, *Liberales Ilustres*, 227; Olivo Lara, "Biografías de Veracruzanos Distinguidos," *Anales del Museo Nacional*, VI (Cuarta Época), 162.

[17]Ricardo García Granados, *La Constitución de 1857 y las Leyes de Reforma en México* . . . , 38.

[18]Miguel filed his resignation in late December, 1856, but Comonfort at first refused to accept it. The conservative *Diario de Avisos* (December 19, 1856) quoted a typical opposition editorial, pleading for Comonfort not to admit the resignation "in the name of all the Liberals, of all the Mexicans who love their native land. . . ."

in the policy of the government? Was the program to be continued, modified, or perhaps reversed? Almost from that moment a new question began to absorb the public mind: What were Comonfort's real intentions? The shift of his weight might suffice to upset the delicate balance and provoke open civil war, if it were placed on the side of the forces of reaction which were striving to bolster the old *status quo* and to retract the advances of the reform effected to that time.

Meanwhile, the nation received the promulgation of the new Constitution (February, 1857) and the announcement of the elections to inaugurate the constitutional order. When Miguel Lerdo issued a proclamation, on June 12, 1857, announcing his decision not to enter the presidential race,[19] even though the radicals had insisted on his candidacy, Comonfort's election was assured.

A few days prior to Miguel's formal announcement three new ministers were appointed to complete the vacancies in the cabinet for the remainder of the interim period which was scheduled to end September 16, 1857. Those appointments were of significance, since the public interpreted the political opinions of the men selected as the reflection of Comonfort's future aims.

Into the ministry of Foreign Relations, one of the key positions at the moment, stepped Sebastián Lerdo, a magistrate of the Supreme Court, rector of San Ildefonso, and best identified as being universally unknown. Because of the crucial state of Mexican international relations and the vague reputation he enjoyed as an efficient administrator of the college, it was presumed that he was competent to fill the high assignment to which he had been called. But none would venture further than a presumption, either on his merits or his political leanings.[20]

Perhaps even more enigmatic than Sebastián's sudden prominence was the total absence of any comment that he was the brother of Miguel, who had been one of the chief topics occupying the press since the publication of the Ley Lerdo. Considering that Miguel had quit the Comonfort cabinet only a few months previously and had been pressed to run in the presidential race by the *puros*, the omission indicated a contemporary ignorance of the affinity of the two men, just as their respective connections with Comonfort indicated the chasm separating their political beliefs.

---

[19]"Manifestación al Público," June 12, 1857, *El Estandarte Nacional* (Mexico), June 17, 1857. See also García Granados, *La Constitución de 1857*, 54.

[20]Riva Palacio (ed.), *México á Través de los Siglos*, V, 245; Rivera, *Historia de Jalapa*, IV, 778; Bancroft, *History of Mexico*, V, 713. The semi-official *El Estandarte Nacional* identified Lerdo merely as a "magistrate of the Supreme Court of Justice."—June 6, 1857.

The MS. of this as well as other later appointments to cabinet posts may be found in *Sebastián Lerdo de Tejada, Su Expediente Personal*, Archivo de Relaciones Exteriores, Mexico, D.F.

In regard to the other two newcomers, Antonio García, the minister of Justice, was , perhaps more obscure than Sebastián Lerdo, but such was not true of the elderly Marcelino Castañeda, who had accepted the portfolio of Government.[21] Being an older statesman with recognized opinions and having served in the constituent congress of 1856–1857, where he had defended staunchly the maintenance of an exclusive Roman Catholic Church in Mexico,[22] he was considered the key to the new cabinet. In general the reaction to the changes lay some place between hesitancy and suspicion;[23] and one observer remarked that "these nominations have been very badly received."[24] A slight revival of confidence occurred a few days later when Castañeda resigned and was replaced by Jesús Terán, governor of Aguascalientes, whom the official press pointedly described as a man of progress and a promoter of reform.[25] The other members of the cabinet were Juan Soto (War), José María Iglesias (Finance), and Manuel Siliceo (Fomento), none of whom was new and consequently evoked no comment.[26]

With but three months before the constitutional régime was to be placed in operation, the new cabinet could amount to little more than a temporary expedient. Iglesias, the minister of Finance, related that Comonfort called the members for collective meetings each day, at which time matters of general import were discussed, while individual problems were handled by conferences between the President and the minister concerned.[27] Yet, it is Lerdo's particular rôle in the conduct of foreign relations which is the primary concern here. He assumed his duties in the midst of a bitter dispute with Spain and at a moment when war seemed imminent. To understand his heritage in the foreign office, it will be necessary to trace the developments springing from an incident which took place six months previously.

Though Spanish-Mexican relations were far from cordial under the dictatorship of Santa Anna[28] and failed to improve during the brief administration of Juan Álvarez, the occasion leading to an

---

[21]*El Estandarte Nacional*, June 9, 1857.

[22]Francisco Zarco, *Historia del Congreso Estraordinario Constituyente de 1856 y 1857*, I, 771 ff.

[23]Riva Palacio (ed.), *Mexico á Través de los Siglos*, V, 245; Gabriel Saldívar (ed.), *La Misión Confidencial de Don Jesús Terán en Europa 1863–1866* (Archivo Histórico Diplomático Mexicano, Ser. 2, No. 1), p. xii.

[24]Vicente Riva Palacio to Mariano Riva Palacio, June 5, 1857, Mariano Riva Palacio Papers, Folder 167, UT.

[25]*El Estandarte Nacional*, June 18, 1857; Rivera, *Historia de Jalapa*, IV, 779.

[26]Niceto de Zamacois, *Historia de Méjico*, XIV, 594.

[27]Iglesias, *Autobiografía*, 27.

[28]See Richard A. Johnson, "Spanish-Mexican Diplomatic Relations, 1853–1855," *The Hispanic American Historical Review*, XXI (November, 1941), 575–576.

open breach did not occur until December, 1856, when a band of robbers assassinated five Spanish nationals at the hacienda of San Vicente near Cuernavaca.[29] Certain details surrounding the assassinations left the surface impression that the attack had been directed against Spanish citizens. At least so the Spanish chargé, Pedro Sorela, ·chose to interpret the incident, although it would appear that the outrage was a normal by-product of the uncertain conditions arising from revolutionary times, particularly the lack of an effective police system. Irascible, impetuous, obviously seeking a justification for a complete rupture of diplomatic relations, Sorela moved rapidly from blunt demands for immediate retribution to unveiled insinuations of complicity against the Mexican government. In early January, 1857, he presented an ultimatum to the Mexican government, demanding not only apprehension and punishment of the criminals but the payment of indemnification within eight days. Although the government did all within its power to conciliate the Chargé and to bring the culprits to justice, such peremptory requirements could not be fulfilled within an arbitrary period of time. Consequently, Sorela called for his passports and departed in a huff, leaving to the Spanish press the task of further warping the story and whipping the Spanish public's natural animosity toward its former colony into a healthy frenzy.[30]

At the time Sebastián entered the cabinet, José María Lafragua, Mexican minister plenipotentiary appointed to settle the problem, had arrived in Spain and was attempting to adjust the difficulties with the Spanish Secretary of State. The mission failed completely, but Lerdo had little if any control over the negotiations, partly because of the time element in overseas communications. Neither had he written Lafragua's instructions,[31] nor was he able to arrange a satisfactory conclusion before he resigned from office; and hence the story of the unfortunate mission need not be discussed here.[32]

[29]The following summary is based on the lengthy account, including important diplomatic correspondence, of José María Lafragua, the Mexican plenipotentiary who was sent to Spain to arrange a settlement of outstanding Mexican-Spanish differences.—*Memorandum de los Negocios Pendientes entre México y España* . . . , especially 1–17. It was published by installments in *La Sociedad*, beginning December 30, 1857.

[30]It should be noted, in order to avoid confusion, that the Spanish Chargé addressed his first protest to Miguel Lerdo de Tejada (December 21, 1856), who was encharged temporarily with the conduct of foreign relations from November 14 to December 24, 1856. See Document 5, Lafragua, *Memorandum sobre los Negocios Pendientes*, 131; *Personas Que Han Tenido á Su Cargo la Secretaría de Relaciones Exteriores desde 1821 hasta 1924* (Archivo Histórico Diplomático Mexicano, No. 6), 22.

[31]Lafragua, *Memorandum de los Negocios Pendientes*, 22.

[32]The British and French ministers at Mexico City offered the services of their governments for mediation of the dispute between Spain and Mexico in notes addressed to Lerdo, dated September 2, 1857, but definitive action on this proposal was still pending when he resigned a few days later.—*José M. Lafragua, Su Expediente Personal*, Segunda Parte, Archivo de Relaciones Exteriores, Mexico, D.F.

One thing should be noted, however: the San Vicente affair was an incident provoking much international concern. That Lerdo was entrusted with foreign relations in a period of dangerous tension was no small honor to an unknown figure in political life. Concealed as it was in the first clause of the Mon-Almonte Treaty and swallowed like the War of Jenkins' Ear by later events, the San Vicente episode was one of the seeds of the Spanish part in the allied intervention of 1862.[33]

Another aspect of Lerdo's short ministry, which is of more interest than significance, was his brief exposure to the fumes of Manifest Destiny, so noxious to Mexico in the recent past. The personification of the aggressive spirit, then nearing its apogee in the rising Republic of the North, was John Forsyth, who arrived in Mexico (October, 1856) as United States minister, with a bagful of real estate proposals and transit contracts, scarcely camouflaged in the form of international treaties. In accordance with his instructions, he repeatedly pressed the Comonfort government to make an "adjustment" of the northern boundary and to grant to the United States transit rights across the Isthmus of Tehuantepec.[34]

Yet even Forsyth's excessive ardor cooled in the face of the resiliency of Lerdo to his offers; and in that policy of unequivocal rejection, the Foreign Minister was in complete accord with President Comonfort, who "would sooner throw himself from the Palace windows" than alienate an inch of Mexican territory.[35] The answer to Forsyth's haggling was precisely stated by Lerdo in a formal note to the United States Minister. In regard to a boundary treaty, the Mexican government "considers inadmissible any plan based upon the cession of any portion of the national territory," while the clauses of the United States draft treaty for transit rights were "stipulations Mexico could not admit insomuch as they depreciate her rights of sovereignty over that Territory."[36]

While Lerdo's conduct of the foreign office, a mere fragment of a broader, disjointed epoch, had no tangible results, at least there were no McLane-Ocampo treaties, for all the desperation of Comonfort's financial position, and war with Spain had been avoided for the time being.

---

[33]Manuel Rivera Cambas, *Historia de la Intervención Europea y Norte-Americana en México y del Imperio de Maximiliano de Hapsburgo*, I, 194; Javier de P. Acevedo, *Europa y México 1861–1862* . . . , 24–25; Luis Pérez Verdía, *Compendio de la Historia de México* . . . , 484.

[34]James Morton Callahan, *American Foreign Policy in Mexican Relations*, 240, 244–245, 247.

[35]Forsyth to Cass, September 15, 1857, William R. Manning (ed.), *Diplomatic Correspondence of the United States: Inter-American Affairs, 1831–1860*, IX, 931.

[36]Lerdo to Forsyth (trans.), September 12, 1857, Manning (ed.), *ibid.*, IX, 927.

The cabinet submitted a collective resignation on September 15, which Comonfort accepted two days later. Judging by the evidence, this event might be passed over as a mere fact. The overt reason given by the ministers for their retirement was the desire to leave Comonfort, now the constitutional president, the freedom to choose a new set of councilors who would be acceptable to the newly-elected congress. The reasoning seemed plausible and was considered valid, perhaps because of frequent repetition.[37] One of the retiring ministers, Manuel Siliceo, related an entirely different story, however, which is valuable for permitting an insight into Lerdo's political opinions at that time. According to Siliceo, the ministers arranged a pretext for public consumption to the effect that

it was necessary to leave the poor President with freedom to call a parliamentary cabinet. This is the apparent reason, but the real and true one is that we [i.e., the cabinet ministers] are neither constitutionalists nor do we believe that you can resolve the situation with the aforesaid Constitution of 1856; not for a moment do we believe that the country is ready to be governed constitutionally; quite to the contrary, according to us. The great reforms which the country needs cannot be effected by congresses but by a liberal dictatorship, blameless and progressive.[38]

There were others intimately connected with events during those days of suspense surrounding the beginning of the constitutional order who confirmed Siliceo's account. One observer went to the length of claiming that the cabinet had exerted pressure on Comonfort to reject the Constitution of 1857 and to continue governing with extraordinary executive powers, but it had failed to overcome his personal antagonism to such a *golpe de estado*.[39] "The present ministers will retire," wrote Pedro Escudero to Mariano Riva Palacio, after an interview with Comonfort on September 9, "since all are in accord with the continuation of the dictatorship by the terms under which it now exists."[40]

Peering beneath the veneer of the official account, one can discern that Sebastián, a key member of the cabinet, must have had little faith in the machinery erected by the Constitution of 1857

[37]Anselmo de la Portilla, *Méjico en 1856 y 1857, Gobierno del General Comonfort*, 262; Zamacois, *Historia de Méjico*, XIV, 644–645; Iglesias, *Autobiografía*, 26–27.

Comonfort's official acceptance of the joint resignation was printed in *El Eco Nacional*, September 23, 1857.

[38]Manuel Siliceo to Manuel Doblado, September 21, 1857, Carlos E. Castañeda (ed.), *La Guerra de Reforma según el Archivo del General D. Manuel Doblado, 1857–1860* (*Nuevos Documentos Inéditos ó Muy Raros para la Historia de México*, Ser. 2, III), 8.

[39]José M. Aragón to Lic. D. Manuel Doblado, September 14, 1857, Castañeda (ed.), *ibid.*, 6.

[40]Pedro Escudero to Mariano Riva Palacio, September 9, 1857, Mariano Riva Palacio Papers, Folder 168, UT.

as a practical expedient for controlling the widespread unrest.[41] Fortunately, his attitude escaped notice, for the Constitution in time was to become enshrined as a national symbol. But considering the exigencies of the moment, one should not condemn too quickly those who desired an extension of strong government. Even with dictatorial powers during the interim period, Comonfort was exhausted in trying to cope with the hydra-like generative power of the reaction. The prospect under the new organic law, with its feeble executive, shackled by a unicameral assembly chosen on the theoretical basis of popular representation, was not a reassuring experiment to those of a moderate leaning, although Comonfort's indecision and later defection to the conservatives cannot be condoned.

With his departure from the cabinet in September, 1857, Sebastián ended a brief and abortive initiation in politics, though he was mentioned afterwards as a possible choice for the succeeding ministry.[42] Since he seemed to be opposed to the Constitution, that was perhaps the most fortunate accident which could have befallen him; for in the few weeks to follow, Comonfort cast off the title of legal president and discarded the constitutional order in exchange for the ragged garment of a revolutionary executive. The event which ended the protracted period of hesitancy and tension occurred in December, 1857, when he accepted the Plan of Tacubaya, an ill-disguised conservative scheme by which the new order was overthrown and the attempt was made to erase the achievements of the reform since late 1855. In this fashion was Mexican society split violently into two factions which resorted to the battlefield as the only method of resolving their ancient conflicts.

As noted previously, the conservatives established their government in Mexico City, upon the principles of religion, privilege, and the old, familiar way of life; while the liberals rested their cause on the much-maligned Constitution of 1857 with all the equalizing reforms which it incorporated and the ideal of popular, representative institutions. They eventually established their government at Vera Cruz under the presidency of Benito Juárez, who fell heir to his office by virtue of Comonfort's desertion and the fact that he was in line to succeed, being president of the Supreme Court of Justice.[43]

The ebb and flow of the struggle which continued for three years with all the characteristics of civil strife came to rest in the triumph.

---

[41]Compare the contrary claim of Enrique M. de los Ríos, *Liberales Ilustres*, 227–228.

[42]*El Eco Nacional*, September 27, 1857; [José M. Aragón?] to M. Doblado, October 14, 1857, Castañeda (ed.), *La Guerra de Reforma*, 17.

[43]Mexico had no other "legal" president until over fourteen years later, when Sebastián succeeded on Juárez's death, through the same medium of the presidency of the Supreme Court, the *de facto* vice-presidency.

of the cause of reform and the Constitution. With victory came a vengeful spirit against those who were in any way connected with the conservative régime or the events leading up to Comonfort's acceptance of the Plan of Tacubaya. A strange political inquisition followed when the only entrée into political life was open support of the liberal cause during the War of the Reform, or freedom from the taint of association with the conservative régime.

Sebastián made no contribution to the eventual victory of the constitutionalists, but he could claim the second credential. For three years he remained in the capital, continuing his neutral duties as rector of San Ildefonso—duties which were never considered political, although the conservative government had supervised the institution. If there was any doubt on the "correctness" of his stance, it was removed during a session of congress in 1862, when he was serving as a deputy. At that time a committee proposed that certain members of the house should be excluded from office and placed outside the forgiveness of the general amnesty if they had in any way served the reaction from 1858 to 1861, or had been involved in the *golpe de estado* of December, 1857, as the Plan of Tacubaya was branded. Not only was the measure rejected but during the course of the debates one of the opposition speakers pointed out that the bill, if passed, could be applied to some "worthy representatives, like Señor Riva Palacio and Señor Lerdo, who have not served the reaction, but the country and only the country, in positions distinct from politics. . . ." One of the proponents of the bill then explained that it was never intended to comprehend "citizens so creditable as Señor Riva Palacio and Señor Lerdo for whom he professed the highest esteem and respect."[44]

Yet Lerdo's aloofness toward politics during the war, while relatively absolute, should be qualified. Under the Plan of Tacubaya, Comonfort was to appoint a council of the outstanding leaders of all parties to assist him while a new constitution was being drafted. Among those chosen was Sebastián Lerdo, who, along with Manuel Siliceo, his former colleague in the cabinet, was named secretary to the body.[45] In addition, a rumor circulated a few days later about Sebastián's appointment to an interim ministry being formed by Comonfort.[46] But the provisional experiment came to a sudden end, Comonfort himself realizing—too late—that he had been merely a tool of the conservatives.

On the other side of the balance, Lerdo gave positive proof that he had no desire to attach his fortunes to the reactionary cause. In December, 1858, a conservative scheme (Plan of Ayotla) developed near Mexico City to overthrow the unpopular president,

---

[44]Session of congress, November 5, 1862, *El Siglo*, November 6, 1862.
[45]*La Sociedad*, December 26, 1857.
[46]*Ibid.*, January 2, 1858.

Félix Zuloaga, and to substitute a more capable leader who was to be selected by a provisional junta. Lerdo was appointed to that assembly, but wisely refused to attend its meetings and even resigned his commission.[47] Thus, the sum of his political activities justify the title "moderate,"[48] but the facts indicate that it should be extended to moderate liberal.

In glancing back upon Sebastián's disconnected and fragmentary political ventures over a period of some five years which was mostly chaos and disorder, one could almost discount them altogether. Still, it is always helpful to see the cross section of a man's opinions as they were at one particular stage in order to understand the extent of evolution at a later time. To Lerdo personally, the most fortunate benefit was negative: he avoided ruining his future by becoming entangled with the losing side or being involved seriously in the Plan of Tacubaya, a graveyard for many promising figures. On the other hand, it might be presumed that his positions on the Supreme Court and especially his cabinet post would have given him a certain prestige, a certain public prominence. It was not so. Whatever gains may have accrued to him were erased by the three-year intermission in normal public life—if there were such a standard—during the civil war; and in 1861 he began again to lay the foundations of his political career as a deputy in congress. From that point there would be no further interruptions. Before tracing in detail his interesting climb, however, it is necessary to pause for a better understanding of the brothers Lerdo, Miguel and Sebastián, and their relationship to each other.

---

[47]*Ibid.*, December 31, 1858; January 1, 2, 1859.

[48]Maurice Elward Caldwell, *The War of "La Reforma" in Mexico, 1858–1861* (Ph.D. thesis, The University of Texas, 1935), 156–157.

Chapter V

Interlude: The Brothers Lerdo

The past has given few examples of two brothers both of whom have attained eminence as statesmen. When such a coincidence occurs, it becomes difficult to deal with one to the complete exclusion of the other. Certain questions are bound to arise. What was the relationship between the two? How may they be compared? What analogies may be drawn of their public careers?

In the case of Miguel and Sebastián, these questions are best answered in a general way by first tracing briefly the chief events of Miguel's career and pointing out specific evidence from which a few conclusions may be drawn. If further excuse is necessary for this pause, other than interest, certainly the historical confusion which surrounds the brothers Lerdo would seem to suffice.

Several references have been made already to the activities in which Miguel had prominence. His life—intense, energetic, and vivid—was like a brilliant flash, fading quickly into obscurity behind the shade of Juárez, perhaps the most enduring and massive figure of nineteenth-century Mexico. To comprehend Miguel's true position, therefore, one must gather a few facts and then seek the opinions of contemporaries. Like his younger brother Sebastián, the story of his life, unavoidably sketchy, must be pieced together painstakingly from fragments scattered here and there.

An outline of Miguel's political offices will demonstrate the concentration of his activity during the short span of about eight years. He appeared to have gained some recognition as early as 1852, when he was an active member of the *ayuntamiento* of Mexico City,[1] but his first real opportunity probably came to him by chance. After the resignation of President Mariano Arista and many devious manipulations behind the scenes, it was decided (in 1853) to recall Santa Anna from his place of exile in Colombia to resume his familiar rôle as chief of the nation. Whether Mexico had succumbed to habit is difficult to say, yet the fatal decision was made and a commission, with the appearance of a coalition of all factions, was appointed to carry the personal invitation to the ex-President. Searching for a representative of the liberal federalists, the interim

---

[1] Ernesto Alconedo, "Miguel Lerdo de Tejada," *Diez Civiles Notables*, 118. Miguel was mentioned frequently in the regular reports on the *ayuntamiento* printed under the column for local news *(Noticias de la Capital)* in *El Siglo*, May–June, 1852.

officials agreed upon Miguel Lerdo, and he seems to have accepted the assignment and to have made the trip to Cartagena.[2]

Soon after Santa Anna's return, Miguel received an appointment as undersecretary of Fomento,[3] a new ministerial department erected in 1853 to promote general economic development and for which Miguel was chiefly responsible.[4] It was a natural child of his fervent devotion, almost a monomania, to the theory that economic-material development of Mexico was the chief antidote for curing her timeless ills.

Miguel's connection with the dictatorship, as already noted, did not affect his fortunes after the triumph of the Revolution of Ayutla; and he continued in the same office in the same department, of which he had been the principal founder, until President Comonfort appointed him minister of Finance to replace the retiring Manuel Payno.[5]

The boundless energy he exerted while holding that post, especially toward implementing the Ley Lerdo, can be gauged in part by the famous *Memoria de Hacienda* which he presented to Comonfort early in 1857.[6] It was a compilation of the progress made to that time in disamortizing the church lands throughout the nation, with all the supplementary decrees, real property evaluations and descriptions, names of purchasers—in short, all available data neatly tabulated—to show the President the results which had been attained.[7]

On leaving office in January, 1857, Miguel retired to private life and finished a book which he had long postponed because of his

---

[2]Juan Suárez y Navarro, *Historia de México y del General Antonio López de Santa-Anna* . . . , I, 227, 228. The author, who. was intimately associated with those events, spoke of Miguel, even at that early date, as a representative of the *"partido puro."*
Miguel mentioned the incident in one of his own works but omitted any reference to himself.—*Apuntes Históricos*, II, 606–607. See also Enrique Olavarría y Ferrari, *México Independiente 1821–1855* [Riva Palacio (ed.), *México á Través de los Siglos*, IV], 804; Guillermo Prieto, *Memorias de Mis Tiempos, 1840 á 1853*, 399–400.

[3]Riva Palacio (ed.), *México á Través de los Siglos*, IV, 811.

[4]In an editorial in *El Siglo*, June 9, 1861, Francisco Zarco commended the success of the new ministry and noted the progress achieved under its direction, "because Sr. Lerdo de Tejada, whose grandiose projects were not a mystery to his numerous friends . . . presided over its organization."

[5]Zamacois, *Historia de Méjico*, XIV, 258. See above p. 34, 34n.

[6]*Memoria Presentada al Exmo. Sr. Presidente Sustituto de la República por el C. Miguel Lerdo de Tejada* . . . ; Phipps, *Some Aspects of the Agrarian Question in Mexico*, 79, 79n.

[7]Although the problems arising from the Ley Lerdo were of first priority, Miguel did not confine his energy to that one aspect of national economy. His reforming instinct spread to such matters as tariff revision, debt consolidation, and postal conventions. For his own summary of these activities, see *Memoria de Hacienda, 1857*, 3–48.

public responsibilities,[8] but he might have been a candidate for the presidency in the elections had he so desired. Considering his tremendous popularity with the *puros* and fame as a reformer, one cannot eliminate completely his chances of success, though any statement in that connection would be highly speculative. Among the reasons for his refusal to participate was a fear that electoral campaigning might further endanger a nation already embarrassed by frequent revolts and torn by irreparable factionalism.[9] In justice to him, there was merit and patriotism in his abnegation at the time, since he held Comonfort's policies in deep distrust.

It is useless to follow the avalanche of press rumors about Miguel's resignation, because he revealed his own opinions of Comonfort, the reaction, and the Ley Lerdo at the very time those events were current history. Miguel believed that if Comonfort, a man "suave and conciliatory," had used his undivided force and energy in destroying the clerical-military reaction,

the struggle would have effected forcibly the complete reform of those two classes which have most abused the patience of the nation, leaving her free once and for all of the great obstacles which have blocked her aggrandizement and prosperity. But for his own misfortune and that of the Republic, General Comonfort lacked the qualities of energy and abnegation necessary to fight for the rights of the nation, and adopting a policy of wavering from one extreme to another, in which he alternated some actions of valor with others of unmitigated weakness, he did no more than maintain the civil war. . . .[10]

In Miguel's way of thinking, Comonfort's weakness fused the opposition into a compact core of resistance, and his blind sustenance of "antiquated ideas" made the funereal consequences of open civil war inevitable. Summing up his denunciation—and here he exposed his belief in popular sovereignty—he stated that Comonfort had supported the reactionaries who refused "to recognize in the Mexican people the faculty which nature had conceded to all human societies of procuring their own well-being and prosperity . . . ."[11]

In regard to the land reform for which he had labored so ardently, unfortunately he mentioned it only in a casual manner, omitting any reference to himself as the author. Yet he placed the blame for the failure to enforce it squarely at the door of the clergy who prodded a devout populace into opposition with truculent preaching and other clerical weapons.[12]

---

[8]See Miguel Lerdo de Tejada, *Apuntes Históricos*, II, prologue and p. 634.
[9]"Manifestación al Público," June 12, 1857, *El Estandarte Nacional*, June 17, 1857.
[10]Miguel Lerdo de Tejada, *Apuntes Históricos*, II, 622, 626. Quotation adapted.
[11]*Ibid.*, II, 627, 634.
[12]*Ibid.*, II, 626–627.

Miguel's retirement in January, 1857, was not to be of long duration . Chosen a magistrate of the Supreme Court in the elections of 1857, he took office in November of that year.[13] Then came the intricate events leading to the Plan of Tacubaya and the outbreak of civil war. While Juárez, who snatched up the legal presidency which Comonfort had tossed aside, made his tortuous way to Vera Cruz via the Pacific Coast, Panamá, and New Orleans, to establish the constitutional government, adventures scarcely less dramatic were happening to Miguel in Mexico City, then in possession of the conservatives.

It is hardly necessary to point out that the capital was not a particularly healthy milieu for the author of the Ley Lerdo; for as a revolutionary agent commissioned by Juárez to foment unrest within the reactionary stronghold,[14] he lived in constant danger. Hounded from place to place by the police, he eventually sought asylum at the American legation, where he found Forsyth, the United States minister, sympathetic to his risks and willing to shelter him as "a guest" under his roof.[15] But Forsyth found his visitor so "hated by the church party" that he prepared to defend the legation ("my castle") against an expected attempt of the conservatives to violate its immunity in order to seize the human prey contained therein.[16]

Confined and hazardous as were his activities, Miguel continued the work for which he had been commissioned; however, after the miscarriage of an audacious republican plot in October, 1858, in which he was acting as the chief coördinator, his residence in the capital was no longer tenable.[17] He vanished from Mexico City about mid-October, shortly before Forsyth's exit, and made his way to Vera Cruz to join "the sick family" *(la familia enferma)*, as the conservative press disdainfully styled the Juárez government.[18]

[13]Dublán y Lozano, *Legislación Mexicana*, VIII, 651; Parada Gay, *Breve Reseña de la Suprema Corte de Justicia*, 50–51.

[14]According to Francisco Zarco, editor of *El Siglo*, three persons including himself, Miguel Lerdo, and Ramón Guzmán, worked together for Juárez in espionage activities in Mexico City in 1858. The principal objective was the purchase of supporters who would be willing "to pronounce" against the reactionary régime.—*El Siglo*, March 19, 1861.

[15]Forsyth to Cass, July 1, 1858, Manning (ed.), *Diplomatic Correspondence*, IX, 1011.

[16]Forsyth to Cass, August 1, 1858, *ibid.*, IX, 1018.

[17]Miguel Blanco, commander of the military troops taking part in this scheme, described Miguel Lerdo's part in *Rectificaciones Históricas, Colección de Artículos Escritos por el C. Miguel Blanco*, especially 65–69, 71–72, 78. Having approached the city from the direction of Morelia, Blanco arrived with his force at Tacubaya, October 14, 1858, the night after Miguel Lerdo departed in search of information of his whereabouts.—*Ibid.*, 78.

[18]*La Sociedad*, October 22, 1858. Miguel's reported locations were occasionally mentioned in the capital while he was en route to Vera Cruz.—*Ibid.*, November 17, December 15, 1858.

The active part which Miguel took in the War of the Reform (1858–1861) was in sharp contrast to that of his brother. Until June, 1860, he served as minister of Finance in Juárez's *familia enferma* at Vera Cruz, the city of his birth. Because of his clear-cut ideas, his reputation as a father of reform, and his generally acknowledged brilliance as a financier and economist, his popularity ascended until those around him in the official circle discovered that they were relegated to the rôles of political pygmies. William Churchwell, the special diplomatic agent of President Buchanan at Vera Cruz, stated that Miguel Lerdo had drafted the "eminently liberal" program of the Juárez régime; and after describing Juárez and Melchor Ocampo, another cabinet minister, he compared them to Miguel, who

has all the brilliant qualities of the other two, is as pure as they, but possesses more of the practical habits which constitute a mind turned towards the actualities of life, rather than towards its dreams.

He is the most popular man among his party, and deservedly considered as the master spirit of the Cabinet. His tendencies are all American; he is the best informed statesman of the political and commercial history and progress of his country.

We should look up to him as the man most reliable in his preferences for us; frank, open, bold, and always ready to approach a question, and to assume a responsibility.[19]

But Churchwell was neither the first nor the last American diplomat to be dazzled by Miguel's talents and personality. The condescending Forsyth, as early as 1856, had considered him "one of the most liberal & enlightened of Mexican Statesmen,"[20] and a little additional personal contact elevated his opinion to "the ablest and most fearless public man I have met in this country, and who is the acknowledged leader of the Puro or Democratic party. . . ."[21] In addition, Robert McLane of treaty fame, who became the United States minister at Vera Cruz in the spring of 1859, thought Miguel "a statesman of a grave and thoughtful character, very radical withal in his opinions, and quite reliant and confident on the ultimate success of the liberal party in Mexico. . . ."[22]

Miguel's list of diplomatic admirers was not confined to those of Yankee origin. George Mathew, the British minister to Mexico, added another verbal trophy by awarding him the title of "the ablest if not the only financier in the Republic. . . ."[23]

---

[19]Churchwell to James Buchanan, February 22, 1859, Manning (ed.), *Diplomatic Correspondence*, IX, 1033, 1034.

[20]Forsyth to Marcy, November 19, 1856, *ibid.*, IX, 863.

[21]Forsyth to Marcy, January 1, 1857, *ibid.*, IX, 877.

[22]McLane to Cass, April 7, 1859, *ibid.*, IX, 1041.

[23]George B. Mathew to Lord John Russell, May 12, 1861, *British and Foreign State Papers*, LII, 250.

While at Vera Cruz, Miguel's activities centered upon finance and diplomacy, two of the thorniest, interconnected problems facing the struggling constitutional government during the civil war. In addition, he made a trip to the United States in the summer of 1859 to raise a loan, but met inevitable defeat, principally because the Buchanan administration was insisting upon a Mexican territorial cession as a *sine qua non* of any kind of financial aid.[24]

Just prior to Lerdo's departure for the United States, Juárez promulgated the long-delayed reforms, separating in detail the church from the state. The most important single measure was the outright confiscation of church real property without compensation, the logical advance from the Ley Lerdo, which the church adamantly had refused to accept. Those measures collectively constituted the most permanent achievement of the civil war, even though, technically speaking, they did not become organic law until many years later. Nor can it be denied that Miguel Lerdo was the chief figure who forced "the cautious, stolid Indian president to act without further delay upon the project to nationalize ecclesiastical properties, which had been pending for months. . . ."[25]

Miguel's political acumen, experience, and popularity led to personal enmities and jealousies within the cabinet, which in the case of Ocampo, eventually degenerated into an open feud. Finding himself isolated on virtually every cabinet question, particularly in regard to proposals for mediating the civil war,[26] Miguel's resignation became a matter of time. The occasion for the rupture with Juárez was Miguel's proposal to suspend payments on the foreign debts for a brief period as an expedient to fill the vacuum in the treasury. "The President agreed to my plan after a long deliberation over the advantages and disadvantages," he explained, but then reversed his decision after the matter had been announced publicly. Thus compromised, Miguel continued, "no other recourse

[24]James Morton Callahan, "The Mexican Policy of Southern Leaders under Buchanan's Administration," *Annual Report of the American Historical Association for the Year 1910*, 145n.

[25]Caldwell, *The War of "La Reforma" in Mexico*, 175. See also Sierra, *Juárez*, 145–146. Complete nationalization was probably Miguel's original objective in 1856, although it was too radical for the Comonfort cabinet at that time.—Romero, *Biografía del Ciudadano Benito Juárez*, 17–18. But compare Ralph Roeder, *Juárez and His Mexico*, I, 206–207. Roeder's entire treatment of Miguel is patently prejudiced, probably for the reason which is most obvious—he competed too well with Juárez for historical glory.

[26]See the entries in Juárez's journal, March 13, April 20, 23, 1860, J. M. Puig Casauranc, *Archivos Privados de D. Benito Juárez y D. Pedro Santacilia*, 270–273; M[iguel] Lerdo de Tejada to Manuel Doblado, July 24, 1860, Castañeda (ed.), *La Guerra de Reforma*, 205.

remained but retirement; not only was I left in a very annoying situation, but furthermore I was condemned to ridicule."[27]

During the six months intervening between Miguel's split with Juárez and the end of the civil war (January, 1861), he retired to private life, although he was connected with another futile attempt to mediate between the opposing factions, a negotiation apparently initiated by Francisco Pacheco, the Spanish minister to the conservative government. Despite Pacheco's claim to the contrary,[28] he seems to have sought the coöperation of Miguel, who properly conveyed the scheme to Juárez. The legitimate President, however, remained intransigent toward any dealings with the conservatives.[29]

With the victory of Juárez and the liberal faction came the announcement of new elections, already delayed because of the war. Oddly, that event fused the political lives of the brothers Lerdo: when one made a permanent exit, the other made a permanent entrance. One of the chief presidential candidates, Miguel died, March 22, 1861, at his home in Tacubaya, stricken by typhus fever.[30] Florid tribute filled the columns of the press for many days, while the government ordered the observance of mourning throughout the republic and passed measures of financial aid for the family of a man who died poor. The deserved recognition of a great reformer, liberal, and statesman attained such a peak of homage that a description could not be magnified out of true proportion. "We can assert without exaggeration," wrote Manuel María de Zamacona, who delivered one of the burial orations, "that Mexico has never seen a funeral so crowded, nor one in which the grievous sympathy of all classes was made so manifest."[31] Another contemporary who witnessed the procession added that "his ability, probity, political and religious tolerance made him worthy of public appreciation. His burial was the most crowded which has ever been seen."[32]

---

[27]M. Lerdo de Tejada to Jesús González Ortega, July 23, 1860, *Correspondence of Jesús González Ortega, 1851–1860,* I (Typescripts, UT). See also McLane to Cass, June 14, 1860, Manning (ed.), *Diplomatic Correspondence,* IX, 1194–1195.

[28]In a speech before the Spanish Senate, Pacheco stated that Miguel Lerdo ("one of the most distinguished persons of the liberal party") had initiated the matter.—Felipe Buenrostro, *Historia del Primero y Segundo Congresos de la República Méxicana . . . ,* IV, 35, 44; but José María Iglesias flatly denied this story on what he claimed to be excellent documentary proof.—*Ibid.,* IV, 77.

[29]*Ibid.,* IV, 193–194, 194n.

[30]*El Monitor,* March 23, 24, 1861. Coming after a protracted illness, Miguel's death was unexpected. Juárez visited him on March 21, and reported his condition much improved.—*El Siglo,* March 23, 1861.

[31]*El Siglo,* March 26, 1861.

[32]Unsigned to Comonfort, April 4, 1861, Comonfort Papers, Folder 17, UT. Roeder goes to some length to ridicule the fabulous tribute paid to Miguel, who "died just in time to save a reputation which remained mythical."—*Juárez and His Mexico,* I, 288. Roeder erroneously dated Miguel's death in February.

There remains a question about Miguel's public life which should be mentioned even though no definitive answer can be given. Would he have been president had he lived on? Justo Sierra, one of Juárez's biographers, believed it probable:

> Lerdo would have been a great president, perhaps better than Ocampo, his rival, because he was cooler, less subject to sentimentality, less impulsive let us say, though also of a soul less grand and of a spirit less brilliant. Who knows [*Quién sabe*]!; and it is useless and puerile to enter upon discourses of this type. . . .[33]

Some key to the relative strength of Juárez and Lerdo may be found in the election returns, although the figures could be no more than an indication: first, because Miguel died in the early stage of the election, and the staunchest supporters do not vote for dead men; and second, a Mexican election (especially one conducted under conditions at the conclusion of a bitter civil war) is always replete with puzzling factors which defy evaluation. Nevertheless, it was highly significant that Miguel had some 1,700 votes to Juárez's 5,100 when the count was made in congress as late as May, 1861.[34] How many of Juárez's votes, assuming a fair election, would have been cast for Miguel Lerdo had he not died?

Whatever may be surmised of Miguel's presidential prospects, Juárez never faced a more dangerous rival, and when he died, *El Impasible* was relieved of "a terrible competitor."[35] Despite the anti-Juarist viewpoint of Villaseñor y Villaseñor, one cannot overlook his suggestive comment that Miguel was not only Juárez's most formidable rival, but could not be disposed of—as Juárez allegedly had disposed of so many others—by being given a slipshod army and having his popularity sapped through inevitable defeat on the battlefield against superior conservative forces.[36] Roeder, too, tacitly recognized Miguel's greatness in the effort he expended to deny it,[37] no doubt because he saw in Lerdo's career a contribution which must be undermined or else Juárez must share a part of his glory.

No sketch of Miguel's life would be complete without at least commenting upon one facet of his versatility, his writings, most of which have been cited previously. Volume I of his first work, *Apuntes Históricos*, appeared in 1850;[38] but the last two volumes

[33]Sierra, *Juárez*, 231.
[34]Session of May 23, 1861, *El Siglo*, May 24, 1861.
[35]Rivera Cambas, *Historia de la Intervención*, I, 397.
[36]Alejandro Villaseñor y Villaseñor, "El Tratado MacLane-Ocampo," *Obras*, I, 154–155.
[37]Roeder, *Juárez and His Mexico*, I, especially 206–208, 288. Although he frequently quotes at some length, Roeder studiedly avoided the contemporary comments on Miguel.
[38]A review was printed in *El Siglo*, November 20, 1850.

were not published until 1857 and 1858, respectively. Meanwhile, he had written *Comercio Esterior de México desde la Conquista hasta Hoy* (1853), dedicated to Santa Anna,[39] *Cuadro Sinóptico de la República Méxicana en 1856,*[40] and the famous official compilation, *Memoria de Hacienda, 1857.*[41] All treat of economic or commercial matters, though they also have much historical value. In addition, they contain detailed statistical data and Miguel's theories on economy in general with pertinent remarks about the particular ills which affected the Mexico of his day. Silva Herzog singled out the *Comercio Esterior* "as already a classic in the economic history of the nation";[42] yet all of Miguel's works are rather widely cited, for some reason or another. To mention a few contemporary commendations, *La Sociedad,* in an article on population, included the *Cuadro Sinóptico* as one of the few basic sources for that subject,[43] while a writer for *El Siglo* praised the same work for its exactness, regretting that Miguel's official duties impeded his scholarly pursuits.[44] Certainly his intellectual interests were the perfect complement of his political aims and no doubt one of the bases for his wide recognition as an economist. And there was so little competition in the realm of practical economy in an age when political theorization held a monopoly. Ignacio Altamirano, the fiery orator from Guerrero, when lamenting the loss of Miguel, summarized the situation aptly: "We have many bookkeepers, but few economists."[45]

With the framework of Miguel's life complete, brief and general as it must be, it is necessary to face a more difficult problem, the relationship to his brother Sebastián. Unfortunately, the evidence is sparse and negative, and consequently there can be little elaboration on the subject, other than collecting the scattered references already made. Still, certain existing conditions aid to fill the gulf left by the absence of documentary material. Almost eleven years separated their ages, a most significant fact, when there was apparently no family tie to overcome the discrepancy.[46] Their respective connections with Comonfort indicated the difference in their

---

[39] A facsimile of the dedicatory letter was used as the cover for *Divulgación Histórica,* IV (April 15, 1943).

[40] A collector's item today, the *Cuadro Sinóptico* sold for two pesos in 1856.— Advertisement, *El Siglo,* May 24, 1856.

[41] In addition to the official publication, the *Memoria de Hacienda* was reprinted in segments in Buenrostro, *Historia del Primero y Segundo Congresos,* VI, 235–615; VII, 3–133.

[42] Silva Herzog, *El Pensamiento Económico en México,* 60.

[43] *La Sociedad,* November 17, 1858. See also Robert Denhardt, "Mexican Demography," *The Pacific Historical Review,* VII (March, 1938), 155.

[44] *El Siglo,* January 26, 1856.

[45] *Ibid.,* September 21, 1861.

[46] Sebastián was born in April, 1823; Miguel in July, 1812.

political viewpoints during the Revolution of Ayutla; and Sebastián's passive part in the War of the Reform, as a rector of a college in conservative-controlled Mexico City, not only extended that feature for three years, but also separated their places of residence. If the above is circumstantial, how can the almost complete lack of material on the relationship be explained? While it must not be assumed that contemporaries failed to recognize the blood relation, those who knew both brothers, personally or indirectly, omitted enlightening comments. For example, Miguel's name was occasionally mentioned in the debates in congress in 1861, when Sebastián was a prominent deputy, yet none of the speakers ever remarked about the affinity, as logically might be expected.

On the other hand, the material indicating some connection is either fragmentary or untrustworthy. In support of their alleged collaboration on the Ley Lerdo, one writer has claimed that the famous Jesuit uncle, Ignacio M. Lerdo, reprimanded them for such an "immediate and direct" attack on the church and excused them from any further personal visits to him.[47] Moreover, in the *Memoria de Hacienda, 1857,* may be found two official notes which Miguel addressed to the "Rector of San Ildefonso" in regard to certain real property holdings of the college.[48.] Such letters would have been sent to any rector of the same college.

Among other bits of information which might be mentioned is a remark of Villaseñor y Villaseñor that Miguel's influence brought about Sebastián's election to congress in 1861. Yet he also added that Sebastián was a moderate,[49] while Miguel's affiliation with the radicals was known to all. At any rate, such influence could only have been indirect, since Miguel was seriously ill during most of the period of voting.[50]

The complete failure to uncover any positive evidence bearing upon the association of the two brothers leads to the conclusion that it either did not exist at all, or was so unimportant that it may be dismissed altogether as a factor of any weight in the life of Sebastián. For all practical purposes, therefore, particularly the question of the direct influence of the older brother upon the younger, they may be considered unrelated.

If the above assumption is premised primarily upon the absence of positive evidence to the contrary, their present historical con-

[47]José M. Bustos, *Biografía de R. P. Soler de la Compañía de Jesús,* 9.

[48]September 26, 1856, January 26, 1857, *Memoria de Hacienda, 1857,* 36–37.

[49]Villaseñor y Villaseñor, "El Tratado Wyke-Zamacona," *Obras,* II, 153.

[50]No mention was ever made of Sebastián in any of the countless press articles on Miguel at the time of his death. The only tangible effect that event had on Sebastián, which is known to the writer at least, was a change in his stationery. He did adopt writing materials with a black border, as custom apparently dictated.—S. Lerdo de Tejada to Mariano Riva Palacio, August 6, 1861, Mariano Riva Palacio Papers, Folder 169, UT.

fusion is more easily understood. Most historians, those of Mexico being no exception, follow the practice of referring to persons by the last name,[51] and thus Miguel and Sebastián have been amalgamated as simply "Lerdo" or "Lerdo de Tejada." This sin of omission, springing from contemporary writers who were undoubtedly conscious in their own minds of the distinction, has been the continuous heritage of readers since. One example will illustrate the practice. Manuel Payno, who knew both men well, had occasion to refer to "Lerdo" several times in a work which he wrote in 1868, but he never mentioned a first name. Since he intermingled references to both brothers, the reader must know in some detail the biographical facts of their lives in order to distinguish one from the other.[52]

Some secondary historians have perpetuated the confusion, not only as a natural outgrowth of its origin, but because detailed biographical data on both men are difficult to locate and certainly cannot be found conveniently in any one place. Had biographies been written on the life of either Sebastián or Miguel, both of whom have merited the attention, or had writers made the attempt to point out the danger by the use of something more than an occasional parenthetical reference to the first name, the complication might never have arisen. Two works in English on United States-Mexican diplomatic relations will serve as excellent cases in point. The index to a book of Professor Callahan (p. 642) lists only "Miguel Lerdo de Tejada," while Sebastián's first name never appears in the text, although the great majority of the citations to "Lerdo de Tejada" apply to the younger brother.[53] On the other hand, the index to Professor Rippy's study lists only Sebastián (p. 400), although the "Lerdo de Tejada" he mentioned as being sent to the United States to negotiate a loan was Miguel.[54]

Continuing the examples in the diplomatic channel, it appeared that even Thomas H. Nelson, United States minister to Mexico after the French intervention, while Sebastián Lerdo was head of the Foreign Office and during the early part of his presidency, either confused Sebastián with Miguel or did not know of the latter's existence. Referring to Sebastián in one of his dispatches, Nelson defined him as the man who "did so much to bring about the secularization of church property in Mexico."[55]

[51]The writer has been forced constantly to correct this natural pitfall in composing the present chapter.

[52]Manuel Payno, *Cuentas, Gastos, Acreedores y Otros Asuntos del Tiempo de la Intervención Francesa y del Imperio*, 921, 925, 929, 930.

[53]James Morton Callahan, *American Foreign Policy in Mexican Relations*. The references to Miguel are on pp. 255, 262, 264; to Sebastián, pp. 249, 328, 343, 351, 363, 364, 378, 384, 480, 481.

[54]James Fred Rippy, *The United States and Mexico*, 223.

[55]Nelson to Fish, Mexico, March 23, 1871, *Dispatches from Mexico*, XLII (MSS.), Archives of the United States, Washington, D.C. (hereafter cited *Mexico, Dispatches*, A.U.S.).

Occasionally the negligence transcends omission to the realm of positive error. Thus, the authors of a recent survey of the history of Latin America stated that Sebastián wrote the Ley Lerdo and apparently they were unaware of the existence of Miguel.[56]

It might be worth while to propose a simple formula for distinguishing between the two brothers. If the key date of 1861 can be remembered, the time when Miguel died and Sebastián began a continuous political career, one can be assured that any accurate references to an "active" Lerdo de Tejada subsequent to that year are to Sebastián. Furthermore, the Lerdo de Tejada so prominent in the public events of 1856 to 1861 was almost invariably Miguel —almost. A warning must be given for the years 1856 to 1858, when Sebastián made his abortive entry into public life; for on two occasions it seemed that the brothers might collide in their appointments or resignations to or from office. Sebastián was *fiscal* and magistrate of the Supreme Court from December, 1855, to June, 1857, while Miguel was elected to the court in late 1857; and Sebastián was minister of Foreign Relations, June to mid-September, 1857, an assignment which Miguel handled in late 1856.

Any comparison of the two brothers would be anachronistic at this time, but some general similarities and contrasts may be pointed out. Both men were outstanding, civilian, liberal statesmen of the nineteenth century and had an interesting relationship to Juárez; both were men of refinement, with keen, educated minds, who displayed no small amount of courage and determination, though each in a different way; both were capable politicians who attained high offices and bountiful popularity; and both suffer the same historical neglect for somewhat similar reasons.

In contrast, Miguel's career was far more concentrated in point of time than Sebastián's and covered a different epoch; and his every energy seemed to be consecrated toward the economic-material improvement of Mexico. One would search in vain to find that singleness of purpose in Sebastián, that intensity and impatience of the reformer who desires the accomplishment of radical changes overnight.

There are other picturesque details about their lives which invite comparison, such as personality, physical appearance,[57] and attitude on foreign policy, among others; but they need not compete for a niche in the hall of fame. For every concession to one, an advantage might be found in favor of the other. They are both strong pillars upon which rests much of the weight of Juárez's fabulous reputation.

---

[56]John Francis Bannon, S. J., and Peter Masten Dunne, S. J., *Latin America, An Historical Survey*, 695, 700.

[57]In physical appearance, judging by the only pose which ever seems to be reproduced of him, Miguel was handsome, urbane, and polished. See the portrait in Sierra, *Juárez*, opposite p. 168.

Chapter VI

The Game of Parliament, 1861-1863

During the years 1861–1863 Lerdo reëntered politics as a congressional deputy; hence, a study of that period of his life falls within the broader framework of the history of congress. Yet even to include the enlarged phase would leave the perspective distorted, since the epoch was important primarily as the background of the French intervention and seldom is considered from any other standpoint. One must keep in mind, therefore, the dominant development in order to orient the significance of the activities of a single deputy in a factious unicameral assembly. While the main events will be interwoven with the specialized story whenever necessary, it will be valuable to sketch the general pattern at the outset, including only the outstanding facts.

The heritage of the Juárez government in 1861 was no bed of roses. A bleeding body politic cried out for coöperation, discipline, and time—time to reorganize finance and administration; time to breathe life into the dormant institutions established under the Constitution of 1857; time to quash the implacable opposition, which refused to accept defeat after three years of civil war; time to answer the blatant complaints of foreign powers; and time to carry out the reforms of church and state which had been the fruit of victory for the liberals.

Unfortunately, not one of these cries was answered. The mushroom revolts of the conservatives continued, reminiscent of the Revolution of Ayutla, while conciliation among factions was relegated to a fanciful theory by the march of events during the first six months of the year. Not only had the liberals suffered two staggering blows in the natural deaths of Miguel Lerdo and Gutiérrez Zamora, the governor of Vera Cruz, but the opposition had levied a left-handed vengeance in the murders of three other outstanding republican leaders, Melchor Ocampo, Santos Degollado, and Leandro del Valle.

Not satisfied with confining their thrusts to the domestic front, the conservatives had their agents abroad, peddling the twin projects of intervention and monarchy at the courts of European powers as the sole means of rescuing Mexico from the Juárez demagogy. Their efforts coincided with the decision of France, Spain, and Great Britain to settle their financial claims and other complaints against Mexico by the efficacious method of force. The decision was embodied in the famous tri-partite Treaty of London (October 31, 1861), each signatory nation having her peculiar pretexts for intervention superimposed over concealed motivating factors.

By January, 1862, just one year after the entry of Juárez into Mexico City following the triumph in the War of the Reform, the three European powers had landed contingents of troops on Mexican soil, lending a veneer of international complication to the always fundamental internal struggle over privilege. When a dispute among the interventors in April ended in the withdrawal of the Spanish and British from the enterprise, the ambitions of Napoleon III, tangibly represented by a large and experienced expeditionary force, were left exposed in a quaint and uneasy mésalliance with the decimated reactionary faction of Mexico. But not until June, 1863, and not until Puebla had twice become a national symbol by impeding the advance of the French troops, did the French commander enter the capital, forcing Juárez and the residual of his republican government in flight along the road to San Luis Potosí. Then the newlyweds settled down to establish a monarchical household, eventually under the nominal control of Archduke Maximilian, and to discover how incompatible were their respective interests.

In the face of foreign danger first and actual invasion and attack later, it is difficult to understand how the men of Mexico were able to enter the game of parliament with a vehemence almost detaching them from those more pressing concerns. The ambitions of congress were hardly appropriate to the exigencies of the time which called for a strong executive free to take decisive action. It should be remembered, however, that men had fought or waited to establish the representative government projected in 1857, and it seemed that nothing would deny them the reward.

Whatever justification may be given for the work of congress, it was again a poor time for experimentation. The vague phraseology of the organic law, the wrangling of the deputies, bloated with theory and lacking parliamentary experience, and the complete absence of anything resembling organized parties and party discipline combined to form a heavy millstone around the neck of President Benito Juárez, who was attempting to cope with the internal and foreign dangers. By calling the elections of 1861, Juárez had opened the glass case in which the Constitution of 1857 had long been preserved, and in so doing he had complied with his constitutional duties. But time and the antics of congress no doubt reminded him of the fable of Pandora's box.

For many years Mexico had been without a central representative institution. True, a constituent congress had met to draft the

Constitution in 1856–1857, and for a few weeks the first congress under that instrument had convened in late 1857, until the Plan of Tacubaya abruptly ended its sessions. Beforehand, under the dictatorship of Santa Anna (1853–1855), and subsequently during the civil war (1858–1861), a congress could not be assembled. Partly because of the long expectation and partly because of the exalted position of the unicameral legislature under the Constitution,[1] the public eagerly anticipated the convening of the congress after the elections of 1861.

That the deputies were inexperienced in parliamentary tactics was a natural outgrowth of the past. Nevertheless, the men who sat in the congresses, meeting from May, 1861, to May, 1863, formed an impressive galaxy, a virtual monopoly of the famous names of the second half of the nineteenth century. There were the Riva Palacios, father and son, who require no introduction; Juan José Baz, the timeless politician; Manuel and Joaquín Ruíz, two of the many cabinet ministers of Juárez; and Romero Rubio, whose reputation sprang from a later period as a supporter of Lerdo and a father-in-law of Porfirio Díaz. The young Díaz himself was a deputy from Oaxaca, although he was absent much of the time for the military campaigns against the French. Ezequiel Montes, Francisco Zarco, Guillermo Prieto, Manuel María de Zamacona, Ignacio Altamirano, and Sebastián Lerdo composed a battery of speakers who vied for renown in the golden age of Mexican oratory. Ignacio Mariscal, José María Mata, Ignacio Ramírez, and Ignacio Zaragoza were among others of an incomplete list whose names glorified the congress of 1861–1863.

Even with an abundance of intellect, it was not difficult to find criticism of the congress when the sum of its work was evaluated. Justo Sierra called it a "neurotic despotism,"[2] while Villaseñor y Villaseñor branded it the worst representative Mexico had ever had, because the members wasted "much time in useless and heated discussions which served only to arouse passions."[3] The deputies themselves were self-condemnatory, like José María Bautista of Puebla, who wondered, at the conclusion of the first session in the summer of 1861, if their activities would be as "sterile" in the fall term.[4] The answer came from one of his colleagues who summarized the concensus among the deputies after a meeting in September: "The session was adjourned at 4:30 in the afternoon. We had the pleasure of hearing the majority of the deputies . . . complain

[1] See García Granados, *La Constitución de 1857*, 44.
[2] Sierra, *Juárez*, 479.
[3] Villaseñor y Villaseñor, "El Tratado Wyke-Zamacona," *Obras*, II, 88.
[4] *El Siglo*, July 30, 1861.

bitterly about the lamentable manner in which time is wasted in Congress over questions of no moment and of no positive result."[5]

For all the factiousness, personal animosity, and haggling over technicalities which permeated the sessions, the deputies had youth, chauvinism, and a zest for playing the game of parliament. Perhaps anticipating his opportunity to sparkle on the rostrum, Altamirano, the great orator of Guerrero, caught something of the spirit of the members when he declared: "I shall also go to the Congress, and the rest of my companions of the deputation [of Guerrero] will all be young, progressive, and enthusiastic. . . ."[6] If ignorant of parliamentary practice, those young men, said Gustavo Baz, had their individualism and a profound faith in patriotic institutions.[7]

The main thread of dissension which tied together the many sessions of congress was the dispute over the nature of government under the Constitution; specifically, what was the proper link between the mighty congress and the weak executive? The problem consistently arose, regardless of the issue under consideration, and there could be no understanding of the attitude of congress without realizing the presence of that struggle in the background. Lacking precedents, the deputies stopped to interpret their system, a pause which might have had a baneful effect on executive action in meeting the foreign invasion.

While there was agreement that Mexico had something resembling responsible cabinet government, beyond a vague generalization the ideas on the rules for the game of parliament were as numerous as the men who were politically conscious. When should a minister resign? When was an interpellation of a minister in congress serious enough to cause his downfall? To what extent was the president responsible for policy? Who should head the ministry? The press, the deputies, and even the president joined in the arguments to offer suggestions on the legitimate rules for the game.

No one seemed to know the final answers, as was shown by the hazy interpretation of Francisco Zarco, a founding father of the Constitution, the compiler of a two-volume work on the debates of the constituent assembly, and a person who should have been an authority on the subject. According to him, Mexico had a government neither of the presidential type nor of the European cabinet-type, but a hybrid of peculiarly Mexican vintage which was strangely difficult to operate. After discussing the ministerial

---

[5]*Ibid.*, September 29, 1861.

[6]Altamirano to Ignacio Ramírez, March 1, 1861, *Correspondence of Jesús González Ortega*, 1861, IV (Typescripts, UT).

[7]Baz, *Vida de Benito Juárez*, 208. For another excellent characterization of the congress, see Miguel Galindo y Galindo, *La Gran Década Nacional . . .* , II, 49.

features of the British and United States constitutions, Zarco decided that:

Neither of these two systems is that established by our Constitution. We will not discuss at the present time its intrinsic merit, but certainly we shall take note that it neither declares the chief of State inviolable, as is done in constitutional monarchies, nor makes him the only one responsible as in the United States. It establishes a mixed system, a complex responsibility, extending to the president and the ministers. This double responsibility makes more serious the ministerial crises, more difficult their solutions.[8]

Having chased himself in unenlightening verbal circles and having convinced the reader of his own confusion in regard to the government of Mexico, Zarco concluded: ". . . what we infer is that under our system the solutions of the [ministerial] crises are more difficult, and also the duties of the opposition are more delicate."[9]

President Juárez, accustomed to freedom of action during the War of the Reform, was also puzzled about the solution, but he refused to relapse into the rôle of a figurehead. During one of the many "ministerial crises" of that period, he called upon Manuel Doblado, the governor of Guanajuato, to form a new cabinet. Doblado insisted upon absolute freedom in choosing his associates for the proposed ministry, since, he claimed, he would bear the brunt of responsibility before congress on matters of governmental policy. To his demand, Juárez replied that he had always chosen his secretaries of State, agreeing to suggested modifications whenever feasible; and, he added,

it is not certain that only the Ministers are responsible as occurs in European systems, since according to our Constitution the President also has responsibility and is not inviolable like the Kings, for which reason the Constitution gives him the faculty of naming and removing freely the Ministers.[10]

Yet congress never relinquished its claim to supremacy under the Constitution, and it persisted in the attempt to erect in modified form a responsible parliamentary system, a unique development leading to constant conflict with the executive, centering in the ministry. The organic tussle was halted by the circumstances springing from the French invasion which forced congress to lodge extraordinary powers in the president. At any rate, such a development was a premature political birth in Mexico for reasons which García Granados has pointed out: "The scrupulous observance of the spirit of our Constitution would have led logically to a government of the parliamentary majority; but a solid majority cannot

[8]*El Siglo,* July 14, 1861.
[9]*Ibid.*
[10]Puig Casauranc, *Archivos Privados de D. Benito Juárez,* 313–314.

exist while parties are lacking in the essential organization and discipline."[11]

Despite their dilatoriness and wrangling, the deputies of the period 1861–1863 left behind them the idea of republican, representative institutions, an idea which lived on through the French occupation. They were the representatives of the people; they were cherished in memory as such. When Maximilian, in 1865, decreed a provisional organic law for his empire, the unanimous public complaint was that he had not written "a single phrase" about a congress, an institution to which the Mexicans were devoted fervently.[12]

One electoral district in the state of Mexico returned a relatively unknown man as a deputy to congress in 1861.[13] His name was Sebastián Lerdo de Tejada. After participating for two years in the game of parliament, he emerged with a national reputation, an enriching experience in parliamentary manipulation, and a broadened horizon of political associations. His reputation sprang chiefly from two sources: first, the number of offices he discharged in the congress; and second, his part in a single event in the fall of 1861, the defeat of a draft treaty between Great Britain and Mexico which was considered vital at the time. Before considering the specific incident, it will be helpful to survey Lerdo's general activities in congress and to define his political affiliation, cutting across the chronological sessions of the two years.[14]

While there was no standard to measure the merits of the various representatives in the competition for prominence, certainly Sebastián Lerdo bowed to none in the variety of his activities. He attended meetings with regularity, although he did not take a bold part in the debates at public sessions, and, in fact, he seemed consciously to hold his ability in reserve. At least, that was the impression of Bautista, his old schoolmate, then sitting with him as a fellow deputy: "For a long time in that Cámara," he wrote, "you did not want to show your great talent, your facility in speaking, your select oratory. . . ."[15] There were others like Mata, Alta-

---

[11]García Granados, *La Constitución de 1857*, 45–46.

[12]Paul Gualot, *L'Empire de Maximilien* (*La Vérité sur L'Expédition du Mexique* . . . , II), 172.

[13]*El Monitor*, March 21, 1861. Lerdo was elected by another district in the same state in the summer of 1862.—*El Siglo*, August 13, September 5, 1862.

[14]Statements not cited are grounded upon conclusions drawn from a detailed analysis of congressional meetings on a day-to-day basis as reported in *El Siglo*. In many instances it has been impossible to give a single reference.

[15]Bautista to Lerdo, September 8, 1876, *Memoria de la Academia Nacional de Historia y Geografía* (No. 2, 1946), 47.

mirano, Zamacona, and Montes who were constantly monopolizing the floor, no doubt enchanted by their own sonorous flights and not without an eye on the gallery. Yet the contrast in Lerdo's method of presentation, cool, logical, precise, and notable for the lack of flowery phrases, was enough to command attention when he abandoned his taciturnity. Sierra left an excellent description of him in relation to other outstanding orators:

Lerdo was, without wanting to be, or knowing it, the model of the new orator. Frequently emphatic, his discourses were bas-reliefs of bronze. The bronze was logic, an inflexible logic which served him marvelously to censor texts and to disarm and conquer persons. He did not wrap his idea in grand and sonorous metaphors like the rhetoricians or the poets of the tribune; he went to the grain; he did not cite the classics like his frequent adversary, the lawyer Montes, who gave discourses in Latin with notes in Castilian, nor did he make of history a sword of fire like Altamirano; he cited the words of the proposals or propositions under discussion, compared them, analyzed them with his dialectic power of the first order. And he was not cold; his word and his voice kindled and his concept shone in each conclusion.[16]

On the other hand, much important business was transacted in secret sessions, and it was in such unrecorded meetings that he apparently proved a powerful speaker. Reporting the rumors of a particularly bitter closed session of November, 1861, *El Constitucional* remarked that Lerdo "had been the hero of the day's work, as he always has been in the discussion of the secret sessions."[17] An action portrait of him had appeared much earlier, describing his congressional agility during the meetings of the previous summer:

Sr. Lerdo . . . has unforgivable sins; in the heated sessions of the permanent deputation he was the most stainless defender of the rights of the assembly; those who believed him weak, pusillanimous, and compliant have suffered a horrible deception; he is an athlete full of courage, robust and fibrous, who does not pause to gather in the gifts which they throw out to him in the ring in order to keep him in expectation: neither employments nor commissions nor raised hopes make his firmness vacillate; he is a gladiator of short stature, who knows how to face danger, without provoking the many others who have fought with indomitable audacity in the parliamentary lists.[18]

Once granted recognition, offices came to Lerdo in abundance. On three different occasions he presided over congress,[19] twice in

---

[16]Sierra, *Juárez*, 292.

[17]Reprinted in *El Siglo*, November 27, 1861. In the same issue a satirical poem was printed about Lerdo's perorations at the closed meetings.

[18]*Ibid.*, September 2, 1861. The permanent deputation was a standing committee composed of a representative of each state and the federal district, which sat during the recess for organizational purposes, principally to spy on the executive for any "usurpations" of authority.

[19]Lerdo's terms as president of congress were as follows: August 29 to September 15, 1861 (extraordinary session); April 14 to May 1, 1862; May 4 to May 31, 1863. See *ibid.*, August 30, September 15, 1861; April 15, May 1, 1862; May 5, 1863; *Diario Oficial de la República Mejicana* (San Luis Potosí), June 16, 1863.

regular sessions and once in an extraordinary session, called, incidentally, because of his insistence as president of the permanent deputation.[20] Since the presidency of congress was elective and rotated monthly, the repetition of the reward indicated that Lerdo was successful in taming the spirited deputies. In addition, he held a fair share of the important committee posts, especially on finance and foreign affairs, and twice served as president of the permanent deputation.[21]

Among the particular assignments which fell his lot were the negotiation and drafting of postal and extradition treaties in collaboration with Charles Corwin, the United States minister to Mexico, who had arrived in the spring of 1861.[22] Both conventions were ratified promptly and enhanced Lerdo's training in diplomacy, a sphere which was to be his exclusively for many years as a cabinet minister under Juárez. Nor were those treaties isolated details. Juárez mentioned them in his speech to congress at the close of its sessions on December 15, 1861, as among the outstanding achievements of the body;[23] and a contemporary American publicist considered them "among the most important" diplomatic conventions ratified by the United States during the Civil War.[24]

Various miscellaneous assignments cropped up sporadically and must have kept Lerdo well occupied, since he was still functioning as rector of San Ildefonso. In accordance with a congressional resolution of April, 1862, he drafted a manifesto to the nation, appealing to the people to take up arms against the French invader,[25] and on several occasions he was appointed to make official visits or to participate in the formal ceremonies of congress.[26] Also, probably because of his prominence in the assembly, he attended occasional private or semi-official celebrations. One of those took place on Juárez's birthday, March 21, 1863, when a number of notables was

[20]Zarco wrote the following comment on the extraordinary session: "If anyone could know perfectly the spirit which inspired this convocation it is, without doubt, Sr. Lerdo de Tejada, since he discharged the presidency of the permanent deputation."—*El Siglo*, September 1, 1861.

[21]*Ibid.*, August 3, 1861, and December 26, 1862.

[22]The English and Spanish texts of those treaties may be found in *Derecho Internacional Mexicano*, I, part one, 272–283. See also Corwin to Seward, December 24, 1861, *Correspondence Relative to the Present Condition of Mexico, Communicated to the House of Representatives by the Department of State*, 37; *El Siglo*, June 2, 1862.

[23]*El Siglo*, December 16, 1861.

[24]"Our Diplomacy during the Rebellion," *The North American Review*, CII (April, 1866), 470–471.

[25]Session of April 28, 1862, *El Siglo*, May 1, 1862. The result, "El Congreso de los Estados Unidos Mexicanos a la Nación," May 9, 1862, merited a supplementary edition of *El Siglo*, May 11, 1862.

[26]See, for example, *ibid.*, November 23, 1861; Buenrostro, *Historia del Congreso*, V, 478–479.

present. At that gathering, the toasts to the President were seemingly endless, undoubtedly acting as a rationalization for the free flow of wine. When the time came for Lerdo to perform, he rose before the guests and made a prophetic statement:

Mexico fought and triumphed in the war of independence, she fought and triumphed in the War of the Reform, and she is fighting and will triumph in a war in which foreign intervention attempts to humble her. I toast because the President of the Republic, just as he has been the leader of a triumphant Mexico in the War of the Reform, will be the leader of a triumphant Mexico in this last war of independence.[27]

Though responsibility fell to Lerdo frequently in congress, his own projects for legislation were apparently microscopic. Only on some rare occasion did he initiate a measure, as in September, 1862, when news reached the capital of the death of General Zaragoza, the national hero after his great victory over the French in the Battle of Cinco de Mayo. It was Lerdo who proposed a comprehensive bill in honor of Zaragoza, granting the posthumous title of Benemérito de la Patria and pensions for the survivors of his family.[28] Undoubtedly, he coöperated on proposals which were initiated in the names of others, as in the case of ex-President Comonfort, who was seeking exoneration through congress for his acceptance of the Plan of Tacubaya, the event which had been the occasion for the outbreak of civil war in 1858. At the request of Comonfort, several lawyers, including Lerdo, Riva Palacio, Pedro Escudero, and Ezequiel Montes, had consented to use their influence to guide his petition through the national legislature,[29] but Lerdo himself was never forward in the matter, while Montes stood forth as the principal spokesman.[30]

Lerdo's political affiliation in the congress was not easy to explain, since Mexican factions escaped precise definition. All members were "liberals," or gave lip service to the reforms and the victory of the Constitution in the War of the Reform, but this did not signify that Mexico enjoyed a one-party system. Within the liberal faction were various degrees of opinion, dividing the members into fluid groups, perpetually fragmenting and realigning. Such terms as *moderado, progresista, exaltado, legalista,* and *oposicionista* were alternately applied to the different segments of the congress, the meaning having significance only in relation to particular issues.

---

[27]*El Siglo,* March 22, 1863.

[28]*El Siglo,* September 10 and 12, 1862; Rivera Cambas, *Historia de la Intervención,* II, 79.

[29]E[zequiel] M[ontes] to Ignacio Comonfort, April 19, 1861, Comonfort Papers, Folder 17, UT.

[30]At the session of May 11, 1861, when Comonfort's petition was first considered, Lerdo spoke briefly in favor of it.—*El Siglo,* May 12, 1861.

A member could change his faction as frequently as he changed his clothing, a fact which rendered ridiculous the fetish of cabinet government. For example, a deputy who attacked the ministry on some issue was usually styled an *oposicionista;* but if successful in his opposition and if he obtained a portfolio in an executive shuffle, the attacker became *ipso facto* a *legalista* or *Juarista.*

Whether a deputy was or was not an opponent of President Juárez seemed to have been the accurate thermometer for gauging his political temperature. Justo Sierra placed Lerdo among the important parliamentary personalities who were "manifestly hostile to Señor Juárez,"[31] although his attitude did not justify so strong a description. What, then, was the origin of the legend? It came from his inflexible opposition to a treaty—the Wyke-Zamacona Treaty—arranged by one of Juárez's ministers, Manuel María de Zamacona, an incident which will be discussed in detail in the proper place. When the event occurred, however, the press support behind the defeated Zamacona loosened a barrage of accusations against Lerdo, attributing to him the desire to antagonize and frustrate Juárez and his government. Eventually, Lerdo broke his customary reserve and answered those charges by explaining his views in full, pointing out that "neither before, nor now have I had the purpose of censuring the President of the Republic, remembering that in the face of similar exigencies, he defended to the ultimate in Vera Cruz the honor and the rights of the nation."[32]

Lerdo's political alignment was never grounded on personal contempt or dislike of Juárez, a man whom he apparently admired, trusted, and respected. The toast to Juárez at the birthday celebration in 1863 has been noted previously, but there were other occasions when he commended the leadership of the Chief Executive. During the customary opening ceremony of a session of congress (April 15, 1862), in which the President of the republic and the President of congress exchanged speeches, Lerdo spoke of Juárez as follows:

. . . the Supreme Magistrate of the Republic has demonstrated before in just as difficult circumstances, and he has returned to demonstrate now, all the illustriousness and energy, all the prudence and irresistible firmness with which he defends the rights and the interests of the nation.[33]

Further proof that Lerdo had no personal antipathy toward Juárez was his absolute neutrality on a unique issue which came to a head in September, 1861. Almost half of the deputies were undoubtedly "manifestly hostile" to the man who had "raised himself

[31]Sierra, *Juárez*, 251.
[32]Lerdo to the editors of *El Constitucional*, December 6, 1861, reprinted in *El Siglo*, December 10, 1861.
[33]*El Siglo*, April 16, 1862.

from a wretched Indian hut to the highest position in the state";[34] and they grouped themselves into a typical personal party behind the dashing Jesús González Ortega, governor of Zacatecas, hero of the decisive battle of the civil war, a former minister in one of Juárez's cabinets, and, in 1861, the newly-installed president of the Supreme Court. When Ortega's popularity reached a peak after his victory over the reactionary chieftain Leonardo Márquez in August, 1861,[35] the opposition deputies took the brash step of addressing a petition to Juárez, suggesting in no subtle terms that he resign the presidential chair to make room for a truly capable leader—Ortega. The document became known as the "petition of the 51," after the number of deputies who signed. In protest, some 52 deputies filed a counterpetition, "abhorring" in seventeenth-century Tory style the thought of such an extralegal move. Lerdo's signature was on neither document, for he had remained aloof from the proceedings along with five or six other colleagues.[36]

In analyzing Lerdo's political beliefs as a deputy, as opposed to his relationship to personalities, his one outstanding conviction was on foreign affairs, represented by a national pride approaching chauvinism. What he believed to be an inroad on the national integrity was the force which pulled him from his shell to denounce the Wyke-Zamacona Treaty, and it was significant that he initiated the heroic award of congress to Ignacio Zaragoza. His speeches, already cited, were pervaded with the same flavor. Moreover, his convictions on domestic questions had matured considerably since 1857, when all were baffled by his unexpected entrance into the Comonfort cabinet; but those convictions were "still not well-defined," according to Villaseñor y Villaseñor, who classed Lerdo among the moderate liberals:

Accepting the theory of consummated facts in regard to the nationalization of ecclesiastical property, he tried nevertheless to regulate it with some restrictions and to modify some articles of the constitution, like the one relating to judicial charges.[37]

The most accurate statement of Lerdo's policies was a program which he presented to Juárez in November, 1861, when he was invited by the President to head a new ministry. His plan of action included the following planks, all of which, he claimed, were approved by Juárez:

(1) To adopt no treaty with any foreign power encroaching upon Mexican sovereignty and independence;

---

[34]"The President of Mexico," *The Eclectic Magazine of Foreign Literature*, LX (November, 1863), 373.

[35]See Galindo y Galindo, *La Gran Década Nacional*, II, 69–70, 74.

[36]For the petitions, see Riva Palacio (ed.), *México á Través de los Siglos*, V, 469–470n; Zamacois, *Historia de Méjico*, XV, 749–752.

[37]Villaseñor y Villaseñor, "El Tratado Wyke-Zamacona," *Obras*, II, 153–154.

(2) To observe faithfully the Laws of Reform, respecting all rights acquired under the nationalization and sale of church property ("It would be immoral and unjust to disavow anything which has been done in conformity to the laws.") ;

(3) To build the treasury balance through further sale of nationalized lands;

(4) To observe scrupulously the amnesty, broadening the provisions to encompass those who desired to take advantage of it in good faith; and

(5) To emphasize reconstruction in the "paralyzed" administration of justice by the creation of a special fund to provide adequate salaries for judges or by reëstablishing the old judicial charges to suitors.[38]

What Lerdo objected to most in the political policy of the government was the limitation of the cabinet to "a small circle" of eligibles who professed to be the exclusive owners of certain republican ideas. In times of foreign danger, he insisted, the government should make use of all available talent, rejecting such artificial stigmata as "moderate," for example.[39]

Nor was he the only one who resented the brand "moderate," a group which suffered, wrote Deputy Ezequiel Montes, "a hatred almost equal" to those who had served the reactionary faction in the civil war. Only the *puros* are in favor, Montes added, and "to them and only to them" are we indebted for the salvation of Mexico.[40] In reviewing some of the epithets applied to the moderates by the extremists after the civil war—"reptiles, band of negations, deserters, imperceptible moles, lovers of halfway measures"— one can understand readily why men objected to being tagged with those adjectives.[41]

It has been pointed out that Lerdo's reputation sprang not only from his varied services in congress but from the key rôle he played in the defeat of the Wyke-Zamacona Treaty, one of the most important issues debated by that body. A brief explanation of the background of the treaty will be necessary to clarify its significance.

Following the civil war, the Juárez government immediately fell heir to a complicated set of foreign problems which strained relations to the breaking point with Great Britain, Spain, and France. In general, the grievances against Mexico were financial, but a

---

[38]Lerdo to the editors of *El Constitucional*, December 6, 1861, reprinted in *El Siglo*, December 10, 1861.

[39]*Ibid.*

[40]Montes to Comonfort, March 17, 1861, Comonfort Papers, Folder 17, UT.

[41]See *El Siglo*, May 2, 1861; June 18, August 30, 1862. For an impartial and sound historical definition of the moderate faction, see Manuel Payno, *Memoria sobre la Revolución de Diciembre de 1857 y Enero de 1858*, 90, 91, 93–94.

number of outrages committed against the nationals of the three European powers reinforced the primary complaints. In part the monetary claims were justified, in part excessive and fraudulent; in part the Juárez government was directly responsible, but the foreign powers were demanding satisfaction for the treaties and outrages of the vanquished conservative government as well. While threats of invasion blackened the air in 1861, they remained threats until the Mexican congress passed the famous law of July 17, 1861, suspending payment on all foreign debts for a period of two years. Using that measure as proof positive of bad faith on the part of the Juárez government, Great Britain, France, and Spain fused their interests in the Treaty of London, signed October 31, 1861, which called for an allied intervention in Mexico and a joint settlement of claims.[42]

Meanwhile, Manuel María de Zamacona, who had assumed the portfolio of Foreign Relations in July, 1861, had undertaken the negotiation of a unilateral settlement with the British minister to Mexico, Sir Charles Wyke. Since Britain was the chief creditor of Mexico, it was believed that a successful agreement on the British claims would disengage that nation from any joint intervention plans and convert her from an enemy into a powerful ally. Although that was wishful thinking, for the Treaty of London was a *fait accompli* before Zamacona completed the draft treaty with Wyke,[43] the fact was unknown in Mexico until invasion was under way.

Zamacona's negotiations with Wyke were painful, since the brusque and dictatorial British diplomat applied the pressure hard and severe to the hapless foreign minister of a people "who can't be trusted." His method had telling effects, resulting in a treaty embodying all the demands insisted upon by the British government. In apparently gruelling conferences spanning a period of some three weeks, he had brushed aside all of Zamacona's defenses. "I must not boast of my success until the Convention is actually signed," he pompously informed the British Foreign Office, "which I hope it [sic] will be within the next fortnight."[44]

The treaty itself, which was not drafted and signed until November 21, 1861,[45] left nothing to be desired by the most im-

---

[42]For a brief account of those developments, see William Spence Robertson, "The Tripartite Treaty of London," *The Hispanic American Historical Review*, XX (May, 1940), 167–189. For a detailed treatment, see John Musser, *The Establishment of Maximilian's Empire in Mexico*.

[43]Riva Palacio (ed.), *México á Través de los Siglos*, V, 481. way.

[44]Wyke to Russell, October 28, 1861, *British and Foreign State Papers*, LII, 382–387.

[45]For the text, see Antonio de la Peña y Reyes, *La Labor Diplomática de D. Manuel María de Zumacona como Secretario de Relaciones Exteriores* (Archivo Histórico Diplomático Mexicano, Ser. 2, No. 28), 97–100; Manuel Payno,

portunate British bondholder. All the ancient agreements for hypothecating portions of the customs revenues to meet payments on the British-held debt of Mexico were to remain in force; additional percentages of the total customs returns were allocated to meet payments on the claims arising from the civil war, not only for acts of the Juárez government but those of the conservative régime as well; and, probably the most insulting provision, British consuls or agents of the bondholders were to be allowed "to intervene" in the customs administration, that is, to inspect the books and records in order to insure compliance in good faith with the treaty stipulations. Finally, British agents had the exclusive right to sell special Mexican treasury certificates to foreign importers for satisfying tariff charges.

The final obstacle to the Mexican ratification of the Wyke-Zamacona Treaty was approval in congress, which, according to one of the deputies, had been obtained confidentially by Zamacona from the individual members.[46] If so, during his parliamentary maneuvers, Zamacona had made the unfortunate mistake of overlooking a "little man, beardless and pale, of penetrating voice,"[47] who headed the congressional committee on foreign relations—Sebastián Lerdo.

In a dramatic secret session on the night of November 22–23, congress voted by a large majority to reject the Wyke-Zamacona Treaty. The principal if not the sole responsibility for the unexpected action rested upon the shoulders of Lerdo. In a powerfully effective speech, he dissected the provisions clause by clause, demonstrating how each was in derogation of Mexican sovereignty. Among several bones in the treaty, that which allowed the British to intervene in the administration of the customs was the hardest for national pride to swallow, and Lerdo made capital of it.[48]

An adherent to the cabinet theory of government, Zamacona drafted his resignation, but first sent one final plea to congress to reconsider the consequences of its action. When that was of no

---

México y Sus Cuestiones Financieras con la Inglaterra, la España y la Francia, Appendix, 95–98. The supplementary edition of *El Siglo*, November 29, 1861, conveniently collected many of the important documents on the negotiation along with the text of the treaty.

[46]Bautista to Lerdo, September 8, 1876, *Memoria de la Academia Nacional de Historia y Geografía* (No. 2, 1946), 48.

[47]Sierra, *Juárez*, 292.

[48]Lerdo's speech was not recorded, but it probably followed closely the adverse report of the committee on foreign relations for which he was given exclusive credit.—Antonio de la Peña y Reyes, *La Obra Diplomática de D. Manuel María de Zamacona*, pp. xv, 101–104. See also Villaseñor y Villaseñor, "El Tratado Wyke-Zamacona," *Obras*, II, 120–122; Sierra, *Juárez*, 292–293; *El Siglo*, November 23, 1861.

avail, he stepped down from office.[49] Meanwhile, Wyke, furious over the rejection, submitted an ultimatum to the Mexican government elevating the British demands even higher as a punishment for defeating his project. In a few days he called for his passports and set out for Vera Cruz, only to discover on arrival that he had been commissioned as representative of the British intervention force.[50]

The aftermath of the rejection was a tremendous public reaction displayed in a protracted debate in the press, individual politicians aligning behind Lerdo or Zamacona according to their opinions on the good or harmful result of the decision. Those infected by the new nationalism with its surging pride stood behind Lerdo, while those who considered the treaty as an unavoidable evil sympathized with Zamacona. But to repeat, the popular concern over the defeat of the convention can be understood only in the light of what men believed—men who were ignorant of the consummation of the Treaty of London. The acceptance or rejection had no effect whatsoever on the British position in regard to the impending intervention; historically speaking, the affair was academic. The definitive proof was contained in a dispatch of Lord Russell, the British foreign secretary, to Minister John Crampton at Madrid, November 28, 1861:

> The terms obtained by Sir Charles Wyke fulfil, generally speaking, the separate requirements of Great Britain; but no security is obtained that those terms will be observed any better than former stipulations and engagements.
> That security, if to be found at all, is to be found in the Convention which Her Majesty has concluded with France and Spain.[51]

The second result of the "overweening pride of the Mexican congress, not to say folly, in rejecting that treaty"[52] was a ministerial crisis which followed Zamacona's defeat and resignation. While the executive upset also elicited a sustained discussion, it was important chiefly as an excellent illustration of the theory of cabinet government of that epoch.

---

[49]Buenrostro, *Historia del Congreso*, III, 677–682; VI, 197; Antonio de la Peña y Reyes, *La Obra Diplomática de D. Manuel María de Zamacona*, 114–118.

[50]Wyke to Russell, November 28, 1861, *British and Foreign State Papers*, LII, 411; Antonio de la Peña y Reyes, *La Obra Diplomática de D. Manuel María de Zamacona*, p. xvii.

[51]Russell to Crampton, November 28, 1861, *British and Foreign State Papers*, LII, 388–389.

[52]Corwin to Seward, November 29, 1861, *Correspondence Relative to the Present Condition of Mexico*, 36.

As the leader of the "opposition" in ousting Zamacona, Lerdo received the first call to form a new ministry.[53] After several days of negotiations, during which Juárez and Lerdo discussed various combinations of ministers, the matter reached an impasse. Characteristic of Mexican politics, the trouble was not over the political program which Lerdo proposed, but over the persons he suggested for the new cabinet.[54]

During the cabinet parleys Lerdo visited Sir Charles Wyke, who was still pouting in Mexico City, to investigate the possibility of a rapprochement on the rejected treaty. Wyke's summary of the interview revealed much about what had happened in congress on the crucial night of November 22–23, as well as Lerdo's prominence in the outcome:

To-day [November 28, 1861] I had a visit from Señor Lerdo de Tejada, the leader of the Opposition in Congress, who called to ask me whether I would consent to any modification in the Convention; as, if I would agree to modify the Articles concerning the repayment of the Legation and conducta robberies, and the powers given to enable our consuls to act as interventors, he would engage to pass it through Congress, and then accept the vacant post of Minister for Foreign Affajrs, which under such circumstances he thought the President would confer upon him.

My answer was a simple one, and to the effect that having already made every concession possible in my negotiations with Señor de Zamacona, I could make no others. On receiving this answer Señor Lerdo de Tejada retired, and with him disappeared every hope of the Convention's ratification.[55]

When Juárez and Lerdo failed to agree upon the persons to compose the new cabinet, Manuel Doblado, *caudillo* of Guanajuato, was summoned for the task. Thus, a strange quirk of fate had determined that Doblado and not Lerdo would be the minister of Foreign Relations who negotiated with the interventor nations after their landings in early 1862; and from those negotiations Doblado extracted his chief title to historical fame.

Within six months after the defeat of the Wyke-Zamacona Treaty, fighting had begun against the invasion force of Napoleon III; but the game of parliament went on, even though Mexican independence was facing its severest trial. Perhaps because the great victory of Cinco de Mayo produced an excess of overconfidence, or because the metropolis seemed distant and protected, the deputies were able to quarrel to the bitter end. Still, the preternatural complacency

---

[53]Six months previously Juárez had offered Lerdo a cabinet post, but he had declined on grounds that he was acting as a legal counsel for ex-President Comonfort, then in exile.—Puig Casauranc, *Archivos Privados de D. Benito Juárez*, 296–297; *El Siglo*, June 25, July 6, 1861.

[54]Lerdo to the editors of *El Constitucional*, December 6, 1861, reprinted in *El Siglo*, December 10, 1861; Puig Casauranc, *Archivos Privados de D. Benito Juárez*, 312, 315.

[55]Wyke to Russell, November 28, 1861, *British and Foreign State Papers*, LII, 411–412.

was not alone reflected in the factiousness of the national representatives: it pervaded all of society in the capital. A traveler arriving in Mexico City as late as September, 1862, remarked about the unusual external calm: "The capital was quiet and peaceful. It seemed utterly shut out from all the excitement created by the invasion, as though, really trusting in its remoteness, its barriers of mountains, its lakes and natural defenses, it defied the foreigner."[56]

Finally, in May, 1863, the game was interrupted rudely by the news of the fall of Puebla and the approach of the French forces. In the face of absolute necessity, the congress reluctantly granted the President extraordinary powers to last for the duration of the foreign invasion,[57] and closed its session on May 31, 1863, with the customary exchange of speeches between the President of the republic and the President of congress. After Juárez's speech, Lerdo, again the presiding officer, answered:

The Supreme Magistrate, who has defended the rights of Mexico in the most difficult circumstances, remains with the full sum of power which the free election of the people and the repeated vote of confidence of the national representation grant to him. It does not doubt that with those attributes and with the patriotism of all good Mexicans, nothing will be omitted from whatever may be necessary to continue fighting worth ly to effect the triumph of the rights, the sovereignty, and the independence of the Republic.[58]

That evening, Juárez, a small coterie of republican advisers and ministers, and a few deputies of congress evacuated the capital and took the road to San Luis Potosí.[59] Lerdo was among the group; he was no longer a passive bystander as in the days of the civil war; and he was to support the republican cause and Juárez with unwavering loyalty over a dangerous road, four years long, which led through the deserts of the north to Paso del Norte before it wound its circuitous route back to Mexico City and triumph.

And the game of parliament? It was interrupted, not ended. On its resumption years later, after the withdrawal of the French, the fall of Maximilian's empire, and when the republic had resumed a normal course once again, Lerdo found himself on the opposite side of the contestants, first as a minister and later as president. Time would prove how much he had absorbed from his experience as a member of that impetuous body.

---

[56]Sara Yorke Stevenson, *Maximilian in Mexico: A Woman's Reminiscences of the French Intervention, 1862–1867*, 74.

[57]*El Siglo*, May 29, 1863. Despite the circumstances, congress debated the grant of power at great length. It appeared to have been the principal topic of the final session.

[58]*Diario Oficial de la República Mexicana*, June 16, 1863.

[59]Riva Palacio (ed.), *México á Través de los Siglos*, V, 585.

Chapter VII

The Nomadic Republic, 1863-1867

The heroic epoch of the French intervention and the empire of Maximilian has held and continues to hold a magnetic attraction for the writers of many nations. Lending itself to a variety of interpretations and surrounded by an aura of romance, tragedy, and grandeur, the period has been a fruitful field for both diplomatic and national historians who have correlated it to innumerable topical studies. The ambitions of Napoleon III; the revival of Latin empire in the New World; the history of monarchical schemes in Mexico; the rebirth of Mexican nationalism; the Monroe Doctrine; the foreign policy of William H. Seward; and Confederate diplomacy during the American Civil War are a few illustrations.

From the standpoint of Mexican history, probably no other era has accumulated so rich a storehouse of materials. Virtually every principal actor in the drama left behind a personal narrative, a set of private documents, or a polemic at the least, and, in addition, secondary writers have bequeathed exhaustive accounts. But however much a truly impartial and analytical synthesis of Maximilian's empire is needed, the historian of today would search rather haplessly to find even minor details to contribute; for Maximilian's every act seems to have been recorded—and debated—from the moment he considered the proffered crown of Mexico until he pronounced his last words before the firing squad at Querétaro.

Empire and intervention form but half of the story, because there were again two governments in Mexico, just as during the War of the Reform. It might be presumed that an era which came to signify the resurgence of Mexican nationalism, the preservation of Mexican sovereignty and independence, the formal death of the monarchical idea, and the glorified victory of democratic institutions and the reforms would be treated from an essentially Mexican viewpoint, at least by Mexican historians; that is, it would be a narrative of events placing the emphasis upon the trials and tribulations of the errant government of Juárez, which survived untold risks and hardships, as it fled from place to place to escape the pursuing French, finally emerging with victory in 1867. Oddly enough, none has considered that aspect worth the telling, as a continuous and detailed story, although for heroism it could compete with the best the empire has to offer. In most cases even the biographers of Juárez have presented but fleeting glimpses of the wandering President, glimpses intermingled in a confusing manner with the tale of empire, and invariably it is Maximilian and his problems which receive the preponderance of attention.

Reversing the orthodox treatment, the plan here will be to follow consistently the flight of the Juárez government, consciously neglecting the empire. The orientation is not artificial, for Sebastián Lerdo was the companion and adviser of Juárez, trekking every mile of the troublous tour with him while acting as minister of Foreign Affairs and Government, a position which corresponded to prime minister. Three civilians—Juárez, Lerdo, and Iglesias—upheld unflaggingly the symbol of republican government and were so tenacious of their bondage that they became known as "the immaculates." The itinerary of those human symbols, their way of life, and the methods under which they operated are all proper subjects for discussion under the heading of the nomadic republic; but first, a structural sketch of the vital and well-known facts of the establishment and agony of empire must be set forth.

Although General Forey had entered Mexico City with his French troops as early as June, 1863, it was not until a year later that Maximilian and Carlota arrived as emperor and empress of their adopted nation. Several months of machinations had been required to create an artificial crown; but under the auspices of Napoleon, the French army, and the resuscitated conservative stalwarts, the sequence of the Regency, the Assembly of Notables, the fictitious plebiscite to express the will of the people for monarchy, and the formal acceptance of Maximilian at Miramar were all consummated without any insuperable snags.

In the meanwhile, Bazaine, combining in himself the civil and military power, had replaced Forey as commander in chief of the French expeditionary force. After a brilliant campaign of late 1863, he not only removed much of the tarnish which French military polish had received during the reverses at Puebla but was able to offer the new sovereign a country which was superficially pacified and largely under the domination of the French. He had also delivered crushing blows to the residual of the organized republican armies, regrouped after the loss of Puebla; and had forced Juárez, his cabinet, and a few faithful followers to dash on from San Luis Potosí, first to Saltillo and then to Monterrey, where the mobile capital was located at the time Maximilian arrived.

With French intervention at its apex and the republican outlook at the nadir, both in morale and resources, the Archduke who came to cultivate the "exotic plant" of monarchy in Mexico had some justification for being optimistic. But the plant itself was atavistic, doomed to failure if only through the workings of time, in part because the conditions of the New World had proved adverse and in part because the hardy democratic weed, lethal to monarchical growths, proved impossible to eradicate.

In addition, the very roots of Maximilian's monarchy were diseased, artificially supported as they were by French military might. The unfortunate association gave the republicans a weapon of nationalism with its verbiage of independence, and, when combined with the democratic ideal and the inherent Mexican suspicion of the foreigner, became in itself a tremendous obstacle to Maximilian. Then, while the French army and the imperial Mexican allies were almost always victorious in major engagements, they could not crush the acephalous and desultory guerrilla warfare of the republicans, who harried their lines of communication, terrorized the towns, and gnawed perpetually at the morale of the empire. Like the democratic ideology, the method of warfare of the republicans was fleeting, abstruse, sporadic: it could not be crushed by a single victory or series of victories; it was the type of native fighting closely approximating the widely-practiced brigandage at which Mexicans excelled.

Besides the government of the republic, its ideology and warfare, Maximilian also faced an entangling net of domestic and foreign problems: external debts, including the commitments to Napoleon; the suave but mounting diplomatic hostility of the United States after the conclusion of the American Civil War; the disputes with the papacy and the Mexican clergy over the restoration of nationalized church lands; the anomalous position of Bazaine, a commander serving two emperors, one real and one nominal; and all the perennial plagues of Mexican governments, especially party factionalism and finance.

During three years Maximilian decreed everything and resolved nothing. He reigned but he did not rule. Personally attractive and gracious, guided by magnanimous intentions, idealistic and impractical, he struggled with conditions which would have baffled any skilled statesman, even one thoroughly versed in Mexican conditions. Time deepened the depressive quagmire in which he found himself and magnified the disputes, the problems, and the breaches in his empire; yet he survived as long as French force was available to support the flimsy structure. When the foreign troops were gone, he refused to see the facts except as he wanted to see them. Adamantly clinging to a condemned crown, he blindly sacrificed common sense to the fetish of his Hapsburg pride until he was driven to grasp the last straw in the wind—the unqualified acceptance of the discredited conservative party. The siege of Querétaro, the last stand of monarchy, and the tragic finale before the firing squad were unnecessary but perhaps fitting conclusions to the chapter of the second Mexican empire.

But Querétaro spelled finis for something more than empire, something which has been obscured by Maximilian's noble departure: the ultimate triumph of the revolution for reforms begun in 1854–1855. The conservative party succumbed with the Archduke never again to contest openly the principle of separation of church and state or the theoretical equality of Mexican classes. Thus the base metal of civil war, confused by the alloy of intervention, returned to civil war on the old model with the departure of the French troops in early 1867, properly terminating on the note of Maximilian, Miramón, Mejía, Méndez, and Márquez.

The peregrination of the republican government, from May, 1863, to July, 1867, was an abstruse hegira from the standpoint of time and place, but it formed the essential background of Lerdo's contribution during the period as Juárez's principal minister.[1] Naïve as the analogy may be, one may consider the topic like a round trip tour under duress. The tour began and ended in Mexico City; the duress which prevented the governmental tourists from vegetating in one place for any extended period of time was usually the pursuit of the French troops or their imperial Mexican allies. While tracing the route and setting forth the factual timetable, it is logical to consider the outstanding problems at each segment of the journey. After more than four years of a seemingly aimless meandering, Juárez, an experienced political *voyageur* even in 1863, had more than proved that Charles II was a novice when he returned to England in 1660, claiming that he never cared to set out on his travels again.

The first stop of the government was at San Luis Potosí, where it arrived in June, 1863,[2] and where the capital remained for almost seven months. After the campaigns at Puebla, the French halted in Mexico City, parleying with the revived conservative faction and making the necessary arrangements to pad a throne for the future emperor. The breathing spell was more than welcome to Juárez, since it allowed for time to reorganize the republican army in preparation for meeting the inevitable thrust north and west by the foreign expeditionary force.

---

[1]The present writer is aware of the exasperation experienced in attempting to ferret out the location of Juárez and his followers at any particular time. The appended timetable should serve as a convenient aid.

[2]Dublán y Lozano, *Legislación Mexicana*, IX, 625. For a description of the first leg of the journey, see *Diario Oficial de la República Mejicana* (San Luis Potosí), June 16, 1863.

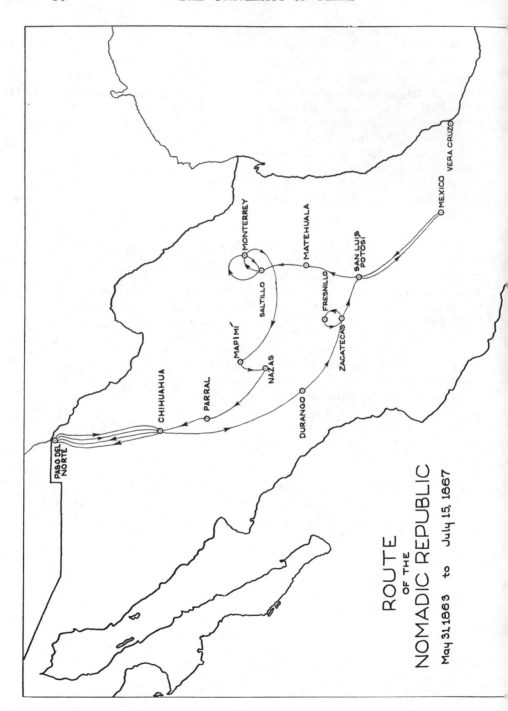

ROUTE
OF THE
NOMADIC REPUBLIC
May 31, 1863   to   July 15, 1867

TIMETABLE OF THE NOMADIC REPUBLIC

Place	Arrived	Departed	Residence Months	Days	Route	Travel Time by Days
Mexico	---	May 31, 1863	---	---	Mexico to San Luis Potosí	9
San Luis Potosí	June 9, 1863	December 22, 1863	6	13	San Luis Potosí to Saltillo	18
Saltillo	January 9, 1864	February 10, 1864	1	1	Saltillo to Monterrey	3
Monterrey	February 12, 1864	February 14, 1864	---	3	Monterrey to Saltillo	(?) 1
Saltillo	February 14, 1864[1]	April 2, 1864	1	16	Saltillo to Monterrey	(?) 1
Monterrey	April 2, 1864	August 15, 1864	4	13	Monterrey to Chihuahua	58
Chihuahua	October 12, 1864	August 5, 1865	8	24	Chihuahua to Paso del Norte	9
Paso del Norte	August 14, 1865	November 13, 1865	2	29	Paso del Norte to Chihuahua	7
Chihuahua	November 20, 1865	December 9, 1865	---	19	Chihuahua to Paso del Norte	9
Paso del Norte	December 18, 1865	June 10, 1866	5	23	Paso del Norte to Chihuahua	7
Chihuahua	June 17, 1866	December 10, 1866	5	23	Chihuahua to Durango	16
Durango	December 26, 1866	January 14, 1867[1]	---	19	Durango to Zacatecas	8
Zacatecas	January 22, 1867	February —, 1867	---	(?)	Zacatecas to San Luis Potosí	(?)
San Luis Potosí	February 21, 1867	July 3 (?), 1867	4	(?)	San Luis Potosí to Mexico	(?) 15
Mexico	July 15, 1867		---	---		

Total time absent: 4 years, 1 month, 15 days.
Estimated time en route: 6 months.
[1] Approximation.

Lerdo had accompanied Juárez as a member of the permanent deputation of congress, and he acted in the capacity of vice-president of that body at San Luis until he entered the cabinet about three months later.[3] While the activities of the deputation were academic in the face of the military conditions, the continued meetings and the futile attempt to convene a congress at San Luis in late 1863 illustrated the theoretical supremacy of the legislative branch in the Constitution.[4] When the imperial forces drove Juárez north in December, the republican element reluctantly accepted the fact that democratic government had to rest unconditionally in the hands of the executive, that congress had to remain dormant until victory was won and the invader expelled.[5]

With the enhancement of the executive came a natural increase in the prestige and significance of the ministers. As previously noted, Juárez had given Lerdo several opportunities in 1861 to join his official family, but in each case the Rector of San Ildefonso had shown hesitancy or unwillingness. In August and early September, 1863, when a new cabinet shuffle was taking place, he again was asked to accept a portfolio. Juárez's insistence combined with what Lerdo considered his patriotic duty under the circumstances overcame his initial refusal;[6] and he entered the cabinet as minister of Justice in September.[7] A few days later he was transferred to the much more important post of minister of Relations and Government, through which he came to be considered the prime minister of Juárez. The lasting core of the cabinet was formed about the same time when José María Iglesias assumed the portfolio of

---

[3]*Diputación Permanente del 3er Congreso de la Unión: Actas del 13 de Junio al 14 de Diciembre de 1863*, 1, 28.

[4]Not until December 8, 1863, was the ephemeral dream of a full congress abandoned.—*Ibid.*, 60.

[5]José María Iglesias, *Revistas Históricas sobre la Intervención Francesa en México*, II, 330–331; Dublán y Lozano, *Legislación Mexicana*, IX, 670–673. The remnants of the permanent deputation of congress again attempted to call a session even as late as March, 1864, at Saltillo.—*Ibid.*, IX, 680.

[6]Circular to State Governors (signed by Lerdo), Paso del Norte, April 30, 1866, Matías Romero (ed.), *Correspondencia de la Legación Mexicana en Washington durante la Intervención Extranjera . . .* , VI, 654. Also printed in *Periódico Oficial del Gobierno Constitucional de la República Mexicana* (Paso del Norte), May 10, 1866. (This journal, which traveled with the Juárez government, will be cited hereafter as *Periódico Oficial* with the place of publication.)

[7]*Diputación Permanente del 3er Congreso de la Unión*, 16. The original letter appointments and correspondence connected therewith may be found in *Sebastián Lerdo de Tejada, Su Expediente Personal*, Archivo de Relaciones Exteriores, Mexico. In addition, all of Lerdo's cabinet appointments are listed accurately in *Secretarios de Estado del Gobierno Mexicano* (MS., UT Library), 47, 65, 67, 68.

Justice and subsequently of Finance.[8] Thereafter, the three civilians, Juárez, Lerdo, and Iglesias, remained together throughout the serpentine peregrination until victory had been achieved in 1867.

While at San Luis, the government emphasized measures of defense, for any offensive military operations on a large scale were outside the realm of consideration. Ignacio Comonfort, the former president who had been reinstated and converted to minister of War, was working in conjunction with Lerdo to bring unity into the high command of the republican army. It must have seemed strange to the former President to receive orders from his former Minister of Foreign Relations,[9] yet the two friends apparently worked together to resolve jealousies among the principal army chieftains. Lerdo himself traveled between San Luis and Querétaro during late September and early October to meet Generals Comonfort, Doblado, and Uraga for conferences on the problems.[10] But the government could do little more than maintain peace in its own ranks and await the forthcoming drive of Bazaine, captive as it was to the voluntary financial donations which the states saw fit to concede.

As long as the republicans possessed some bargaining power in the form of organized forces in the field and before Bazaine basked in the flush of his military victories of late 1863, all hope for some agreement with the invader had not faded. The French Commander in Chief was not averse to accomplishing his aims by diplomacy as a substitute for arms, and it was common knowledge that feelers were being circulated to inveigle the republican military leaders to the side of the projected empire.[11]

More important were the notices of Manuel Siliceo, a moderate liberal in Mexico City who conferred with Bazaine[12] and then passed along information to Ignacio Comonfort that a confidential agent would be sent to treat with the republicans at San Luis: "I know

[8]Lerdo to Romero, San Luis Potosí, September 12, 1863, Romero (ed.), *Correspondencia de la Legación Mexicana*, III, 597; Iglesias, *Revistas Históricas*, II, 131, 225; Riva Palacio (ed.), *México á.Través de los Siglos*, V, 618. For the interesting personal animosities behind the cabinet changes, see José Rocha, *Galería de los Hombres Ilustres del Estado de Guanajuato*, I, 31.

[9]An interesting example was Lerdo's advice to Comonfort on intelligence reports received from occupied Mexico City.—Lerdo to Comonfort, San Luis Potosí, October 27, 1863, Comonfort Papers, Folder 23, UT.

[10]Lerdo to General José L. Uraga, San Luis Potosí, September 23, 1863; 6/98, No. 613; Lerdo to Juárez, Celaya, October 1, 2, 1863, 6/99, No. 614, 6/100, No. 615, Archivo de Benito Juárez, Biblioteca Nacional de México, México; Juárez to Comonfort, San Luis Potosí, September 28, October 1, 1863; Comonfort to Lerdo, Querétaro, November 1, 1863; Lerdo to Comonfort, San Luis Potosí, November 3, 1863, Comonfort Papers, Folder 23, UT.

[11]Siliceo to Comonfort, Mexico, October 1, 1863, *ibid.*, Folder 23, UT. Time was the essence of any bargain with Bazaine, wrote Siliceo, and, he added, that "opportunity will not return. . . ."

[12]Siliceo to Comonfort, Mexico, October 22, 1863, *ibid.*, Folder 23, UT.

that a commissioner will leave, probably in tomorrow's diligence, to meet with you, Doblado, Lerdo, and Uraga: I do not know precisely the object and terms of the commission, and for this reason I am not informing you about them."[13] Comonfort in turn advised Lerdo of the machinations in Mexico, and the two decided to await developments as well as the arrival of the commissioner, leaving the initiative to Bazaine.[14]

The agent turned out to be Napoleón Saborío,[15] a former congressional colleague of Lerdo, through whom Lerdo proposed the final official offer to treat with the French for an honorable settlement of differences. There could be no treaty with the French, Lerdo wrote Saborío, except on the *sine qua non* of absolute respect for the independence of Mexico and the right to choose freely her form of government, "so that the negotiations are limited to points which may be considered relatively secondary."[16] Armed with that letter, Saborío arrived at the headquarters of Bazaine, who, in the midst of his military glory, answered with a haughtiness which parried that of Lerdo. In regard to the terms of mediation set forth by Sr. Lerdo de Tejada with "the Liberal Government as it is called," he told Saborío, it would be impossible to treat except "solely on the basis of pure and simple adhesion to the Intervention."[17] Thus ended the last perfunctory effort to break the *impasse*. The issue was unequivocally defined and there was no room for compromise of any kind.

Was Juárez ignorant of Lerdo's terms for mediation, as has been implied?[18] No positive proof can be shown that the President authorized the letter; yet he was with Lerdo and there was nothing in the conditions which in any way could have compromised his honor. In the light of Lerdo's unfailing loyalty to Juárez, it would be hazardous to conjecture that, as minister of Relations and Gov-

---

[13]Siliceo to Comonfort, September 29, 1863, *ibid.*, Folder 23, UT.

[14]Comonfort to Siliceo, San Luis Potosí, October 6, 1863, *ibid.*, Folder 23, UT.

[15]Lerdo to Comonfort, San Luis Potosí, October 25, 1863, *ibid.*, Folder 23, UT.

[16]Lerdo to J. Napoleón Saborío, C. de U., Potosí, November 28, 1863, Genaro García (ed.), *La Intervención Francesa en México según el Archivo del Mariscal Bazaine* [*Documentos Inéditos ó Muy Raros para la Historia de México*, XVII],. 19–20.

[17]Napoleón Boyer to Sr. Saborío, December 10, 1863, *ibid.*, 70–71. Boyer, the chief of staff for Bazaine, was merely passing along the instructions of his commander.

[18]Roeder, *Juárez and His Mexico*, II, 544. Roeder stated that Juárez was in flight from San Luis and his whereabouts was unknown, presumably while the exchange with Bazaine was pending; however, Juárez was still there at the time and for several days after the mission of Saborío had ended.

ernment, he had acted treasonably or without the full approval of his chief.[19]

The months of false security for the republican government at San Luis ended in December with the approach of the army of General Tomás Mejía, who was supporting the intervention, but Juárez, Lerdo, and the rest of the officials did not fly precipitately northward. Instead, they waited not far from the city for an impending battle which never took place. When the republican army failed to engage Mejía, evacuating the city to him,[20] the government accepted facts and continued on to Saltillo in the state of Coahuila-Nuevo León.[21]

Having anticipated the necessity of a rapid change of location, the government desired to move the capital to Monterrey, the stronghold of Santiago Vidaurri, one of the most powerful local dictators in the nation. In actuality, he operated the state of Coahuila-Nuevo León as if it were his vast, personal fief. Lord Vidaurri had shown himself strangely uneasy at the prospect of the embarrassing visit of the central government to his domains, and, in turn, the orphan institution of Juárez had justification for quaking at the prospect of throwing itself into the jaws of that citadel of personalized localism.[22] The fears were in no manner mitigated when Minister of War Comonfort was unexpectedly assassinated in November, since the government might have relied upon his friendship with Vidaurri to insure coöperation with Juárez.[23]

---

[19]Saborío, apparently deceived of Bazaine's real purposes, had proceeded to inform Lerdo of the "generous intentions of the intervention"; but the skeptical Lerdo demanded an explanation of the true objectives, fearing they would be prejudicial to the national independence.—José Napoleón Saborío to Colonel Boyer, San Luis Potosí, December 1, 1863, García (ed.), *Documentos Inéditos ó Muy Raros*, XVII, 48–52. At any rate, Lerdo never took the initiative of sending Saborío to deal with Bazaine, as Rivera Cambas has stated.— *Historia de la Intervención*, II, 363.

Captain Blanchot, a French officer present during the campaign, felt that the incident was crucial and that it was a great mistake to cast aside the golden opportunity to negotiate with the "prime minister of Juárez."—Colonel Ch. Blanchot, *Memoires, L'Intervention Française au Mexique*, II, 104–107.

[20]Rivera Cambas, *Historia de la Intervención*, II, 373.

[21]Juárez and the cabinet left San Luis in the afternoon of December 22, 1863.—Juárez to Santacilia, December 24, 1863, Puig Casauranc, *Archivos Privados de D. Benito Juárez*, 25.

[22]As early as December 10, Juárez had agreed with his son-in-law that Vidaurri must be attracted to the cause or "eliminated."—Juárez to Santacilia, December 10, 1863, Puig Casauranc, *ibid.*, 17. See also Frank Lawrence Owsley, *King Cotton Diplomacy: Foreign Relations of the Confederate States of America*, 119–120, 128.

[23]For data on Comonfort's untimely death, see Iglesias, *Revistas Históricas*, II, 197–198; Riva Palacio (ed.), *México á Través de los Siglos*, V, 620.

As if to test the dangerous path leading to Monterrey, Juárez located first at Saltillo (January 9 to February 10, 1864),[24] awaiting the reaction of Lord Vidaurri to his projected transfer. Meanwhile, the local chieftain blew hot and cold in his letters to Juárez, all of which spelled, in the light of subsequent events, a bitter hostility to the encroachment of the central government upon his special sphere of action.[25] In truth, his loyalty to the republic was to be reckoned in direct proportion to the government's geographical distance from his own fief and its inability to interfere with his prerogative as the local *caudillo*.

Ultimately, Juárez, Lerdo, and Iglesias decided to place Vidaurri's temporizing to the only accurate test by directing their steps to Monterrey, sending General Doblado of Guanajuato ahead with his division of soldiers to prove that the republican government was not yet totally subject to the whims of petty chieftains.[26] The treacherous Vidaurri managed to gain control of the artillery of Doblado on the wily pretext that he intended to use it for salvos to celebrate Juárez's arrival; but it was a far more practical purpose for which the purloined cannon were destined: to indicate with brutal frankness that there was insufficient room for localism and centralism to cohabit in the same vicinity.

Learning of the legerdemain when encamped outside the city of Monterrey,[27] Juárez conferred with his ministers and the decision was made to brave the lion's den. On the morning of February 12, the government entered an ominously silent city after a heavy downpour which prognosticated the result. Following three days of residence in Monterrey, in a highly explosive atmosphere which found the opposing elements of Juárez and Vidaurri bristling at each other from armed camps, Juárez and his company were forced to return to Saltillo when the balance of military power swung in favor of Vidaurri.[28]

---

[24]Iglesias, *Revistas Históricas*, II, 224–225; Pedro Pruneda, *Historia de la Guerra de Méjico desde 1865 á 1867* . . . , 229; Rivera Cambas, *Historia de la Intervención*, II, 388.

[25]See Vidaurri to Juárez, February 8, 1864, Santiago Roel (ed.), *Correspondencia Particular de D. Santiago Vidaurri, Gobernador de Nuevo León, 1855–1864*, I, 258.

[26]Among the many works covering the dispute between Vidaurri and Juárez, the official account of Lerdo, upon which the following summary is based primarily, is the most complete and accurate.—Circular, Saltillo, February 26, 1864, *Colección de Leyes, Decretos y Circulares Expedidas por el Supremo Gobierno, 1863–1867*, I, 225–260. See also Iglesias, *Revistas Históricas*, II, 252; Sierra, *Juárez*, 367.

[27]*Colección de Leyes* . . . *1863–1867*, I, 243.

[28]Iglesias, like Lerdo, a participant in the dispute, told his version of the sequence of events in an article written at Saltillo on February 26, the same date as Lerdo's circular.—*Revistas Históricas*, II, 245–257. Juárez's views may be pieced together from a letter to his wife, Margarita Maza de Juárez,

Despite Juárez's loss of prestige as a result of the episode, the political contest was not finished, and at least the government abandoned the policy of wooing Vidaurri, substituting a method he could better comprehend—that of pronouncing him a traitor to the cause.[29] Mustering all possible forces and ' making use of popular opposition to Vidaurri, the government, after forcing him to flee from Monterrey, returned to his city for a more permanent stay in early April, just before Maximilian reached Mexico to begin his personal rule.[30] The capital was once again in a durable resting place where it remained until mid-August. The attitude of Vidaurri, who later defected to the empire, illustrated merely one of many similar if less important wedges of personal localism which split republican unity, hampered its military efforts against the French, and endangered the errant central government.

As long as Juárez remained at Monterrey, the government retained control of northern customs revenues, easy means of communication with the United States, and a hinterland which was not wealthy but adequate to permit the development of forces to threaten the empire.[31] Naturally, Bazaine and Maximilian determined to strike, to eliminate the breeding ground for republican revival, and to force the *de jure* government out of the country if possible. One of Vidaurri's followers, a Colonel Quiroga, who had professed loyalty to Juárez after the flight of his chief, tacked his sails to catch the imperial wind which was blowing northward in the form of advancing French columns. The treason of Quiroga with his large armed force brought about the hasty departure from the city of Juárez, Lerdo, Iglesias, and the rest of the tiny bureaucracy (August 15, 1864), although the withdrawal was already contemplated because of the drive of the enemy. Nevertheless, it was Quiroga's unexpected attack on the small escort force of the government which again endangered the lives of the President and his cabinet. Fortunately, Lerdo acted with foresight and caution on one occasion, preventing Juárez from exposing himself unnecessarily to the street fighting which was taking place between Quiroga's force and the outnumbered presidential escort.[32] Also, he appeared to have prepared the carriage so that the ministers could tumble in and beat

February 12, 1864, and his correspondence with Vidaurri while in Monterrey, dated February 13, 14, 1864, Roel (ed.), *Correspondencia de Vidaurri*, I, 259, 261–262.

[29]Dublán y Lozano, *Legislación Mexicana*, IX, 675–676; Bancroft, *History of Mexico*, VI, 131, 131n.

[30]*Colección de Leyes . . . 1863–1867*, II, 18–21.

[31]Sierra justly criticized Juárez for not retiring to the northern states immediately after the evacuation of Mexico City and before the republican armies had been squandered in useless engagements.—*Juárez*, 369.

[32]Leonardo S. Viramontes, *Biografía Popular del Benemérito de América Benito Juárez*, 211.

a hasty retreat out of town in the midst of the spirited skirmish.[33] Without claiming any honors for the retirement, Lerdo described the details and also the attack of Quiroga upon the escort the following day when the government party was several leagues from Monterrey, an attack in which one of the loyal soldiers lost his life and two others were wounded.[34]

Summing up four and one-half months of residence at Monterrey, the Rector of San Ildefonso, who no doubt had discovered life in the north a striking departure from his neatly arranged routine in the metropolis, praised the government for its discretion in dealing with the local state authorities and for its energy in collecting and supporting combat units. Furthermore, the central government had carried out the program without "taking a single peso from the state's own revenues," at least until May. It was a good example to the people, declared Lerdo, as well as a contrast to the methods previously employed by the traitor Vidaurri, who had milked the inhabitants of his fief for all they would give. When the federal government finally had to resort to a heavy loan, just prior to the departure, "in truth it was not badly received, because it was distributed most equitably through the use of a junta of merchants and proprietors of Monterrey. . . ."[35]

Matured by a rough initiation into the crude concept of federalism in Nuevo León—"freedom from outside restraint, local independence, license even"[36]—Lerdo informed Matías Romero, the Mexican representative at Washington, of his practical observations: "I believe that the majority of the inhabitants of Nuevo León can be considered civilized and of good sentiments or at least those of Monterrey and the principal settled places; I believe also that the majority has not held hostile ideas toward the Government. . . ." But Vidaurri and his proselytes had practiced such a "system of terror" that most of the people, fearing his eventual return to power in the state, were afraid of retribution in case they coöperated with the federal government. "I would have to write a great deal, if I desired to give you an approximate idea of that part of the popu-

---

[33]Rafael de Zayas Enríquez, *Benito Juárez, Su Vida—Su Obra*, 189–190.

[34]Lerdo to Romero, Nazas, Durango, September 22, 1864, Romero (ed.), *Correspondencia de la Legación Mexicana*, IV, 540–541. See also Iglesias, *Revistas Históricas*, III, 19–20. Francisco Mejía, a member of the presidential escort, left an account of the event in his diary, *Épocas, Hechos y Acontecimientos de Mi Vida, y los Que Fuí Actor y Testigo* (MS., UT Library), 62.

[35]Lerdo to Romero, Nazas, Durango, September 22, 1864, *Correspondencia de la Legación Mexicana*, IV, 541.

[36]J. Lloyd Mecham, "The Origins of Federalism in Mexico," *The Hispanic American Historical Review*, XVIII (May, 1938), 171. Professor Mecham's definition of federalism as understood in Mexico coincides precisely with the defections which the Juárez government faced in the northern states during the intervention.

lation in which Vidaurri has his partisans. I shall only say to you that they nourish all the sentiments of greatest hatred against the men and things of the interior of the Republic. . . ."[37]

The itinerary from Monterrey to Chihuahua, requiring two months' time (August 15 to October 12) and traversing four states and an estimated 300 leagues, was one of the most difficult legs of the entire peregrination.[38] It was dangerous and replete with hardship, pathos, and discouragement. The spirits of the triumvirate and the few faithful of the republican government reached the nadir, for all that was left to them at the end of the trail was a segment of desert with scanty resources in a distant corner of their cherished *patria*. Danger harassed them at the outset, as shown by the attacks of Quiroga, and hardship was evidenced in many forms, causing the wholesale desertion of the fleeing federal army which had rendezvoused with the government and its cavalry escort at a point near Saltillo. The army had remained intact until it reached the edge of the desert, when some 600 or 700 dropped out of the ranks, according to Lerdo's estimate.[39] Nor could it have been anything but misery to cross a desert region in the travel-weary coach which Juárez, Lerdo, and Iglesias used. Water was always a precious item, while the meals of the President and his two ministers frequently consisted of the dried biscuit carried in the coach, supplemented, when fortune favored, with the roast beef offered by the hospitable owner of a *rancho* along the route.[40] Yet the diet of dust and sand must have been plentiful at all times as the presidential coach bounced along with the cavalry over scarcely discernible trails which wandered across broad stretches of monotonous desert.[41]

The journey has also been described as one of pathos and despair, but such adjectives rest not alone upon mere implication from the fact that the loyal peered through one of the gloomiest clouds of the intervention period. On the eve of the Battle of Majoma (September 21, 1864), in which the last sizeable force of the republic was scattered, the government travelers paused at a lonely hacienda in

---

[37]Lerdo to Romero, Nazas, Durango, September 22, 1864, Romero (ed.), *Correspondencia de la Legación Mexicana*, IV, 541–542.

[38]For Lerdo's account, see Lerdo to Romero, Nazas, Durango, September 22, 1864, *ibid.*, IV, 540–544; Lerdo to Romero, Chihuahua, October 16, 1864, *ibid.*, IV, 545–546. See also Lerdo's circulars, Monterrey, August 15, 1864, Nazas, Durango, September 21, 1864, *ibid.*, IV, 539. Iglesias' account may be found in *Revistas Históricas*, III, 19–49.

[39]Romero (ed.), *Correspondencia de la Legación Mexicana*, IV, 543.

[40]Viramontes, *Biografía Popular de Juárez*, 212–213.

[41]Romero (ed.), *Correspondencia de la Legación Mexicana*, IV, 543. For a synthesis of the reaction of American travelers to this area, see Glenn S. Dumke, "Across Mexico in '49," *The Pacific Historical Review*, XVII (February, 1949), 35–40.

northern Durango, on the banks of the Nazas River, to celebrate the birthday of Mexican independence. The remembrance of the gilded heroes—Hidalgo, Morelos, and Guerrero—was undoubtedly a lugubrious pill for those stalwarts struggling in the second war for independence. José María Iglesias was able to describe their modest festivities in poetic terms, despite the external circumstances:

The solemnity of the occasion was grandiose by its very simplicity. The mountains which narrowed the horizon raised themselves majestically, like silent witnesses to that important spectacle. The moon, peering between the clouds which had concealed it a moment before, bathed the Nazas, which flowed a short distance away. The picture of the audience, formed on the step at the door of the hacienda, was composed of the government, of the small number of loyal followers who had accompanied it on its third peregrination, of the soldiers of the battalion of Guanajuato, of the corps of mounted riflemen, the faithful escort of the Supreme Magistrate of the nation, and of the simple inhabitants of the hacienda, who for the first time, without doubt, were attending such a celebration.[42]

With less of the poetic in his veins, Lerdo possessed the steely stoicism which wasted little time on sentiment or self-pity. A few days after that evening and in the middle of the miserable journey, he wrote: "However bad our situation may be, we have all been able to foresee it and we have all known for some time that what is needed is more time and more constancy."[43]

Repeating the tactics used outside San Luis Potosí, the government awaited at Nazas the outcome of the battle between the republican division commanded by General González Ortega and the French forces spearheading into the northern part of Durango. The opponents joined in the Battle of Majoma, and the result was the disintegration of the last respectable force which the republic had in the field. Strategically speaking, the military plans after the battle had to rest in the hands of local chieftains practicing a scattered warfare from Chihuahua to Oaxaca and Guerrero; while the government had only one choice—to retire to the protective isolation in the state of Chihuahua and attempt to give unity to the struggle to the extent which geographical limitations would permit. As Gualot aptly stated, "Juárez dived in the solitudes of Chihuahua, vast territory little more than desert, which pertained to Mexico only in a geographic sense."[44]

For a period of more than two years, from October, 1864, to December, 1866, Juárez, Lerdo, and Iglesias upheld the symbol of the republican government within the desert state of the north,

---

[42]Iglesias, *Revistas Históricas*, III, 25–26.
[43]Lerdo to Romero, Nazas, Durango, September 22, 1864, Romero (ed.), *Correspondencia de la Legación Mexicana*, IV, 544.
[44]Gualot, *L'Empire de Maximilien*, 70.

poor in resources and population but rich in enthusiasm for the cause of independence. In a relative sense, the government, relying on the coöperation of the people of Chihuahua, found a stabilized situation at last, and there the triumvirate expended their energies to vitalize the feeble resources in order to counteract the universal demoralization among the republican elements. When many others gave up and accepted actively or passively the consolidation of Maximilian's empire under the guidance of the French, they struggled on in the northern outpost, at least never openly admitting the apparent futility of carrying on. Reading between the lines, however, one can discern that there was occcasional discouragement. After reaching Paso del Norte in August, 1865, Iglesias wrote: "The present situation of the supreme government is certainly exposed to danger and difficulty, and it would be puerile to deny it. Its resources are scanty: the foreign invasion has tossed it from place to place, even to the ultimate extreme of the republic."[45] Then, scraping the bottom of the barrel of morale, he added with courage:

We write this at 500 leagues from the ancient capital; surrounded by the desert on all sides; . . . we write while errant, almost proscribed between dangers and calamities. And we write, nevertheless, with serene pulse and tranquil conscience, because we have not lost faith in the cause which we sustain; and even when one guides a desperate cause, there will always be pride in the days of life which remain to us, of having defended it in the supreme moments of its misfortunes and its extinction. God protect the cause! God save it![46]

If the Juárez government found a permanent home in the state of Chihuahua, that was true only in a general sense. The travels had not ended, for the capital twice was located at Paso del Norte (present Juárez), on the very periphery of the nation, because of the unpredictable tactics of the French, who twice captured and twice evacuated the city of Chihuahua. Probably the hostility of the United States to the empire prevented the French from striking the last few miles, either to drive Juárez across the international boundary or into some desert hideout, like a bandit fugitive. The Chihuahua circuit, a vicious circle when computed statistically, totalled three entries and departures into and from the capital itself and two entries and departures into and from Paso del Norte. The French troops supporting Maximilian had thus come within a few leagues of crushing the personal symbols of the opposing central government. Lerdo, who penned the official circulars to state governors, informing them of the constant changes, performed

[45]Iglesias, *Revistas Históricas*, III, 472.
[46]*Ibid.*, 473.

that duty so frequently that his reports appeared like standardized forms.[47]

Before considering the outstanding governmental problems in which Lerdo figured during the residency in Chihuahua, it would be interesting to investigate some of the external aspects of daily life, public and private, of the famed triumvirate. While on the road, especially after entering the confines of Chihuahua, the people and local officials showed spontaneous enthusiasm whenever the presidential coach hove in sight. Writing from Nazas, Lerdo declared that "not only has the Government been well received but with genuine enthusiasm";[48] and once in Chihuahua itself, he elaborated that at Nazas and beyond, the reception of the President had been "general and enthusiastic." "Unfortunately, the resources of this State are not large; but at least we have seen that the President and the cause of the Republic hold the best sympathies throughout the State."[49]

Special receptions, banquets, and parades were usually prepared for Juárez; and although he was the focus of those arrangements, Lerdo and Iglesias were always present, always an integral part of the program. The frequent arrivals of the government at Paso del Norte or Chihuahua provided excellent excuses for the citizenry to dust off the champagne stockpile or delve into the wine cellar for whatever might be located there.[50]

In addition, Juárez's birthday, approaching a national holiday by that time, was another excellent opportunity for moments of frivolity to dispel the gloom surrounding the cause of nationalism.

---

[47]For the circulars, see *Periódico Oficial* (Paso del Norte), September 7, 1865; *ibid.* (Chihuahua), November 21, 1865; *ibid.* (Paso del Norte), January 1, 1866; *ibid.* (Chihuahua), June 20, 1866; *Colección de Leyes . . . 1863–1867*, II, 251, 295–297; Romero (ed.), *Correspondencia de la Legación Mexicana*, VI, 346–347, 368–370, 377, 693–694. Exact dates of arrival at either Paso del Norte or Chihuahua are entered on the chart of the peregrination.

Other convenient data on this phase of the travels may be found in Puig Casauranc, *Archivos Privados de D. Benito Juárez*, 80, 95, 102, 104, 108; Galindo y Galindo, *La Gran Década Nacional*, III, 340–343.

[48]Lerdo to Romero, Nazas, Durango, September 22, 1864, Romero (ed.), *Correspondencia de la Legación Mexicana*, IV, 543.

[49]Lerdo to Romero, Chihuahua, October 16, 1864, *ibid.*, IV, 546.

[50]I. S. Bartlett, a newspaper correspondent and customs official at Franklin, Texas, across the river from Paso del Norte, gave an interesting description of Juárez's first arrival at the "slumbering" Mexican village and the bustling excitement which resulted. When Bartlett visited Juárez at Paso del Norte a few days later, the President had champagne to serve.—I. S. Bartlett, "President Juárez at Old El Paso," *Bulletin of the Pan American Union*, XLI (November, 1915), 646, 648. For one of Juárez's descriptions of a reception, see Juárez to Santacilia, June 18, 1866, Puig Casauranc, *Archivos Privados de D. Benito Juárez*, 153–154.

The party of March 21, 1865, at Chihuahua, found Lerdo at the top of the list of men scheduled to give toasts at the gathering. All the local functionaries were present, and, in justice to them, their constituency had given remarkable coöperation to the beggar central government. Lerdo rose to toast them in words which were sweet nectar to the insatiable thirst of local pride. Sounding the phrases dear to the native sons, tossing out melifluous morsels to the ravenous localist appetites, he perorated many times upon the prefacing phrase "Honor to Chihuahua" for this, for that, and for the other. But it was not monotonous to the hierarchy of Chihua-huenses present, and Lerdo's finale provoked a pandemonium of enthusiasm: "I toast, gentlemen, to the State of Chihuahua, free and sovereign among the states of the Mexican Republic!" Shouts, bravos, and the national anthem merged in the joy, as men rushed to the rostrum to grasp Lerdo's hand, embrace each other, or engage in quasi-evangelical antics which spring forth when state and national harmonies blend so well.[51] Obvious as was the purpose, Lerdo's speech showed that he was gaining insight into the force of localism. One day he must cope with the problem as president of the republic.

The daily routine of the official family of three was far less colorful, however. The taciturn Juárez described it adequately as "an errant life in these deserts where there are no diversions of any species."[52] Isolated from home, friends, and families, virtually cut off from contact with the outside world, the petite ministry carried on the burden of administration and policy with a modicum of assistance. It was wait and work with whatever resources could be obtained. Naturally the three men became inseparable companions, eating together, living together, and sharing their frugal pleasures, like cigars or mail from the United States which they anticipated with the impatience of children. Once when speaking of "friends" Lerdo and Iglesias, Juárez wrote to Santacilia: "Every mail day we read your letters together with great pleasure. . . ."[53] On another occasion, he mentioned a box of cigars which Santacilia had sent from New York: "I expect that Sr. Lerdo has just taken out his cigars. . . . D. Sebastián has been very contented and satisfied."[54]

---

[51]*Periódico Oficial* (Chihuahua), March 28, 1865; Romero (ed.), *Correspondencia de la Legación Mexicana*, VI, 109–110; Prida Santacilia, *Siguiendo la Vida de Juárez*, 207–208.

[52]Juárez to Santacilia, Paso del Norte, September 27, 1865, Puig Casauranc, *Archivos Privados de D. Benito Juárez*, 93.

[53]Juárez to Santacilia, Paso del Norte, April 6, 1866, *ibid.*, 133.

[54]Juárez to Santacilia, Chihuahua, October 15, 1866, *ibid.*, 187. Francisco Bulnes' criticism of Juárez and the luxurious life of the peregrinating government, which "from the material point of view was enviable," was a half-truth and patently unfair.—Bulnes, *El Verdadero Juárez y la Verdad sobre la Intervención y el Imperio*, 821–826.

It was during those months of intimacy that Lerdo gained the ascendancy over Juárez as his leading adviser, a marked influence which was to last many years. The sway which one man may exercise over another is not, of course, a factor which lends itself to scientific measurement. Juárez and Lerdo might have shed some light on the perplexing question by scattering a few revealing personal comments here and there, but both remained silent. Still, the solutions to the great problems of state during the intervention, as will be shown, carried with them the deep stamp of Lerdo's mind, although a president must accept the ultimate responsibility for his acts; and further, the idea was broadcast widely by the close of the period that Lerdo's administrative, diplomatic, and political talents were the foundation stones which complemented Juárez's recognized tenacity and faith for the republican cause. While the association no doubt was mutually influential and advantageous, Juárez alone reaped the historical harvest of glory.[55]

A few illustrations will serve to demonstrate the contemporary position which was conceded Lerdo as the chief lieutenant of Juárez. Not only did French historians refer to him as the prime minister of the wandering President,[56] indicating that his prominence had filtered all the way back to Mexico City, but the famous Castelnau mission of late 1866 and early 1867 also revealed how great was the trust which Juárez placed in him.

General Castelnau, aide-de-camp of Napoleon III, who arrived in Mexico in October, 1866, with broad, discretionary powers, was instructed to find some escape hatch for France from the Mexican embroglio and the crumbling empire of Maximilian.[57] Ephemeral as was his scheme, Castelnau proposed to cashier Maximilian and to establish a provisional government headed by a liberal—anyone but Juárez—through whom the French could treat, salvage some of Napoleon's blemished prestige, and obtain a measure of the financial aims which had been the original pretexts for intervention. Among the feasible choices for an interim executive of the liberal party, Castelnau favored Lerdo de Tejada for reasons which were significant: "Endowed with a great intellect, of good character, of an energy which excludes neither moderate ways nor a spirit of conciliation, he appears to me the man who offers us the most guarantees, and who ought to be the most easily accepted by

[55]Countless biographies, sketches, monographs, special studies, general histories, and documentary collections have centered around Juárez's life, but only a few cursory sketches are available on the life of Sebastián Lerdo.

[56]Blanchot, Memoires, L'Intervention Française, II, 104; Gualot, L'Empire de Maximilien, 26; Gualot, Fin D'Empire, 213–214.

[57]The data on the Castelnau mission are taken from the detailed study of Louis Sonolet, "L'Agonie de L'Empire du Mexique, d'après des Lettres et des Notes Inédites du Général Castelnau," La Revue de Paris, IV (July-August, 1927), 590–603, 605–616.

Juárez."[58] The certainty with which Castelnau wrote proved that Lerdo's fame had traveled far, despite the confinement in Chihuahua.

From the republican camp itself came flashes of jealousy of Lerdo's affinity to the President. Guillermo Prieto, one of Juárez's ardent apostles, bitterly attacked Lerdo after his (Prieto's) break with Juárez in late 1865. While his comments were polemical, they disclosed a wounded vanity springing from Lerdo's primacy in the mind of the Chief Executive.

He [Lerdo] discredits or hates all of the men of the reform; his beautiful ideals are. . . : [as in text] As suspicious as he is ignorant, as able through his talent as he is vain and impotent, he holds hatreds and rancors almost clerical, all the while he neither believes in anything, nor feels any affection for anybody: this man is the tutor of Juárez; and the one who has formed a vacuum around him, and he is the one on whom our destinies are going to depend.[59]

Even the wife of Juárez's faithful minister of Finance, José María Iglesias, felt the sting of envy toward Lerdo, who had relegated her spouse to a subordinate rôle in affairs of state. Writing to Iglesias from distant Mexico City, she judged resentfully that "he has worked so much less than you and has had the fortune of obtaining as his share the signing of certain documents which all the periodicals have published, and through them everyone knows that he [Lerdo] is at the side of Sr. Juárez."[60]

As for Juárez himself, his mind and its inner workings were surrounded by such a thick crust that even his biographers have been baffled perpetually in their attempts to penetrate to the inner sanctum. Justo Sierra, for example, denied that he was "sub-

---

[58]Castelnau to Napoleon III, October 28, 1866, quoted by Emile Ollivier, *L'Empire Libéral, Études, Récits, Souvenirs*, IX, 96. Roeder quoted this dispatch at greater length, though he did not identify it as such or cite his source.—Roeder, *Juárez and His Mexico*, II, 648. Sonolet quoted the complete report, but his version, presumably taken from the papers of General Castelnau, did not include Lerdo's name; however, the man whom Castelnau referred to as "the second personage of the liberal party" (p. 611) could have been only Lerdo.—Sonolet, "L'Agonie de L'Empire du Mexique," *La Revue de Paris*, IV, 605–616. In his story of the incident, Gualot included Lerdo's name. —*Fin D'Empire*, 213–214.

[59]Prieto to Chiquitín, May 6, 1866, *El Diario del Imperio* (Mexico), August 7, 1866. The letter fell into the hands of the imperialists and was printed for propaganda purposes. It was reprinted in *Periódico Oficial* (Chihuahua), September 22, 1866; consequently, the President was aware, no doubt, of the remarks about Lerdo's alleged tutorial influence. Compare with Prieto's flattering remarks on Lerdo's service during the intervention as written in a textbook intended for public consumption.—*Lecciones de Historia Patria Escritas para los Alumnos del Colegio Militar*, 420.

[60]Doña Juanita Iglesias to José María Iglesias, Mexico, September 6, 1866, Archivo de Fernando Iglesias Calderón, Legajo 4, A.G.N.

ordinated to the Rector of San Ildefonso," implying that the reputed personal influence was nine-tenths rumor,[61] but others concede Lerdo a fair share of the moral and intellectual support of the republican effort against intervention.[62] The intermittent references which Juárez made to Lerdo in his personal correspondence indicated respect and a close personal tie;[63] and it should be noted that not only during the intervention but long afterward Juárez looked upon Lerdo as a person indispensable to his cabinet. At least by 1867, toward the end of the intervention, Lerdo was a man to be reckoned with on any major political problem.

In regard to the operation of government in the north, too frequently historians have glided over the surface of the topic, leaving the false impression that Juárez, Lerdo, and Iglesias simply roosted in Chihuahua until Maximilian was defeated, by time, by his own deficiencies, and by the operation of international factors, such as United States' hostility and the evolution of France's domestic and foreign position after the Battle of Sadowa. Admittedly, the withdrawal of the foreign troops was the key to republican victory, yet the maintenance of a *de jure* central government and the limited direction it gave to the scattered guerrilla forces were factors that should be considered in preventing the consolidation of empire in Mexico and consequently the net result.

While no detailed study of the Juárez government can be presented here, some general features must be understood to comprehend the vital phases which Lerdo handled as minister of Government and Foreign Relations. The size of the ministry, for one thing, was a handicap, forcing upon a handful of men all the mechanics of drafting decrees, circulars, and official correspondence. At one time, the combined ministry under Lerdo consisted of himself and one assistant, while no department had more than two subordinates.[64] That was the "hierarchy of officials" of which

---

[61] Sierra, *Juárez*, 399. But he contradicted himself later, stating that the two men "appeared one and the same in their intentions. . . ."—*Ibid.*, 482–483.

[62] For a few illustrations, see Galindo y Galindo, *La Gran Década Nacional*, III, 651n; Roeder, *Juárez and His Mexico*, II, 577; Gualot, *L'Empire de Maximilien*, 26; Payno, *Cuentas, Gastos, Acreedores . . . del Imperio*, 928, 929. The military chiefs of the republic, said Payno, were bound "by a species of copper wire, which held the moral entity called the Republican Government, represented by an antagonist of Napoleon in Juárez and a minister who was called Lerdo."

[63] Puig Casauranc, *Archivos Privados de D. Benito Juárez*, 109, 125, 133, 146, 147, 155, 187.

[64] Lerdo to Romero, Chihuahua, March 27, 1865, Romero (ed.), *Correspondencia de la Legación Mexicana*, VI, 118. A list of the civilian employees, exclusive of the ministers, the so-called "immaculates" who continued to serve the government during the peregrination, was printed in *El Siglo*, July 16, 1867.

Bulnes complained without justification.[65] The division of functions among the ministers has been noted previously, but, practically speaking, the duties overlapped and the triumvirate discussed and resolved all major questions in common. The means for disseminating official policy and decrees as well as the propaganda organ was the *Periódico Oficial,* scheduled to appear twice weekly, which traveled with the government from Monterrey to Chihuahua to Paso del Norte and back to Chihuahua. Lerdo always enclosed copies of the paper in his diplomatic pouches to Romero as the most convenient method of briefing the representative at Washington on governmental measures; while Iglesias filled many of its columns with diatribes against Maximilian, the French, and the empire in general.[66]

Isolation in the northern deserts magnified the communication problem out of all proportion, and Lerdo constantly struggled for solutions under the ever-changing conditions. Actually, Romero at Washington was the center of communications for the United States, Europe, and even Mexico, the government at Chihuahua being a distant outpost on the shaky network. After Lerdo informed Romero of the fall of Guaymas to the French (1865), through which port duplicate dispatches had been sent from Washington via the Mexican consul at San Francisco,[67] only one relatively certain channel with the outside world was accessible to the government: from Chihuahua (or Paso del Norte, depending on the location of the capital) to Franklin, Texas (near present El Paso), to Santa Fe, to Kansas City, and into Washington, or vice-versa. Since the route was tedious and dangerous, Lerdo was often without news for five, six, or more weeks after Romero had posted it in Washington. Thus, when the triumvirate gathered to open the mail packets after the arrival of the diligence from Franklin, they were reading and learning of events which were not current but ancient history. Some news filtered in by way of travelers from the interior of Mexico and occasional letters came from that direction; but the information was always stale and frequently of doubtful reliability. It was also difficult for Lerdo to maintain contact with the northern military commanders engaged in field operations distant from the capital. Once he advised Mariano Escobedo, one of the principal republican generals, that the government had received no word of his whereabouts for almost a month and a half.[68]

---

[65]Bulnes, *El Verdadero Juárez,* 822–823.

[66]Iglesias' articles were compiled later in the three-volume work cited frequently as *Revistas Históricas.*

[67]Lerdo to Romero, Chihuahua, April 19, 1865, Romero (ed.), *Correspondencia de la Legación Mexicana,* VI, 139–140.

[68]Lerdo to Escobedo, Chihuahua, August 25, 1866, Archivo de Fernando Iglesias Calderón, Legajo 12, A.G.N.

As minister of Government, Lerdo had to cope with the thorniest problem of intervention from the republican standpoint: defection on all levels among civil and military ranks. The government necessarily depended upon local chieftains who controlled local administration and resources, and "the most tenacious fight which Juárez sustained was with the anarchy that sapped his own party."[69] The *caudillos*, willing to coöperate with the government to the extent that such action coincided with their personal interests in retaining independence from outside control, would just as quickly turn against the Juárez federalism to block any encroachment from that direction on their private spheres of sovereignty. The most famous of those *caudillos* and the outstanding example of defection during the intervention was Santiago Vidaurri of Coahuila-Nuevo León; yet there was a multitude of others throughout the northern states, wherever the federal régime entered or attempted to intervene directly in the conduct of local affairs—in Tamaulipas, on several occasions, in Sinaloa, and Sonora. That aspect of affairs, though never publicized, made one of the less patriotic pages in the record of victory over empire. In fact, the dividing line between patriotism and personalism was fluid, although Justo Sierra defined it accurately as the national *caudillos* on one hand—great leaders like Porfirio Díaz and Mariano Escobedo, who were working sincerely with Juárez for nationalistic reasons—and the caciques on the other, who worked against the French and Maximilian only because they opposed the interference of the empire in their fiefs.[70]

Fortunately for the government and especially for reducing Lerdo's problems, Chihuahua displayed an unparalleled spirit of coöperation and loyalty. Juárez and his ministers gathered in conference with the local officials soon after the first arrival at the state capital in 1864, to allow them a voice in raising local military forces and in the distribution and collection of taxes.[71] No doubt that was intended as an anodyne for the state of siege Lerdo was soon to promulgate, by which local executive and legislative branches were suspended and all political and administrative rights were lodged in the resident central government.[72] The government's appoint-

---

The above summary was based primarily on the diplomatic correspondence between Lerdo and Romero. Professor Frazer has also pointed out the time element in communications as a factor in Lerdo's conduct of foreign affairs.— Robert W. Frazer, "The Ochoa Bond Negotiations of 1865–1867," *The Pacific Historical Review*, XI (December, 1942), 400; "The United States, European, and West Virginia Land Company," *ibid.*, XIII (March, 1944), 35.

[69]Rivera Cambas, *Historia de la Intervención*, II, 548.

[70]Sierra, *Juárez*, 452–453. Historically speaking, the attitude was nothing more than the continuance of the peculiar Mexican definition of federalism.

[71]Iglesias, *Revistas Históricas*, III, 41.

[72]Lerdo to the Governor and Military Commandant of Chihuahua, November 18, 1864, *Periódico Oficial* (Chihuahua), November 25, 1864.

ment of prominent local leaders for administration, the glory which the people of the poor, neglected state seemed to feel in playing host to the central government, and such flattering phrases as Lerdo doled out for their provincial pride, as at the birthday celebration in March, 1865, undoubtedly helped to assuage the pain arising from the loss of autonomy.

It was the handling of defection at the center, however, which was the brilliant contribution of Lerdo to the survival of Juárez as president and possibly the *de jure* existence of the federal government. The ancient Mexican political disease, which may be styled presidential fever, did not cease its ravages with the intervention. Uncomfortable and totally uninviting as the presidential chair appeared during that period, it remained the crowning prize for the ambitious.

By far the most dangerous threat to Juárez and to his government centered around the machinations of Jesús González Ortega which transpired during the residence in Chihuahua. A military hero who had given valuable services in the War of the Reform and at the siege of Puebla, Ortega had within him the troublesome and human embers of presidential aspirations which had never died out since the days of the "petition of the 51," when he had been proposed as a substitute for Juárez after the election of 1861. A *caudillo* governor of Zacatecas, Ortega was impulsive and lacked the suave political acumen of a Manuel Doblado, for example. After his disastrous defeat at Majoma (September, 1864), he followed the government to Chihuahua, residing in a private home and maintaining no intercourse with the government officials.[73] There he brooded some weeks before the wheels of his mind formulated a legal approach to the office of president.

One day in November Lerdo received a letter from Ortega, reminding the government that he was president of the Supreme Court of Justice and consequently vice-president of the nation, and inquiring whether Juárez was ready to hand over to him the post of chief executive. Ortega had calculated that Juárez's legal term (four years) would end on November 30, 1864.[74] That query was the spark which set off a battle of manifestoes and legal sophistry, causing many personal animosities. More serious, however, was the breach which it made in republican unity, for several followers joined Ortega in what amounted to a civil strife behind the republican lines, giving joy to the imperialists and impeding the war effort seriously.

---

[73]Juárez to Santacilia, Chihuahua, December 22, 1864, Puig Casauranc, *Archivos Privados de D. Benito Juárez*, 30.

[74]Ortega to Lerdo, November 30, 1864, Romero (ed.), *Correspondencia de la Legación Mexicana*, IV, 559–561; *Periódico Oficial* (Chihuahua), December 3, 1864.

Ortega, who had made the mistake of filling his letter with constitutional dogma, was scarcely a match for a man with a trained legal mind like Lerdo, who, with cutting logic, transposed his support of Juárez into a written reply which left no doubt in the mind of the ambitious General about his practical chances of gliding into the presidency on verbiage. In his answer, Lerdo first shattered Ortega's flimsy claims: (1) Though Juárez had been declared elected in June, 1861, the actual term did not begin until December 1 of the year, and in no case should the four-year period be diminished. Consequently, the current constitutional term would end on November 30, 1865, not November 30, 1864. (2) Juárez had been invested with extraordinary powers by a representative national congress for the duration of the war, and he alone, therefore, had the right to interpret any debatable points in the organic law. (3) As Ortega had claimed, under Article 81 of the Constitution, should elections not be held and a new president not be installed by December 1 of an election year, then the old executive would automatically cease to function and the president of the Supreme Court would assume the office ad interim until the elections were held. But, countered Lerdo, that clause was intended "only to prevent the president from abusing the influence of his power," and not to cover an absolute impediment to elections as had arisen from the circumstances of the French intervention. Considering all the above reasons, Juárez should continue in office until it was possible to hold national elections.

Then Lerdo, who had completed only his negative attack, began to topple the rickety legal ladder which Ortega had built to the presidency. In effect, he asked: Who was this person claiming the executive office through the technicality of his position as vice-president? A man who had accepted the office of governor of Zacatecas in 1863 without obtaining the proper license of the federal government, an act in direct violation of a constitutional provision. As a result, Ortega had forfeited his presidency of the Supreme Court; still, the philanthropic Juárez "has agreed to use his ample powers" to reinstate Ortega in his judicial position. Thus, Ortega, who had premised all his presidential pretensions on his *de facto* vice-presidency, awakened to discover that only through charity was he to be restored to that lowlier office. Finally, Lerdo concluded by touching the crux of the matter: Juárez was respected, trusted, and "generally recognized" by the republican chieftains, and on that basis he should continue to stand as the symbol of central government.[75]

---

[75]Lerdo to Ortega, November 30, 1864, Romero (ed.), *Correspondencia de la Legación Mexicana*, IV, 561–565; *Periódico Oficial* (Chihuahua), December 3, 1864.

What happened subsequently is one of the most controversial and well-known aspects of the republican phase of the intervention. After apparently accepting the government's determination, Ortega requested a license to return to the interior of Mexico and recruit fresh forces to fight the empire. Included in the license was a clause which permitted him, if necessary to avoid enemy lines, to pass through the United States on his journey southward. Ortega left Chihuahua for the United States where he eventually established in New York City, recruiting foreign troops, falling under the influence of other disaffected, anti-Juarist republicans, and accumulating debts which compromised the honor of the Juárez government, since he still held the cloak of high official position. Those developments occurred between November, 1864, and November, 1865, while the government was still in the state of Chihuahua.[76]

With Ortega's unorthodox conduct as a perfect pretext, Lerdo issued the famous decrees of November 8, 1865, accompanied by his lengthy circular to state governors.[77] The first decree extended the tenure of Juárez indefinitely until the conclusion of the war; and the second, unnecessarily ruthless, removed Ortega from office, virtually outlawed him, and ordered his immediate arrest and trial whenever he set foot upon national territory. The circular was an elaborate review of the Ortega question, with all the details, as well as a legal rationalization for the stance of the government and the fiat extension of presidential tenure.

It would be useless to dissect the unfortunate *dénouement* of the episode, which has been done so partially by the proponents of one side or the other. Ortega again began to brood (in New York) upon the harsh treatment to which he had been subjected. In a short while he had gathered about him other opponents of Juárez, the best known among them being Guillermo Prieto, Miguel Negrete, a former and discredited minister of War for Juárez,[78] and General Patoni of Durango. After a series of escapades along the Texas border, which General Sheridan of the American "Army of Observation" helped to foil,[79] and further vituperous ex-

---

[76]The principal monograph in defense of Ortega was written by his grandson.—José González Ortega, *El Golpe de Estado de Juárez, Rasgos Biográficos del General Jesús González Ortega*. A concise, impartial summary of the complicated dispute with Juárez may be found in José Bravo Ugarte, *Historia de México*, III, 321–323.

[77]Romero (ed.), *Correspondencia de la Legación Mexicana*, VI, 359–366.

[78]The *Periódico Oficial* (Paso del Norte), June 7, 1866, recorded the results of an interview between Prieto and Juárez on December 8, 1865, just prior to their break. Not only was Lerdo at loggerheads with Prieto, but with Negrete also. See Doroteo Negrete, *La Verdad ante la Figura Militar de Don Miguel Negrete*, 177–178. The malcontents composing the Ortega plot, therefore, were as much the personal enemies of Lerdo as of Juárez.

[79]P. H. Sheridan, *Personal Memoirs*, II, 224.

changes between Lerdo and Ortega in the form of manifestoes,[80] Ortega and his helpmate Patoni eventually made their way to Zacatecas (January, 1867). They were arrested promptly by the Juarist Governor and retained in prison long after the war had ended—and after Juárez had been elected constitutional president in 1867.[81]

Historians generally have warped the question to whet the particular axes which they were grinding. Biographers favorable to Juárez have maligned Ortega as a traitor, while those taking the opposite viewpoint denounce Juárez and Lerdo for their cruelty toward a national hero. Juárez is painted as a dictator, lusting for power and determined to crush all obstacles in his path. Intermingled with those conclusions there is invariably a surplus of banter and falderal about constitutional clauses, mostly derived from the circulars of Lerdo.

In order to determine Lerdo's importance, first as an influence on Juárez's decision and second on the entirety of the issue, it is necessary to attempt an impartial conclusion on the over-all significance of the affair. In any estimate, Ortega's great military services to the republic should never be discredited; yet he had many blots on his political record and often had been openly insulting to Juárez, a personal factor which should not be overlooked.[82] In the strictest constitutional sense, the president of the Supreme Court should have succeeded to the presidency on December 1, 1865, but, as Lerdo had pointed out, Ortega's claim to the office had been compromised by his own actions.

Brushing aside the subterfuge of constitutional technicalities, the issue was determined on very practical grounds. Ortega was flighty and undependable, while Juárez had proved his political

---

[80]Circular to State Governors (signed Lerdo), Paso del Norte, April 30, 1866, Romero (ed.), *Correspondencia de la Legación Mexicana*, VI, 636–656; Iglesias, *Revistas Históricas*, III, 646–654.

[81]Governor Miguel Auza to Lerdo, Zacatecas, January 8, 1867; Lerdo to Auza, Durango, January 10, 1867, *Colección de Leyes . . . 1863–1867*, III, 148–152. In addition to the works cited, consult Rivera Cambas, *Historia de la Intervención*, II, 545–546, 630–631; III, 157–160; Zamacois, *Historia de Méjico*, XVIII, 1723–1727.

[82]The "petition of the 51" should be recalled, as well as a speech which Ortega made when taking the oath of office as president of the Supreme Court in August, 1861. In addition, he had resigned from Juárez's cabinet in April, 1861, in a manner which was rude to Juárez without provocation. Also, he had joined with Doblado to request Juárez's resignation in the gloomy days of early 1864 after the French campaign had scattered the republican armies. Nor was his military record unscathed. Both Lerdo and Juárez criticized his tactical blunders and leadership during and after the Battle of Majoma. Lerdo summarized the accumulated grievances of the government against Ortega after the siege of Puebla in a letter to Romero, Paso del Norte, January 27, 1866, Romero (ed.), *Correspondencia de la Legación Mexicana*, VI, 465–468.

morality and Gibraltar-like qualities in supporting the cause of republicanism. The test of the right or wrong of the November decrees was the test of public opinion; and that force, as Juárez accurately defined it, was lodged in the local chieftains who were fighting the war against the empire and whether they would continue to support him as their leader.[83] Throughout the scattered areas of republican resistance came the reiteration of loyalty to Juárez, while Ortega found support only among the outcasts, the discredited, the exiles. Hence, Juárez, who had retained the loyalty of the chieftains to that point, was authorized to continue as the trustee of the cause; in short, it was no stage to exchange the known for the unknown element, to trade horses in mid-stream.[84]

Whether Lerdo influenced Juárez to stay in power was premised upon the assumption that Juárez ever considered resigning. According to Manuel Ruíz, the only magistrate of the Supreme Court at Chihuahua when the November decrees were issued, and a man who defected soon after their publication, Juárez had determined not to continue in office after his constitutional term had ended. At the insistence of Lerdo and Iglesias, however, the few high officials present submitted their opinions on the matter in writing. As a result, Juárez reversed his original decision and "adopted the opinion of Sr. Lerdo," who drafted both decrees of November 8, 1865, as well as the circular in explanation.[85] Furthermore, Roeder declared that Juárez went through a prolonged mental dilemma, torn between his devotion to legal principles, which dictated his resignation, and his political instincts, which dictated that he continue in office to avoid "the danger of disrupting the defense of the country at the most crucial period of the war. . . ."[86] But viewing Juárez's career as an entity—his actions during the War of the Reform and his subsequent tenacious grasp of power until death, as well as his stolidity during the intervention—one can only conclude that he clutched the presidency with the firmness of mortmain and that he never hesitated about retaining the office. Thus, those presumed inner struggles did not

---

[83]Juárez to Santacilia, Paso del Norte, March 30, 1866, Puig Casauranc, *Archivos Privados de D. Benito Juárez*, 131.

[84]Pantaleón Tovar, a republican exile in New York, brilliantly argued the government side on the above grounds, though in much different phraseology. —Tovar to Lerdo, New York, April 3, 1866, *Suplemento al Primer Cuaderno de Documentos Publicados por el General González Ortega, para Esplorar la Opinión de Sus Conciudadanos en Favor de una Rebelión contra el Gobierno Nacional de México*, 19–21.

[85]Manuel Ruíz, *Exposición Que el C. Lic. Manuel Ruíz, Ministro Constitucional de la Suprema Corte de Justicia de la Nación, Presenta al Soberano Congreso* . . . , 8.

[86]Roeder, *Juárez and His Mexico*, II, 614. Another recent biographer of Juárez subscribed to a similar opinion.—Pere Foix, *Juárez*, 201–202.

mesh with his acts. As Carlos Pereyra declared: "It is a fact that the consecration of Juárez to the [liberal] credo which he served always coincided with his personal interest."[87] Juárez was probably a victim of the monomania that he was indispensable to the salvation of Mexico and perhaps never separated completely that belief from his personal ambitions which were built on gradiose scale.

There was little doubt, however, that Lerdo stood forth as Juárez's principal collaborator in the arbitrary extension of tenure, and it should be noted that the decision was contained in Lerdo's letter to Ortega as early as November, 1864. If Juárez knew from the start what his ultimate decision would be, it was Lerdo who wrote the polished decrees, supplied any necessary moral support, and reasoned out the intellectual apologies and constitutional interpretations. Lerdo was the brain of the procedure, even though Juárez called the documents of November 8, 1865, "my decrees."[88]

Lerdo's motives can be conjectured only from a series of indications. Although he denied Ortega's charge that he was possessed of a congenital thirst for office, the satiation of which depended upon Juárez's survival,[89] undoubtedly he had become attached to his high position and growing influence over the President. Furthermore, if Juárez had died suddenly, there was strong reason to believe that he would have preferred Lerdo as his successor. While the decrees anticipated the default of the President through death and promised to name a successor, that action was never taken; but, based solely on conjecture, Juárez and Lerdo may have had a confidential understanding that Lerdo should fill the president's chair in case of the death of the incumbent. Certainly that contingency was in the forefront and a vital concern after Ortega was eliminated. However that may be, the republican triumvirate survived its most difficult internal threat in a prolonged test which showed Juárez and Lerdo in their closest teamwork. No doubt personal and patriotic motives intermingled in the minds of both men, but history has decided that those motives—fortunately—paralleled.

The other phase of governmental duties which fell within Lerdo's sphere of responsibility was the conduct of foreign affairs. Like almost every honor derived from the republican victory over empire, the credit for an "immaculate" external policy pyramided to Juárez's glory; and, as president, he admittedly accepted the

[87]Carlos Pereyra, *México Falsificado*, I, 145.

[88]Juárez to Santacilia, Paso del Norte, March 2, 1866, Puig Casauranc, *Archivos Privados de D. Benito Juárez*, 125.

[89]Circular to State Governors (signed Lerdo), Paso del Norte, April 30, 1866, Romero (ed.), *Correspondencia de la Legación Mexicana*, VI, 654; *Periódico Oficial* (Paso del Norte), May 10, 1866.

burden of ultimate accountability. On the other hand, the man who comprehended the problems and who drafted the clear-cut instructions and diplomatic notes to Romero at Washington was Sebastián Lerdo. For reasons which will be explained below, it would appear that he was also the initiator and watchdog of the general diplomatic program, answerable not alone for the mechanics of diplomatic exchanges but to an extent for Juárez's adoption and strict observance of a line of action laid down in late 1864.

Limited by the isolation, the long delays in communications, the poverty of the treasury, and, most important, the lack of any real bargaining power, the diplomatic objectives which Juárez and Lerdo attempted to promote were naturally concentrated. Excepting the mission of Jesús Terán, the special republican agent in Europe, all effort was directed in and toward the United States, the aims being to obtain all possible moral and physical aid from the Northern Neighbor, to prevent the recognition of Maximilian, and retain the sympathy of the United States for Juárez.

The famous instructions which Lerdo sent to Romero in December, 1864, form an accurate abridgment of the broad framework of the republican foreign policy:

(1) In order to expel a powerful foreign invader from Mexican soil it would not be "inconvenient" for the Mexican government to accept aid from a foreign nation under terms which would not be prejudicial to the national honor and interests.

(2) The government, which had unqualified confidence in the intelligence and experience of Romero and appreciated his knowledge of the United States, could not foresee the diverse problems bound to arise; therefore, it left him free to work at Washington within the broad framework of his general instructions.

(3) While particular decisions must necessarily be left to Romero's discretion, it was best to stipulate positively the ironclad rules which were not to be violated under any circumstances— rules set forth by the Mexican congress in the grant of extraordinary powers to the executive: ". . . [the government] will always abstain from any treaty or convention which does not preserve the integrity and independence of the national territory, or one in which another government might pretend to hold any species of intervention whatsoever in the Republic."

(4) Any future arrangement with the United States could have the character of a military alliance

or could even have the character of a treaty in which the Monroe Doctrine is elevated to the position of a permanent principle which would impose without exception the obligation of mutual aid to repel European intervention of any kind in matters exclusively American. . . .

(5) Whatever particular contracts for loans, military supplies, or foreign troops might be agreed upon, the Mexican security for

repayment must "always avoid every hypothecation or compromise of any part of the national territory which could be the occasion for some future cession of the same." In bargaining for United States' aid of whatever category, the guiding principle must always be to reduce the ultimate burden and danger to the republic.[90]

Within those fixed boundaries, Lerdo released the Washington representative to pursue every possible physical or moral support which the United States saw fit to concede. History has acknowledged in glowing terms the record of Romero's superhuman energies and his meticulous care for details in order to invigorate the instructions and to keep the Mexican question in the forefront at Washington. The written testimony of his robot qualities was compiled by himself in the *Correspondencia de la Legación Mexicana en Washington durante la Intervención Francesa,* a work of ten volumes in small print, most of them stocked with his own intricate activities which indeed were "marvels of industry."[91]

With rare exception, Lerdo waited, receipted for Romero's reports. and after careful scrutiny sent Juárez's and his own commendations to Romero for the wise handling of numberless major and minor problems. Occasionally, Lerdo elaborated the basic instructions, as in 1865, when he stipulated that any volunteer force recruited in the United.States to aid the republican cause must have the official stamp of approval of that nation as well as her guarantee that such force would not threaten the autonomy, the democratic institutions, or the existing republican government of Mexico.[92]

Only once did Lerdo issue anything resembling a sharp rebuke to his faithful agent at Washington, and that was when Romero had taken part in planning ·an "unofficial" feeler to determine whether the United States would give "efficacious aid" to Juárez in return for a slice of Mexican territory. Lerdo then cautioned Romero, in a brusque note which was unequivocal, referring him to the rules of December 30, 1864, and reminding him that "the Government must comply with its sacred duty," which meant absolutely no alienation of national territory.[93]

It may be argued that Seward's velvet diplomacy of bringing increasing pressure upon Napoleon III after the Civil War to force the withdrawal of the French troops was a purely national policy, unaffected by the exhausting services of Romero, working under the

[90]Lerdo to Romero, Chihuahua, December 30, 1864, Romero (ed.), *Correspondencia de la Legación Mexicana,* IV, 565–567.

[91]Dexter Perkins, *The Monroe Doctrine, 1826–1867,* 437–438. See also Bulnes, *El Verdadero Juárez,* 827; Victoriano Salado Álvarez, *Memorias,* I, 379.

[92]Lerdo to Romero, Chihuahua, March 29, 1865, Romero (ed.), *Correspondencia de la Legación Mexicana,* VI, 121–123.

[93]Lerdo to Romero, Chihuahua, January 26, 1865, *ibid.,* VI, 34.

terms set forth by Juárez and Lerdo.[94] It may be argued, too, that the weight of United States' sympathy, the moral shield of the army on the Rio Grande, and the physical assistance granted from time to time[95] were purely coincidental to and not the result of the foreign policy of the government at Chihuahua. But none can disparage the combined efforts of Lerdo and Romero, who did so much with a miserable paucity of diplomatic raw materials.

As already noted, history has recognized the importance of Juárez and Romero in Mexican foreign relations during the intervention. With Lerdo, it has been less kindly. Again, it is the problem of evaluating the influence of one man upon another. That Lerdo performed all the yeoman administrative service of the foreign office was undeniable; and Romero himself acknowledged that the correspondence he received from Lerdo (1865–1867) showed a "determination and efficacy" which "is inspired by a fixed plan in whose unfolding is demonstrated a grand intellect and patriotism; there is not in the whole of it . . . a single note, or a single word whose publication could be considered prejudicial to the national interests. . . ."[96] Sierra appended his appraisal to the effect that there was "a scrupulousness which floated in all the instructions of Sr. Lerdo de Tejada. . . ."[97]

Yet to what extent should credit be distributed between Lerdo and Juárez, first for the conception and second for the unblemished observance of the main thread of the policy of which Mexicans were so proud,[98] a policy which demanded the sanctity of every inch

---

[94]A contemporary example of the purely national interest of the United States in the Mexican question was the following comment of an anonymous author written before the French departure: "We seek not the annexation of Mexico with its ignorant population and quarrelsome factions. We are not advocates of that misinterpretation of the Monroe doctrine which compels the United States to fight the battles of other nations."—"Our Diplomacy during the Rebellion," *North American Review*, CII (April, 1866), 469–470.

[95]General Philip Sheridan, commander of the "Army of Observation" on the Rio Grande, made some interesting comments on the clandestine aid given the Mexican republicans along the border as well as an evaluation of the significance of his large army as a moral factor protecting the Juárez government.—*Personal Memoirs*, II, 216, 224–228. See also Clyde Augustus Duniway, "Reasons for the Withdrawal of the French from Mexico," *Annual Report of the American Historical Association for the Year 1902*, I, 328. Professor Duniway's classic article, which diminished the rôle of the United States in the French withdrawal, should be read in the light of Dexter Perkins' reinterpretation.—Perkins, *The Monroe Doctrine, 1826–1867*, 514–525.

[96]Romero (ed.), *Correspondencia de la Legación Mexicana*, I, Introduction, pp. xiv–xv.

[97]Sierra, *Juárez*, 383.

[98]Fernando Yglesias Calderón wrote a detailed study to glorify the contribution of the Juárez government toward effecting the withdrawal of the French and defeating the empire, the avowed purpose being to deprecate the credit which certain Mexicans had conceded to the United States. It was typical of a proud nationalism born of the intervention.—*Rectificaciones Históricas, El Egoismo Norte-Americano durante la Intervención Francesa*.

of Mexican territory regardless of the critical conditions and dire need of United States aid? Without detracting in any way from the apex which Juárez reached in Mexican nationalism as a result of the intervention, it was probably his minister of Foreign Relations who at least shared in the formulation of the immaculate diplomatic conduct and insisted that it be followed. Both men had old records on the subject. Under difficult circumstances in the past, Juárez had accepted the practical expedient of real estate dealings or insulting foreign conventions, like the McLane-Ocampo Treaty, the Wyke-Zamacona Treaty, and its twin, the Wyke-Doblado Treaty. Faced with the worst situation of his career, in a desert corner of the republic, he suddenly decided that the government would sink or swim in its territorial entirety and not by doling out segments to gain material aid from the outside. How account for that *démarche* except by the fact that the Rector of San Ildefonso was a dominant influence at his side?

Sebastián Lerdo had his record on foreign affairs, too, and it will be recalled that the record held the strongest characteristic of his career. It demanded the honor of Mexico at any price, as evidenced by his chauvinism in congress while defeating the Wyke-Zamacona Treaty in 1861, or earlier, by his adamant rejections of Forsyth's proposals for territorial cession in 1857. Consequently, when Juárez insisted that there would be no loans or other aids from the United States unless obtained "without sacrificing an inch of our territory, and without diminution of the national dignity,"[99] perhaps he was parroting ideas which had a part of their roots in the brain of Sebastián Lerdo.

One humorous sidelight which entered the stream of diplomatic correspondence between Chihuahua and Washington was the arrival of Santa Anna at New York in 1866. Already a shopworn political relic and rapidly becoming the whipping boy of Mexican historians, he obstreperously proclaimed his devotion to the republican cause and his desire to sacrifice himself by entering the ranks of Juárez. His application was made through Romero at Washington and forwarded to Lerdo, whose disgust could scarcely be concealed. At the last moment, replied Lerdo, "he had come to offer his services, when he has seen that the ultimate hour of intervention will soon be striking." Even on the ridiculous assumption that the ex-Dictator's intentions were in good faith, the government wanted none of his stench to pollute the cause or alienate trusted followers; for "as a militarist, he has betrayed all the governments which have employed him; as a chief of government, he has betrayed all the parties which have supported him; and as

---

[99]Juárez to Santacilia, April 6, 1865, Puig Casauranc, *Archivos Privados de D. Benito Juárez*, 53.

a Mexican, finally, he has betrayed the cause of his native land."[100] Not confined to diplomatic language, Juárez gave a terse résumé on the depths to which the outcast Santa Anna had sunk: "That personage is a political cadaver which no one is capable of reanimating."[101]

No treatment of republican foreign affairs during the intervention would be complete without at least a mention of the roving European agent, Jesús Terán. He was sent by Juárez to exert whatever influence he could upon European courts to encourage the withdrawal of the French troops from Mexico. Terán's activities had little if any bearing on the eventual decision for retirement, but his travels and interviews with outstanding European officials were nevertheless colorful. His dispatches were directed to Lerdo via Romero at Washington, and it was Lerdo who drafted his credentials as an agent to Great Britain and Spain as well as occasional instructions to guide his conduct.[102] It is interesting to recall that the two men had been colleagues in the Comonfort cabinet of June-September, 1857.

Terán attended to his duties conscientiously, traveling back and forth across Europe, to Rome, to Cádiz, to Paris, to Vienna, or to wherever he felt his arguments might be heard by willing ears in official circles. Among the men before whom he protested the foolishness of empire and predicted its impending doom were Cardinal Antonelli, papal minister of State, Drouyn de l'Huys, the French minister of Foreign Affairs, and General John M. Schofield, a special agent of the United States at Paris who was also protesting the presence of the French in Mexico on behalf of his government.[103]

Perhaps Terán's most significant interviews were the two with the Baron du Pont at Vienna, Maximilian's former private secretary, before whom he advocated the withdrawal of the French troops and the Emperor Maximilian upon an honorable arrangement with Juárez before it was too late, before the imminence of

---

[100]Lerdo to Romero, Chihuahua, July 6, 1866, Romero (ed.), *Correspondencia de la Legación Mexicana*, VI, 706, 707. See also *Periódico Oficial* (Chihuahua), October 22, 1866; Rivera Cambas, *Historia de la Intervención*, III, 271–273, 271–273n.

[101]Juárez to Santacilia, Chihuahua, June 22, 1866, Puig Casauranc, *Archivos Privados de D. Benito Juárez*, 156. For the eventual capture, tr al and exile of Santa Anna (1867), see Zamacois, *Historia de Méjico*, XVIII, 1664–1668, 1701–1705.

[102]For the credentials, see Gabriel Saldívar (ed.), *La Misión Confidencial de Don Jesús Terán*, 6–11. Lerdo later advised Terán not to make use of those papers but to represent himself simply as an "Agent of the Government of the Republic. . . ."—Lerdo to Terán, Chihuahua, July 22, 1865, *ibid.*, 23–24.

[103]*Ibid.*, 28, 55–63, 67 72. Schofield told the story of his mission in "The Withdrawal of the French from Mexico," *The Century Illustrated Magazine*, N.S., XXXII (May–October, 1897), 128–137.

republican victory had drained away all bargaining power. The republican method of guerrilla warfare, Terán told Du Pont, could not be bested:

This system [of guerrilla warfare] is much more dreadful, in as much as it never reveals its power; it obtains victory by the force of defeats, and the conqueror each day believes the triumph certain, until slow consummation and annihilation come to release him from the error. Mexico achieved her independence with eleven years of continuous defeats; in the same manner she effected the reform in three years; and thus she will now save her independence and her institutions.[104]

That sage piece of advice was forwarded to Maximilian but unfortunately went unheeded, just like the counsel which Terán had given to the Archduke at Miramar in 1863, when the project of monarchy was still in the embryonic stage.[105] Although the accurate prognostications of Terán fell into ears which listened patiently but refused to accept cold truths, many would have done well to have acted upon them, not the least of whom was the doomed Maximilian himself. When the day of judgment arrived for the Emperor, at Querétaro in 1867, Lerdo made excellent use of Terán's original warning at Miramar to refute the pleas for leniency made on behalf of the Archduke.[106]

By the beginning of 1867, the situation confronting the imperial-republican opponents had altered radically. Not only had Juárez and his ministers survived the worst of their trials, but time was playing in their favor. Behind the effective shield of United States' moral protection, the republican military forces had displayed an amazing power of resurgence under the leadership of General Mariano Escobedo and the direction of the minister of War, Ignacio Mejía, who had joined the official family at Paso del Norte in late 1865. By the turn of the year all the northern states had again fallen under republican domination, while similar success had crowned the *caudillos* of the south, especially Porfirio Díaz, who had raised an army on his own initiative after his escape from imprisonment at Puebla in 1865.

Conversely, the exotic empire was disintegrating rapidly as its vital prop, the French expeditionary force, was being reconcentrated for embarkation. When the last French soldier had departed

---

[104]Terán to Lerdo, Vienna, July 30, 1865, Saldívar (ed.), *La Misión Confidencial de Don Jesús Terán*, 31–32.

[105]Maximilian to Baron du Pont, December 8, 1864, quoted by Galindo y Galindo, *La Gran Década Nacional*, III, 353–355.

[106]Mariano Riva Palacio and Rafael Martínez de la Torre, *Memorandum sobre el Proceso del Archiduque Fernando Maximiliano de Austria*, 31–32 (hereafter cited *Memorandum sobre el Proceso*).

and Bazaine had bidden farewell to the scene of his four-year baptism in empire building for two emperors simultaneously (March, 1867),[107] the odds had turned overwhelmingly in favor of the republicans. The fall of Maximilian, who had rejected stubbornly the efforts of General Castelnau to salvage him despite his pride, was crystal clear. A brief hour for death throes, and the empire and its meager force of conservatives would be crushed. The masquerade ended with the French retirement, unveiling the Mexican scene for the indigenous civil strife resembling the earlier period of the Revolution of Ayutla and the War of the Reform.

With victory on the horizon, the nomads of the north—Juárez and his ministers—packed their bags and the government archives, bade farewell to their philanthropic host, the state of Chihuahua, and began the journey south in December, 1866.[108] Pausing in Durango briefly,[109] they moved on to Zacatecas in late January, 1867, where they were welcomed by the shouts of a joyful populace.[110]

Then occurred one of the most thrilling incidents of the entire peregrination. Although in death throes and controlling little more than a few large cities, the fading empire showed that it still possessed the venom for a final sting. Out of nowhere General Miramón pounced upon Zacatecas with an imperial force, almost capturing a priceless booty in the persons of the President and his ministers. Only a coincidence and a chance miscalculation saved the government. Miramón had ordered a cavalry troop in 'pursuit of the government coaches, but for the first time in their travels, Juárez, Lerdo, and Iglesias had mounted horses to clatter out of town ahead of the rifle shots of the enemy. The carriages, containing only government files, had been directed along one of the routes leading out of town, while the horses bearing the triumvirate had taken another. By the time the fact was discovered, they

---

[107]Facts, figures, and dates on troop embarkations were given by Gualot, *Fin D'Empire*, 263–264. Blanchot, who was with the last troop contingent to leave, gave his interesting ruminations on departure "without regret" from Vera Cruz.—Blanchot, *Memoires, L'Intervention Française au Mexique*, III, 475–476.

[108]Lerdo to Romero, Chihuahua, December 9, 1866, Romero (ed.), *Correspondencia de la Legación Mexicana*, VI, 887; Juárez to Santacilia, Chihuahua, December 7, 1866, Puig Casauranc, *Archivos Privados de D. Benito Juárez*, 195.

[109]Romero to Lerdo, Washington, January 29, 1867, Romero (ed.), *Correspondencia de la Legación Mexicana*, IX, 95–96; Juárez to Santacilia, Durango, January 1, 1867, Puig Casauranc, *Archivos Privados de D. Benito Juárez*, 197. Romero had received notice that the government was scheduled to depart Durango on January 14; but Pruneda entered the date as January 16.— Pruneda, *Historia de la Guerra, 1861–1867*, 410.

[110]Juárez to Santacilia, Zacatecas, February 2, 1867, Puig Casauranc, *Archivos Privados de D. Benito Juárez*, 201. Juárez, stated that the arrival date at Zacatecas was December 22, an obvious error for January 22.

had made good their escape, although the pursuers trailed them some three leagues. However ungraceful a figure they must have cut, galloping across the plains on conveyances most unfamiliar to their anatomies, the change had spelled the difference. "Had we delayed leaving the Palace [at Zacatecas] a quarter of an hour longer," Juárez estimated, "we would have given a brief moment of pleasure to Miramón, but we escaped because the hour had not yet struck."[111]

Miramón's splendid display of surprise tactics was artificial. Forced to retire from Zacatecas a few days later, he met the main force of the republican army in the Battle of San Jacinto in which his weary imperial troops were mauled and dispersed.

Meanwhile, Juárez and his ministers returned to Zacatecas, where they found Maximilian's order for their trial in event of capture—a compromising piece of intelligence on the eve of the Emperor's own downfall[112]— and in a few days they continued to San Luis Potosí.[113] The upheaval at Zacatecas, a near disaster, had caused the scattering of many government documents and, in addition, interrupted Lerdo's contact with Romero at Washington for a period of several weeks.[114] From late December, 1866, until late April, 1867, he found it impossible to send any dispatches to the United States, a source of no small concern to Romero.[115]

At San Luis the stage was set for the final and probably most dramatic event of the empire: the trial and execution of Maximilian. First, however, the Archduke, relying on the advice of his conservative counselors, decided to lead personally the remnant of his troops against the army of Escobedo, against overwhelming numerical odds. The campaign ended, for all practical purposes, in the siege and capture of Querétaro, resulting in the internment of Maximilian, his key supporters, and his army, although the

---

[111]Juárez to Santacilia, San Luis Potosí, March 25, 1867, ibid., 207–208. See also Juárez to Santacilia, Zacatecas, February 2, 1867, ibid., 201–202; Iglesias, Autobiografía, 39; Viramontes, Biografía Popular de Juárez, 233–234.

A number of writers have erred on the Zacatecas escape, stating that Juárez saved himself "by the speed of his carriage," probably because Miramón used that very phrase in a telegraphic message which he sent to Mexico via Querétaro on January 27, explaining the incident to the Emperor.—Diario del Imperio, February 6, 1867.

[112]Maximilian to Miramón, Mexico, February 6, 1867, quoted by Gualot, Fin D'Empire, 269–270; E. Masseras, Un Essai D'Empire au Mexique, 159–160.

[113]Juárez to Santacilia, San Luis Potosí, February 22, 1867, Puig Casauranc, Archivos Privados de D. Benito Juárez, 205.

[114]Lerdo to Romero, San Luis Potosí, April 22, 1867, Romero (ed.), Correspondencia de la Legación Mexicana, X, 533.

[115]Romero to Lerdo, Washington, May 19, 1867, ibid., IX, 466.

lugarteniente, Leonardo Márquez, held out in Mexico City until late June against the besieging army of General Porfirio Díaz.

Like the ultimate military events and all else pertaining to the empire, the story of the trial and execution of Maximilian, Miramón, and Mejía (Tomás) has been repeated to the point of monotony. Forgetting the record of bloodshed which formed the history of Mexico during the three years of Maximilian's rule, the world focussed its sympathy on the doomed man, lending an international significance to the events at Querétaro.

It is needless to tell the factual story of the trial, the legal-constitutional arguments presented by the prosecution and defense, or the broader principles of international law, humanitarianism, and republican reputation which were intermingled throughout the various stages of the proceedings and in the pleas for pardon after the three prisoners had been sentenced to execution. The pros and cons in regard to the sacrifice of Maximilian still may be argued without definitive solution, although later historians have been more moderate in the treatment of Juárez for his decision to deny a pardon. The viewpoints of apologists and denunciators may be located readily for both sides, but the most accurate contemporary account and the only one which had any claim to impartiality was that of two of Maximilian's defense lawyers, Mariano Riva Palacio and Rafael Martínez de la Torre.[116] Acting as a liaison team between Maximilian at Querétaro and the government at San Luis Potosí, they had an opportunity to become acquainted with the principals and the reasonings on both sides of the question; and, while honestly desirous of saving Maximilian, they had excellent reputations among the republicans and were openly sympathetic with the republican cause.

Although the primary concern here is to extract Lerdo's influence on Juárez's final decision, some major points about the trial must be clarified. On one hand, the summary military tribunal convened by Escobedo on the order of the government was a

---

[116]*Memorandum sobre el Proceso*. This work, published soon after the events took place, was and remains the classic of the trial and execution. The following recent accounts summarize the episode on the basis of the best contemporary materials: Roeder, *Juárez and His Mexico*, II, 665–673; Count Egon Caesar Corti, *Maximilian and Charlotte of Mexico*, II, 809–824; Montgomery Hyde, *Mexican Empire: The History of Maximilian and Carlota of Mexico*, 281–292. Roeder's pages have the advantage of brevity and the author's inimitable style; but Hyde's, though colorful, fail to account in any way for the rôle of Sebastián Lerdo, a major defect in the present writer's opinion. Though a much older publication, Ollivier's synthesis of the trial is relatively impartial and compensates for Hyde's omission.—Ollivier, *L'Empire Libéral*, IX, 488–517.

perfunctory gesture, or better still, a farce,[117] in order to salve international opinion which weighed heavily in favor of the blue-eyed emperor. The government possessed more than adequate legal apparatus to justify Maximilian's execution, however, in the vague and comprehensive law of January 25, 1862, for summary judgment of those attempting to overturn the republic or collaborating with the invader.[118] Furthermore, there was moral justification to be derived from Maximilian's own "Black Decree" of October 3, 1865, calling for summary execution of republican soldiers, and from his order to Miramón at Zacatecas to try and sentence the President and his ministers if apprehended. On the other hand, the fate of Maximilian did not rest on the decision of the military court, which was a foregone conclusion, but on whether Juárez would weaken and grant a pardon.[119]

Turning to the individuals who have been charged with the brunt of responsibility for Maximilian's death, Juárez, as the only man legally capable of issuing a pardon, has received the major attention; secondly, Juárez and Lerdo as collaborators; thirdly, Lerdo alone as the man behind the scenes; and finally, Escobedo, the republican general who supervised the trial at Querétaro.[120]

Actually, nothing could release Juárez from the formal responsibility for the execution; but there was strong reason to believe that Lerdo was the real intellectual, moral, and nationalistic force behind his ultimate determination. That opinion has been denied

---

[117]In regard to the order for the trial, Juárez declared: ". . . the government has desired that a formal judgment be given in which charges against and the defenses of the criminals are proved. Thus, all imputation of precipitateness and rancor which bad faith may want to attribute to the government will be removed."—Juárez to Santacilia, San Luis Potosí, May 22, 1867, Puig Casauranc, *Archivos Privados de D. Benito Juárez*, 218. See also Frederic Hall, *Life of Maximilian I* . . . , 284; Bertita Harding, *Phantom Crown: The Story of Maximilian & Carlota of Mexico*, 320.

[118]Dublán y Lozano, *Legislación Mexicana*, IX, 367–371. Such was the scope and phrasing of the law that anyone could have been convicted of any crime under its provisions, provided the authorities so desired.

[119]No one ever expressed much concern about the fate of Mejía and Miramón, but obviously, if Maximilian were given grace, it followed that the same should be granted to those two companions and to many others among his supporters who had proved themselves anathema to the republicans. Otherwise, a premium would have been placed on the blue blood of a Hapsburg over that of a Mexican, a premium which a nationalist like Lerdo would not have been able to concede.

[120]It is interesting to note that Lord Acton, a British contemporary of the event, hesitated between Juárez and Lerdo and then decided that Escobedo was probably the "real author" of the execution.—John E. E. D. Acton, "The Rise and Fall of the Mexican Empire," *Historical Essays & Studies* (ed. by John Neville Figgis and Reginald Vere Laurence), 171.

emphatically,[121] but remembering that Lerdo was nearing the apogee of his influence over Juárez, the following salient facts cannot be cast aside:

(1) The two defense lawyers for Maximilian used their major efforts to influence Lerdo at San Luis Potosí, not wasting any of their limited time on the superficialities of the Archduke's defense at Querétaro. When Lerdo gave them his personal opinions for absolute conformity to the harsh law of January 25, 1862, opposing any delay in the trial itself, they both lost heart and agreed that their battle for the Archduke's life was nine-tenths lost. On completion of the first, exhausting, three-hour interview with Lerdo, he ushered them immediately to Juárez's quarters. "But we encountered in the President the same calm reasoning which Sr. Lerdo had maintained, expressed in different words."[122]

(2) Virtually all of the important correspondence, telegrams, and requests for interviews with Juárez in regard to the trial and pardon, private or diplomatic, were funneled through Lerdo; and furthermore, he formulated the official dogma of his government, rationalizing the necessity of the death sentence.[123]

(3) Lerdo's personal viewpoint was undoubtedly for death and expressed before the capture of Maximilian. It was the opinion of a chauvinist, who would exonerate the sovereignty of Mexico and the blood which had been strewn across her soil for four years because of foreigners by destroying the men who were the symbols of that travesty.[124] After the Battle of San Jacinto, in which a large number of French prisoners were executed en masse by Ecobedo,[125] Lewis D. Campbell, accredited minister of the United States to the Juárez government, residing indolently at New Orleans, wrote to Lerdo protesting the atrocity. In addition, he expressed the hope on behalf of his government that, in event of Maximilian's capture, he would be given "the humane treatment which was accorded prisoners of war by civilized nations." In his reply, Lerdo first justified the execution of the French "fili-

---

[121]Francisco G. Cosmes, *Historia General de Méjico* . . . , XIX, 10–11. Cosmes added, however, that in dealing with secondary figures among the imperialists, "it can be assured that the influence of Lerdo inclined the mind of the President toward rigor." See also Rodolfo Reyes, *Benito Juárez, Ensayo sobre un Carácter,* 150.

[122]*Memorandum sobre el Proceso,* 22–24.

[123]See *ibid.* Other convenient documentary collections on the trial and execution may be found in *Colección de Leyes . . . 1863–1867,* III, 210–245; Romero (ed.), *Correspondencia de la Legación Mexicana,* X, 16–27, 52–59.

[124]See Lerdo's calculated replies to the defense lawyers and Baron Magnus, the Prussian Minister to Maximilian who joined in the pleas for pardon, in *Memorandum sobre el Proceso,* 22–24, 58–59, 65–68.

[125]Rivera Cambas, *Historia de la Intervención,* III, 487–488, 488n.

busters" of Miramón's army captured at San Jacinto and then expounded his opinions in regard to Maximilian:

The French forces having been withdrawn, the Archduke Maximilian has desired to continue shedding futilely the blood of Mexicans. Excepting three or four cities still dominated by force, he has witnessed the entire Republic rise up against him. Despite this, he has wilfully continued the work of desolation and ruin of civil war without purpose, surrounding himself with the men most noted for their spoliations and ponderous outrages and with those most stained in the misfortunes of the Republic. In case the persons over whom such a responsibility weighs are captured, it does not appear that they can be considered as simple prisoners of war, since they are definitely responsible to the law of nations and to the laws of the Republic. The Government, which has given numerous proofs of its humanitarian principles and of its sentiments of generosity, has the additional obligation of considering, according to the circumstances of the case, that which the principles of justice demand and the duties to which it must conform on behalf of the Mexican people.[126]

Those were the sentiments of Sebastián Lerdo. There was nothing in the trial, in the official reasoning of the government, or in Lerdo's later replies to Riva Palacio and Martínez de la Torre which was more than an elaboration of those fundamental points. To repeat Lerdo's famous discourse before the defense lawyers— "Now or perhaps never can the Republic be consolidated"—[127] would be redundant. It was difficult to deny that he was the intellect of the decision, or that the trial was other than a gesture, a sop to foreign nations.

(4) There were many who stated directly or implied that Lerdo was the chief mental persuasion on Juárez. What anguish the President suffered remained a mystery, but undoubtedly he was wearied and enervated by weeping women like Agnes Salm-Salm and the hysterical wife of Miramón, who dragged her two children before him. Many felt that he leaned toward clemency; others denied it absolutely; but John W. Foster, the United States minister to Mexico when Lerdo was president, was convinced by the many stories he heard from the lips of the principal figures of the intervention that Lerdo "was generally credited with deciding the fate of Maximilian."[128]

Finally, much credence has been given to the supposition that Juárez was helpless to act other than he did, that he was chained by "public opinion," especially the demands for execution on the part of the army. Of course, Juárez himself explained to Agnes Salm-Salm that he acted not as a person or according to personal

---

[126]Lerdo to Lewis D. Campbell, San Luis Potosí, April 22, 1867, Romero (ed.), *Correspondencia de la Legación Mexicana*, X, 537.

[127]*Memorandum sobre el Proceso*, 65–67. A translation of the discourse may be found in W. Harris Chynoweth, *The Fall of Maximilian, Late Emperor of Mexico*, 152–155.

[128]John W. Foster, *Diplomatic Memoirs*, I, 48. See also Sierra, *Juárez*, 471–472; Ulick Ralph Burke, *A Life of Benito Juárez, Constitutional President of Mexico*, 160n.

inclination but to fulfill his inexorable duty to the laws and to the people. But where was that popular demand? How was it expressed? What effort was made to obtain any test of public opinion? Whatever the strength or leaning of that nebulous factor, it held no significance whatsoever unless the republican government sincerely desired to spare Maximilian. On the contrary, Juárez ordered a peremptory trial and hastened the procedure to a logical conclusion, proving that the quick dispatch of the captured prize was the real purpose. Otherwise, the army of Escobedo would have been ordered on to Mexico City and kept occupied in aiding Díaz, then besieging the capital, instead of remaining at Querétaro to meddle in the trial.

Nor is it feasible to argue that Juárez remained aloof from counsel, making independent decisions on so grave a question, because he was a human being and because each step was accompanied by ministerial conferences, even the final three-day postponement on execution of the sentence.[129]

In concluding the interpretation of a highly controversial matter, it can be said with impunity that if Lerdo was not largely responsible for Juárez's final disposition of the case, at least Maximilian had not the slighest chance for pardon with the opinion of the "Prime Minister" resting in the scales against him.

Maximilian, Miramón, and Mejía were executed at dawn on June 19, 1867, and two days later the imperial garrison at Mexico City capitulated to General Porfirio Díaz. Yet the journey lacked one last leg for completion. The President and his ministers, for the final occasion, packed their bags to return from San Luis to the once familiar scene of the ancient metropolis. Pausing at Chapultepec in mid-July, on the request of the *ayuntamiento* of Mexico City to allow time for preparations,[130] they made the triumphal entry on July 15. Lerdo, sun-tanned and robust from his experience,[131] rode with Juárez, Iglesias, and Mejía (Ignacio) in an open carriage through one of the gates of the city. Parades, flag-waving, popular ovations, and speeches composed a day of glory for the victorious underdogs: a day of well-deserved interest on a four-year investment in nomadic republicanism, four years of defection, danger, desert, and defeat.[132]

---

[129]Memorandum (signed Ignacio Mejía), San Luis Potosí, June 16, 1867, Romero (ed.), *Correspondencia de la Legación Mexicana*, X, 57–58; *Colección de Leyes . . . 1863–1867*, III, 239–242.

[130]Juárez to Santacilia, Chapultepec, July 13, 1867, Puig Casauranc, *Archivos Privados de D. Benito Juárez*, 222–223. The exact date of departure from San Luis is not known to the present writer, but the presidential party had arrived at Dolores Hidalgo (Guanajuato) on July 4.—*El Siglo*, July 17, 1867. Juárez was still at San Luis on July 2.—*El Globo* (Mexico), July 3, 1867.

[131]Baz, *Vida de Benito Juárez*, 287.

[132]For the festivities, see *El Siglo*, July 15, 16, 1867; Viramontes, *Biografía Popular de Benito Juárez*, 244–246; Zamacois, *Historia de Méjico*, XVIII, 1656–1657.

The year 1867 marked the substantial close of the reform initiated in 1854 with the Plan of Ayutla. It was also the great epoch of nationalism and national exoneration. All the stains and insults heaped upon Mexico, as summarized by Manuel Payno, had been cleansed with the victory of 1867:

Day by day, year by year, our national reputation, because of the dispatches of [foreign] ministers, of the accounts of travelers, of the letters of adventurers . . . was appearing under an aspect so unpleasant, so distorted, that the critical judgment of even the most philosophical and studious men rated us on a par with certain Asiatic peoples, captive to the most absurd superstitions, submerged in the most complete ignorance, and delivered unto the most bloody barbarism. After Baron Humboldt, for whom Mexico must erect a statue as a proof of her gratitude, and Ward, the first English diplomatic agent, the more benevolent writers conceded to Mexico a beautiful earth, a suave climate, and a great abundance of mines. All is good in Mexico, they added, except the people.

Then, during the period immediately preceding the intervention, Payno continued, came a fresh bevy of degrading comments from the pens of foreign diplomats:

The Mexicans are totally inept at administration. Those who are not inept are malicious.

The public rents are the patrimony of the employees, of the military, and of the contrabandists who collaborate with the highest functionaries to diminish and appropriate the customs revenues for themselves.

The governments do not understand how to legislate or administrate. All is disorder, confusion, impediments, delays, and bad faith.

The Mexican army is undisciplined, cowardly, immoral, and a foreign force is necessary for some years to govern the country.

The Mexicans need a strong, unitary government; and freedom of the press and the representative system are still very delicate fruits for a population so crude and barbarous.

Foreign residents are molested, insulted, robbed, and assassinated inhumanely in Mexico.

The governments of Mexico which call themselves liberal are the epitome of immorality and bad faith; one cannot even depend on their promises or conclude any treaty. It is necessary to take all their revenues by force, to establish justice for ourselves by our own hands, to recover boldly the honor of our insulted flags, and to avenge the insults and affronts to our nationals.

Such were the ideas about Mexico, repeated in the press, in the legislative chambers, and in the Secretariats of State at Paris, London, and Madrid, and such were the causes which determined the intervention and later the establishment of a monarchy with a foreign prince.[133]

Such were the national stains atoned for by the defeat of intervention, empire, and Maximilian—and Sebastián Lerdo could claim a share in the process of erasing them.

The students of San Ildefonso held a special celebration in honor of Lerdo, their prodigal rector. Among those giving poetical eulogies in praise of his services to Mexico was the young Justo Sierra.—*El Siglo*, July 18, 21, 23, 1867.

[133]Payno, *Cuentas, Gastos, Acreedores . . . del Imperio*, 916–917.

Chapter VIII

From Prime Minister to President, 1867-1872

The period intervening between the end of the French intervention in 1867 and the inauguration of the dictatorship of Porfirio Díaz in 1876—sometimes called the restoration—was composed of the last administration of Benito Juárez and the single term of Sebastián Lerdo. Essentially it was a time of transition in which old problems remaining from the epochs of the Reform and the Empire were resolved. Meanwhile, there was arising a new philosophy growing out of a markedly different orientation on political questions. Coinciding with those subtle yet perceptible changes, a young leader emerged who seemed to personify the dogmas of positivism, materialism, order, peace, and economic progress. His name was Porfirio Díaz.

The hang-over problems pressed hard upon the restoration government, which concentrated its chief energies upon them, not by choice but because circumstances so dictated. After thirteen years of turmoil and militarism, tempered solely by intermittent periods of partial civil strife, the program of peace could be insured only by continued warfare. The republican armies numbered an estimated 80,000 patriots, adventurers, and brigands in 1867, all of whom were obstreperous in their demands as place seekers or pension hunters. About 20,000 of that group were moulded into a loyal federal army and kept occupied (while gorging half of the national revenues) with the thankless task of taming the other 60,-000, many of whom joined bands of pillagers or political discontents. Although the lawless elements maintained a perpetual state of ebullience in the country, the new model army was an unusually efficient machine, time and again destroying incipient revolts and carrying far and wide the torch of respect for the national government. Of necessity there was much bloodshed and also much injustice to those who deserved to have recognized, in some tangible way, their services during the intervention; still, the dearth of funds in the treasury was an undeniable fact, and past patriotism could be no license for perpetual *pronunciamientos* in the future, if the government were to survive.

Second in importance to the struggle for peace and order was the definite trend toward centralism. Often thwarted and forced into devious channels, the current pressed forward, eroding by degrees the strongholds of localism which were found in the state régimes. To reunify Mexico under a centralist government, to destroy the feudalistic federalism existing in fact, was largely a process of transforming the state governors or *caudillos* into obedient agents of central authority. When Díaz seized power in 1876, he found the metamorphosis in advanced stages, although he himself was to consummate the work by carrying it forward to the extreme. From Juárez and from Lerdo, he inherited the pattern, the precedents, and even the constitutional forms to make the task much easier.

In addition to constitutional reform which would bolster not only the central government but the executive branch in particular, there was the task of rebuilding the disrupted administrative machinery, of augmenting the national income, of dealing with those who had collaborated in the ephemeral scheme of empire, and of writing into the organic law the separation of church and state.

But what of conforming to the new philosophy which demanded of the government a "positive" economic program in order to give impulse to the development of a Mexico reputed to contain fabulous treasures in material resources—a fallacy which men had compounded since the days of Cortés? The failure of Juárez and Lerdo, especially Lerdo, to transform Mexico overnight into a balanced, prosperous, streamlined nation, economically speaking, was an Achilles heel for the opposition which hammered the mark with a persistent and largely unjustified zeal. Modest as were the beginnings in such fields as railroad and telegraph building, educational expansion, and the reknitting of commercial and diplomatic ties with Europe, the surprising thing was that the government could accomplish anything, with peace and order requiring so much money and attention. Perhaps, then, it is time for historians to analyze and commend the cautious steps taken from 1867 to 1876 in the economic and social spheres, instead of comparing arbitrarily the statistical data on the Mexico of 1911, at the close of the Díaz régime, with that of 1876, when Lerdo left the presidency. Perhaps in the light of the Revolution of 1911, there was in Lerdo's policy more of foresight and common sense than the decadence and inertia which were generally attributed to him.

As for the political history of the period under consideration, it is largely the story of three ambitious men, three among many: Juárez, Lerdo, and Díaz. It is the story of their followers, methods, and the factors which influenced their respective fates. In regard to Mexico's destiny in general and the presidential chair in particular, Juárez believed he was indispensable; while Lerdo regarded himself as infallible and Díaz as inevitable. Thirty-five years of fact proved that Díaz's self-appraisal was the closest approach to truth, but from the standpoint of tenure, Juárez was the most successful, since his grip on power was loosened only by death in 1872. Lerdo then stepped into office by virtue of his *ex officio* position of vice-president, to be eliminated four years later by a freakish Mexican revolution which ended with Díaz having cleared the path of competitors to begin his rule of three and one-half decades.

While the nine years which marked the culmination and end of Lerdo as a political figure logically may be divided into two periods, his rise to the presidency and his own administration, it should be remembered that the period is a compact unit, revealing continuous trends and methods, both under Juárez and Lerdo, modified slightly by the differences in the personalities of the two men. The reason probably was that Lerdo, as chief of the Juárez cabinet during most of the last administration of the Indian President, collaborated with his superior on general policies. Nor did the advent of Díaz inaugurate any striking political innovations. His régime was merely an emphasis toward the extreme of the centralizing trends already well under way, without the respect for certain political liberties, such as freedom of the press, of speech, and of assembly, which were allowed the opposition under Juárez and Lerdo.

Before launching the detailed development of the general pattern outlined above, one must understand clearly the distortion of the historical literature describing the restoration years. No really fair analysis is available either for the last administration of Juárez or that of Lerdo. Juárez's biographers glide over the period quickly, half ashamed and usually apologetic, while the few accounts of Lerdo's administration are little more than polemics, drafted by men who were his bitter enemies. Finally, it should be noted that almost all the contemporary accounts, whether monographs or general histories, were written under Díaz; and it was not healthful at that time to wax other than derogatory toward Lerdo, although moderate praise was permissible toward Juárez.

To spin the myth that the millenium had arrived with Díaz, it was essential to paint Lerdo's administration—for sensational contrast—in the violent colors of corruption, decadence, venality, and tyranny; for Díaz, the symbol of order and progress, had ascended to power through revolution, the antithesis of the philosophical dogma of obedience to constituted authority which he preached. Rather pathetic, those Porfirist historical acrobats. They were masters of subterfuge and contradiction. Indeed, they had too much to explain and rationalize in the background of their hero, when they faced the problem of expounding the policies he eventually adopted. Yet so gross have been the cumulative layers of their historical distortion, piled high during thirty-five years of dictatorship, that the truth may never be recognized about the nine-year period of transition. If that were possible, one would see the restoration as an era of discipline, continuity, and, above all, tolerance in the face of exasperating problems. Despite the superficial aspect of constant chaos and revolt, there was no need to apologize for either the Juárez or Lerdo administration. Many of the remarkable accomplishments under Díaz were possible probably because those men helped to prepare the way. That more was not realized was a failure which belongs, in large part at least, at the doorstep of Díaz and his following, who formed the core of unending turbulence.

The immediate exigency which the Juárez government faced after the return to Mexico City in 1867 was the calling of elections to fill the national offices of president, deputies, and magistrates of the Supreme Court. Again it was time to animate the Constitution of 1857, which had never been in operation, except for two brief intervals, since the date of its promulgation. The anticipated election aroused great public interest, not only because it symbolized the reinstallation of constitutional government after so many years of fighting for that right, but also because it was a necessary stamp of validity to the national government's acts since the date of the arbitrary extension of Juárez's tenure at Paso del Norte in November, 1865. The reëlection of Juárez to the presidency, therefore, was virtually a nationalist dictate, both as a deserved prize in recognition of his services against the intervention and as a *tabula rasa* for the execution of Maximilian.

Society was impatient for the executive to issue the electoral decree *(convocatoria)*. What would it contain and how would it be phrased? Even the delay of one month aroused speculation and suspicion which were reflected in the press. Those attitudes were justified, for something unusual was in the offing.

The electoral *convocatoria* of August 14, 1867, was drafted and promulgated by Sebastián Lerdo de Tejada in his capacity of minister of Relations and Government.[1] As everyone expected, it called for the primary and secondary elections, but it also proposed five unexpected constitutional amendments in the form of a plebiscite which "the people" were to accept or reject as general propositions at the same time they balloted for the candidates: (1) the establishment of a senate, which meant the substitution of a bicameral for a unicameral national legislature; (2) the addition of a two-thirds suspensive veto to the constitutional powers of the president; (3) the adoption of the principle that all executive reports to congress should be in writing, as opposed to the verbal interpellation of ministers; (4) the drafting of limitations on the right of the permanent deputation of congress to call special sessions; and (5) the determination of the presidential succession beyond the president of the Supreme Court. In addition, the *convocatoria* granted the

---

[1] Dublán y Lozano, *Legislación Mexicana*, X, 44–49.

voting franchise to the clergy and empowered federal employees to sit as deputies in congress.

The public reaction, "a terrible tempest of protests,"[2] was immediate and violent, from both the partisans and enemies of Juárez, spreading like an "electric spark" throughout the capital.[3] The press hammered out a monotonous chant about the unconstitutional method of revising the sacred code—unconstitutional because Article 127 set forth that an amendment should be passed by a two-thirds vote of the congress and ratified by a majority of the state legislatures, not by a national plebiscite.[4] In vain did the official journal, *Diario Oficial*, try to stem the adverse tide rising against the program, although it pointed out rightfully that the reforms were not attacked on their intrinsic merit but upon the technicality of violating a constitutional procedure.[5]

To a lesser extent the opposition raged about the concession to the clergy, a class in complete discredit because of its part in bringing on foreign intervention and empire. Pantaleón Tovar, an editorialist for *El Siglo*, did an exemplary job of waving the bloody shirt for the Jacobin liberals:

To those men [the clergy] who have proved that they have no more opinions or beliefs than money, are we to hand over, what! to give them participation in the government of a soil which they betrayed? To those men whose covetousness brought the intervention upon us, and with it robbery, assassination, and the burning of towns . . . ?

If there are those who have forgotten their [the clergy's] crimes, we can be assured that the country could not forget them.[6]

And it was the concession to the clergy in the *convocatoria*, coupled with Lerdo's theological training and his former position as rector of San Ildefonso, which earned him the epithet "Jesuit," a tag which his enemies never wearied of repeating, although his later actions as president gave the lie to the common belief in his clerical partisanship.[7]

Subtle and bombastic lampoons against the government for its brain child continued unabated and could be illustrated *ad infinitum*. A clever cartoonist for *La Orquesta* amused his clientele by depicting the *convocatoria* as a cat, always present with Juárez and

---

[2]Ciro B. Ceballos, *Aurora y Ocaso*, 29.
[3]*El Siglo*, August 21, 1867.
[4]*Ibid.*, August 19, 1867.
[5]*Diario Oficial* (Mexico), August 22, 1867.
[6]*El Siglo*, September 9, 1867.
[7]*El Siglo*, for example, ran a clever article entitled "List of Objects, Things, and Persons Which Could be Suppressed with Convenience in Our Society," and the list included, among other items, the *convocatoria* of 1867, and "the Jesuits who may be in the ministry."—*Ibid.*, September 13, 1867. The reference was to Lerdo. See also Zayas Enríquez, *Juárez*, 229; Cosmes, *Historia de Méjico*, XIX, 58.

Lerdo, whether they were caught under a literal "rain of protests"[8] or were engaged in scissoring the Constitution of 1857.[9] *El Siglo* made a hypothetical survey to discover the attitudes of various professional and social classes on the *convocatoria* and learned that the doctor saw in it the symptoms of a "ministerial crisis," while the physicist predicted that, according to the law of gravity, "Juárez will fall by the weight of his *convocatoria.*"[10]

So universal was the denunciation of the cabinet for the constitutional trespass that Juárez issued a manifesto, reiterating his devotion to the law and accepting full responsibility for the proposed amendments as

the expression of my most intimate convictions. I have been moved to propose them by an extended consideration of events in the past, by the experience of some years of government, and by the examples of our own history and that of other republics, which have in their sound institutions a permanent guarantee of liberty, a pledge of peace, and a source of greatness and prosperity.[11]

But to tamper with the Constitution, long "consecrated as the emblem of the nation and the bloodied banner of the people,"[12] was to wound unnecessarily the idealistic elements. It appeared to be the negation of all which Juárez had stood for during the wars of reform and intervention. Consequently, the marriage of the election to proposals for transcendental constitutional changes, to be effected by an arbitrary amendment procedure, was definitely a blunder bound to miscarry. In his speech at the opening of congress on December 8, 1867, Juárez admitted as much, renouncing any intention of counting the plebiscite section of the returns. At the same time he firmly defended the merit of the reforms and announced that the government would submit them to congress in a thoroughly constitutional way.[13] Not until 1874, however, when Lerdo was president, was a part of the program realized with the adoption of the senate. Thus was checked at the outset of the restoration an excellent scheme for centralization which was the most sweeping positive reform promoted by the government from 1867 to 1876. It was necessary to discover other methods within the existing frame of government in order to augment the executive power at the center. But as a medium for personal attacks, the premature *convocatoria* never lost its popularity with the opposition which centered its main thrust at Lerdo.

---

[8]*La Orquesta,* August 31, 1867.
[9]*Ibid.,* August 24, 1867.
[10]*El Siglo,* September 28, 1867.
[11]*Diario Oficial,* August 22, 1867; Dublán y Lozano, *Legislación Mexicana,* X, 67–68.
[12]Emilio Rabasa, *La Organización Política de México,* 155–156.
[13]*El Siglo,* December 9, 1867.

The orthodox interpretation of the *convocatoria* and the accepted result of its admitted infringement of the Constitution have been that it caused a cleavage in the liberal party at a time when its members were knit solidly into a unit after the triumph of Juárez. Were that interpretation true, then the chastisement of Lerdo for his misfire could not be too severe; but the orthodox conclusion is too shallow to bear close inspection. Throughout the independence epoch, the liberal party had shown that it had not the vaguest concept of the word "unity." At best the liberals had formed a tenuous emulsion from time to time, which usually cracked apart under any rigorous test. Although the liberals in 1867 had eliminated their arch enemy, the conservatives, they were ready at the first signal for fragmentation into two personal groups, the supporters and the opponents of Juárez and his counselor, Lerdo. If national decorum demanded an instant of reverence for Juárez's services, both he and Lerdo had accumulated many enemies. Those enemies waited in ambush for a plausible occasion to initiate the open attack, and Lerdo handed them a perfect one in the *convocatoria*. A contemporary publicist perceived the situation exactly: "At the termination of the war of intervention, the liberal party was divided into two factions called ministerial and opposition. The *convocatoria* was the pretext not the cause of said division." Since party development, he added, was present "in the nature of things," the latent opposition was "close to being manifested as soon as circumstances would permit it, and the *convocatoria* presented an opportunity."[14]

Although Juárez had taken the unique step of shielding his Prime Minister by accepting full responsibility for the proposals in his manifesto, and Iglesias had declared officially that he had voted in favor of every clause during the preliminary cabinet discussions,[15] Lerdo was the brain of the program, as the "intelligent and intriguing counselor" of Juárez.[16] The best proof that Lerdo conceived and sold to Juárez his product for centralization and strong executive government was neither the dominance he enjoyed as a counselor nor the scourging he took from the contemporary writers, although either would be sufficient evidence to confirm his responsibility. Actually, the *convocatoria* was the record of his experience with a convention parliament in 1861–1863, each of the

---

[14]Editorial of Emilio Velasco, *ibid.*, January 6, 1871.

[15]*Ibid.*, August 24, 1867.

[16]Ricardo García Granados, *Historia de México desde la Restauración de la República en 1867 hasta la Caída de Porfirio Díaz*, I, 54–55, 56; Sierra, *Juárez*, 479; Sierra (ed.), *México Su Evolución Social*, II, 418; Augustín Rivera y Río, *La Revolución Mexicana en 1876*, 15; Vicente Riva Palacio, *Historia de la Administración de D. Sebastián Lerdo de Tejada*, 20–21; Cosmes, *Historia de Méjico*, XIX, 41.

five reforms representing a governmental weakness with which he had had intimate association as a deputy.[17]

Lerdo tacitly related his mature reflections on that earlier congressional experience in his famous circular to state governors of August 14, 1867, the indispensable explanation of the reforms proposed in the *convocatoria* of the same date. Even Lerdo's enemies, even the staunchest supporters of the Constitution of 1857, must have admired that remarkable piece of constitutional literature. Coming from the pen of Lerdo, it should stand as one of the great critiques on the Constitution of 1857 and as the most valuable single source for his centralistic ideas of government; moreover, it illustrated his keen intellect, an intellect trained to use the subtle devices of sophistry.[18]

One by one, Lerdo discussed the individual amendments proposed, refuted all anticipated, contrary arguments, and concluded by reasoning the necessity for the revisions to the organic law:

(1) In regard to the general need for the five amendments: "The normal progress of administration demands that the legislative power is not everything, and that in the face of it the executive does not lack all independent power." ". . . for normal times, the despotism of a convention[19] can be as bad, or worse, than the despotism of a dictator. Reason counsels and the experience of the most advanced countries teaches that the peace and well-being of society depend on the convenient equilibrium in the organization of public powers."

(2) In regard to the establishment of a senate: It was prosaic to brand an upper house aristocratic and stifling to energetic action, and such reasoning was spurious. A senate not only corresponded to the federal theory of government[20] but also provided a body of mature and reflective statesmen who could check precipitate action in the lower house.

(3) In regard to the two-thirds suspensive veto as an added power of the president: That power was incorporated into the United States Constitution and the Mexican Constitution of 1824, but as the Constitution of Mexico then read, the executive could be eliminated from all voice in legislation, even from giving an opinion, by simple majority vote of the assembly.

(4) In regard to the executive-legislative relationship: Executive reports to congress should be in writing, either from the president or his ministers. Since the Constitution of 1857 was silent on the

---

[17]See Chapter VI.

[18]For the circular, see Dublán y Lozano, *Legislación Mexicana*, X, 49–56.

[19]Lerdo was referring to the unicameral assembly which was theoretically omnipotent under the Constitution of 1857.

[20]Note that Lerdo did not trespass on the sacred principle of federalism, intrenched in Mexican ideology by this date.

point, such a principle, if adopted, would be merely an addition to the organic law; and further, that was the practice of the United States on whose plan of government Mexico had modeled her own system more closely than on "that of the representative monarchies of Europe." Lerdo's purpose did not appear to be one of mere convenience, but to quash the ministerial instability springing from the inchoate development of parliamentary government. Undoubtedly recalling some of the violent scenes in the congresses of 1861–1863, in which he had taken no small part, he made unequivocal his desire to sever that rudimentary institution and to disengage the president and his cabinet from dependence on the legislature:

"The hindrance which the prolonged tenure of bad ministers causes can be very serious; but the incessant change of ministers is also sufficiently serious." It was absurd to permit any one deputy "to vex" the ministers with interpellations "at any hour and without reason. Everyone can recall some deplorable scenes in Mexico in which the dignity and credit of the legislative and executive have suffered on account of some private interests, with serious prejudices to the public welfare."

(5) In regard to restricting the powers of the permanent deputation of congress: Lerdo pointed out the unfortunate experience in 1861, when a special session was called by a handful of deputies for no loftier a reason than to attack the President. Unless the Constitution were amended on that point, the votes of as few as seven deputies could suffice to bring about "the convocation of congress in extraordinary session."[21]

(6) In regard to defining the presidential succession beyond the president of the Supreme Court: Should both president and *ex officio* vice-president default simultaneously, it was essential that the successor be designated in advance in order to avoid "serious inconveniences." By "serious inconveniences" Lerdo undoubtedly meant civil war provoked by a mad scramble for the presidential prize. The nation should rectify the deficiency in the organic law before the emergency arose, at which time it might be too late.

As has been pointed out, the opposition shied from attacking the merits of the five proposals, since they were basically sound and desirable, but sank its teeth into two more or less technical counts: the unconstitutional amendment procedure and the concession to the clergy. Lerdo must be given full credit for anticipating those flank attacks, for he had prepared his defenses—and, if necessary, a strategic retreat—in the circular of August 14. Those defenses, incapable of stemming the tide of opposition, were both

---

[21]The presence of congress was always a handcuff to the ministers, a stumbling block to energetic administrative action, and a source of embarrassment to the executive in general. The proposal was obviously centralistic, intended to limit congress, if possible, to the regular sessions.

admirable and humorous and displayed a mind nimble in the employment of artifice.

The urgent necessity of the times demanded that rapid action be applied to the reforms, Lerdo claimed. Since an election had to be called in any event, no question of disturbing the public peace was involved. It would be ridiculous, as some might pretend, to deny the "right of the people," by means of a plebiscite, to authorize congress to amend the Constitution on some general points determined in advance; and "if the majority of the people do not vote in favor of the reforms, no harm will be caused." To those who might absurdly claim that a constitutional provision on amendment procedure was superior to the "free will" of the majority of the people (that is, voting by plebiscite), he would simply quote Article 39 of the Constitution: "The national sovereignty resides essentially and originally in the people. All public power springs from the people and is instituted for their benefit. The people have at any time the inalienable right to alter or modify the form of their government."

As for the voting concessions to the clergy, Lerdo was prepared for the outcry of the Jacobins with the simple answer that the clergy were citizens and should exercise their rights of citizenship openly and directly, not surreptitiously through an indirect influence on elections and the elected.

Why is it necessary to dissect the *convocatoria* of 1867 and Lerdo's explanatory circular in such detail? Not only was the thwarted program one of the most important issues of Juárez's restoration term, but it was the guide to Lerdo's centralistic aims for his own presidency. Because of the *convocatoria* and Lerdo's undeniable authorship, he himself became a major political issue, with the opposition continually attempting to destroy his preëminence in Juárez's cabinet, until the time when he resigned in January, 1871. To repeat, there was no single document which so clearly or completely revealed Lerdo's centralistic philosophy of government. In a life which was so much shadow and rumor, largely absorbed by the figure of Juárez, the value of such rare materials, whereby the one may be separated rather precisely from the other, cannot be overestimated. In the words of Emilio Rabasa:

Of the conviction of Lerdo on the ineffcacy of the Constitution for stable and efficient government, we have not only h's testimony but a reasoned expression in the circular which accompanied the *convocatoria* of 1867 . . . a circular which is a finished chapter of political science, sufficient to demonstrate the lofty talents of its author, his exceptional knowledge of the matter, and the delicate touch with which he was capable of censuring that which he desired to become respectable [*i.e.*, the Constitution of 1857].[22]

---

[22]Rabasa, *La Organización Política de México*, 155.

While the plebiscite section of the *convocatoria* was forgotten for the moment, the national elections were held, returning Juárez to the presidency with a sweeping majority of the vote. He was not without a modicum of competition, since the touted General Porfirio Díaz garnered a small portion of the ballots, which probably signified that Juárez's control of the nation was far from absolute.[23] But among the many candidates for the vice-presidency, that is, presidency of the Supreme Court, none had an absolute majority; consequently, the decision was thrown to congress, which voted by state deputations on the two top contestants, Lerdo and Díaz. Lerdo was the victor by a vote of seventeen to six,[24] thanks less to his popularity than to the unity of the Juarist party. From the standpoint of legal qualification, Lerdo of course, was the logical choice. Yet it should be remembered that the presidency of the court was principally an office of political not juridical significance. The decision, coming from a congress which Juárez and Lerdo manipulated,[25] indicated that the Indian President clearly preferred Lerdo as his successor.[26]

Out of the elections, Lerdo emerged as a tripedal political creature, since he was elected initially a deputy to congress, even before his election as president of the court. That meant he had inserted one foot in each of the branches of the government, executive (minister of Relations and Government), legislative, and judicial.[27] Duality of federal office was permissible upon special license of the branch concerned, which prerequisite not only presented an occasion for the opposition in congress and in the court to needle Lerdo by turns, making his personality one of the chief questions of 1868, but seemed to verify the common belief in his prepotent position in the highest circle of government.

Immediately after congress convened in December, 1867, the executive requested a license for Deputy Lerdo to continue as minister of Relations and Government. Although the question was sterile, once Lerdo had informed congress that he chose the judicial

---

[23]Juárez received 7,422 electoral votes; Díaz, 2,709.—*El Siglo*, December 20, 1867.

[24]*Ibid.*, December 20, 1867.

[25]A few days prior to the opening of congress, Lerdo wrote to his good friend General Mariano Escobedo: "Nothing in particular is happening here now. The congress will be installed in two or three days. At present the opposition does not amount to even a third part."—Lerdo to Mariano Escobedo, December 2, 1867, Archivo de Fernando Iglesias Calderón, Legajo 12, A.G.N.

[26]While still invested with extraordinary powers, Juárez, prior to the elections, reconstituted the Supreme Court on a temporary basis. He named Lerdo president, revealing his personal choice for the office.—*Colección de Leyes . . . 1863–1867*, III, 303.

[27]In an editorial of January 10, 1868, Zarco called Lerdo a "trinity," referring to his plurality of office.—*El Siglo*, January 10, 1868.

position in preference to that of deputy,[28] it was too succulent an opportunity for the enemy to overlook. Congress did not grant the license until a full month had passed and not until an excess of the venom against "the Jesuit" had been released on the floor of the house in debates over the concession.[29] The speeches did serve to show that the matter of the license was tied intimately to the prevailing idea of cabinet responsibility to the majority of congress. Zamacona, an opposition leader in the house, believed that the license, if granted, would be equivalent to a "vote of confidence" for Lerdo, who had suffered a "ministerial defeat" in the *convocatoria* of August.[30] Several days later, Deputy José María Mata denounced Lerdo as the evil soul of the government, whose unvaried intent had been to destroy "the foundations of our constitutional edifice" ever since he had entered Juárez's cabinet.[31]

Despite all the verbiage, the administration still held a strong majority of the deputies; but no sooner had Lerdo passed successfully through the congressional wringer than he faced a miniature convention in the Supreme Court. Having taken the oath of office as president on June 4, 1868, he fell under its jurisdiction. Once again a license was necessary if he were to continue in the cabinet.[32] His enemies on the court, counting upon a majority, determined that they would not fail in the same terrain as congress, and from June until early September no dispensation was forthcoming for Lerdo to return to the ministry. In taking such a position, the magistrates had departed from all semblance of an independent judiciary to advance their political rôle in the Constitution by presuming to fix the composition of Juárez's council. One writer properly styled the judges of the court as "ministerial" (pro-Lerdo) and "opposition."[33]

In July, while the license question was in abeyance and while Lerdo actually presided over the court, a case arose on the constitutional right of the tribunal to review court-martial hearings. The various opinions expressed were acrimonious, and the personal friction among the magistrates was patent, clearly springing from the attitudes toward Lerdo. A reporter at the sessions left the following account of what took place:

Defeated on the major question, the Lerdist magistrates managed to carry the secondary issue, because one of the "opposition" members shifted to their side. After the close vote, Justice Cardoso (an

---

[28]Session of congress, December 26, 1867, *ibid.*, December 27, 1867.
[29]See the congressional debates printed in *El Siglo*, December 11, 1867, to January 10, 1868.
[30]Session of congress, December 10, 1867, *ibid.*, December 11, 1867.
[31]Session of congress, January 7, 1868, *ibid.*, January 8, 1868.
[32]*Ibid.*, June 5, 1868.
[33]*Ibid.*, July 19, 1868.

anti-Lerdist) exclaimed: "I solemnly protest against the validity of that decision: I so declare, and I wish it to be recorded that I consider [the decision] anti-constitutional, and no one can make me recognize a judgment which is not competent."

Justice Lerdo: "It will be necessary to submit to the will of the majority."

Justice Cardoso: "The majority has no imperium over my conscience as a man."

A few days later, Lerdo corrected a statement made by another anti-Lerdist member, León Guzmán: ". . . said gentleman did not intend to say . . . anti-constitutional . . . but, better stated, extra-constitutional. . . ." Guzmán abruptly interrupted the President of the Court: "I do not authorize or recognize in Señor Lerdo the faculty of interpreting, commenting, or deducing anything about my statement."[34]

But Juárez was not to be denied the presence of "the Favorite" at his side. While the ministry of Government was filled from January to September by Ignacio Vallarta, an influential politician from Jalisco, the portfolio of Relations was left vacant, as if to anticipate the return of its old incumbent. Moreover, it appeared that Lerdo's influence in government had continued unbroken, despite his formal absence from the cabinet. Vallarta, though a popular minister, resigned in disgust in early September, for "considerations of public interest and demands of personal delicacy."[35] Though the language was abstract, everyone knew that Vallarta had refused to subordinate himself to Lerdo's leadership.[36]

Soon after Vallarta's departure, the President again filed the request for Lerdo's license from the court, and that body, seeing its attempt to eradicate Lerdo's influence had failed, surrendered by conceding a permit which should have been perfunctory from the outset. One of the anti-Lerdist magistrates explained that he had reversed his opinion on the license since denial had provoked neither a change in policy nor a change in the cabinet, and consequently further refusal would no longer be a matter of "principle" but solely one of his personal opposition to Lerdo.[37] Francisco Zarco,

---

[34]*Ibid.*, July 19, 1868.

[35]Vallarta to the Undersecretary of Foreign Relations, September 1, 1868, *ibid.*, September 4, 1868. See also Zarco's editorial in the same issue.

[36]García Granados, *Historia de México*, I, 72; Cosmes, *Historia de Méjico*. XX, 117. Rivera y Río stated that Lerdo had attempted to convert Vallarta into "his clerk," like all the other cabinet ministers.—Rivera y Río, *La Revolución de 1876*, 49–50. However that may be, the two men were the bitterest political enemies ever afterwards.

[37]Statement of José María del Castillo Velasco, *El Siglo*, September 10, 1868; Cosmes, *Historia de Méjico*, XX, 113–115.

editor of *El Siglo,* summarized the extended struggle which at last had been resolved:

> By what has just taken place, it is seen that the President has felt the services of Señor Lerdo indispensable, and for that reason he absta:ned from form:ng a new cabinet, hoping to overcome, as he did overcome, the resistance of the Supreme Court. This now explains the continuance in the cabinet of the rest of the Lerdo ministry.[38] They were soldiers who did not believe their chief [Lerdo] lost or a prisoner, but who saw him surrounded in an ambush from which they hoped he could free himself.[39]

Elaborating Lerdo's contest with the court, Zarco concluded:

> According to certain rumors, the ministerial crisis has been only on the surface, like an interlude or entr'acte through which the government has passed, since at bottom Señor Lerdo has continued prepotent in the situation. Hence, it is undoubtedly more worth while that Lerdo return to the ministry, as a true minister, because the lucid situations are better than the shady ones, and because it is better to have responsible ministers than intimate counselors.[40]

Lerdo had thus weathered the "terrible tempest" which shattered over his head from the *convocatoria* of 1867 and had emerged victorious in the battles of the licenses, holding firmly to his post of chief of Cabinet, despite the persistent sniping of the enemy, in the press, in congress, and in the court. Technically, his tenure was not unbroken, and both congress and the Supreme Court had made sustained efforts to crush his influence with Juárez. Both attempts had failed miserably.

Lerdo's rôle in the ministry was two-sided: his specific duties as minister of Relations and his position as chief of Cabinet, the second being of immeasurably greater importance. Yet because of his responsibility for defining Mexican foreign policy during the restoration period, in collaboration with Juárez, that phase cannot be ignored altogether.[41] At best, the story of foreign relations for those years was notably uninspiring, although historians have given Lerdo more unqualified praise for his conduct on that score than on any other.[42]

---

[38]Ignacio Mejía (War), Blas Balcárcel (Fomento), Matías Romero (Finance), Ignacio Mariscal (Justice and Public Instruction). Lerdo returned to Relations, while Iglesias soon assumed the post of Government vacated by Vallarta. Note that Zarco speaks of the ministry as pertaining to Lerdo.

[39]*El Siglo,* September 11, 1868.

[40]*Ibid.,* September 11, 1868.

[41]The following general statements on foreign policy are based largely on: *Mexico, Dispatches* (1867–1871), A.U.S.; *Plumb Papers,* VII–XII; Genaro Estrado (ed.), *Un Siglo de Relaciones Internacionales de México (á través de los Mensajes Presidenciales),* (Archivo Histórico Diplomático Mexicano, No. 39), 106–112. See also the materials cited p. 202n.

[42]See Cosmes, *Historia de Méjico,* XIX, 211. Cosmes was bitterly anti-Lerdist in his viewpoint.

At the end of the intervention the bottom suddenly dropped from Mexican relations with Europe, relations which had been in the forefront of both domestic and foreign issues long before 1861. Into the vacuum came the all-absorbing interest of reconstruction. It must have seemed strange to the Mexican of 1867 that there was no threat of invasion, no foreign debt to fret about, and no customs revenues hypothecated to foreign powers to undermine the chief source of the national income. Of course the government could not wipe the slate clean of valid international obligations, but certainly they were in the background and in a state of suspended animation.

Under the light of past experience, Lerdo established a European policy which amounted to a modified isolation, characterized by dignity, pride, and aloofness. Simply stated, the policy was grounded on the premise that most of the nations of western Europe had disavowed the legitimacy of the republic by recognizing the spurious régime of Maximilian; therefore, diplomatic ties could be renewed only after the European nations had made the advances and upon an equitable adjustment of the old conventions. In other words, the Mexican inferiority complex and national pride dictated that she stand quietly and await proposals from Europe, which would signify a tacit admission of the Old World's sins against the honor of Mexico.

At the same time, an effort was made to leave the clear impression that Mexico was not the land of Xenophobia,[43] and that she would welcome the resumption of friendship and commerce with Europe.[44] "It is indispensable to concede to Don Sebastián Lerdo de Tejada," declared Cosmes, "the merit of having been the initiator of that new international policy which sanctioned the moral independence of Mexico before the powerful European nations."[45]

Since the policy was composed of attitude and inactivity, little can be said to describe its working; however, two incidents arose soon after the government returned to Mexico City which will serve as illustrations: the return of Maximilian's body to Austria and the withdrawal of the British diplomatic officials.

In early September, 1867, Vice-Admiral Tegetthoff of the Austrian navy arrived in Mexico with verbal instructions to claim and transfer Maximilian's remains back to Europe. Interpreting the private nature of the mission as an inference of disrespect toward the republican government, Lerdo informed Tegetthoff that no obstacle would be placed in his way, provided he obtained a written request for his purpose, either from the Austrian government or the Hapsburg family. When the Austrian Chancellor complied with

[43]Editorial of Francisco Zarco, El Siglo, August 13; 1868.
[44]Editorial of Emilio Velasco, ibid., December 21, 1871.
[45]Cosmes, Historia de Méjico, XIX, 913.

the demand, forwarding a note to Lerdo couched in polite and cautious terms, the Mexican government procured every convenience for Tegetthoff's departure.[46]

The other incident mentioned, involving the withdrawal of the British diplomatic officials from Mexico, was the last formal exchange between the two countries for a period of several years. The matter came to a head when British Consul Glennie of Mexico City, while intervening in Mexican litigation on behalf of one of his nationals, was informed by the court that his official capacity was no longer recognized. On inquiring of Lerdo about the exact nature of his status, he learned that there was nothing personal involved, but "solely the general policy laid down by the' [Mexican] Government. . . ."[47] Lerdo explained to Glennie that:

the Government of the Republic consider that they cannot recognize the offic'al character of the Agents of such Governments as placed themselves in a state of hostility towards the Government of the Republic or had disowned the Government thereof, by recognizing the so-called Government which was sought to be established in Mexico by the foreign intervention, or permit Consular duties to be exercised by such persons.[48]

As a result of that attitude, the British Foreign Secretary soon forwarded an order for the departure of the British legation in Mexico, then headed by R. T. C. Middleton.[49] In complying with the requests for passports, Lerdo attempted to make the departure of the British as free of friction and ill-feeling as possible: "The position in which the Mexican Government saw itself placed, and is still placed," he advised Middleton, "in regard to those Powers [which recognized Maximilian], has not been the result of its will." The Mexican government "has had, and still has, the intention, when those Governments may desire to treat again with the Republic, not to place any difficulty in the way of so doing in just and proper terms."[50]

Although the negative position adopted toward Europe was based on patience and the healing quality of time, it was not altogether sterile of results. When Lerdo left the cabinet in 1871, rep-

[46]Mexican historians tend to dwell upon the details of that minor episode, illustrative of national sensitivity. All accounts praise Lerdo for his "correctness" in handling the affair. For details see García Granados, *Historia de México*, I, 60–68; Zamacois, *Historia de Méjico*, XVIII, 1690–1693, 1712–1718. The diplomatic correspondence between Chancellor Beust, and Lerdo was printed in *El Siglo*, November 11, 1867. Cf. Samuel Basch, *Recuerdos de México* . . . (trans. from Italian to Spanish by Manuel Peredo), 303–305; José Román Leal, *México Constitucional*, 50, 187.

[47]Consul Glennie to Mr. Middleton, August 27, 1867, *British and Foreign State Papers*, LVIII, 683.

[48]Lerdo to Glenn'e (trans.), August 30, 1867, *ibid.*, LVIII, 686.

[49]Lord Stanley to Mr. Middleton, October 25, 1867, *ibid.*, LVIII, 687–689.

[50]Lerdo to Middleton (trans.), December 11, 1867, *ibid.*, LVIII, 703.

resentatives of the German Confederation, Italy, and Spain were residing in Mexico once again.[51]

In contrast with the European outlook at the close of the intervention, the relationship with the United States was and continued to be friendly. In addition to the establishment of the Mixed Claims Commission for the adjustment of private claims which had accumulated since the Treaty of Guadalupe Hidalgo,[52] the outstanding example of the new era of good feeling between old international enemies was the visit of William H. Seward to Mexico in late 1869, apparently intended to dissipate any Mexican fear of latent American aggression. One of the highlights in the tour of the former United States Secretary of State was a banquet given in Mexico City in his honor, and, as might have been expected, Lerdo was present and one of the principal speakers.[53] It is interesting to note that Lerdo, sometimes called "the Seward of Mexico,"[54] roundly praised the Mexican policy of the American Secretary of State during an interview in which United States Chargé Edward Lee Plumb presented his credentials:

The expressions of Mr. Lerdo de Tejada in the conversation I then had with him were of the strongest character in acknowledgment of the wisdom of the policy that has been pursued by the United States. . . . His language impressed me with the belief that this government is deeply sensible of the benefits it has received from that of the United States.[55]

When Lerdo finally resigned from the ministry of Relations, the United States Minister to Mexico, Thomas H. Nelson, wrote to him that he regretted the conclusion of their eighteen months of personal relationship in which Lerdo's attitude on all types of questions was "characterized by the utmost frankness and evident desire to arrive at just conclusions."[56]

---

[51]Cosmes, *Historia de Méjico*, XX, 874–886; Roeder, *Juárez and His Mexico*, II, 703–704.

[52]See *El Siglo*, December 23, 25, 26, 1868. Lerdo appeared before congress in secret sessions to promote the ratification of the treaty. See also Walter Flavius McCaleb, *The Public Finances of Mexico*, 133.

[53]Details of Seward's visit to Mexico may be found in Cosmes, *Historia de Méjico*, XXI, 39–50. Lerdo issued the formal invitations for the celebration, one of which was addressed to General Vicente Riva Palacio (dated November 22, 1869).—Vicente Riva Palacio Papers, Folder 183, UT.

[54]*The Two Republics* (Mexico), February 22, 1868 (reprint from the *New York Tribune*).

[55]E. L. Plumb to Charles Sumner, October 10, 1867, *Plumb Papers*, VII.

[56]Thomas H. Nelson to Sebastián Lerdo de Tejada, January 19, 1871, *Sebastián Lerdo de Tejada, Su Expediente Personal*, Archivo de Relaciones Exteriores; Nelson to Fish, January 23, 1871, Enclosure "B," *Mexico, Dispatches*, XLII, A.U.S.

But General William S. Rosecrans, Nelson's predecessor as chargé d'affaires, felt a militant antipathy toward Lerdo, expressed in several of his dispatches. On one occasion he wrote:

Beyond the *convocatoria* of 1867 and the formulation of a negative yet dignified foreign policy toward Europe, it became difficult
to determine the real genius of executive policy. Was it Juárez or
Lerdo? Once again, just as during the intervention, their individual
rôles were virtually impossible to strain one from the other. Juárez
was no puppet, but he was undoubtedly sensitive to the influence of
his ministers. He was a brilliant statesman of inertia, obstinacy,
inaction, and tenacity, not a leader who conceived and gave impulse to programs, reforms, or ideas. That task reverted to the men
who surrounded him, and he acquiesced in or rejected their leadership. Many ministers came and went over the span of fourteen
years, but Lerdo came and stayed. No other chief counselor of
Juárez held such sway during such an extended tenure, nor did
any other seem to enjoy such a free rein in the over-all conduct of
affairs, despite the persistent and concentrated attack of the opposition against him. In the absence of any records of cabinet meetings or intimate insight into the thoughts of those two great figures,
the length of their relationship looms large as one approaches a
terrain which must of necessity be tread with hesitancy. But whatever else may be said of him, Lerdo was certainly the Buckingham
of Mexican history.

One external aspect of administration which magnified Lerdo's
prominence during the restoration years was the old idea that
cabinet government existed under the Constitution of 1857. Since
Lerdo was unquestionably the "chief of Cabinet," almost all complaints were channeled in his direction, Juárez being responsible
indirectly by failing to perceive the unpopularity of his alter ego
and to replace him with another who could hold the confidence of
"public opinion," a vague term which Mexican journalists and
statesmen used and abused constantly. Hence, the question of the
licenses, which arose consecutively in congress and in the court in
1867 and 1868, was a ministerial crisis of the first water, as already
pointed out.

To comprehend how Mexican politicians interpreted their system
of government under an organic law which was pliable enough
to permit the growth of a cabinet or presidential régime, it is
necessary to investigate the statements of contemporary writers.
Cosmes best exemplified the uncertainty which prevailed at that
period in regard to the nature of the executive and its relationship
to the unicameral legislature. Was there or was there not, he
asked, "a minister who [was] chief of Cabinet?" Was he responsible for "the program" of the administration? Exactly what

"My convictions are that he controls President Juárez and that he is just as
much our opponent and the opponent of all foreign influence and immigration
as he can be consistently with his policy of 'Status quo' and 'Mexico for me
and the Mexicans.' "—Rosecrans to Seward, February 10, 1869, *ibid.*, XXXV,
A.U.S.

was the president's position? None of those questions could be decided, he answered, by the "literal sense" of the Constitution but by "political customs, parliamentary habits, and even by motives of personal delicacy."[57]

In his discussion of the "prime minister" and his cabinet, Cosmes' explanations were more specific. The prime minister did not possess the authority to direct individual ministers, but he was the official who joined with the president in selecting the cabinet members and whose general political ideas dominated in the council. Dissonance between executive and legislative branches, "public opinion," or a parliamentary defeat could provoke a "partial or total" change in the cabinet, depending on the nature of the question at hand.[58]

Vague as were his interpretations, Cosmes' ideas shed light on the nature of the relationship between Juárez and Lerdo and were typical of the formative stage of the organic law and of the prevailing opinions of the time. It may be seen that under such a system Juárez would be a figure somewhat aloof and beyond the range of the lowlier level of the political pool, while Lerdo would be thoroughly immersed.

Far less helpful were the ideas of Francisco Zarco, one of those in the thinning ranks of the fathers of the Constitution. Time, however, had rendered Zarco's opinions more confusing than they had been in 1861–1863. When Lerdo's license was under discussion in congress, he commented that the composition of the cabinet "should indicate the policy of the administration." It mattered little whether the members of the ministry were selected from among the deputies. The essence of the system was the cabinet which should count "on the support of a majority in congress." Zarco endorsed cabinet unity and responsibility, yet the "president alone" was the chief of the cabinet.[59] Obviously, such a mechanism was clogged with incongruities, but in any event the focus was on the ministry in day-to-day operation, not upon the president.

Yet neither Zarco nor any other journalist could check the flood of the opposition which continued to consider Lerdo the evil brain of the government. The official organ, *Diario Oficial*, once made a feeble and belated effort in that direction. Mexico was not, it editorialized, a constitutional monarchy under a prime minister, but a republic like the United States, where the president was responsible for all governmental acts and defined the policy which was continuous regardless of changes in the cabinet. Therefore, no basis

[57]Cosmes, *Historia de Méjico*, XX, 103–104.

[58]*Ibid.*, XX, 104–108.

[59]Editorial of Francisco Zarco, *El Siglo*, January 2, 1868. Zarco was a deputy in congress at the time.

existed "for attributing to Señor Lerdo de Tejada the exclusive responsibility for the acts of the executive. . . ."[60]

Ridiculing that defense, the opposition press refused to believe that anyone but Lerdo was the motor of the "centralistic" administration of Juárez. Although the President might accept ultimate responsibility, "Señor Lerdo has been the author and stage director of the despotic constitutional tragedy of which we have been the victims. . . . Señor Juárez has been the impresario and first hero who selected the drama and has desired to illuminate his abilities at tragedy. . . ."[61] After eliminating the polemic from the charge, there probably remained an analogy which separated as accurately as possible the careers of Juárez and Lerdo.

The scope of Lerdo's general influence was not altogether a topic of conjecture, nor could it be concealed, as he undoubtedly desired, behind the closed doors of cabinet meetings. The custom of ministerial interpellation, which congress delighted in and Lerdo despised,[62] continued after the intervention, conforming to the idea of cabinet government. Iglesias, a member of the cabinet over which Lerdo presided, thus described that facet of the ministers' duties:

The principal occupation of the ministers consisted in frequent attendance in Congress, where their intervention in the debates was necessary, either to give them a proper direction, or to answer the incisive attacks of the opposition deputies. . . .[63]

That Lerdo appeared before congress for a question hour from time to time in order to explain issues which pertained to his particular department (Foreign Relations) held nothing at all surprising, whether the topic concerned the budget, a boundary dispute with Guatemala, or the violation of customs authority by a British mail packet.[64] It was significant when he was called from his inner sanctum to explain or rationalize policies adopted by the executive which had not the vaguest connection with foreign affairs. Lerdo's occasional appearances before the legislature, therefore, served not only to illustrate the "vigorous dialetic peculiar to him" as he faced with poise what "was more than a Congress, a Convention, since the debates sustained in it always were characterized by

[60]*Diario Oficial*, July 23, 1870. It was possible that Lerdo himself ordered the drafting of the article.

[61]*El Mensajero*, January 31, 1871.

[62]It will be recalled that one of the amendments proposed in the *convocatoria* was the substitution of written for verbal reports of the executive to congress.

[63]Iglesias, *Autobiografía*, 50.

[64]See *Diario de los Debates*, May 18, 1870, 5th Congress, II, 421–422; *ibid.*, November 26, 1869, 5th Congress, I, 494–495, 497–498; session of congress, March 18, 1868, *El Siglo*, March 19, 1868.

heated passion";[65] but also the grasp which he maintained over general conduct of government.

On several occasions Lerdo entered congress to explain some incident involving federal-state relations, and his discourses revealed that he was no admirer of localism and had no tolerance for the habit of military uprisings. A typical case had arisen in Guerrero, where General Jiménez had flouted the authority of General Diego Álvarez, designated by the central government as the legitimate governor of the state. Jiménez had gone so far as to call elections in his own name to fill the local offices. In ordering Jiménez to the capital to answer for his conduct, Lerdo informed the deputies that the executive was doing no more than punish, properly and prudently, a violation of the central authority.[66] He returned to the chamber a few days later to touch the heart of the issue:

. . . the broader point of view in which the question ought to be seen is one of achieving the principle of obedience to legitimate authority, of giving death to military insurrections. That is what congress should see. On approving the elections carried out by Jiménez, which are not in the final analysis more than an army mutiny, the congress will be endorsing upheavals against order, and the matter in regard to Guerrero would be a bad precedent, which perhaps would compel the national representation to sanction other similar acts.[67]

Lerdo concluded by calling the attention of congress to similar, current revolts against the "legitimate" authorities of Yucatán and Sinaloa, in which the rebels had promised loyalty to the central government if granted recognition. But the executive had not and would not recognize the representatives of force in any form, especially those who had overthrown constituted authority; nor should congress, he warned, lend its support to "military mutinies," because to do so would defeat the "principle of respect for authority emanating from the laws."[68]

In January, 1870, Lerdo was before congress on a question affecting internal peace and order which was far more serious, since the revolts under discussion were aimed at the destruction of the central government. Requesting that congress grant the executive "extraordinary faculties" to deal with the rebels effectively, he stated, in a speech long remembered:

The Government is certain of reëstablishing order; it holds not only with certainty but with infallibility that it must subject the disturbers of public peace to the imperium of the laws, although it may have to repeat what

---

[65]Ceballos, *Aurora y Ocaso*, 48, 51. Quotation adapted. Ceballos' description applied to the 4th Congress, but was apropos of all the restoration congresses.

[66]Session of congress, January 11, 1868, *El Siglo*, January 12, 1868.

[67]Session of congress, January 30, 1868, *ibid.*, January 31, 1868.

[68]Session of congress, January 30, 1868, *ibid.*, January 31, 1868. For similar statements of Lerdo in congress, see *ibid.*, February 12, 1868.

it did during the War of the Reform and during the intervention, because it is resolved to put an end to the system of *pronunciamientos* and to the pretension of overcoming legal authority by means of force.[69]

Lerdo's cardinal belief in respect for law and order, his violent dislike of the ingrained Mexican habit of *pronunciamientos*, and his advocacy of centralistic government and federal support to the "constituted" local authorities—which in turn were obedient to the center—no doubt gained for him the reputation of a centralist and a destroyer of state sovereignty.[70] Still, those ideas seemed to be leaving their impressions on executive policy toward the primary problem during the restoration years: internal peace and order.

Lerdo's encounters with congress were not limited to topics dealing with foreign affairs and internal unrest. The outstanding economic project of the restoration period was the completion of the Mexico-to-Vera Cruz railroad, a project with a history dating back to 1857.[71] In 1868, the government renegotiated the contract with the British company which was engaged in its construction, and the revision was submitted for the approval of congress.[72] The opposition gathered sufficient votes to defeat the new government contract and substituted one of its own, drafted principally by Manuel María de Zamacona.[73] The cabinet faced a serious crisis in the bill of the opposition, and two ministers, Balcárcel (Fomento) and Iglesias (Government), entered the debating to defend the government.[74] It was Lerdo, however, who presented the final plea for the cabinet, calling for the defeat of Zamacona's bill. At the conclusion of his speech, he announced that the ministry believed passage of the substitute measure would signify a "vote of censure." Although Zamacona's counterproposal was defeated in the division taken

---

[69]*Diario de los Debates*, January 10, 1870, 5th Congress, I, 831. It should be noted that a speech allegedly delivered by Lerdo before congress on November 17, 1871, which Castillo Negrete selected for reprinting as an outstanding oration, was not given by Lerdo but by Ignacio Mariscal. See Emilio del Castillo Negrete, *Galería de Oradores de México en el Siglo XIX*, III, 32–40.

[70]A typical denunciation may be found in Cosmes, *Historia de Méjico*, XX, 655.

[71]Background sketches on the railroad may be found in Gustavo Baz and E. L. Gallo, *History of the Mexican Railway* (trans. by George F. Henderson), 13–16; Fred Wilbur Powell, *The Railroads of Mexico*, 99–103. The lithographs of the various engineering structures, in the work written by Baz and Gallo, present an effective pictorial study of the difficulties in building the road.

[72]The status of the company and the progress made on the railroad, as of 1868, were summarized in a propaganda pamphlet issued by the company at the time the new contract was up for approval in congress, and an excellent map of the route, showing sections completed and those under construction, was appended.—Supplement to *El Siglo*, October 19, 1868.

[73]See the congressional debates as reported in *ibid.*, September 23, 28–30, October 2, 1868.

[74]*Ibid.*, October 15, 1868.

immediately afterward, Lerdo had been the secretary who apparently had risked the survival of the ministry.[75]

Often an interpellation would degenerate into a bout of personalities, or, when guided by a clever antagonist, would ensnare a minister by leading him into an unanticipated bypath. In early 1868, Zamacona, Mata, and others of the opposition, plotting such a trap, disinterred the Ortega question in which Lerdo was a major accomplice. Lerdo sprang the trap planned for him, but simultaneously caught the opposition in congress in a clever web of logic.

First, Lerdo admitted that congress never had come forward with an express declaration of its attitude toward Juárez's extension of tenure in November, 1865, or toward the imprisonment and suspension of General Ortega in his rights of citizenship; however, the legislature's silence signified consent, and the statute of limitations had run. In other words, congress might have ordered Juárez to deliver the presidency to Ortega on December 8, 1867, on first convening after the intervention, for otherwise

the congress would be an accomplice in the violation of the Constitution. After the election of the president of the republic, congress could also have done a similar thing by not making a verification of the election [of Juárez] and by calling Ortega to be encharged with the government. It did not do so; therefore, it must be understood that congress is in conformity with the suspension of General González Ortega in his rights of citizenship. On the contrary, if the legal argument is carried forward as the said General González Ortega understands it, not even congress itself would be representative of the country. . . . I request congress to keep in mind that said Señor [Ortega] is an officer who placed himself in rebellion against the government and who is comprehended in the circular and law I have cited.[76]

The opposition had no answer to that sinuous logic, nor did it care to be a party to an admission of its own illegitimacy. The matter was dropped suddenly, in deference to Lerdo's "ingenuous sophistry,"[77] while the enemy went in search of other devices to embarrass the Prime Minister, devices which could not be converted into boomerangs.

Another personalized clash occurred in congress when Lerdo, after finishing with an interpellation, "took advantage of the occasion" to correct some derogatory remarks which were being cast at Matías Romero, then minister of Finance, for his acceptance of a piece of national property in partial payment for several years of unpaid salary as a diplomatic representative. Lerdo delivered a eulogistic discourse to cleanse Romero's honor, extolling him before the deputies as a model of patriotism and service.

---

[75]Session of congress, October 20, 1868, *ibid.*, October 21, 1868.
[76]Session of congress, February 26, 1868, *ibid.*, February 27, 1868.
[77]Villaseñor y Villaseñor, "El Golpe de Estado de Paso del Norte," *Obras*, II, 383–384.

Deputy Prieto called for the floor in turn, declaring that the payment to Romero was "unjust and arbitrary," despite the diplomat's acknowledged patriotism, because there were veterans, orphans, and widows, turned down by the treasury, "who do not have the fortune of being ministers or who do not possess the eloquence of Señor Lerdo." Although the flank attack came unexpectedly, Lerdo, forced to defend his cabinet, branded the statements of Prieto as unfair and inexact, adding that the government had turned away no creditor or patriot: "On the termination of the war, the government had to diminish the armed force, because it was not possible to support an army of fifty to sixty thousand men." In so far as widows and orphans were concerned, the government had handled their cases with "the greatest equity." Thus, far astray had meandered a debate which began by Lerdo's harmless attempt to explain the justice in paying back salary to a public servant![78]

Excepting those topics already discussed, little additional evidence can be brought to bear on Lerdo's true influence over policy. Government being a highly personalized institution in Mexico, the dearth of private correspondence relegates conclusions to the realm of the problematical. Some strong indications of how extensive was Lerdo's invasion into the guidance of affairs may be found in the letters he wrote to Mariano Riva Palacio, governor of the vital state of Mexico during most of the period under consideration.

Lerdo and Mariano were old acquaintances who combined official and personal matters in their correspondence. Once Mariano was attempting to negotiate the surrender of Sotomayor, the ringleader of a group of bandits within his constituency. In order to bring the chieftain within the orbit of the law, Francisco Limón, the *jéfe político,* in direct charge of the arrangements, recommended a pardon and personal guarantees in return for the surrender.[79] The suppression of banditry, one of the persistent problems of the restoration, fell within the scope of the federal authority, and hence the matter came to Lerdo's attention. Typical of his old San Ildefonso justice, he wrote to Riva Palacio in appreciation of the good intentions of the *jéfe político,* "but I do not see the possibility of doing more than what has been done in previous cases." The central government had upheld a policy toward banditry under which there could be no exceptions, and "he [the *jéfe político*] should understand that I may do no more because it is absolutely impossible."[80] A few days later, the *jéfe político* confided to Gov-

---

[78]Session of congress, January 18, 1868, *El Siglo,* January 19, 1868.

[79]Francisco Limón to Governor Mariano Riva Palacio, April 16, 1870, Mariano Riva Palacio Papers, Folder 171, UT.

[80]Lerdo to Mariano Riva Palacio, April 21, 1870, *ibid.,* Folder 171, UT.

ernor Riva Palacio that he had received a note from Lerdo, containing the refusal of the general government to concede his petition for special favors in the case of Sotomayor, "being founded on reasons excessively justified. . . ."[81]

An identical case came up about the same time which Riva Palacio handled through Ignacio Mejía, the minister of War. Yet Mejía did not determine the disposition of it, either on his own authority or in collaboration with the President, as might have been expected. It was decided by the President, to be sure, but in a junta of ministers.[82] Although Lerdo's name was not mentioned expressly by Mejía, it appeared more than a mere coincidence that the cabinet, acting as a body, applied the same rule of "no exceptions" which Lerdo had dictated in the incident of Sotomayor. At least, the cabinet, which one of its members admitted was acting in a joint capacity on "all serious affairs,"[83] was also functioning as a unit in carrying out detailed matters of policy.

Many were the occasions when Lerdo sent requests to Riva Palacio to place certain recommended persons in public offices in the bureaucracy of the state of Mexico.[84] Patronage favors were mutual, however. Once Mariano asked Lerdo to fix congress' attention on his favorite project, the Mexico-to-Toluca railroad, in order to obtain the concession from the federal government. While the agenda of congress was especially crowded at the moment, Lerdo replied in a way which proved that he was the proper person to seek when one desired to manipulate the deputies: "Although I rather doubt that it will be possible," he replied smugly to Riva Palacio, "[congress] being occupied with the affair of Tehuantepec; nevertheless, I shall procure [the consideration of your proposal] with great pleasure. . . ."[85]

Then, there were other ingredients in the oil of political friendship—the *amigo* of that personalized machinery of government, as Andrés Molina Enríquez styled it[86]—of which Lerdo appeared to supply his share. When the Minister of War inadvertently irritated Riva Palacio with a telegraphic order bluntly phrased, Lerdo applied his diplomatic touch—and his knowledge of practical

[81] Francisco Limón to Mariano Riva Palacio, April 24, 1870, *ibid.*, Folder 171, UT.

[82] Ignacio Mejía to Mariano Riva Palacio, March 19, 1870, *ibid.*, Folder 171, UT.

[83] Iglesias, *Autobiografía*, 50.

[84] Lerdo to Mariano Riva Palacio, November 28, 1870, Mariano Riva Palacio Papers, Folder 171; February 21, July 20, August 20, 1871, *ibid.*, Folder 172, UT.

[85] Lerdo to Mariano Riva Palacio, October 4, 1870, *ibid.*, Folder 171, UT.

[86] Andrés Molina Enríquez, *Los Grandes Problemas Nacionales*, 67.

psychology—to smooth the feathers of the ruffled Governor of Mexico:

> Señor General Mejía will write to you . . . so that you will not retain any bad interpretation of the telegram.
> I shall make only a little complaint [to you] in a few words, and I consider it work to write myself.
> Any bad impression which you may have had or may have, supposing that any of us in the general government might forget, even for a moment, all the consideration which you deserve personally and officially and in every way and under all circumstances, is an injustice.
> You and I being old friends, I can come straight to the point.
> When one receives a letter or similar thing from persons whose affection and consideration cannot be doubted, and one finds something explained poorly or stated badly [as in Mejía's telegram], it should be attributed to any involuntary motive whatever, and not to bad intention.
> But if it does not admit of a good explanation in any manner, then one ought to answer that it is not well stated and not cavil against friends.
> I shall rest content that you think as well of us as we think of you.[87]

Again, he wrote to his close friend General Escobedo, commander of an army division, presumably to calm the General's impatience over delays in promotions for subordinate officers. Lerdo explained that he had taken the matter directly to Juárez and that Mejía's tardiness was due not to negligence but illness.[88]

The final facet of Lerdo's rôle in the cabinet from 1867 to 1871, which must be treated briefly in order to demonstrate the prepotency attributed to him, was the obstinate attack of the opposition press. Though evidences of the journalistic aggression have been cited already, the prominent threads of the press attack throughout those years formed a fabric with a pattern all of its own. Inimical editors never wearied either of writing or allotting space for polemical articles, satirical poems, and brutal cartoons directed at Lerdo, "the Jesuit, the evil genius of government, the Mexican Machiavelli, the seminary politician, the destroyer of the Constitution, the germ of unrest, the immaculate of Paso del Norte, the favorite of Cura Juárez," as he was tagged variously with an impressive list of unsavory pseudonyms.[89]

Generally speaking, the attack was without real substance, based as it was on assumption and surmise; for secrecy surrounded the

---

[87]Lerdo to Mariano Riva Palacio, March 16, 1870, *ibid.*, Folder 171, UT. The letter was written in Lerdo's nervous scrawl.

[88]Lerdo to Escobedo, September 15, 1867, Archivo de Fernando Iglesias Calderón, Legajo 12, A.G.N. The material available on the personal relationships which Lerdo maintained at various levels of government is rare indeed, which explains the disconnected nature of the foregoing illustrations; but the present writer feels that they indicate what probably existed on a vast scale.

[89]*El Padre Cobos*, edited by Ireneo Paz, and *La Orquesta*, edited by Vicente Riva Palacio and others, were the leading anti-Juarist papers of the early restoration epoch, devoted largely to satirizing Lerdo.

cabinet whose members maintained a tight security on their joint discussions. As a result, the press diatribe was vague and negative, offering no positive substitutes for the program which it attempted to undermine, except for changes in the personnel of the cabinet. When all the fat had simmered from the polemical writings, the complaints were probably more a matter of personality than principle, or, to borrow a hybrid term from Francisco Bulnes, the rivalry between "los *in* y los *out*."[90] Lerdo was among "the ins" of government, apparently controlling an extensive block of patronage, and not only influential with Juárez but clearly the dominant figure in the ministry. Resentment and envy—and not a little of fear and respect—were natural by-products of that special position, which were manufactured by "the outs"; and those politicians who experienced such human sentiments found their most soothing outlet in the press of the times.

Perhaps the cleverest satire was hatched in the editorial office of Ireneo Paz, the director of *El Padre Cobos,* an ardent supporter of Porfirio Díaz and a man without scruples, whether plotting military insurrections or drafting violent newspaper copy. But despite his monotonous and certainly crude burlesque, it should be noted that Paz held a healthy respect for "Don Sebastián Lerdo de Tejada, a man very intelligent and full of ambitions, the chief of Juárez's cabinet, and the only terrible one among all our [the Porfirists'] adversaries for his refined perspicacity."[91]

From the date of its foundation, *El Padre Cobos* was placed, ironically, under the protection of Lerdo, "the prime minister, the alter ego of the President,"[92] and the editor reserved a special space in the upper left-hand corner of the front page of each semiweekly issue to "prick" Señor Saint Sebastián [Lerdo], who was pierced figuratively with a poem and literally in a cartoon by means of the "arrows" forged by "Padre Cobos."[93] Week after week "Padre Cobos" shot his brace of barbs, which did not have the desired effect of destroying Saint Sebastián politically. "Thirty-four arrows!" once exclaimed "Padre Cobos" despondently, after as many shots, "and [Saint Sebastián] so tranquil!"[94]

The poignancy of the cartoons was indeed the cleverest feature of Paz's press. One of the best examples was a scene of Juárez, blindfolded, addressing congress in the usual ceremonial speech at the close of a period of sessions: ". . . I assure you [the deputies],"

[90]Francisco Bulnes, *El Verdadero Díaz y la Revolución,* 40.
[91]Ireneo Paz, *Algunas Campañas, Memorias,* II, 294.
[92]*El Padre Cobos,* February 21, 1869.
[93]The last of those "arrows" was printed in the issue of January 22, 1871, at the time Lerdo left the Juárez cabinet.
[94]*Ibid.,* June 20, 1869.

read the caption, "that the policy of my beloved minister [Lerdo] will make you happy. Amen."[95] In another edition, Juárez is shown driving the "coach of state" relentlessly toward a precipice. Across the gorge was the tombstone of the Constitution of 1857. Lerdo was standing by Juárez, dressed in a general's costume and leering wildly, ready to shove him over the cliff:

Juárez: "Don Sebastián, the situation is critical."

Lerdo: "Go on! Not even you comprehend my policy."[96]

"Padre Cobos" once dreamed of having spied upon a secret meeting of Juárez's cabinet. He related the aberration to a brother monk as follows:

Juárez was presiding at the head of his counselors, silent and immobile, except for his eyes which showed gleams of "satisfaction" elicited by the discussion in progress. At his feet sat Lerdo, "on a very large cushion," presiding over the ministerial reports, while "the other ministers were more retired" and seated "on smaller cushions."

Mejía, the minister of War, reported on the numbers of the opposition which he could destroy daily in order to pacify the enemies of the government. Lerdo interrupted by directing the Minister of Government to expedite a circular to the effect that there would be no official interference in the approaching elections.[97]

Minister of Government: "Nothing more than one circular?"

Lerdo: "Or two, it is the same."

Minister of Government: "The fact is, I find myself inclined to expedite even four."

Lerdo: "In proper time; it is always best to begin with the first."[98]

The journalistic thrusts at Lerdo were of a rich assortment, however, varying from the modest and indirect, to the openly violent. La Iberia, the moderate paper directed by the Spaniard Anselmo de la Portilla, stated:

Few are those persons who must deal with Señores Lerdo, Iglesias, and Romero who will not leave delighted with their excellent educations, their affability, and even with their own affairs expedited; and nevertheless, no government has faced such tremendous opposition.[99]

Other papers discharged their accusations more bluntly. When Lerdo held a plurality of offices after the election of 1867, La

---

[95]Ibid., June 6, 1869.

[96]Ibid., March 28, 1869. The cartoonists always made capital out of Lerdo's prominent, almost protruding eyes.

[97]Government interference in elections was notorious, but the incumbent administration always gave lip service to freedom and impartiality in supervising them.

[98]El Padre Cobos, March 18, 1869.

[99]La Iberia quoted by Cosmes, Historia de Méjico, XXI, 32–33.

Orquesta, listing them with rancor, warned him flatly: ". . . but your policy turns our stomach." Good patriots "have seen in you a constant threat to the Constitution and to democratic principles. It is necessary that you prove they are deceived."[100] The chief organ of the Porfirist faction, on the other hand, employed indirection to launch its calumnies against Lerdo—for political reasons; hence, it reprinted a speech delivered by a partisan at a club gathering. Lerdo, claimed the speaker, had hidden himself for many years

behind the parapets at San Ildefonso in the capacity of rector, teaching himself the exercise of tyranny through his students, applying the *palmeta* and other improper punishments of the culture of our century, and establishing a religious intolerance by which the students were obligated to confess and assist at the Eucharist.[101]

Judging by the cumulative attack of the opposition press, the prevailing though hazy conception of cabinet government in which a prime minister was more or less directly responsible for policy, Lerdo's recognized primacy in the cabinet, his part in such major questions as the *convocatoria* of 1867, the formulation of foreign policy, and his relationship with congress—judging by all those factors primarily, it can be stated unconditionally that he was, next to Juárez, the key figure in the governmental program from 1867 to 1871. Whether Juárez should be an exception is not only a fascinating question but one which cannot be answered in the affirmative with any degree of certainty; whether Lerdo was really the genius of government and actually held a prepotent influence over the Indian President in the general guidance of affairs could at best be a conjecture. At any rate, Juárez's national reputation and the moral strength which his character imparted to the administration during that hectic period of revolts were vital forces not to be discounted. Each man, Lerdo and Juárez, had certain valuable talents to contribute, talents which probably were more complementary than competitive. The fact remains, however, that Lerdo, as a president himself, guided his own, highly personal administration much as he allegedly had conducted that of Juárez in his rôle of chief of Cabinet.[102]

---

[100]*La Orquesta*, December 21, 1867.

[101]*El Mensajero*, January 31, 1871.

[102]For some interesting comparative comments of contemporaries on the enigmatic relationship between Juárez, Lerdo, and other ministers, see Sierra, *Juárez*, 225; Paz, *Algunas Campañas*, II, 238; Zayas Enríquez, *Juárez*, 270–271; Riva Palacio, *Historia de la Administración de Lerdo*, 19. It should be noted that this topic remains one of the great controversial issues surrounding the epoch of Juárez.

Lerdo's resignation from the cabinet was provoked by a personal-political breach with Juárez, an event bound to transpire and which was determined in point of time by the national elections of 1871. The fundamental cause was obvious to everyone: the intimate link between the two men could not withstand the strain while they competed openly for the presidency. Indeed, the situation was anomalous until Lerdo resolved it by stepping down from his high post in the council in January, 1871.

Long before his resignation was filed, Lerdo had offered to retire, as he confidentially informed his friend, Mariano Riva Palacio, governor of the state of Mexico:

As I revealed to you when we took leave of each other before your departure for that city [Toluca], I believed that I should separate from the ministry, through the fear that my remaining would be badly interpreted in and.out of congress, when my major desire has been, and is, not to give any occasion, voluntarily or involuntarily, that may cause any difference or disorder in the advance of the administration.

Nevertheless, the President has believed that I should not resign, and it did not seem to him the opportune time to modify his ministry.[103]

In the same letter, Lerdo revealed a touch of self-condemnation which indicated that he was only superficially loyal to Juárez while secretly nursing the thought of his own candidacy: "If I am wrong in remaining, my excuse will be that I do not impose, but on the contrary, I subordinate my will."[104]

That presumption was confirmed by one claiming to be a friend and admirer of Lerdo:

The truth which few know about . . . is as follows: Don Sebastián will leave the ministry and certainly will go to the United States and afterward to Europe. To the present this is not verified; but *that is the belief* which soon . . . must be realized.

Then the writer added that the separation was not "a dispute with Don Benito, at least ostensibly; it appears that questions of suspicion in connection with the approaching elections have determined it."[105]

So, Lerdo continued in the cabinet under what must have been a delicate situation until a definite excuse arose for his absolute separation. The occasion was the election of the *ayuntamiento* of Mexico City in December, 1870, during which the electoral body bifurcated, each segment claiming to be the legitimate authority

---

[103]Lerdo to Mariano Riva Palacio, September 22, 1870, Mariano Riva Palacio Papers, Folder 171, UT.

[104]Lerdo to Mariano Riva Palacio, September 22, 1870, *ibid.*, Folder 171, UT.

[105]Lu's (?) to Vicente Riva Palacio, September 1, 1870, Vicente Riva Palacio Papers, Folder 183, UT.

and each electing a set of officers. Since one group was known to be Lerdist and the other Juarist in political sentiment and since the *ayuntamiento* supervised the presidential elections in the capital, the solution of the impasse held much significance; and Juárez handled it so as to make clear that he intended to cling to the presidency and to use his decisive official influence toward that end by uprooting all potential opposition.[106]

Whatever ray of hope Lerdo may have entertained that Juárez would not attempt to perpetuate himself in power was at last liquidated.[107] He tendered his resignation in terms which politely pointed out the uncertainty of the previous months in the cabinet:

Since the Sunday of July 3 of the past year, I had the honor of informing the Citizen President of the republic that for my own personal reasons, among them failing health, I desired to separate from the ministry of Foreign Relations.

I again expressed the same desire last September, and afterward had occasion to manifest in the council of ministers that I judged my separation opportune on the termination of the period of sessions which the congress of the Union was then holding.

This end having arrived, I have had to respect, as a just cause of delaying, a recent and regrettable event very deserving of consideration.[108]

Juárez accepted the resignation, thanking Lerdo tersely for his "important services to the country, especially in her moments of conflict and during the unfortunate days through which she has passed."[109] And thus dissolved the most enduring political team established during the epoch of Juárez. For more than seven years

---

[106]The disputed *ayuntamiento* election, briefly stated above, was a long and complicated political issue. In a fair "legal" struggle in congress in the spring of 1871, the Lerdists forced Juárez to recognize their council as the legitimate one and to install it formally. But no sooner had congress adjourned than Juárez forcibly ousted the Lerdist body, replacing it with one composed of his own supporters. For details, see Cosmes, *Historia de Méjico*, XXI, 745–746, 772, 1057–1059; *El Mensajero*, June 11, 14, 1871; *El Siglo*, January 2, 3, 5, June 10, 1871; Nelson to Fish, December 29, 1870, *Mexico, Dispatches*, XLII; June 10 and 12, 1871, *ibid.*, XLIII, A.U.S.

[107]Zayas Enríquez stated that Lerdo asked Juárez to resign his candidacy in order to avoid the impending revolution being plotted by the faction supporting Porfirio Díaz. Juárez answered with "his recognized firmness, as he had answered so many times: that he was not resigning, because the law and his duty prohibited. . . ."—Zayas Enríquez, *Juárez*, 236–237. See also Zayas Enríquez, *Porfirio Díaz* (trans. by T. Quincy Browne, Jr.), 102–103. Lerdo was known to have visited Juárez as late as March 3, 1871.—*El Mensajero*, March 4, 1871.

[108]Lerdo to the Minister of Government, January 14, 1871, *El Siglo*, January 18, 1871. The "recent and regrettable event" was the *ayuntamiento* dispute. Lerdo also informed Mariano Riva Palacio of his resignation, but the letter containing the information was notably unrevealing.—Lerdo to Mariano Riva Palacio, January 17, 1871, Mariano Riva Palacio Papers, Folder 172, UT.

[109]Manuel Saavedra to Lerdo, January 17, 1871, *El Siglo*, January 18, 1871.

the two men had been associated intimately in the daily direction of government, and it was perhaps regrettable that the breach was premised on the discord of personal ambitions. In Juárez's way of thinking, however, the presidential chair was his exclusive sinecure on a lifetime calculation, while any other contender, regardless of ability, past loyalty, or services, was presumably *ipso facto* guilty of a high personal treason. After destroying his competition by one means or another for thirteen years, Juárez saw Lerdo transformed from an intimate friend and counselor into just another traitor with ambitions. Time had rendered the President neither less effective in destroying his competitors nor less greedy in clinging to office, as the election of 1871 demonstrated.

For a brief moment, the press concentrated on the resignation and then turned its full attention toward the campaign of 1871. In fact, Lerdo's departure from his official position was the signal for bringing into the open an independent political faction in support of his candidacy for president.[110] The satirical *El Padre Cobos*, reluctant to trust the rumor that Lerdo was resigning "any more than that Don Benito has lost his love for the presidential chair," captured the crux of the event in a clever dialogue between Juárez and Lerdo, entitled "His Majesty and the Favorite":

Juárez: "Speak to me of whatever you wish but do not touch upon the presidential chair."

Lerdo (reminding Juárez of how long he had secured him in that chair) : "Already you have had thirteen years of governing, compatriot, and it is necessary to make the public comprehend little by little that you continue to be indispensable."

Juárez: "What do thirteen years amount to? I have eaten them like a cake with sugar icing and with the same facility I shall eat another thirteen."

Lerdo: "Yes, I already know that you are a good gastronomist in that matter of eating years."[111]

Yet it was General Ignacio Mejía, the minister of War, who told the most intimate story of the rift which had occurred within the government family. He wrote Mariano Riva Palacio that for some time three parties had been developing in congress which were denominated "Lerdists, Juarists, and the old opposition." While the Lerdists supposedly had been friendly toward the government, their attitude on major questions had been inconsistent, preventing a

---

[110]*Ibid.*, January 18, 20, 1871. *El Siglo* reviewed the press reaction to Lerdo's resignation in its issue of January 18, 1871. See also *El Mensajero*, January 13, 14, 18, 1871.

[111]*El Padre Cobos*, January 8, 1871. The cartoon depicting the breach showed Lerdo gleefully breaking the iron chain and bracelet which bound his leg to that of Juárez. The President was hiding his face in a handkerchief and weeping.—*Ibid.*, January 15, 1871.

"compact majority capable of supporting the government. . . ."
Mejía had called Lerdo's attention to that problem, requesting
that he force "those who called themselves his friends [*i.e.*, the
Lerdists]" either to join the Juarist party or to enter "the open
opposition." Mejía's plea had been unsuccessful. Then, Iglesias
and Lerdo left the cabinet in close succession:

Those who call themselves Lerdists take [Lerdo] as a candidate for president,
and in my judgment they have harmed him as they have harmed the country
already. With this conduct they enervated useful works in congress and today
they divide the better element of the liberal party. . . . I had answered that
Don Sebastián would not separate from the cabinet, and that he would be our
[the cabinet's] reserve for an unfortunate case such as that which threatened
the President in his illness,[112] or, better, to enter that position at a later period
with the acquiescence of all. Now that they [the Lerdists] have taken him in
order to present him as a competitor of Señor Juárez, it already appears to me
that they have nullified him, because it will be very difficult for him to compete;
and if by a chance his candidacy should triumph, his administration would
cause a real harm.[113]

The words of Mejía were of some weight, since he was probably
the most capable man in the ministry next to Lerdo. Obviously,
Lerdo was being groomed for the presidential succession, provided
his patience would endure the span of Juárez's life; but his position
was compromised by the actions of those who "called themselves
his friends." And Mejía's pregnant remark—that it would be
"very difficult for him to compete"—was not only a veiled com-
mentary on official interference in elections but an accurate fore-
cast of the results: Mejía would be manipulating the units of the
federal army on polling day in behalf of the reëlection of Juárez.

The campaign and election which continued through the first six
months of 1871 were perhaps as colorful as any ever staged in the
independence period of Mexican history. Three factions entered the
race, taking their names from the respective candidates whom they
backed for the presidency: Juarist, Porfirist,[114] and Lerdist. The
Juarists counted on the larger portion of the bureaucracy in federal
and state offices in addition to the federal army, always a major and
usually a decisive factor in the final result, through direct interference in the balloting and by enforcing the loyalty of the state
governors.

---

[112]Juárez had suffered a severe illness in late 1870.

[113]Ignacio Mejía to Mariano Riva Palacio, January·26, 1871, Mariano Riva
Palacio Papers, Folder 172, UT.

[114]The Porfirists, whose candidate was Porfirio Díaz, adapted his first name
for their party, since " 'Diazist' would be an impossible word."—Zayas Enríquez, *Porfirio Díaz*, 113n.

The Porfirists had mingled such motley elements in their ranks that they were the most heterogeneous of the three groups.[115] They counted upon the military discontents outside the regular army, some of the idealistic young liberals, the outcasts of the old conservative party, the multitude of enemies accumulated by both Juárez and Lerdo, and a large group of disappointed place seekers, the "outs" of the political world. Their leader was young General Díaz, a hero for his military service during the intervention and Juárez's only opponent in the election of 1867. Under the astute tutelage of Justo Benítez, his alter ego, Díaz had retired from the army to his ranch of La Noria in Oaxaca, soon after the close of the foreign war, to work the soil like "Cincinnatus," which certainly he was not,[116] while clever campaign managers—Benítez, Paz, Zamacona, and others— religiously polished his military glory to many times its natural brilliance and praised his patriotism to a point of boredom. Actually, the Cincinnatus act was a mask for covering Díaz's congenital ambition; and his secluded retreat at La Noria was a convenient headquarters for plotting under the aegis of his brother Félix, governor of Oaxaca. Although Díaz until 1871 kept his own slate technically clean of revolution, he permitted his name and his national reputation to serve as the ideology of countless *pronuciamientos* during the chaotic restoration years. If, then, he was theoretically free of blame for the unrest plaguing the government, he was morally responsible; for he could have rendered a great service to the nation by issuing an unequivocal statement to the effect that he was not a promoter of revolution nor would he permit his name to serve as the magic for any attempt to overthrow established authority by violent means. By not so doing, the opposition welded a Morton's Fork with which to prod the administration. The frequent revolts, so it claimed, were symptomatic of the evils of the Juárez-Lerdo régime; and when the government acted quickly and often harshly to crush those movements, it was branded as a brutal tyranny. To what extent the opposition itself, under the titular leadership of Díaz, was responsible for the government's difficulties in consolidating peace and order has never

---

[115]Although one can find the facts about the Porfirist party in any of the biographies on Díaz, the most valuable and fascinating account is that of Ireneo Paz, *Algunas Campañas*, II, III. Paz was associated with all the early Porfirist machinations and knew personally all the leaders. The following statements are based on this work, which was continued in Paz, *Porfirio Díaz, 12a Leyenda Histórica*, I.

[116]The first comparison of Díaz to Cincinnatus with which the present writer is familiar appeared in *La Orquesta*, September 7, 1867.

been determined, but it certainly appeared to be a cause of primary significance.[117]

The Lerdist party[118] assumed the character of its chief, being composed of men of property, a few capitalists, the intelligentsia, the socially prominent, and a minority of the bureaucratic element which Lerdo had erected in governmental posts during his long tenure as chief of Cabinet. But by far the most conspicuous element was drawn from the professional classes, especially lawyers and writers. A few key personalities must be mentioned as the most outspoken of the Lerdist supporters and the real stage managers of his campaign and later his presidential policies.

Ramón Guzmán and Manuel Romero Rubio stood at the top of the list as the Lerdist strategists in the difficult game of directing congress. Both were men of means, but while Guzmán had accumulated a fortune as a capitalist and banker, Romero Rubio was a socialite lawyer who had been educated at San Ildefonso along with Lerdo. Also in congress supporting Lerdo were such men as Isidro Montiel y Duarte, legal publicist and scholar, Dr. Hilarión Frías y Soto, and Vidal Castañeda y Nájera. In the ranks of the journalists, poets, and writers, Lerdo counted on the staff of El Siglo, which included Jesús Castañeda, Emilio Velasco, Julio Zárate, and José María Vigil.[119] From among his old cabinet companions, Lerdo carried with him, when he resigned, only José María Iglesias, who was a man widely respected for his moderation, administrative experience, and erudition.[120]

---

[117]Why could Juárez not establish peace and order, asked Zayas Enríquez? And his answer: "Principally because we Porfirists, with our continual revolutions, would not permit him to do so."—Zayas Enríquez, Porfirio Díaz, 112n.

Referring to the years 1867 to 1876, Bulnes spoke of Díaz's "sad career of disturber. . . ." In addition, he gave the date for the termination of the "immaculate" part of Díaz's life: "General Díaz was also one of those imbeciles who until 1867 believed in liberty."—Bulnes, El Verdadero Díaz, 38. Finally, he styled Díaz "the indefatigable perturber of the public peace since 1869."—Bulnes, ibid., 20.

[118]The following synthesis of the Lerdist party is based not only on a variety of sources but also on indirect evidence such as congressional divisions, the composition of the Lerdist ayuntamiento of 1870–1871, and a number of manuscript letters. For a few reliable references, general and specific, see El Siglo (for the entire year of 1871); Emilio Ordaz, La Cuestión Presidencial, 11; Cosmes, Historia de Méjico, XXI, 336–342; Bancroft, Vida de Porfirio Díaz, 481–484; Riva Palacio, Historia de la Administración de Lerdo, 29–30, 215–224; Bancroft, History of Mexico, VI, 377–378.

[119]Zárate and Vigil were famous Mexican historians, each contributing a volume to the famous general set, México á Través de los Siglos, edited by Vicente Riva Palacio.

[120]Iglesias claimed that he retired to private life during the elections in order to remain neutral, since he was a friend of both Juárez and Lerdo.—Iglesias, Autobiografía, 53–54. Iglesias' statements of his own political motives are notoriously untrustworthy, however. That he was a Lerdist seemed confirmed when he was elected president of the Supreme Court soon after Lerdo became chief executive. See also Nelson to Fish, December 29, 1870, Mexico, Dispatches, XLII, A.U.S.

Turning to the state governments, Lerdo had erected a formidable personal structure which was nullified largely by the intervention of Juárez before the elections and after Lerdo had resigned. At one time, however, Lerdo could have depended on the support of Governor Escobedo of San Luis Potosí, Governor Francisco Leyva of Morelos, Governor Florencio Antillón of Guanajuato, Governor Antonio Tagle of Hidalgo, and Governor Romero Vargas of Puebla. Had those officials been left unmolested to dictate the vote in their constituencies for the Lerdists, even discounting Lerdo's loss of the *ayuntamiento* in Mexico City, Lerdo probably would have carried an election which was bound to be thrown into the lap of congress for final decision.

Lerdo himself was a civilian statesman of great talent, vast experience, sound education, and impeccable manners and speech, concealing only in part his boundless self-confidence and conceit. Endowed with all the social amenities, he was in truth a Mexican version of Lord Chesterfield. It was only natural that those of the upper and upper middle classes who valued such qualities in a statesman would flock to his political banner. The Lerdists may have been justified in styling themselves "the party of intelligence," since they did seem to have a virtual monopoly on intellect, but at the same time the accusations hurled by opponents that they were aristocratic and arrogant probably were equally deserved.[121]

During the campaign, the factions developed rudimentary organizations which were almost national in scope. If the balloting followed the stereotyped pattern of fraud and official interference, Juárez left the opposition free to promote their respective candidates, at least academically speaking.[122] Throughout the country, political clubs sprang up, papers were founded "to postulate" one or the other of the three contenders, and a full-scale propaganda attack was launched by each of the factions. Upon the press of Mexico City, which became a sort of national party headquarters, fell the burden of leadership and coördination of the scattered local activities for each party. For the Juarists, that duty was discharged by the subsidized press, especially the *Diario Oficial* and *La Paz;* for the Porfirists, *El Mensajero* was the principal organ;[123] while the Lerdists used *El Siglo* for the same purpose.[124]

[121]Cosmes, *Historia de Méjico*, XXI, 337.
[122]Even Ireneo Paz, the violent anti-Juarist publicist, admitted that from 1867 to 1872 the journalists "could write freely."—*Algunas Campañas*, III, 21.
[123]For an analysis of the campaign policies and editorial direction of *Él Mensajero*, see Walter V. Scholes, "*El Mensajero* and the Election of 1871," *The Americas*, V (July, 1948), 61–67. See also Paz, *Algunas Campañas*, III, 27–32. Paz was not only editor of *El Padre Cobos* but also secretary to the editorial staff of *El Mensajero*.
[124]A complete listing of the papers which supported Lerdo's candidacy may be found in *El Siglo*, July 1, 1871.

A preliminary electoral battle, coinciding with the other phases of the campaigning, took place on the floor of congress in a combined special and regular session in the spring of 1871, ending just a few weeks prior to election day. Virtually every question considered by the deputies had some connection with the approaching tempest; and to gain a majority the so-called "Lerdist-Porfirist League" was founded by which the deputies representing the two unofficial factions united to frustrate the government and to achieve some advantages in the elections. In a Girondin sort of way, the strange alliance was successful: for example, the Lerdists triumphed, with the aid of the votes of Porfirist deputies, in forcing Juárez to install their *ayuntamiento* in Mexico City; but the crafty President trumped up an excuse to oust that body immediately after congress adjourned. Similarly, all the fruits of victory which the League produced were sterile, for Juárez had the funds and machinery of government to expend on his reëlection, resources which far outweighed in practical value the legislative maneuvers of the League. From the beginning of the session, stated Cosmes, "it is almost certain" that Juárez had not the least intention to obey the dictates of the opposition in congress. As he once expounded to a partisan: "It is one thing to legislate and another to enforce the laws. He who laughs last laughs best. . . ."[125]

In reality, the Lerdists and Porfirists were strange bedfellows, having absolutely nothing in common except their opposition to Juárez's reëlection. Defeated at the polls, the Porfirists raised the age-old cry of fraud and followed it up with revolution. The Lerdist party, on the other hand, made clear from the outset that it was a party of peace regardless of the outcome, and it constantly reiterated the assertion throughout the six months and more when the electoral struggle was raging.[126] Bitter as were the Lerdists against "some procedures of the government," their formula was always "complete submission to the law; neither revolution nor despotism." Furthermore, their peaceful if rancorous acceptance of Juárez's reëlection made their actions speak well for their words.[127]

The program of the Lerdist party, as set forth in *El Siglo*, was noteworthy, less as an intrinsic part of the campaign itself than as confirmatory evidence of Lerdo's dominant influence on government during the previous four years. Significantly, the Lerdists openly endorsed Lerdo's policies as a minister and announced that his election would mean no fundamental changes in those policies. Nor did the Lerdist press intend to insult Juárez or diminish his

---

[125]Juárez quoted by Cosmes, *Historia de Méjico*, XXI, 970.

[126]*El Siglo*, May 11, June 3, July 26, August 26, September 7, 1871.

[127]*Ibid.*, September 7, 1871; Nelson to Fish, August 30, 1871, *Mexico, Dispatches*, LXIII, A.U.S.

deserved reputation. It was not Juárez, personally, but the principle of a second reëlection which the Lerdists denounced as undemocratic.[128] In addition, the Lerdists published a formal platform which incorporated among its seventeen planks Lerdo's dignified foreign policy toward Europe, promotion of free public education, the "inviolable right of property . . . as the foundation of the social order," a *laissez faire* attitude toward economic projects, and a number of other vague promises.[129]

Considering the principal premise of peace at all cost, regardless of the outcome of the election, the Lerdist party in methods, composition, and program was consistent with Lerdo's own beliefs, personality, and official record in the government. But the direct part which Lerdo played in supervising the political propaganda flowing from *El Siglo,* the direction he gave to the congressional struggles in the spring of 1871, and other possible liaison activities he may have carried on with the party chiefs who were conducting his campaign remained a mystery. It should be recalled that he was again serving as president of the Supreme Court after resigning from the cabinet in early 1871. That he stood aloof from the acrimony of the campaign, not stooping to participate directly, was a tribute to his sense of discretion and dignity. Since he never considered himself bound by any party obligations after assuming the presidency in 1872, it would appear that he passively acquiesced in the activities of the party which borrowed his name and promoted his candidacy, instead of giving it personal leadership.

The outcome of the election, the victory of Juárez, certainly should not have been a "mystery to anyone."[130] Despite fraud, force, and Mejía's use of the federal troops "to perpetuate Don Benito in power,"[131] no single candidate captured a majority of the electoral vote, which the electoral committee in congress counted as follows: for Juárez, 5,837; for Díaz, 3,555; and for Lerdo, 2,864.[132] Consequently, the decision was made by congress, and since the Juárez deputies could muster a majority, they were able to impose their candidate on the country for an additional four years.[133] The formal consummation by congress of a highly suspicious victory was made in the face of a strong minority which

[128]Editorials of Emilio Velasco, *El Siglo,* January 13, 14, 1871.

[129]*Ibid.,* supplement of February 2, 1871. When one of the Juarist papers questioned the Lerdist platform as not that of Lerdo himself, *El Siglo* replied feebly: ". . . he [Lerdo] has not contradicted us. . . ."—*Ibid.,* February 4, 1871.

[130]J. M. Aguirre de la Barrera to Mariano Riva Palacio, October 4, 1871, Mariano Riva Palacio Papers, Folder 173, UT.

[131]Isidro Montiel y Duarte to Mariano Riva Palacio, July 21, 1871, *ibid.,* Folder 172, UT.

[132]*Diario de los Debates,* October 7, 1871, 6th Congress, I, 315.

[133]*Ibid.,* October 12, 1871, 6th Congress, I, 391.

abstained from voting and whose angry protest against the electoral farce was registered in silence. Just before the final count was taken, Roberto Esteva, a Porfirist deputy, announced:

It is a notorious fact that Don Benito Juárez has not asked the public suffrage for his favors, but he has violated it. That was the prologue of the comedy. His actions have been unfolding successively, and now the conclusion is written beforehand. And since the author of the electoral farce has 105 deputies as collaborators in the work, to attempt to introduce a revision in that conclusion would be in vain. It is evident that within a few moments Don Benito Juárez is to be elected president of the United States of Mexico, against law and justice; this will be an illegal fact, but it is a fact, and in such an unhappy situation, one so bitter and sad for the independent deputies, silence is more eloquent than words. I prefer to remain silent.[134]

Although an ardent Lerdist, Deputy Montiel probably reflected a general sentiment when he wrote:

In regard to the political chronicle, I should say without temerity that it can be assured that Señor Juárez does not have a majority in the elections which have taken place.
Now who will compete with him? I do not know, but whoever it may be, I shall vote against the reëlection, because a president for eighteen years would make himself appear a great deal like one of those who are called Majesties, whom the Mexicans are not accustomed to tolerate.[135]

Unsuccessful at the polls, the Porfirist faction resorted to the tested Mexican expedient of revolution to gain control of the machinery of government. A few days before Juárez was declared reëlected by congress, an abortive and bloody uprising occurred in the shadow of the national palace in Mexico City, which General Rocha quashed ruthlessly and quickly. Then, in early November, Díaz dropped the mask of "Cincinnatus" and issued from his ranch in Oaxaca the plan of La Noria, calling for the overthrow of Juárez and claiming absurdly that "if triumph crowns our efforts, I shall return to the peace of my home, preferring in any event the frugal and tranquil life of the obscure laborer to the ostentations of power."[136]

Although the efficient Mejía was prepared for the Porfirist plot and set for nipping the revolution as soon as it budded,[137] that

---

[134]*Ibid.*, October 12, 1871, 6th Congress, I, 388. Bancroft was correct in describing the elections as abominably fraudulent, but he was guessing when he added: ". . . and with certainty it can be presumed that the true vote was for Díaz."—Bancroft, *Vida de Porfirio Díaz*, 485.

[135]Isidro Montiel y Duarte to Mariano Riva Palacio, July 21, 1871, Mariano Riva Palacio Papers, Folder 172, UT.

[136]Quoted by Cosmes, *Historia de Méjico*, XXII, 59–60. For the entire plan, see *ibid.*, XXII, 54–62. Edward L. Plumb, former United States chargé to Mexico, accurately described the Plan of La Noria as "absurd."—Plumb to J. Sanford Barnes, November 18, 1871, *Plumb Papers*, VIII.

[137]Ignacio Mejía to Mariano Riva Palacio, August 11, 12, 1871, Mariano Riva Palacio Papers, Folder 172; *idem.* to *idem.*, October 3, 5, 23, 24, 1871, *ibid.*, Folder 173, UT.

issue continued in the forefront of national life for several months to come. When Juárez died, Díaz was still at large attempting to consolidate his scattered rebel elements for renewed attacks against the government, even though the federal army had smashed the main forces gathered together under the banner of La Noria.

In the final analysis, Juárez's decision for reëlection was a political error of the first magnitude, but not because of the methods he used to realize that end. Lerdo and Díaz and their respective followers had no grounds for complaint on that score, both using the governmental resources to perpetuate themselves in the presidency when the opportunity arrived. But since Juárez himself appeared to be exceedingly unpopular in 1871, he could have performed a patriotic service by stepping down from office after thirteen years of tenacity, thus removing all pretext for revolt. Furthermore, such a step taken by a man of his national moral strength might have established something of a precedent for the future. And he could have used his position to dictate a successor who need not necessarily have been Lerdo. Undoubtedly, all factions would have praised that iota of abnegation on his part. By blindly casting aside the great opportunity, however, he made obvious the primacy of his personal ambitions and partially justified the revolutionary program of the Porfirists. Moreover, he rendered his entire career suspect: What part of it was motivated by patriotism and what part by personal greed? Was Juárez a statesman in the broader sense of the word or just the most successful politician who had ever entered upon the historical scene of independent Mexico? There was no great nationalistic goal to coincide with and to justify his personal ambition in 1871, as there had been throughout the previous phases of his career.

However that may be, Lerdo faded rapidly from prominence in the political arena after his defeat in the elections of 1871. Juárez left him unmolested in the office of president of the Supreme Court,[138] of which two years of the six-year term remained to be served. Still, none had ever struck *El Impasible* on his sensitive spot—his exclusive right to the presidency—and survived to be of any consequence in national politics thereafter. Nor was there reason to believe that Lerdo would be an exception to Juárez's long string of victims. It appeared that Sebastián would complete his term on the court, while his name diminished in the national picture. For all practical purposes, then, the year 1871 seemed to

---

[138]David Hannay concluded that Juárez did not remove Lerdo for fear of driving the Lerdists into open support of the Revolution of La Noria.— *Díaz*, 143. In the absence of positive evidence to the contrary that assumption appeared logical. Actually, the personal relationship between Juárez and Lerdo, after Lerdo resigned from the cabinet and ran in the election, remained another mystery.

mark the end of the unusual political rôle of one Don Sebastián Lerdo de Tejada.

It was close to midnight on July 18, 1872, when Ignacio Mejía arrived at the home of Sebastián Lerdo. Although the hour was a strange one for visiting, Sebastián was in the habit of retiring late, and besides the call was of an official nature. Initially, Mejía informed Lerdo that President Juárez was seriously ill; but when Sebastián, "deeply moved," prepared immediately to go to the Palace, the Minister of War told him the full story of Juárez's death which had occurred just a few minutes prior.[139]

Juárez's permanent departure provoked a brief interlude of silence and respect for a man whose resiliency and endurance had transformed him into a veritable institution, a man whose name was to be attached to an entire epoch of Mexican history. Almost a generation had grown up without knowing any other as chief executive. So, everyone closed his eyes to the bitterness springing from the recent electoral struggle to speak kindly words of the departed, for the dead can do no political harm.[140]

The most direct result of Juárez's death was to extract Lerdo de Tejada from the heap of political derelicts and to align him in the highest office of state, a post he undoubtedly had coveted for some time. None could contest the legality of his short interim presidency, which followed immediately, since he had been chosen *ex officio* vice-president (president of the Supreme Court), not in the disputed contest of 1871, but in that of December, 1867. Consequently, he rose to power by the operation of an event and was theoretically unencumbered by party obligations or by any question of legal right.[141]

With those favorable factors Lerdo could include his reputation for talent, his administrative experience, and the fact that he brought with him a breath of freshness into government. After all, the country had wearied and grown stale on Juárez, whose stolid, ponderous personality had lent a half-morbid air to politics. If the truth could be seen underneath the layers of eulogistic hypocrisy which surrounded the funeral services, the most widespread sentiment was probably relief at Juárez's passing; and that was a

---

[139]Octavo Paz (ed.), *Album a Juárez*, 32; Riva Palacio, *Historia de la Administración de Lerdo*, 42. The detailed story of Juárez's death may be found in Cosmes, *Historia de Méjico*, XXII, 304–350.

[140]Hannay, *Díaz*, 148.

[141]See *La Voz de México* (Mexico), July 20, 23, 1872; Emilio Ordaz, *La Cuestión Presidencial*, 13; Riva Palacio, *Historia de la Administración de Lerdo*, 62–63.

natural advantage to Lerdo. Expressing that feeling, a resident of Guadalajara wrote:

Congratulate Señor Lerdo for me on his advent to the presidency and tell him that I wish him success in all his determinations. His entrance to power has been generally well received here because it is believed that the revolution [of La Noria] will no longer have any plausible pretext. Society expects much of him, not in the political but in the administrative sense. All recognized that Señor Juárez was a notable man, but at the same time they agree that he did not make us happy. His long administration was a constant series of revolutions. He destroyed the old edifice; it concerns Señor Lerdo to build the new one. We all expect peace and good administration from his government.[142]

But *política* could not be relegated to a secondary rôle, and never in his career did Lerdo prove himself a more clever strategist than during the interim presidency. Of the three factions which had participated in the tumultous campaign of 1871, the Porfirists had fallen into complete disgrace by turning to revolution against "the tyrant Juárez." While the credit for breaking the back of the revolt belonged to Juárez and the army, Lerdo was to reap the harvest of glory, since scattered rebels were still at large attempting to recoup their losses and give new vigor to the uprising. Ireneo Paz, arch intriguer of the Porfirists, was with Díaz hiding out under the protection of the bandit cacique of Tepic, Manuel Lozada, at the time the news of Juárez's death reached him. He admitted that it was a disconcerting blow to the crestfallen "Cincinnatus"; for the *raison d'être* of revolt had vanished with the Indian President. Nevertheless, Díaz made his way to Chihuahua to join the rebel force of Donato Guerra—which had enjoyed some minor military successes in that frontier state—in order to have some bargaining power with the new President.[143]

In regard to the other two factions, the Lerdists were as jubilant and expectant of appointments as the Juarists were uneasy about losing the ones they possessed by virtue of their departed leader. Such was the triangular political heritage of Lerdo when he stepped into office in July, 1872.

No sooner had Juárez's funeral services ended than Lerdo acted decisively to insure his popularity and to restore complete peace, placing his main site on the consolidation of his position. First, he

---

[142]Vicente Ortigosa to Mariano Riva Palacio, July 26, 1872, Mariano Riva Palacio Papers, Folder 174, UT. For the factors in Lerdo's early popularity, see Riva Palacio, *Historia de la Administración de Lerdo*, 52–55; Bancroft, *Vida de Porfirio Díaz*, 488.

Among the letters of congratulation to Lerdo was one from U. S. Grant, president of the United States.—U. S. Grant to Sebastián Lerdo de Tejada ("Great and Good Friend"), October 7, 1872, *Sebastián Lerdo de Tejada, Su Expediente Personal*, Archivo de Relaciones Exteriores.

[143]Paz, *Algunas Campañas*, III, 319, 322–323, 334–335.

issued a manifesto to the nation, promising to govern during the interim period in accordance with the Constitution and the laws, especially those of the reform, and with absolute respect for all individual guarantees. There was also a most significant political comment:

In the provision for public duties and employments, I shall heed only honor, aptitude, and true merit. I shall take into consideration the present employees, in whom such qualities concur, not harboring . . . dispositions against anyone, whatever may have been his political antecedents. In the exercise of the supreme power I should not be an organ or a representative of a political circle, but the representative of the entire nation. I should not be the chief of a party, but an impartial and just executor of the law.[144]

Although some of the phrases had an old ring, they were injected with real meaning by Lerdo's good faith in complying with them and in promulgating, on the same day, the order of the permanent deputation of congress for a special presidential election to be held in October.[145]

Lerdo then turned to the Porfirist faction and offered a general amnesty for political crimes which, on acceptance, would restore the rebels to full rights of citizenship, including that of participation in the elections slated for October.[146] The only conditions were forfeiture of rank, titles, pensions, and other military awards. To the public the decree appeared to be a gesture of magnanimity on the part of the new President, but underneath it was a masterful political stroke, amounting to a momentary mortal wound to the Porfirist body politic. One by one Díaz's military henchmen crumbled away to accept the offer, while he held out in Chihuahua, prating about the harshness of the terms and demanding modifications of the amnesty, all of which Lerdo modestly refused.[147] The longer Díaz held out and the more manifestoes he issued, the more he showed in the colors of a disgraced military mountebank, lusting for power. Typical of the verbiage of Cincinnatus was his manifesto to the "regenerative army" of September 13, 1872. Despite the "present brilliant condition of our armies," he lied, ". . . we will renounce the power of our bayonets before the altar of peace," provided the government would substitute "frank conciliation" for the "humiliating pardon" it had presented; "but, if on the contrary, the government believes the ostentation of power and the luxury of blood which characterized the past administration [of Juárez] constitute the path which it should follow, we shall

---

[144]July 27, 1872, *Diario Oficial*, July 28, 1872.

[145]*Ibid.*, July 28, 1872; Dublán y Lozano, *Legislación Mexicana*, XII, 237.

[146]*Diario Oficial*, July 28, 1872; Dublán y Lozano, *Legislación Mexicana*, XII, 236–237.

[147]Riva Palacio, *Historia de la Administración de Lerdo*, 65; Cosmes, *Historia de Méjico*, XXII, 129; Paz, *Algunas Campañas*, III, 333.

pursue that which our duty points out to us."[148] "In these documents Don Porfirio only proved . . . that after all he too was in the year 1872 a Mexican politician. The one substantial word which stands in the midst of a flow of verbiage was the demand that the amnesty should be amended in his favour."[149]

At last Díaz submitted in what must have been as crushing a blow to his ego as it was to his national reputation. But his resignation to the "humiliating pardon" came not "as a sacrifice to his country's welfare,"[150] not to give Lerdo "a lesson in patriotism," and, above all, not as an act "inspired by the purest love for his country" which "placed him far above Lerdo in the concept of the people endowed with proper judgment."[151] The brutal truth was that Díaz's position was untenable: he either had to accept the amnesty on Lerdo's actually generous terms or face a quick annihilation, for General Rocha was poised with the flower of the federal army ready to strike the disorganized rebel band in case of further delay. Even the most flattering of Porfirist historians, after weaving all kinds of contradictory falsehoods about the incident, reluctantly blurted out the truth:

> If one examines the matter closely, it will be seen that nothing was more advantageous for Lerdo than that the revolutionists remain with arms in their hands. Before the nation they appeared as ambitious, common men who had rebelled only to satisfy personal aspirations, and, taking the question to the sphere of facts, the triumph of the government was certain.[152]

In the words of Ireneo Paz, who accompanied Díaz through that dark age of *Porfirismo*, the General's prestige and his following had suffered a blow from which recovery was to be counted in years: ". . . suddenly the Porfirist bonds dropped ninety-nine points."[153] Just before signing the amnesty and during a final conference with his few faithful followers, Díaz admitted that "we must consider ourselves also routed in politics. At least, we can do very little in the month which remains before the elections."[154]

Perhaps Lerdo should have been less complacent about his competition. Perhaps, too, it was Lerdo's amnesty "which saved Díaz" and gave him the opportunity for resurrection many years later;[155] yet Lerdo was justified in believing in 1872 that he had dealt the Porfirists a definitive blow: "The politicians of Mexico, on seeing

---

[148]Quoted by Cosmes, *Historia de Méjico*, XXII, 418–419.
[149]Hannay, *Díaz*, 148–149.
[150]Zayas Enríquez, *Díaz*, 112.
[151]Cosmes, *Historia de Méjico*, XXII, 426.
[152]*Ibid.*, XXII, 426–427.
[153]Paz, *Díaz*, I, 174.
[154]Díaz quoted by Paz, *ibid.*, I, 170. Paz was present at the conference. See also Quevedo y Zubieta, *El Caudillo* . . . , 221.
[155]Mateo Podan, *Porfirio Díaz Debe y Haber*, 275.

that the *Caudillo* of April 2 [Díaz] was returning conquered, considered him dead; but . . . the dead in politics are in the habit of reviving."[156]

While dispatching the revolutionary element, Lerdo had not neglected to handle his own and the old Juarist groups. The problem was altogether different, however, requiring the intrigue and diplomacy at which he excelled. In a word, Lerdo maintained the *status quo*, leaving the Juarists in office, exactly as he had promised in his manifesto of July, 1872, and keeping his own followers hopeful, if impatient. "It did not appear that Juárez had died," said Cosmes, "since the entire administration was found in the hands of his most devoted partisans."[157]

After the brutal treatment of the Lerdists, it might have seemed strange that Lerdo did not wreak wholesale vengeance on the old Juarists, ripping them from office all the way from the cabinet to the lower levels of the administration. On the other hand, there were several feasible explanations of his clever strategy:

(1) He himself was much at home with the old Juárez cabinet over which he had presided for so many years.

(2) His own faction was, after all, little more than a fragment of Juárez's party, and he was obviously attempting to fuse the two pieces into a unit behind his own leadership. Lerdo apparently had left behind him no irreparable breach with his old official friends when he stepped out of the cabinet. Ignacio Mariscal, a former Juárez minister and one of his last major appointees— minister of Mexico to the United States—explained Lerdo's providence to a New York reporter:

When Señor Lerdo de Tejada became politically estranged from President Juárez, I felt it my duty to my country to strongly side with the latter, and in consequence became politically opposed to Señor Lerdo; but this, I gladly say, did not at all interfere with our social and personal relations. We have remained good friends. When I was so unfortunate, a few months ago, as to lose my mother, Señor Tejada gave me several proofs of his friendship, which I shall never forget.[158]

(3) By keeping the old Juárez cabinet, Lerdo not only quashed any possible opposition—the Juarist party was then leaderless and all potential leaders were in the cabinet—but he dangled before them a hope of continued tenure.

(4) He left the appearance of respect for the method by which he had ascended to office, that is, by the operation of accident and law, not by election; hence, he was not free, technically, to make his own choices for administrative posts.

---

[156]Nemesio García Naranjo, *Porfirio Díaz*, 186.
[157]Cosmes, *Historia de Méjico*, XXII, 384.
[158]*The New York World*, August 1, 1872.

(5) He was attempting to disengage himself from all party connections and obligations: "In the exercise of the supreme power I should not be an organ or a representative of a political circle, but the representative of the entire nation. I should not be the chief of a party, but an impartial and just executor of the law."[159]

If the Lerdist faction, or "those who called themselves his friends," as Mejía had styled them, grumbled and nursed their aspirations, he owed them nothing for his position. He was chief executive through his presidency of the Supreme Court, for which he was indebted to Juárez. Juárez was dead, so God appeared to hold the reversionary interest. Moreover, the Lerdists would continue to support him as long as they hoped for office and as long as there was no one else to attract their backing.

Whatever may have been the motives in Lerdo's devious reasoning processes, the test of his delicate political balance was the election of October, 1872. The returns from all sections of the country were almost unanimous for the only candidate in the race. While the election of 1871 was unique for campaigning and vituperation, the presidential election of 1872 was unique for almost opposite reasons. There was but one candidate, for all practical purposes, and one party; and there was no question of legality, no claim of fraud or official interference, as Iglesias pointed out:

Without the necessity, then, of any pressure, and solely through the irresistible influence of a true popularity, he [Lerdo] could be said with justice to be elected by the people, a functionary surrounded in 1872 by the prestige of all parties.[160]

On November 16, congress verified Lerdo's election,[161] and on December 1, he took the oath of office as constitutional president. In his inaugural speech before congress, Lerdo informed the deputies:

Happily, the zeal of the government to realize the union of all the Mexicans under the aegis of the law has not been fruitless. I feel an inexpressible satisfaction in being able to say that the civil war has ended and that the confidence in which peace will be consolidated has been reborn. These inestimable benefits are not alone due to the straightforward policy of the government, but principally to the patriotism of the citizens, without whose efficacious coöperation all my efforts would have been sterile.

[159]Manifesto of July 27, 1872, Diario Oficial, July 28, 1872.

[160]Iglesias, La Cuestión Presidencial en 1876, 62. To the present writer's knowledge, only one historian has asserted that the presidential election of 1872 had even a tinge of official pressure. Wilfrid Hardy Callcott stated: "That the electoral procedure was questionable cannot be doubted. In fact, in large areas (some claim in almost half the nation) no polls were opened."— Callcott, Liberalism in Mexico 1857–1929, 89. Citing the work of Iglesias above, Callcott extracted a statement which his authority intended for the election of 1876, not that of 1872.

[161]Diario de los Debates, November 16, 1872, 6th Congress, III, 520. Lerdo had garnered 9,520 electoral votes; Díaz, 604.

And the President of congress replied:

Congress recognizes that your prestige has begun to revive the public credit, that the prudent methods of the inter.m administration have reëstablished harmony between the governors of the States and the federal government, and that they have served to maintain the good relations which link us with some foreign powers. . . .[162]

In truth, "the six months which the interregnum of Lerdo had lasted was the age of gold of his administration."[163]

But spontaneous praise came from a variety of sources. Porter C. Bliss, secretary of the American legation in Mexico, wrote:

The unanimity with which Mr. Lerdo has been chosen is without a precedent in Mexican annals, and the nation now entertains the brightest hopes of the preservation of peace and the consequent immense development of the resources of the country.[164]

Thus, at the outset of his constitutional presidency, Lerdo mounted the pinnacle of his popularity. The nation stood behind his leadership with a unity which it probably had never known, while peace reigned throughout the republic. The "Jesuit" rested on the peak of his career; "Cincinnatus" was deep in the black hollow of his own. It was a glory the like of which even Lerdo's old companion, the taciturn Juárez, had never experienced.

The surge of national confidence sought an outlet for expression, discovered in the formal opening of the Mexico-to-Vera Cruz railroad.[165] The inauguration of the fabulous engineering feat, symbolical of a Mexico awakening to the importance of economic questions, consisted of a nine-day journey which the constitutional President led to the port of Vera Cruz and back to the capital. All along the route, going and coming, the population turned out to give the new Chief Magistrate an acclaim "which was neither feigned nor purchased."[166] A lavish round of fêtes and entertainments of a great variety filled every hour of the excursion. At

---

[162]*Ibid.*, December 1, 1872, 6th Congress, III, 682, 683.

[163]Cosmes, *Historia de Méjico*, XXII, 399.

[164]Bliss to Hamilton Fish, December 3, 1872, *Papers Relating to the Foreign Relations of the United States . . . 1873*, I, 635 (hereafter cited *U.S. Foreign Relations*).

[165]The following sketch of the inaugural has been based upon the accounts of Cosmes, *Historia de Méjico*, XXII, 465–476; José F. Vérgez, *Recuerdos de Méjico*, 24–112; *El Domingo* (Mexico), January 12, 1873. Cosmes reprinted the telegraphic reports of Alfredo Bablot, a journalist who accompanied the presidential party during the excursion. Vérgez was a Cuban journalist, invited to participate in the celebrations. Both accounts contain many fascinating details which must of necessity be eliminated here.

[166]*El Domingo*, January 12, 1873.

Vera Cruz, Lerdo boarded a Spanish warship as guest of the Spanish Minister to Mexico, where host and guest outdid each other in attempting to smooth the scars of the past between their two nations. While aboard, Lerdo took advantage of the generosity of the Spanish captain to enjoy his first seagoing "voyage," a short cruise along the coast lasting the larger part of an afternoon. The return to the capital from Vera Cruz was a repeated run of the gauntlet of festivities, without a single incident to mar the brilliance of the tribute.

The pinnacle of popularity was lofty, and Lerdo had attained it quickly. How his pride must have swelled to unimaginable proportions—it was capable of great expansion—to see the throngs of admirers, to read the flattery spread thick across the pages of the press, and to sense the general feeling of optimism in a country finally at peace.

His decline was relatively steep, graded in point of time by a four-year administration. Unfortunately, the unity was neither natural nor built on permanent foundations. Never again would he experience the brilliance of that transitory moment, the climax of his entire career; but that he had achieved it at all, even for a moment, was a tribute to his unusual political skill.

Chapter IX

The Presidential Administration:
A Topical Survey

No Mexican president has been more maligned, misunderstood, and misrepresented than Sebastián Lerdo de Tejada. It is inconceivable that a man who gave Mexico her first large taste of peace, served on a platter of tolerance and liberality, should be disposed of historically with a few terse sentences to the effect that he was indolent, exclusive, tyrannical, and Jacobin. From whence came those distorted adjectives? They were mostly the outpourings of Lerdo's political enemies, who made—and were left in complete freedom to make—a blind and systematic attack against his administration. Unfortunately, later writers have accepted the products of an inimical press with a sublime naïvete. There can be no history, however, without an evaluation of materials; there is, consequently, no history of the administration of Sebastián Lerdo.

Before embarking on a survey of Lerdo's term in office, it is well to realize that he had certain fixed concepts on central government and definite ideas in regard to the proper sphere of administrative activities. Though well grounded in political theory, he was a product of practical experience and shaped his program within the mould of his personal conception of the national interests for the Mexico of his day.

What were the objectives, then, of the schoolmaster-lawyer President and where may they be discovered? Part of them were expressed and may be found in specific documents, like the Manifesto of July, 1872, the Magna Carta of Lerdismo;[1] others must be pieced together painstakingly from the policy statements concealed in the *Diario Oficial*, the executive organ, and, for all practical purposes, the voice of Lerdo himself, explaining his actions to as many of the politically conscious of the Mexican public as he could reach; while the remainder must be gleaned from his actions and his past career.

Transcending all other points in his platform and forming its indispensable base was the tenet of peace and order. Initiated under Juárez and arrogated by Porfirio Díaz, oddly enough, as the first sacrament of his régime, the dogma of peace was also Lerdo's religion of state. Without peace nothing was of value. On taking the oath of office in 1872, he informed the deputies that: "I feel an

---

[1] *Diario Oficial*, July 28, 1872.

inexpressible satisfaction in being able to say that the civil war
is ended and that the confidence in which peace will be consolidated
has revived." He concluded his speech by adding:

All my hopes and all my efforts will be directed so that, when I end the period
of my administration, I may contemplate the Republic enjoying, in full peace,
the benefits which liberty procures, which the law guarantees, which enlightenment develops, and which the patriotism of the people conserves.[2]

The idea of peace was one which Lerdo reiterated periodically:

. . . since the President of the republic took possession of power, his principal
anxiety was not only to reëstablish peace, but to avoid the causes or disturbances which would be able to upset it.
To this national aspiration, he directed all his efforts, and, up to the present,
he has had the satisfaction of seeing it realized. Señor Lerdo has believed
and still believes with profound conviction that the essential base for the unfolding of improvements and the aggrandizement of the republic consists
of peace. . . . Railroads, colonization, telegraphs, and all things which alter the
condition of a nation are not possible of realization if there is no peace and
stab.lity: a government can do nothing better than to guarantee this indispensable base of prosperity and well-being.[3]

That was "the point of departure for the policy of Señor Lerdo,"
and "he will not vacillate before any obstacle in order to conserve
inalterable the base of all public welfare: the public peace."[4]
    The indistinguishable twin of the "invariable proposition" of
peace was a bizarre precept to the Mexican—respect for the law.
Steeped in a legal milieu, firmly convinced that the law was an essential social discipline, aware that his people had considered it
too often as verbiage made for exceptions, he desired to uproot the
older practices and implant firmly the second principle of his program. It is necessary to recall the rectorship of San Ildefonso to
understand that Lerdo's devotion to the written rule was no innovation when he ascended to the presidency. While he sat as chief
magistrate, he would grant dispensations to no one and concessions
to no class, for no excuse existed for nonconformity to "the laws":
"One of the most characteristic qualities of Señor Lerdo is energy
. . . but energy in all which signifies compliance with the laws.
Thus, Señor Lerdo has not let himself be dominated by any party
or by any man. . . ."[5]
    It is worthy of note that peace and order of a type which Mexico
had not known since independence prevailed for three and one-
half years under Lerdo's guidance. Except for an uprising in
Tepic, which was checked quickly in 1873, the sporadic state quarrels, mostly of a local nature, and religious unrest in Michoacán in

[2]*Diario de los Debates*, December 1, 1872, 6th Congress, III, 682.
[3]*Diario Oficial*, August 10, 1874.
[4]*Ibid.*, August 10, 1874. See also *ibid.*, January 5, 1875.
[5]*Ibid.*, May 24, 1873.

1875, no insurrection marred Lerdo's term until the national revolution of Porfirio Díaz in early 1876.

Descending from the general sphere of principles, Lerdo specifically promised, on taking office, to keep vigil over the Laws of Reform and to insure the observance of the personal guarantees in the Constitution and in the ruling statutes: freedom of speech, of assembly, of conscience, and of the press. He complied with those promises in consonance with the spirit and letter of the law. Judging by his actions, he considered the fulfillment of that part of his program as the greatest glory of his administration: he considered the safeguarding of personal rights as the real thirst of the Mexican people, accepting at face value the seriousness of the ideology behind thirteen years of revolution. The suppression of those rights under Díaz's rule, after four years of practical use and abuse of them under Lerdo, seemed to prove that he was at fault in his evaluation. At any rate, tolerance and liberalism were two additional characteristics of his administration, the Chief Magistrate setting the example as a believer in "the rights of man."

Lerdo's relationship to factions of the liberal party, as pointed out previously, was the strangest ingredient of his program. Repeated monotonously throughout his term was his desire to raise the presidential chair above the grasp of parties. Not that he opposed factions or desired to crush any political circle, as he once made clear,[6] but he wished to be free from entangling obligations and to place his achievements in the light of national aspirations.

On economic questions, Lerdo approached pure *laissez faire* doctrine. While he felt that the government should provide peace, order, and a framework of legislation conducive to spirited economic activity, and, in addition, foster certain physical improvements such as the means of transportation and communication,[7] it should not be "a tutor or species of proxy" for private capital. According to all "modern economic principles," the purpose of governments did not penetrate the realm of the "contractor, the impresario, or the director of workshops," fields which lay within the zone of individual initiative.[8]

---

[6]". . . the President is very far from trying to destroy, or desiring that any circle or party be destroyed. . . ."—*Ibid.*, May 7, 1873.

[7]*Diario de los Debates*, December 1, 1872, 6th Congress, III, 682.

[8]*Diario Oficial*, March 11, September 9, 1875. It was probably Lerdo's *laissez faire* doctrine which provoked Vicente Riva Palacio, the first minister of Fomento in the Díaz revolutionary government and an outspoken opponent of Lerdo's economic policy, to write: ". . . the development of human activity should not be left solely to individuals, since governments . . . have the unavoidable obligation of not remaining stationary, especially when marked inclinations toward progress are noted in the nation."—Vicente Riva Palacio, *Memoria Presentado al Congreso de la Unión por el Secretario de Estado y del Despacho de Fomento* . . . (1877), 7–8.

Other goals which Lerdo envisioned but could not express openly because of Mexican ideological sensitivities may be implied from his previous career and the history of his presidency. He promoted strong central government, dominated by a powerful, personalized executive and operated by a civilian bureaucracy, which would relegate the army to a subordinate rôle.[9] Liberal to a point of exaggeration, Lerdo was also centralistic to the core, attempting to spread the tentacles of the national government underneath the attachment to localism; but he always worked cleverly under a cloak of the legal forms, trying to conceal the extension behind a camouflage of respect for state sovereignty. Despite the bitter opposition of the press, the hostile minority in congress, and the political pretensions of the Supreme Court, he managed to carry the presidency to its furthest point of advance under the Constitution of 1857, inadvertently preparing the way for the autocracy of Díaz and at the same time disproving the axiom that a centralist inevitably must be conservative.

To trace the roots of Lerdo's concepts of government lies more within the field of psychology than history; yet it is necessary to recall his background as a general explanation. Central government in Mexico was more the personality of the man at the helm than relatively fixed institutions anchored in the traditions of the people. Lerdo's program—stable, effective national government, personal domination by the executive, peace, order, respect for the letter of the law, and emphasis upon personal rights—was, after all, a logical product of his education and career. Moulded in the cosmopolitan environment of the metropolis, he seemed to have an undivided attachment for the great political, social, and economic center of the nation—a truly national outlook on things. Unlike many Mexican statesmen who began their careers in state politics, Lerdo always had been associated with the national government. Consequently, his sentiments were national, leaving little slack for sympathy with localist views.

One of the mysteries of Lerdo's administration was his attitude toward political factions. As frequently stated, he desired to rise above factionalism, to disassociate the presidency from any political

---

[9]Lerdo was credited with being antimilitaristic and even of having a healthy repugnance for "the Generals." See José C. Valadés, *El Porfirismo, Historia de un Régimen: El Nacimiento*, 200; Zayas Enríquez, *Porfirio Díaz*, 110–111.

It was rumored that Juárez, Lerdo, and Iglesias, the triumvirate of the intervention, had agreed among themselves that the presidency should not fall into the "hands of a soldier."—Zayas Enríquez, *Juárez*, 232. Once, after witnessing a military parade with Juárez, Lerdo, so it was told, turned on his heels, remarking disdainfully: "I do not like soldiers."—Quevedo y Zubieta, *El Caudillo* . . . , 173.

ties. The aim was not only convenient but also practicable, working well for a period of several years; however, Lerdo's failure to modify his attitude, as circumstances required, was a cause of serious discontent, eventually alienated a large segment of his support, and must be counted among the major causes of his downfall in 1876.

Lerdo appeared to envision himself as a species of one-man civil service bureau, free to make his appointments from among the so-called liberals according to his personal judgment or fancy: "In the filling of public offices and employments, I shall heed only honor, aptitude, and true merit," he announced in his Manifesto of July, 1872, and, he continued:

I shall take into consideration the present employees [*i.e.*, the old Juarists] in whom such qualities concur, not harboring . . . dispositions against anyone, whatever may have been his political antecedents. In the exercise of the supreme power I should not be an organ or representative of a political circle, but the representative of the entire nation.[10]

Since there had been so many manifestoes cluttering the pages of Mexican history, most of which were taken deservedly with the proverbial grain of salt, little weight appeared to have been attached to the one which Lerdo had issued on assuming the presidency ad interim. With the passage of time, however, as the weeks turned into months and the old Juarist officials retained their posts, the grumblings of party became more severe and the stark seriousness of Lerdo's pronouncement more apparent. The President had not converted the public offices into a fleshpot of spoils, bragged the *Diario Oficial*, and with a few exceptions, all the old Juarists had remained, from "the ministers to the porters. . . ."[11] "No change has yet occurred in the cabinet of President Lerdo," observed United States Minister Thomas H. Nelson in early 1873. "The old ministers of President Juárez remain undisturbed, which causes much complaint and criticism among the immediate friends and partisans of the President."[12]

At the time of Juárez's death, the cabinet was composed of José María Lafragua (Foreign Relations), Ignacio Mejía (War and Marine), Blas Balcárcel (Fomento), and Francisco Mejía (Finance). Since appointments were pending for the two vacant positions, the incumbent undersecretaries, José Díaz Covarrubias (Justice and Public Instruction) and Cayetano Gómez Pérez (Government) remained encharged with those ministries. Adding insult to injury, Lerdo left the undersecretaries untouched and re-

---

[10]*Diario Oficial*, July 28, 1872.
[11]*Ibid.*, March 13, 1873.
[12]Nelson to Fish, March, 1, 1873, *U. S. Foreign Relations, 1873*, I, 656. See also Riva Palacio, *Historia de la Administración de Lerdo*, 98–101.

fused either to appoint them full ministers or to fill the vacancies.[13] Thus, during a large part of Lerdo's presidency, two of the choice political fruits wasted in the hands of men who did not possess the prestige of cabinet rank. Furthermore, after the death of Lafragua in late 1875,[14] the department of Foreign Relations remained in the care of an undersecretary, Juan de Dios Arías.[15]

Excepting Ignacio Mejía, the ministers were old civilian bureaucrats, experienced in the routine of administration, whom Lerdo had known and associated with for many years; and only Mejía, who in truth was more a man of "bureaucratic sagacity" than a typical military figure,[16] was of any real significance, because of his prestige among the ranking army officers and because of his presidential ambitions which blossomed at an inopportune moment in 1876. Certainly, Lerdo could have discharged those men without personal embarrassment when he acceded to office in 1872, for at the time they had presented a collective resignation. In his enigmatic way, Lerdo had refused it politely, assuring them of their security in office for the time being, since he wanted "to study things" before making any abortive changes.[17]

Perhaps it would be of historical interest, but not importance, to describe the individual ministers. Of course, the cabinet, like Lerdo, faced all kinds of ugly and unjustified attacks from the press, attacks which were ridiculous, exaggerated, and sometimes bordering on the obscene;[18] but no longer was there any talk of a puppet president, a prime minister, or a chief of the cabinet. Lerdo retained the old ministers as administrators in the strict sense of the term, not as intimate counselors whose opinions would have weight on the ultimate formation of his policies. In fact, he seemed to make a special point of explaining that none shared "the secrets" of Señor Lerdo, including the members of the cabinet.[19] When *El Siglo* began to harp upon Ignacio Mejía's "superior influence" in

---

[13]Lerdo replied to the press attack about the matter of the undersecretaries with a characteristic aloofness: The President would appoint full ministers "when he believes it convenient. . . ."—*Diario Oficial*, January 9, 1874.

[14]For Lafragua's death, see *ibid.*, November 15, 17, 18, 1875.

[15]Cosmes described the ministers with a typical invective: Lafragua was "a true exhumation"; Francisco Mejía "was positively a nullity," etc.—*Historia de Méjico*, XXII, 292–295. See also the comment of Ramón Prida, *De la Dictadura a la Anarquía* . . . , I, 46.

[16]Valadés, *El Porfirismo, Nacimiento*, 11.

[17]*Diario Oficial*, August 2, 1872; *La Voz de México*, July 21, 1872.

[18]Virtually any issue of *El Padre Cobos* or *El Ahuizote*, both illustrated papers and the most notorious representatives of the opposition press, would confirm the point.

[19]*Diario Oficial*, June 17, 1873. The satirical press frequently portrayed the ministers as echoing Lerdo's remarks in chorus, illustrative of their blind obedience to the President. See, for example, *El Ahuizote*, April 10, 1874.

the department of War, the *Diario Oficial* retaliated bluntly that those who made such foolish declarations "either do not know the elevated and energetic character of Señor Lerdo or feign not to recognize it, in order to presume that he is a tool or instrument of anybody. . . ." Then the government organ went on to elaborate:

When Señor Lerdo desires, or when it appears convenient to him, he can change his cabinet and without doubt he will do so freely and spontaneously, as he performs all his acts; but not bowing to officious indications or being inspired by such passionate as unfounded appreciations which possess a great deal of the personal.[20]

The major controversy of a purely political nature during Lerdo's administration was defined early in the cabinet and its composition. Since the ministerial posts constituted the choice plums of office, carrying with them prestige, patronage, and close association with the President, there were many who desired to partake but few plums were available for distribution. The Lerdists, stunned by their leader's failure to call them to his side in the offices of the executive branch, long refused to believe that Lerdo's decision was other than transitory. Finally, an interesting event came to pass in October, 1873, which set the stage for sweeping away all illusions on a point of policy that Lerdo seemed to feel had been made explicit in his Manifesto of July, 1872.[21]

The incident was a banquet given by Lerdo to entertain a large group of friends, mostly deputies in congress, at the famous restaurant of the day, the Tívoli de San Cosme.[22] Among those present were the old party leaders who had styled themselves Lerdists during the presidential campaign of 1871—the men who had worked feverishly for Lerdo's election. It will be remembered that their ravenous political appetites had gone unsated, though Lerdo had been in the presidential chair for more than fifteen months.

As was customary at that period, a round of toasts made up the program. Lerdo, as host, initiated the speaking; Castilla y Portugal, one of Lerdo's old classmates, followed soon afterward, dwelling upon the student days at San Ildefonso and Lerdo's arduous application to studies; Juan José Baz eventually took his turn, praising the Chief Magistrate for amalgamating the factions of the liberal

---

[20]*Diario Oficial*, June 15, 1873.

[21]See *ibid.*, September 12, November 18, 1873; April 3, 1874.

"Señor Lerdo promised to be the chief of the nation and not of a determined political circle. He has complied with that promise.

"Little of politics and much administration [*poca política y mucha administración*] requested the entire nation, and, so, why do the opposition papers now desire that we have much of politics?"—*Ibid.*, March 8, 1873.

[22]The following account, where not otherwise cited, is based on an article of Alfredo Bablot, a journalist present at the gathering. It was reprinted in *Diario Oficial*, October 29, 1873.

party in congress. The celebration seemed to be progressing well in the elegant atmosphere of the Tívoli, when Romero Rubio rose to speak. It had fallen his lot to make the presentation of a beautiful watch "brought especially from London" by the Lerdists as a gift for the occasion. There were no stenographers present, making verbatim records of the statements, but during his peroration, Rubio made certain implications about the cabinet and "indirectly echoed the dominant desires in all society today about a greater activity in the administration, which may remove the public power from the morass into which it has submerged." Understanding perfectly the intent of the allusion, Lerdo "believed it his duty to explain his policy."[23]

According to Alfredo Bablot, a journalist at the gathering, "it can be said without fear of equivocation that few times has the illustrious Chief of State, the great political orator, been more eloquent, more able, more expansive, and more resolved in his manifestations." Bablot's impression was not only an insight into Lerdo's polish with the spoken word, but, far more important, the President's own recapitulation of his program:

. . . we had the pleasure of studying and admiring the most beautiful and superb discourse a democratic governor could pronounce. A man of deeds, Señor Lerdo does not digress on nebulous theories; his word goes straight to the point, and his expressions have the immortal stamp of an ancient apothegm. He analyzes his policy, examines national opinion, weighs and considers it, and places himself at the head of the modern advance.

Standing before that large, distinguished audience, no doubt in an ominous atmosphere, since many political hopes were pinned upon the words to come, Lerdo explained once and for all just what he expected to accomplish as chief magistrate. He said that "his administrative creed was condensed in his program of July [i.e., the Manifesto of July, 1872], and that it was very easy to understand those points. . . ." In complying with the Constitution and the Reforms, "the norm of his conduct was this: 'Not one step backward.' (At this point a frantic round of applause responded to his words.)" Then, he continued, "he was not a man of party and he believed that in his high position, emanating from the will of the people, he should heed the people without lending himself to a predilection for this or that circle."

Lerdo had said a great deal, but he had not finished. On the matter of state sovereignty, he had no intent to diminish it "in the least," but

neither would he permit any undue violation of the rights and prerogatives of the government of the Union to upset the legal harmony of the republic. Finally, [he said] that the law and only the law would reign in Mexico

[23]The quoted statements are from *El Siglo*, October 27, 1873.

during his administration and that the legitimate interests of the people would have in him the most zealous guardian, the firmest supporter.

It is difficult to recapture the tenseness of those few moments at the most significant party gathering of Lerdo's administration, or to comprehend the magnetism of Lerdo's trenchant remarks. Bablot admitted frankly: "Our words are pallid for reproducing that magnificent, democratic eloquence which Señor Lerdo made us consider as a man of state who has few rivals in the world."

But all were not pleased as they filed from the Tívoli that October night. Many carried in their chests the gall of resentment and disappointment. The editorial staff of *El Siglo*, a substantial part of Lerdo's support in 1871, gave voice to its wounded pride the following day:

> Since Señor Lerdo rose to power, he has made a constant boast that he was not a man of party. . . . We refuse to associate ourselves with a policy in which there are only interests, in which there are no sentiments, and which gives humiliation to political friends for recompense.

Lerdo's friends had interpreted his speech as "an offense and they esteemed that their own dignity was separating them from the President, when, for him, friends and enemies are equal."[24]

Although the staff of *El Siglo* veered sharply into the hostile camp of the opposition, Lerdo kept most of his old supporters throughout his term of office, especially Romero Rubio and Ramón Guzmán, whom he used effectively as the manipulators of a rubber stamp congress. In addition, he placed Joaquín Othón Pérez in the key post of governor of the Federal District, while General Mariano Escobedo continued either as governor of San Luis Potosí or commander of one of the army divisions. Those four men and two or three other obscure persons formed what Ireneo Paz styled the "kitchen cabinet";[25] but while Lerdo was on seemingly intimate terms with many political figures, it was probable that the *Diario Oficial* was correct in stating that none shared "the secrets" of the Chief Magistrate.

Against a pulverizing attack from an ever-enlarging circle of hostile papers, Lerdo clung tenaciously to the old Juárez cabinet—defunct men, docile tools, mummies, political exhumations, as they were styled variously[26]—until the midnight hour of his tenure. Not until August, 1876, did he sweep them from office to be replaced by

---

[24]*Ibid.*, October 27, 1873.

[25]See Paz, *Díaz*, I, 181–187.

[26]For example, Blas Balcárcel, the minister of Fomento, was invariably depicted as a simpleton, in cartoons especially. "All the world complains," smiled Don Sebastián, in another of the satirical dialogues of *El Padre Cobos*, that he had retained "a minister so simple; but I shall tell you frankly that that is the way I want it."—*El Padre Cobos*, October 26, 1873.

more intimate associates, a few weeks prior to the congressional verification of his reëlection in that year.[27] Exactly why he took his adamant stance on the question was a secret he apparently carried to the grave. Iglesias, president of the Supreme Court during Lerdo's administration, merely shook his head and answered that it was a mystery which was "incomprehensible to all";[28] the historian Bancroft wisely glided over the enigma by stating that Lerdo's measures "were ofttimes dark";[29] while the prejudiced contemporary revolutionist, Vicente Riva Palacio, saw in the "absurd partnership" of Lerdo and the old ministry of Juárez nothing more than a "caprice" which demonstrated the President's penchant for intrigue.[30] One of the staunchest of Lerdo's followers, Dr. Hilarión Frías y Soto, explained the matter on the basis of Lerdo's unbounded pride. According to the story he told, presumably after Lerdo's death,[31] both Ramón Guzmán and Romero Rubio approached the President ad interim the day after Juárez's death, showing "visible signs of jubilation," having assumed that the cabinet would be shuffled immediately with the portfolios falling in the clutch of the principal Lerdists. Incensed by their over-zealousness for office and contemptuous of their lack of decorum, Lerdo was determined to prove to the world that none could influence his decisions, even those close friends. When Frías y Soto, Guzmán, and Rubio left Lerdo's home that day, after a perceptibly icy reception, Dr. Frías knew that "the inconvenient step of my friends" would cost them the cherished cabinet posts;[32] and his prognostication proved accurate for four years.

Obviously, if intimate associates could not fathom Lerdo's motive, a definitive solution is impossible. The logical reasons for Lerdo's refusal to change the ministry during the period of the interim presidency have been enumerated previously, reasons which would

---

[27]García Granados, *Historia de México*, I, 142–143; Richardson to Fish, September 7, 1876, *U. S. Foreign Relations, 1876*, 411–412.

Emilio Velasco, a former Lerdist, explained Lerdo's motive for the unexpected cabinet shakeup with the rancor peculiar to the disappointed place seeker: "Self-love was what moved Lerdo to slight his friends; self-love is what moves him to call them to his side. Self-love counseled him to declare himself chief of the nation and not the chief of a party; self-love counsels him today to place himself at the head of a party which has just falsified the public suffrage. Previously, his self-love repugned the idea of appearing dominated . . . ."—*El Siglo*, September 2, 1876.

[28]Iglesias, *La Cuestión Presidencial en 1876*, 27.

[29]Bancroft, *History of Mexico*, VI, 392.

[30]Riva Palacio, *Historia de la Administración de Lerdo*, 160.

[31]Cosmes, *Historia de Méjico*, XXII, 356–360. Cosmes claimed that he heard the story directly from Frías y Soto. Ramón Prida, who made the same assertion, related a similar tale, but his version differed somewhat in details from that of Cosmes.—Prida, *De la Dictadura a la Anarquía*, I, 40.

[32]Cosmes, *Historia de Méjico*, XXII, 360.

remain valid even after his election: the desire to retain the backing of the Juarists; his old friendship with the incumbents in the
ministerial posts; and his faith in the efficacy of dangling the hope
of office before the so-called Lerdists. Nor can Frías y Soto's explanation be discounted, for Lerdo was, above all else, proud, aloof,
and subtle and had the desire to dominate those around him. On
the other hand, there were other equally plausible and perhaps
more substantial explanations for his political conduct.

Lerdo disliked the idea of cabinet government and the constant
turnover in the ministry, which he had expressed in the circular
of August 14, 1867, accompanying the *convocatoria* of that year.[33]
Since he had dominated the Juárez ministers as chief of Cabinet,
none could accuse him of being a puppet to any one of them, as had
been the frequent charge against Juárez during his political association with Lerdo. Furthermore, he had combined the position
of president with his old post of prime minister, fusing the two
offices; at least, so it appeared as long as the old secretaries of
State were retained. That was exactly what happened. If the
cabinet was attacked brutally, there was at least no more jargon
about a puppet president and a chief of Cabinet. Quite to the contrary: the old Juarist ministers were branded invariably as docile
instruments of Lerdo's will. Perhaps, then, those were the occult
purposes which he had in mind—to subordinate and stabilize the
ministry and to lift the presidency into the undisputed possession
of all ultimate executive responsibility.

Yet it also should be remembered that there were but six cabinet
posts available for distribution, while Lerdo had far more than
six supporters who would have considered themselves eligible.
Would the discontent of those persons slighted have vanished had
Lerdo followed any other course than he did, that is, of leaving all
the Lerdists out of office instead of all but six? Probably not; nor
would a change have brought the placid political mirage which the
opposition always implied. Past experience had shown Lerdo that
the shuffling of the ministry was far from a panacea. It was a self-
perpetuating vice, each modification carrying the demand for
another in turn. The party history of the entire period was, then,
primarily composed of the desultory complaints of the disappointed
spoilsmen against a man who "insisted on a policy *sui generis*, entirely of his invention, and who governed without parties, without
a program, and without the law."[34] Thus, one of the truly significant constitutional changes which Lerdo effected, his unrecorded,
mortal wound to the cabinet idea of government under the Con-

[33]"The harm which the prolonged tenure of bad ministers may cause can
be very serious, but also the incessant change of ministers is sufficiently serious."—Dublán y Lozano, *Legislación Mexicana*, X, 53.
[34]*El Monitor*, February 20, 1877.

stitution of 1857, was attained at the cost of friendship and popularity. The disappointment of the place seekers in time became a dangerous structural defect in his own support, eventually breaking open into a wide fissure through which the Porfirist rebels crawled in 1876 to establish the new order of Díaz.

Lerdo was a firm believer in what commonly has been styled centralism, but, better translated, signified a stable, effective central government capable of extending its authority to the most remote, frontier state. Because of Lerdo's conviction in the supremacy of federal over local interests whenever a clash occurred, his administration was largely a study of the subtle and clandestine methods which he adopted to promote centralization; and, in turn, that necessitated an understanding of the relationship of the national executive to the state governments and of the executive to the other two branches at the center, the legislative and the judiciary. It should be noted that the two topics are separated only for convenience, since federal and state government were in practice as hopelessly confused as were political factions with governmental machinery.

The problem is complex for two reasons: first, the Constitution of 1857, with its advanced concepts of separation of powers, universal manhood suffrage, individual guarantees, and the delicate division of authority on federal lines, was as distant from actual practice as infinity is long and served only to confuse the issues; and second, the terms in which men voiced their theories or viewpoints on government, in congress and in the press, were ridiculously remote from the existing social, economic, and political conditions then prevailing in Mexico. To place a Mexican presidential administration "on the ground" requires, therefore, a keen eye to perceive the impalpable beneath a maze of official documents and vitriolic press reports, replete with verbiage which was highly misleading and which only the naïve would accept at face value. Suffice it to say that under Lerdo, as under Juárez before and Díaz after him, there was no "universal manhood suffrage"; there were no "free elections"; and there were no parties in any true sense of the word. Those were nebulous goals for the distant future, but impossibilities when only the "scarcest number" of the population was sufficiently educated to take an interest in politics.[35]

Lerdo's relations with the states, on which rested the foundations of stable government, must be viewed not alone from the standpoint of the governors with whom he was friendly but also from the view of those with whom he apparently fell at odds.[36] Despite the

---

[35]Rabasa, *La Organización Política de México*, 171; García Granados, *Por Qué y Como Cayó Porfirio Díaz*, 5–7.

[36]See Rabasa, *La Organización Política de México*, 153.

undoubtedly justified claims of a wailing opposition—wailing about Lerdo's violation of state sovereignty[37]—he always worked within the forms of the law, shedding responsibility upon congress for ordering the federal troops to intervene in a local dispute. Actually, Lerdo was not precipitate in dealing with inflammatory state conflicts,[38] and furthermore, he made ample use of the government press, the *Diario Oficial*, to fabricate beautiful legends about his respect for local prerogatives: "The President has demonstrated in a manner translated into deeds that all his ambition is that the states may be organized and advance tranquilly in the midst of peace and order."[39] Or, in reply to a complaint against the governor of Sinaloa, Lerdo's indignant rebuttal was:

Sinaloa, like all the states of the federation, is governed by means of its own laws and authorities. Señor Lerdo, as president of the republic, *can not* and *should* not inquire into how the people of Sinaloa are governed in their interior régime. . . . Does the [complainant] desire to make the President responsible for the internal acts of the Governor of Sinaloa? This would be a constitutional absurdity.[40]

Again, when Lerdo was accused of failing to prevent General Francisco Leyva, one of his favorites, from perpetuating himself in the governorship of the state of Morelos, the Chief Executive answered suavely that he had no authority over the internal affairs of states, either on electoral methods or otherwise. The states must seek redress through the federal courts or their own legislatures.[41] When accused of influencing the elections of Zacatecas, Lerdo denied the accusation, giving an explanation which should have salved the most ardent localist: "The people of Zacatecas are entirely free to elect the agents who are most suitable to them."[42]

Yet the satisfying answers of the *Diario Oficial* could not be trusted. A citizen of the same state of Zacatecas wrote that if it were not for Lerdo's machinations in the constituency, aimed toward dictating the elections, the "really popular" candidate would win easily; but "according to all appearances and all rumors, the

---

[37]The *Diario Oficial* fought back against the press attack, against "that zeal [sarcasm] which dominates the Executive of centralizing the entire system, which in this epoch is called 'the Policy of Señor Lerdo.' "—*Diario Oficial*, January 17, 1874.

[38]See an editorial of José María Vigil, praising Lerdo for his attitude on the Coahuila question of 1873.—*El Siglo*, September 23, 1873. The government did its best to publicize executive impartiality in regard to state quarrels. See, for example, *Diario Oficial*, November 16, 1873.

[39]*Diario Oficial*, January 22, 1874.

[40]*Ibid.*, March 21, 1874.

[41]*Ibid.*, June 25, 1873.

[42]*Ibid.*, July 15, 1874. The above are scattered but representative examples of the executive's consistent lip service to federalism.

center is undertaking to impose a governor on the state." "What reason is there for imposing a governor on the state who is not the one whom the people request? Following that frequently repeated phrase—*Reason of State*—we now say: Reason of the presidency."[43] And one of the prominent local leaders of Zacatecas turned against Lerdo in the revolution of 1876, "because my State has found itself under an arbitrary order created by Lerdo . . . represented by a crowd of common speculators who thrive by the shelter of a government weak and consequently inept."[44] Obviously, much occurred behind the scenes which never found its way into official documents.

Two factors, hazardous to trace and evaluate, were especially important in the state-federal harmony: friendship between the president of the republic and the governors of the states and geography. Lerdo, again like Juárez before and Díaz after him, had to depend on "a species of feudalism," as García Granados styled it,[45] in which there was a mutually beneficial contract between himself and the local lords. The President (the liege lord) extracted coöperation from the governors for carrying out his mandates, and he also appeared to dictate the deputies whom the governors "elected" to the national congress (suit to court), deputies who would acquiesce in his program. In return, the governors received freedom within their own fiefs and federal military aid (or nonintervention) when their local enemies threatened. Friendship went far toward insuring the smooth operation of the system, but in the final analysis the practical expedient of the federal army was at the President's disposal to reinforce the *amigo* of government.[46] If a governor became recalcitrant toward the central régime, geography played a major part by delaying the movement of federal troops into the disaffected area; and time was often of the essence in limiting the repercussions of a local revolution.

Lerdo was successful in aligning the governors of the powerful central belt of states in support of his administration, governors who, for the most part, held office throughout his term as presi-

---

[43]S. Carrillo to Vicente Riva Palacio, May 27, 1874, Vicente Riva Palacio Papers, Folder 184, UT.

[44]T[rinidad] G[arcía] de la Cadena to José María Iglesias, November 21, 1876, Archivo de Fernando Iglesias Calderón, Legajo 14, A.G.N.

[45]García Granados, *La Constitución de 1857*, 123.

[46]The Mexican concept of federalism did appear to have many of the elements of feudalism masquerading under the cloak of republican ideology. It should be remembered that the country was preponderantly agrarian, local chieftains were potent quantities, and the personal element in government was the most outstanding characteristic. But a noticeable institutional change was taking place after 1867, being effected by the growing strength and dependability of the federal army, the "retainers" of the president. That force was working a shift in the balance of power between the states and the national government.

dent: Francisco Leyva of Morelos; Rafael Carrillo of Michoacán; Alberto García of Mexico; Ignacio Romero Vargas of Puebla; Florencio Antillón of Guanajuato; Francisco Landero y Cos of Vera Cruz; Manuel Hernández Marín of Durango; Mariano Escobedo of San Luis Potosí; and even Diego Álvarez of Guerrero. It must be admitted that the tacit understandings which Lerdo had with those men in regard to electoral control and determining the lists of deputies to be selected "by the states" for the national congress naturally could not be broadcast in a country which gave an eloquent voice to democracy; hence the real operation of the mechanism cannot be traced in public documents. But the mere existence of those governors in office and the existence of a majority in congress consistently servile to Lerdo's dictates and composed of his personal friends were two facts which left the road open to only one logical conclusion—that such collusion did exist. Seldom can the investigator uncover positive evidence, however, other than the generalized complaints of the opposition. When Lerdo once made an elaborate tour from Mexico City to the caves of Cacahuamilpa in northern Guerrero,[47] his party "embraced" eight governors from the important central states. United States Minister John W. Foster, who attended the outing, was impressed by the fact. "It is a notable indication of the peace of the central States of the country, that the President and eight governors could absent themselves from their capitals without any apparent inconvenience to the public service."[48] Perhaps Foster should have noted that peace was assured as long as Lerdo was successful in cultivating the *amigo* of government.

Although Lerdo maintained firm control over the powerful central states, that was not always the case on the periphery. Among the outstanding conflicts which arose in local areas, and usually due to purely local causes,[49] were those in the states of Coahuila, Yucatán, Oaxaca, and Jalisco, all of which were distant from the center geographically.[50] Excepting Jalisco, each of those cases de-

---

[47]See *Diario Oficial*, February 14–17, 21, 22, 1874; Riva Palacio, *Historia de la Administración de Lerdo*, 404–405; *El Padre Cobos*, February 22, 1874 (cartoon).

The journey, of a purely "private" nature, offered Lerdo's enemies an excellent motif for protesting against the extravagance of the Executive. Since it was such a flimsy cause of complaint, reasoned the *Diario Oficial*, "no better eulogy could be made to the administration of Señor Lerdo. . . ."—*Diario Oficial*, February 27, 1874.

[48]Foster to Fish, February 28, 1874, *U. S. Foreign Relations, 1874*, 732.

[49]Herbert Ingram Priestley, *The Mexican Nation, A History*, 372; Bancroft, *History of Mexico*, VI, 408.

[50]Bravo Ugarte made a convenient list of the local disputes during Lerdo's administration, alleging that "*the anarchy in the states* was provoked almost always by the centralizing action . . . of the Executive of the Union."—*Historia de México*, III, 360.

veloped around a dispute between the state executive and legislative powers over the control of governmental machinery, generally arising on the pretext of a disputed election. The course of events would soon lead to open warfare between the disputing parties and the consequent disappearance of local order. Lerdo usually awaited an opportune moment, until one or both factions had appealed for federal aid,[51] and obtained a legal authorization from congress to intervene with federal troops. Then he appointed an arbiter of his own designation to restore "the constitutional order" in the disaffected area. It may be assumed with certainty—but not easily proved—that the new state régime thereby erected was one in complete consonance with the President. While the general pattern as outlined above was monotonous and always accompanied by a dreary labyrinth of garbled facts and opinions, each case varied considerably in detail and could be elaborated at length. Occasionally, the original disputants in the states would bifurcate or trifurcate, adding to the confusion. Yucatán at one time had three governors and three legislatures, all claiming legitimacy.[52]

However well Lerdo concealed his intervention with legal forms, however justified he was in stopping the degenerate local squabbles, the opposition invariably appealed to the ancient argument of state sovereignty.[53] Lerdo was a despot, a dictator, a destroyer of precious local liberties. When the government asked congress to authorize the appointment of a "provisional governor" for Yucatán, one hostile deputy, in a speech florid with frequent allusions to "the examples of usurpation of the Citizen President," rang the

Riva Palacio discussed the state questions at some length in his *Historia de la Administración de Lerdo*, always with the predetermined purpose of attacking Lerdo. Characteristic of the haphazard organization of the work, the references are scattered, but, for a sampling, see pp. 465–472.

[51]The Coahuila dispute was a good example of Lerdo's caution on local problems and his feigned devotion to federalism. During the early stages of the question, he informed congress that he trusted the local authorities would be able to resolve their own problems peacefully: "Although . . . federal aid was requested [by the Coahuila factions], the Executive has felt that it should abstain from imparting it . . . considering its abstention in highest conformity to our federal system, even considering the affair as a question of the internal constitutional law of the state, which, it is to be desired, may have a prompt and peaceful solution solely through its own power."—*Diario de los Debates*, September 16, 1873, 7th Congress, I, 113.

[52]Cosmes, *Historia de Méjico*, XXII, 592; Riva Palacio, *Historia de la Administración de Lerdo*, 404; Bravo Ugarte, *Historia de México*, III, 360. The method of the "double legislature" was invoked by the Lerdist party in Jalisco during the elections of December, 1875, to wrest control of the state government from the iron grip of Lerdo's enemies, led by Ignacio Vallarta.— Luis Pérez Verdía, *Historia Particular del Estado de Jalisco . . .* , III, 435.

[53]One of the principal themes of the opposition paper *El Padre Cobos* was Lerdo's support of servile state governors and his interference in states where the local régime was hostile to the central government.

changes on the ever-popular appeal to the spirit of localism: "Perhaps that fatal policy of provisional governors will triumph," he admonished, and, if so, it would be necessary for the deputies to return to their constituencies and announce that:

Now you are not free; write the epitaph of the sovereignty of your States on the frontispiece of your [state] palaces; and there where it says: "Palace of the Government of the Free and Sovereign State of ————" write some other words which will contradict those. . . .[54]

Among the cases of federal intervention in local affairs, that of Jalisco differed somewhat, since the governor, Ignacio Vallarta, was known to have been hostile to Lerdo.[55] Superficially, accord prevailed between the two men until Vallarta's gubernatorial term ended in February, 1875, at which time Lerdo was determined to install his own partisan in the state house at Guadalajara. Since Vallarta had a firm grasp on the state electoral machinery, the President was forced to send General José Ceballos into the area to accomplish the purpose. As a result, the spirit of the Jaliscienses, especially Vallarta's following, was roused—localism appeared to be a powerful force in the area—and the elections went to the enemies of Lerdo.[56] The allegedly harsh military rule which followed gave an inexhaustible supply of fuel to the opposition and added one more briar to Lerdo's crown of thorns as a tyrant.[57] In exoneration of state pride, some industrious native son laboriously collected enough documents to fill two volumes, proving "the ominous tyranny of Señor Lerdo and his proconsul, Señor Ceballos," whose "most horrible dictatorship" broke "our Magna Carta into a thousand fragments."[58]

Before completely accepting one side of the avalanche of localist sentiment, one should remember that Vallarta's methods for gaining and retaining power in Jalisco were neither different nor less clouded than those which his sympathizers condemned.[59] Despite

[54]*Diario de los Debates*, April 24, 1874, 7th Congress, II, 204–205.

[55]See Moisés González Navarro, *Vallarta y Su Ambiente Político Jurídico*, 20; Pérez Verdía, *Historia de Jalisco*, III, 405; *El Padre Cobos*, March 7, May 30, 1875; Salado Álvarez, *Memorias*, I, 252.
It will be recalled that Vallarta left the Juárez cabinet in September, 1868, because he refused to accept Lerdo's primacy; but when Lerdo and Juárez parted in 1871, Juárez forcibly ejected the Lerdist governor of Jalisco and aided Vallarta to entrench himself in power in the state.

[56]*Diario Oficial*, March 2, 4, 1875; Pérez Verdía, *Historia de Jalisco*, III, 430, 434–441; Foster to Fish, February 2, 1876, *U. S. Foreign Relations, 1876*, 392.

[57]Cosmes, *Historia de Méjico*, XXII, 676–678.

[58]*Colección de Artículos y Documentos Relativos a los Atentados Cometidos en Jalisco por D. Sebastián Lerdo de Tejada y D. José Ceballos, desde Junio de 1875 hasta 6 de Enero de 1877*, I, 4.

[59]See Pérez Verdía, *Historia de Jalisco*, III, 430.

overwhelmingly favorable and always fraudulent state electoral counts, the party of Vallarta was far from enjoying the unanimous support of the local population. In 1872, one of Vallarta's enemies wrote from Guadalajara:

Friend D. Ignacio Vallarta moves along very unfortunately in his government. I do not know what has happened, but the fact is that all classes of society are discontented with him; he has shamed all the interests and it can be assured that the General Government, in order to capture the good will of the Jaliscienses, will have to do no more than the contrary to what Vallarta wishes.[60]

Closely connected and aggravating Lerdo's trouble with Jalisco was the question of Tepic. At one time a canton of Jalisco, it had fallen under the control of a barbarous Indian cacique, Manuel Lozada,[61] whose word for many years had meant life and death to most of the inhabitants and whose cruelty was a legend among the populace of the rugged region.[62] Last of the true caciques of the Pacific Coast, he had from time to time given a nominal recognition to the central governments of Maximilian and later Juárez. Actually Lozada was a bitter enemy of nationalism and erected his fief into an asylum for political discontents and revolutionists. Ireneo Paz more than once fled to his protection, while the eulogists of Porfirio Díaz preferred to forget that "Cincinnatus" humbly sought the bandit's aid during the Revolution of La Noria in 1871–1872.[63]

Soon after Lerdo became constitutional president, Lozada sent a special commission to Mexico City, demanding privileges for Tepic which amounted to a continuance of his *imperium in imperio*. The answer which Lerdo gave, fitting his centralistic outlook and respect for the law, "was firm and decided; to the effect that the constitution and the laws must prevail throughout the whole republic, and that the government could make no exceptions."[64] That reply was the occasion for Lozada to launch an open revolt.

[60]Vicente Ortigosa to Mariano Riva Palacio, August 22, 1872, Mariano Riva Palacio Papers, Folder 174, UT.

[61]Lozada was known as the "Tiger of Alica," after the name of the sierra over which he prowled.

[62]A detailed account of the Tepic military campaign and the defeat, capture, and execution of Lozada may be found in Cosmes, *Historia de Méjico*, XXII, 138–168; 564–572. Cosmes described the "Tiger of Alica" as an "Indian of genius who was without doubt the type most worthy of study of the various ones who figure in the annals of caciquism in Mexico."—*Ibid.*, XIX, 190. For the origins of Lozada's career, see Riva Palacio (ed.), *México á Través de los Siglos*, V, 254, 254n; Zamacois, *Historia de Méjico*, XIV, 646–648.

[63]Paz, *Algunas Campañas*, III, 270–271, 297, 305–306, 310–311, 315–316.

[64]Nelson to Fish, January 31, 1873, *U. S. Foreign Relations, 1873*, I, 647. See also *Diario Oficial*, January 28, February 1, 1873; Cosmes, *Historia de Méjico*, XXII, 145–146.

Endorsing a "plan" of national scope which contained some religious and conservative provisions,[65] he led his copper horde down from the sierra to the gates of Guadalajara, before being checked by the federal army in the Battle of Mojonera, January 28, 1873.[66] Determined to remove that stain of autonomy from the federal honor, Lerdo spared neither federal funds nor troops to pursue the Indian Cacique into his mountain fastness. After a rigorous campaign in difficult terrain, lasting several months, Lozada himself was captured and executed (July, 1873).[67] The achievement was one of the unqualified glories of Lerdo's term and one of his major contributions to the strength of national government; for Lozada's death signified the termination of "the state of independence in which a considerable part of the coast of the Pacific had remained during some forty years."[68]

But the subsequent dispute over the disposition of Tepic presented one of the clearest cases of Lerdo's centralistic tendencies in his dealings with the states. Jalisco, which had never relinquished her claim over the canton, demanded immediate reincorporation of the area. Lerdo ignored the fiat, however, and retained Tepic as a military district during the remainder of his administration.[69] Beneath the veneer of clever justifications, Lerdo's real purpose appeared to have been the establishment of an outpost of federal strength in a distant area which was a hotbed of localism. Characteristic of the man, he tried to place the responsibility for the peculiar status of Tepic at the door of congress. In his message to the deputies, September, 1873, he pointed out the continuance of armed bands in the mountains of Tepic and the need for the federal government to restore the administrative system there prior to relinquishing control. Despite those circumstances, he added, it would be in the province of the deputies to decide about the status of the region, that is, whether it was to be administered by the executive or returned to Jalisco.[70]

However much the denial of their sovereign territory rankled in the chests of the Jaliscienses, Lerdo could always point to congress as the proper place for them to seek redress; he could always gently remind the native sons of the state of Jalisco that the federal government and army had reconquered Tepic for the nation and

[65]Alfonso Toro, *La Iglesia y el Estado en México* . . . , 441–443. The plan was reprinted in *Diario Oficial*, January 28, 1873; Pérez Verdía, *Historia de Jalisco*, III, 408–414; Cosmes, *Historia de Méjico*, XXII, 501–506.
[66]A map of the battle and the report of the victorious general were printed in *Diario Oficial*, February 18, 1873.
[67]Pérez Verdía, *Historia de Jalisco*, III, 417, 420–424; Cosmes, *Historia de Méjico*, XXII, 564–572.
[68]Cosmes, *Historia de Méjico*, XXII, 572.
[69]See Riva Palacio, *Historia de la Administración de Lerdo*, 117–118.
[70]*Diario de los Debates*, September 16, 1873, 7th Congress, I, 114.

that the state of Jalisco had contributed virtually nothing toward that end.[71] Despite the excellent legal position of the President, the Jalisciences held Lerdo responsible for denying them a cherished plot of former soil, and no doubt the rancor resulting from the Tepic issue largely provoked their hostility toward him.[72]

In general, it can be said that Lerdo, in extending the effectiveness of central government through the states, worked moderately, carefully, and always under a disguise of the forms of the law. In addition, he consistently fortified himself with an excellent set of excuses and legal fictions to explain interference in the states, providing more than ample lip service to the theories of federalism. As will be explained later, Lerdo advocated and effected the addition of a senate to the national legislative power on the perfect pretext that it would complete the federal concept of Mexican government at the center. What he really desired and obtained in the senate was a more facile instrument for intervening in the states to promote peace and the stability of his régime. Because of the velvet quality of his methods, which probably deceived no one, the opposition was forced to generalize its attack by simply calling him a perverter of state sovereignty. Perhaps his subtle methods also explain why it is so difficult to perceive the fundamental yet invisible change taking place in the relationship between the federation and the states. It is significant to note in passing that when Lerdo faced two revolutions simultaneously in 1876, one was launched in Oaxaca and fomented in Tamaulipas and Nuevo León, where geography played an important part; while the other was hatched under the aegis of the governor of Guanajuato, illustrating a breach of the neo-feudalistic contract—a breakdown in the *amigo* of government.

Throughout his years in office Lerdo kept a firm grip on congress, converting it into a servile tool of his will. The solid majority which he controlled in the legislature was not a reflection of his "popular support," but represented his control over the state governors, who returned coöperative deputies to the national capital, and also the efficacy of the federal army in swaying elections in his favor. The executive initiated most of the major legislation, on constitutional reform, economic and educational promotion, state-federal relationships, and special measures for the maintenance of peace and security. Making use of his intimate accomplices, Ramón Guzmán and Romero Rubio, Lerdo bent congress into the

---

[71]*Diario Oficial*, August 28, December 8, 1874.
[72]Pérez Verdía, *Historia de Jalisco*, III, 425; Priestley, *The Mexican Nation*, 371.

brace of his program, extracting from the national representatives the essential endorsement for his actions.

The opposition, well aware of the servile relationship, was busy attacking it in the usual dreary and unimaginative manner. A cartoon entitled "The Powers of the Republic," describing in animal form the opposition's view of the organs of the central government, pictured congress as a lamb and the ministry as a turtle;[73] while the President, on the other hand, boasted of "a power which the Czar of all the Russias does not count upon."[74]

The hostile editor Juan N. Mirafuentes synthesized over four years of press complaints against Lerdo's control over the deputies. The President, "interested in covering his despotism with the mantle of legality," had coverted congress into "a political farce," acted out by men of his own selection who were "the blind instruments of his will."[75] "Some time ago," asserted Mirafuentes, "Minister Lerdo said: let us make congresses according to our will, and thus we shall convert the caprices of despotism into constitutional precepts. Today Señor Lerdo is going to crown his work of usurpation."[76]

Occasionally, *El Ahuizote,* the most obnoxious of the opposition papers, attacked the prostrate congress with satire:

It is assured that the President is going to concede political rights to women, so that the next congress may be composed of pretty young girls. We shall be overjoyed that it may happen thus, because the women of today are more independent than the men, and they will oppose the seductions of Don Sebastián with greater resistance.[77]

While Lerdo managed to mould the pliable congress to his will, the time factor was important, since congressional procedure was slow and tedious. During the processing of legislation, the opposition, which always existed, was permitted to lash out against the executive in whatever terms and at whatever length it chose. Congress, it was true, was largely an academic debating society, filling many exhausting volumes "of that species of archive which practically no one reads and which is called *Diario de los Debates*";[78] but it was also a sounding board, focusing opinion upon the executive and bringing its acts under periodic scrutiny. By respecting the forms of the law, the freedom of the press, and the freedom of speech in and out of congress, Lerdo held out the promise of a

---

[73]*El Padre Cobos,* November 11, 1875.
[74]*Ibid.,* September 19, 1875.
[75]*El Ahuizote,* May 1, 1874.
[76]*Ibid.,* February 13, 1874.
[77]*Ibid.,* February 20, 1874.
[78]Prisciliano Díaz González to Vicente Riva Palacio, January 14, 1875, Vicente Riva Palacio Papers, Folder 185, UT. Díaz González was an opposition deputy during Lerdo's administration.

healthful political progress for the future, which his adversaries never appreciated and never took into account when they accused his administration of decadence, torpor, and delay.

The most permanent legislative monuments of Lerdo's term were constitutional additions, the outstanding one being the constitutionalizing of the Laws of Reform. Decreed by congress on September 25, 1873, and promulgated on October 5 of the same year, the measure

marked the end of an epoch in the ecclesiastical history of Mexico. Henceforth there was no open attempt of the clergy to dominate politics. Church and State were definitively separated. The Reform had won at last, for notwithstanding its disregard during the subsequent Díaz period, its existence as constitutional law was a constant deterrent to extravagant clerical pretentions. No longer did the clergy dare to campaign for the establishment of a medieval theocracy. They declared themselves as being eminently satisfied if accorded the guarantees of a free Church in a free State.[79]

Indeed, the five terse provisions of the measure were a synopsis of thirteen years of strife and bitterness: (1) church and state were declared separated; (2) marriage was declared a civil contract; (3) no religious corporation was to acquire real property or mortgages thereon except for that which was immediately in use for religious purposes; (4) a simple promise to tell the truth was to be substituted for the religious oath before the courts; and (5) no contract, pact, or covenant, whether for religious, economic, or educational purposes, which in any way diminished the "liberty of man," was to be recognized as valid in the eyes of the law.[80]

Perhaps because the church had expected a partisan in Lerdo, it complained bitterly of his zeal to accomplish the technical conclusion of the Reform, while his enemies complained that he pressed the measure for vanity and popularity and to compete with Juárez for a place in history.[81] The fact remained that the organic incorporation of the principles won after many years of costly struggle had long been neglected and was a praiseworthy object.[82] Nor did it seem inappropriate—and certainly not inconsistent with his Manifesto of 1872—that Sebastián had erected the formal monument to a work on which his brother Miguel had been a masterbuilder.

[79]J. Lloyd Mecham, *Church and State in Latin America: A History of Politico-Ecclesiastical Relations*, 455.

[80]Dublán y Lozano, *Legislación Mexicana*, XII, 502–504; J. Pérez Lugo, *La Cuestión Religiosa en México, Recopilación de Leyes . . .* , 239–240. An English translation may be found in *British and Foreign State Papers*, LXVII, 268–269.

[81]The attack against Lerdo's church policy will be discussed in a subsequent section of the present chapter.

[82]As early as 1868, Francisco Zarco, a founding father of the Constitution of 1857, had declared that the Laws of Reform should be constitutionalized. —*El Siglo*, February 5, 1868.

The following year (December, 1874) congress passed a detailed enabling act to implement the Laws of Reform, an act which concluded the major ecclesiastical legislation of Lerdo's term.[83] It prohibited religious instruction in public schools, the wearing of ecclesiastical garb in public, and the holding of religious festivities and services outside the privacy of temples. In addition, it included a number of minor restrictions on such matters as the ringing of bells, all of which the church found derogatory and onerous.

Although there was little of principle involved in the constitutionalizing of the Reform, the principles having been accepted almost universally after the defeat of Maximilian, the deputies showed their love of oratory and the favor of the gallery in the long debates over the various provisions, which illustrated the general dilatoriness surrounding congressional procedure.[84]

The second constitutional reform of Lerdo's administration was the addition of a senate to the existing unicameral national legislature. No other piece of legislation so clearly demonstrated his desire to stabilize the central government and to solidify peace at the expense of state anarchy. Not a reform which arose suddenly, the attempt to erect a senate had a devious history dating back to the *convocatoria* of 1867, a document generally attributed to the genius of Lerdo. But if Lerdo conceived the amendment and finally succeeded in attaining its realization, Juárez supported it during his last administration; and, when he died in 1872, it remained one of his unrealized objectives.[85] At the time congress began to debate the "important matter" in 1870, Juárez wrote that the executive had proposed the addition of a senate "without any other purpose than that of assuring peace in the future on solid foundations."[86] In the last opening address he was ever to deliver to a Mexican congress, Juárez declared, in regard to the pending constitutional proposals:

Among the reforms to which I allude, the creation of a senate, which will moderate and perfect legislative action, figures in the foreground. . . . It would also be desirable that [the senate] be encharged with resolving the differences which arise among the powers of the States, and which, due to the

---

[83]Dublán y Lozano, *Legislación Mexicana*, XII, 683–688; Mecham, *Church and State in Latin America*, 454–455; *Diario Oficial*, December 16, 1874.

[84]For example, see *Diario de los Debates*, April 24, 28, 1873, 6th Congress, IV, 219–225, 272–274. There was even a protracted discussion at the last moment over whether the Laws of Reform should have a preamble.—*Ibid.*, September 25, 1873, 7th Congress, I, 189–193.

[85]Sierra, *Juárez*, 485.

[86]Benito Juárez to Mariano Riva Palacio, April 15, 1870, Mariano Riva Palacio Papers, Folder 171, UT. Juárez's enthusiasm for the amendment bill was expressed in another letter to Mariano Riva Palacio, April 22, 1870, *ibid.*, Folder 171, UT.

absence of a competent authority to resolve them, place the general peace of the Nation in danger.[87]

Following the defeat of the *convocatoria* of 1867, the senate scheme lay dormant until a congressional committee introduced the bill in December, 1869. From that point until Juárez's death, it suffered a stormy career at the mercy of congress' complicated procedure, long-winded debaters, and the obstructionists who were opposed. Finally, a new senate bill was introduced in 1873 and was passed by the necessary two-thirds vote on April 9, 1874, after surviving the labyrinth of debates during several sessions. When congress met for the fall period in 1874, a majority of the state legislatures had ratified, thereby making possible the final congressional decree and the promulgation by the executive in early November, 1874. The first senate was not to convene, however, until the fall term of 1875.[88]

In its outward appearance, though not in details, the Mexican senate was patterned substantially after the North American model. It provided for two senators from each state and the Federal District, elected for a term of four years by the same electoral bodies which chose the deputies, one-half of the number to be renewed every two years. In procedure and exclusive powers, it was also similar to its counterpart in the United States; but there was no real comparison, since the elections, parties, and other political institutions and practices of the two nations differed so markedly.

What, then, was the true import of the senate and what was the explanation for Lerdo's zeal to effect the change? Firstly, the senate was composed of a small group of men, virtually hand-picked, whom the executive could control easily. In effect, it was a veto power to muzzle the larger and more unruly chamber of deputies, over which presidential control was more precarious. That was why Juan José Baz desired three senators from each state instead of two: the greater the number the less "the danger of exposure" to executive domination. "The Senate is always an element of despotism," Baz warned resignedly, "and now that we must have this despotic element, let us make it so that it will be the least prejudicial possible, because the Senate which we are going to have is a true absurdity."[89] Moreover, the senate provided the President with some fifty well-paid sinecures to distribute among his par-

---

[87]*Diario de los Debates*, April 1, 1872, 6th Congress, II, 6.

[88]*Ibid.*, October 30, 1874, 7th Congress, III, 459–460. The congressional record for this session gave a short history of the bill. See also *Diario Oficial*, April 9, October 31, 1874; Riva Palacio, *Historia de la Administración de Lerdo*, 423.

For the amendment, see Dublán y Lozano, *Legislación Mexicana*, XII, 635–641; *Diario Oficial*, November 15, 1874.

[89]*Diario de los Debates*, January 17, 1874, 7th Congress, I, 1223, 1224.

tisans, as the opposition mourned. A cartoon in *El Padre Cobos* captured the point perfectly. Entitled "Caesar and His Senate," it depicted Lerdo as Caesar, standing among his close friends, Rubio, Guzmán, Escobedo, and others, all of whom had been "elected" to the new legislative organ first convening in September, 1875.[90] "Padre Cobos" himself, with his trenchant political vision, explained that the senators would come "to earn 3000 little pesos a year" so that they could "eat peacefully for four years."[91]

But the fundamental significance of the senate was as a legal device of the executive for intervening in state conflicts.[92] The two exclusive powers granted to the senate which merited attention were: (1) the right to declare when the executive and legislative powers of a state had "disappeared" and to authorize the president to appoint a provisional governor who would call new elections and reëstablish the normal operation of state constitutional machinery; and (2) the right to resolve the conflicts arising between the executive and legislative branches within a state on appeal of either of the parties concerned; or, in case the dispute had reached a point of armed conflict, to intervene without appeal, through the instrumentality of the federal executive of course.[93]

In practice, the senate, another tool of the executive, would become the arbitrator of state politics, enabling the president "to establish centralism in fact and to cement the Dictatorship. Such was the work of Juárez and of his minister and successor, Lerdo de Tejada, which General Díaz was to take advantage of with greater success."[94]

Whatever charges were flung at Lerdo for the creation of the senate, it was, remembering the state conflicts during his administration and that of Juárez, a necessary element of stability. Since the first senate did not convene until the twilight of his term and the dawn of the Díaz revolution, Lerdo failed to benefit from the legal engine which he had built to destroy localism.[95] He bequeathed it inadvertently to his nemesis, Porfirio Díaz, as García Granados has pointed out. Far more than his handling of local conflicts, including the question of Tepic, the senate reform demonstrated Lerdo's ambition to found a stable, national régime.

Not only on constitutional reform but on other measures as well, congress followed on the leash of the executive, although there were no doubt many raw throats after protracted debates about the annual budgets and the numerous contracts for railroad concessions, drafted by the government and submitted to congress for

[90]*El Padre Cobos*, October 28, 1875.
[91]*Ibid.*, January 28, 1875. See also Paz, *Algunas Campañas*, III, 346.
[92]García Granados, *Historia de México*, I, 110.
[93]Dublán y Lozano, *Legislación Mexicana*, XII, 639.
[94]García Granados, *Por Qué y Como Cayó Porfirio Díaz*, 7.
[95]Rabasa, *La Organización Política de México*, 154.

approval. After the waste of much time and breath, the determination of the deputies almost invariably coincided with the desire of the President, which should not have been surprising. Satirizing the many hours which the deputies wasted in quibbling about the budget, *El Ahuizote* printed an account of a mock session in which Ignacio Mejía, the minister of War, appeared in the chamber to defend his departmental request of 12,000,000 pesos for the approaching fiscal year. After interpellations, debates, and committee revision, the estimate was reduced to 11,999,999 pesos![96] Such was the independence of congress in the eyes of the opposition.

In addition to constitutional reforms and the legislation on railroads and telegraphs, which will be discussed separately, the most notable law passed from 1872 to 1876 was probably the Stamp Act *(Ley de Timbre)*, which was not placed in operation until January, 1875.[97] Conceived by Juárez's minister of Finance, Matías Romero, a similar law had been passed as early as December, 1871; but the lack of equipment to produce the stamps had prevented it from becoming operative. As in the case of the senate, Lerdo laid the groundwork for the *Ley de Timbre* and permitted Díaz to reap the harvest. The measure was a real effort at broad, internal taxation, which, it was hoped, would rescue Mexico from her prostitution to dependence for national revenues on the fluctuating foreign customs duties, frontier and maritime.[98] Although time served to defeat the President on his major financial project, José Valadés has noted that:

> . . . it was only during the rule of Don Sebastián Lerdo de Tejada that the bureaucratic party attempted the formation of the State over the base of power of the bureaucrat, fixing as a first means a system of national tribute, which was the revenue from stamps. If President Lerdo, the first practicer of systematization of bureaucratic power, had continued to extend this power, he would have fabricated the foundations of a national State, without having the subversive dangers of the military party.[99]

Finally, there were the transitory laws requested by the executive to obtain "extraordinary faculties" in the branches of Finance and War, which authorized the employment of extra-constitutional devices like forced loans, confiscation of property, and forced recruiting. "Extraordinary faculties" freed the executive to deal effec-

---

[96]*El Ahuizote*, May 22, 1874.

[97]Dublán y Lozano, *Legislación Mexicana*, XII, 647–671. After a year's experience, the executive revised the law in certain details.—*Ibid.*, XIII, 13–36.

[98]Pablo Macedo, *Tres Monografías Que Dan Idea de una Parte de la Evolución Económica de México*, 427, 431–432, 434–435. The *Diario Oficial* stated that the *Ley de Timbre* was "the product of a long and conscientious study which would systematize and moralize the collection of taxes. . . ."—*Diario Oficial*, January 1, 1875.

[99]Valadés, *El Porfirismo, Nacimiento*, 200.

tively with revolutionary conditions, and Lerdo possessed them from May, 1875, until he was forced to flee from Mexico City in November, 1876.[100] Closely allied, though less transcendental, was the law authorizing summary trial of highwaymen and kidnappers, which was extended at one-year intervals throughout Lerdo's term to combat the prevalent insecurity, especially in rural areas.[101] Such unusual measures in part mirrored the confidence of congress in the moderation of Lerdo and in part his complete control over that body. At least, United States Minister John W. Foster, an impartial observer, was able to see the beneficent effects of the law for the summary punishment of highwaymen and kidnappers;[102] and he also remarked about Lerdo's cautious application of the "extraordinary faculties":

> Thus far it is to be noted that the President has made very little use of the "extraordinary faculties," and especially not in a very arbitrary manner; and the friends of the measure claim that its good effect is not so much in its exercise as the fear which its possession by the President inspires among conspirators and revolutionists.[103]

In comparing the governmental methods and positive legislative goals of Juárez and Lerdo, the striking continuity in the policies of the two men becomes apparent. To borrow the words of Emilio Rabasa:

> The dictatorship of Juárez continued under the government of his successor, the system being altered in as much as [Lerdo] would soften it in external appearance and in the methods preferred, with the steadiness of the diplomat of refined education, and the pride of a man essentially cultured and certain of the superiority of his understanding.[104]

And Lerdo applied methods in essence equivalent to those of Juárez in attempting to insure the stability of his government:

> . . . to take possession of the legislative Power in order to disarm it, and to subordinate the [state] governors in order to avoid possible rebellions, and to dominate all elections. The result was a dictatorship less ostensible, but just as accomplished as the former one.[105]

On specific measures, like the constitutionalizing of the Laws of Reform, the creation of the senate, and the *Ley de Timbre*, it is even easier to discern the consummation by Lerdo, as exclusive master of the presidential chair, of much of the work initiated or

---

[100]*Diario de los Debates*, May 25, 1875, 7th Congress, IV, 586; Dublán y Lozano, *Legislación Mexicana*, XII, 792; XIII, 43, 84–85.

[101]Dublán y Lozano, *Legislación Mexicana*, XII, 443–444, 577, 715.

[102]Foster to Fish, February 28, 1874, *U. S. Foreign Relations, 1874*, 732.

[103]Foster to Fish, November 8, 1875, *ibid., 1876*, 387.

[104]Rabasa, *La Organización Política de México*, 153.

[105]*Ibid.*, 154.

attempted during the last years of the Indian President, when
Lerdo was at his side as chief of Cabinet.[106] Once again that enigmatic query intrudes: Who was the key figure of the early restoration years, Juárez or Lerdo?

If Lerdo was able to shape the pliable congress according to his
dictates, he found in the Supreme Court one of the chief obstacles
to his administration. In fact, it was the court, led by its president,
José María Iglesias, which fomented dissension, demanded an
absurd political dominance under the Constitution of 1857, played
directly into the hands of the plotting Porfirist faction, and, in the
final analysis, was a basic cause of Lerdo's downfall.

To understand the import of the executive-judiciary conflict, it
is essential to foreshadow the events of 1876. In that year, Iglesias,
president of the court and vice-president of the nation, declared
Lerdo's reëlection illegal and went into open revolution against the
government. Although he spent the balance of his days—after defeat at the hands of the Díaz revolutionists—prating about the
"legality" of his position and refusing to admit that in fact he had
joined the ranks of the barracks pronouncers, he actually had split
the unity of the government at a crucial point, apparently to advance his personal ambitions for the presidential chair. In the light
of these developments, it is difficult not to conclude that Iglesias
combined his high official position, his national reputation, his
friendship with Lerdo, and a ridiculous legal theorem to build up
his own party within the government circle, especially by arro-
gating to himself the discontented Lerdists. Simply stated, the
judiciary conflict of 1874–1876 was the historical background for
a political revolution, propelled by the ambitions of Iglesias for
the presidency and the discontented place seekers of the old
Lerdist party whom he gathered around him.

Soon after Lerdo became constitutional president, it was necessary to fill the vacancy he left behind him as president of the
court. Although several persons competed in the election to fill the
office, including Vicente Riva Palacio, Iglesias was the victor; and
being the intimate associate of Lerdo, it was generally conceded
that he was the President's preference.[107] At any rate, an event
occurred about a year after the election which undoubtedly was

---

[106]See Porfirio Parra, *Estudio Histórico-Sociológico sobre la Reforma en
México*, 160–161.

[107]For the election, see Cosmes, *Historia de Méjico*, XXII, 495–500; Nelson
to Fish, March 1, 1873, *U. S. Foreign Relations, 1873*, I, 655–656. Cosmes'
partiality for Iglesias may be explained by the fact that he was one of
Iglesias' supporters in the revolution against Lerdo in 1876.

as disconcerting as surprising to Lerdo, for Iglesias turned out to be the Sir Edward Coke of Mexican history.

In the spring of 1874, the Supreme Court granted the *amparo*[108] to a group of *hacendados* in the state of Morelos who claimed: (1) that they had been taxed under a law passed by an illegally constituted state legislature and promulgated by an illegal governor (Francisco Leyva); and consequently (2) that they had been deprived of their rights as granted under Article 16 of the Constitution, *viz.*, that no man was to be denied of property unless by a written mandate issuing from a competent authority.[109]

The basic issue was not whether the *hacendados* paid the tax: the crux of the decision of the Supreme Court was that it declared a state governor illegitimate on the famous theory advanced by Iglesias, the "incompetency of origin." In other words, the Supreme Court had staked out an exclusive claim as the final arbiter of all state elections and electoral colleges. But was the claim limited to state elections? Exactly where lay the boundary of Iglesias' theory? If it permitted the court to depose a governor on grounds of an illegal election, could it not do the same in the case of the deputies elected to the national congress or even the president himself?[110] When Iglesias asserted his right to inherit the presidential chair in 1876, he did so on the bizarre extension of his own ridiculous theory that he alone as president of the court—not the court acting as a body—had the right to declare the reëlection of Lerdo "incompetent of origin," even though the Constitution vested the right of verifying the presidential election in congress.

Since the court depended on the executive and its agents to enforce the decision in the Morelos case, Lerdo was able to apply inertia to calm the inflammatory issue. When a second and almost identical case arose in Puebla, on which Iglesias and the court held in the same manner,[111] the alarmed President and deputies passed a law declaring that electoral colleges alone could resolve the legitimacy of popularly-elected authorities, state or federal, and denying the right of any "power, authority, or funtionary of the federation" to revise or place in doubt "the titles of legitimacy

---

[108]*Amparo*, as applied here, was a form of judic'al relief issuing from the federal courts to complainants who could prove that their individual constitutional rights had been infringed by the state or federal authorities. See Russell H. Fitzgibbon, "Glossary of Latin-American Constitutional Terms," *The Hispanic American Historical Review*, XXVII (August, 1947), 577.

[109]Iglesias, *La Cuestión Presidencial en 1876*, 5–8; Iglesias, *Autobiografía*, 58; Rabasa, *La Organización Política de México*, 309.

[110]Rabasa, *La Organización Política de México*, 310–311, 313–314. Bravo Ugarte stated accurately that Iglesias' theory "would have destroyed the stability of all the political organization of the country."—Bravo Ugarte, *Historia de México*, III, 365.

[111]Iglesias, *La Cuestión Presidencial en 1876*, 9–10; Cosmes, *Historia de Méjico*, XXII, 682–683; *El Padre Cobos*, March 14, August 22, 1875 (cartoons).

of a federal or state functionary proceeding from that declaration."[112]

Had men based their opinions on practicality or sound judicial thinking, Iglesias would have been submerged in a sea of ridicule and protest; for no elected officeholder, on the strength of the theory of "incompetency of origin," could have felt secure against an omnipotent political god—the court. On the contrary, Lerdo's enemies capitalized on his "growing unpopularity" and so-called "despotic tendencies," placing the court and especially Iglesias on a pedestal as a humanitarian bulwark, "protecting the persecuted against tyrannical authorities. . . ."[113] Consequently, the court decisions, which stirred discontent and unrest, were debated heatedly in the press, in clubs, and in the forum,[114] provoking unwarranted criticism against Lerdo. Despite the legal-constitutional palaver, the conflict between the court and the executive was primarily political; and it was hardly a coincidence that Iglesias, in his two decisions granting the *amparo* to citizens of Morelos and Puebla, had declared "incompetent of origin" two loyal Lerdists in state gubernatorial positions—Francisco Leyva and Ignacio Romero Vargas.[115]

In the *amparo* cases and the upheaval which followed, Iglesias found a fertile soil in which to plant his presidential ambitions. In the "incompetency of origin" he not only raised the banner of his revolutionary party of "legality," beckoning for all the discontented to look to him, but also found a method of fomenting trouble for Lerdo.[116] Had Iglesias looked about him more carefully, however, he would have discovered an element in the background smiling: the Porfirists, who would take advantage of his yeoman service in cracking the unity of the government.

Although Iglesias had declared publicly that he would give his vote "according to the circumstances of each case," despite the law of May, 1875, invalidating the court's right to revise elections;[117] although he had stooped to enter the press battles raging around his decisions;[118] and although he had made the maximum effort to

[112]Dublán y Lozano, *Legislación Mexicana*, XII, 727; Iglesias, *La Cuestión Presidencial en 1876*, 11; Iglesias, *Autobiografía*, 59–60.

[113]García Granados, *Historia de México*, I, 114–116. "Today no one takes the absurd theory of Iglesias seriously," stated García Naranjo.—García Naranjo, *Porfirio Díaz*, 188.

[114]Rabasa, *La Organización Política de México*, 309.

[115]See a cartoon in *El Padre Cobos*, May 24, 1874, on the Morelos *amparo*.

[116]Ordaz, *La Cuestión Presidencial*, 18–23.

[117]*Diario Oficial*, June 4, 1875; Iglesias, *La Cuestión Presidencial en 1876*, 16–18.

[118]Iglesias, *La Cuestión Presidencial en 1876*, 6–7.

A supporter of Iglesias' judicial theory wrote him that he should have limited his answers to the executive and should not have excited "major dissension" among the branches of the central government.—Rodolfo Sandoval to José María Iglesias, September 28, 1875, Archivo de Fernando Iglesias Calderón, Legajo 14, A.G.N.

endanger the executive, Lerdo maintained a temperate attitude toward him throughout the quarrel. Naturally, the President refused to order the federal army into Puebla and Morelos to oust the key Lerdist governors there—that would have been political suicide.[119] But he did publish the executive opinion on the Morelos *amparo*: ". . . the President believes . . . that the final declarations of an electoral body, legally constituted, cannot be revised by any other power. . . ." Furthermore, he wisely dressed the reasons for his views in the popular garment of federalism:

The President believes that this principle [the right of the Supreme Court to revise elections] would be contrary to the foundation of our popular, representative system, on which the federal and local constitutions are supported; that it would diminish the sovereignty of the states in that which concerned solely their interior régimes; and that it would disturb the equilibrium in the relat.ons between the Union and the federal entities.[120]

The real climax of the Iglesista plot came in 1876 with open revolution, but a premature showdown took place when Iglesias attempted to resign in May, 1875. It is interesting to note that the President of the court later attempted to rationalize his conduct for the benefit of posterity by pointing to that resignation as proof of his lack of ambition,[121] his willingness to retire to private life, and, in short, as undeniable evidence that all his actions had been dictated by the "granite wall of his conscience."[122] After several conferences with Lerdo, in which the President insisted that harmony could be maintained despite the court issue,[123] and during which "he [Lerdo] tried to convince me [Iglesias] with all the subtlety of his genius that all my doctrine on the faculties of the court was vicious," the President of the court agreed to remain in office.[124] In justifying his conduct and explaining his personal motivation, Iglesias uncovered the nucleus of the executive-judiciary conflict. His *decisive reason* for remaining with the court was the insinuation of the opposition press that the revolution had lacked a rallying point but would discover one in him when he resigned from the government circle. "I did not want to give, I could not give, a banner to the revolution," announced the Incorruptible with coun-

---

[119]"Señor Lerdo is too judicious to give aid to the Supreme Court. . . ."— *El Monitor*, March 3, 1875. See also *Diario Oficial*, March 4, 1875; Cosmes, *Historia de Méjico*, XXII, 655–658.

[120]*Diario Oficial*, May 29, 1874.

[121]The basic thread of Iglesias' *La Cuestión Presidencial en 1876* was: "never have I been subject to ambition" (p. 5).

[122]Justo Sierra, *Evolución Política del Pueblo Mexicano*, 436. It must be pointed out that Sierra, like Cosmes, took the side of Iglesias in the revolution against Lerdo in 1876.

[123]Iglesias, *Autobiografía*, 62.

[124]Iglesias, *La Cuestión Presidencial en 1876*, 14–16; Iglesias, *Autobiografía*, 61.

terfeit innocence.[125] That he had done so and desired to do so, however, were best demonstrated by his actions and not by his fatuous words.

On the other hand, Lerdo's desire to keep Iglesias in the fold probably was based on practical reasons, although there appeared to have been an admixture of friendship. Once out of his official position, Iglesias would have been not only a potent presidential rival but also a hero-martyr of the unscrupulous executive.[126] To avoid those dangers in part and in part because he may have felt that Iglesias was sincere in regard to the judicial theory, Lerdo doubled himself to conciliate his old friend. Furthermore, though Lerdo was not a man of sentimental attachments, he no doubt wished to avoid a public breach between himself and the companion with whom he had associated intimately for many years, with whom he had shared the baptism of hardships through the intervention, and with whom he had coöperated in the Juárez cabinet during the trying years of the restoration period. The *Diario Oficial* made every effort to prove that there was no personal disaffection between the President of the nation and the President of the court, and it tried to salve Iglesias' supposedly hypersensitive dignity.[127] In addition, after all the sensationalism arising from the various aspects of the court conflict, Lerdo still showed solicitousness for Iglesias' welfare by ordering the director of the Military Medical Corps to Jalapa to attend the Magistrate, who happened to be ailing in late 1875:

According to what I told you by telegram, on account of your illness, Dr. Francisco Montes de Oca is going to give his services to you if they are convenient.

You know the intelligence and well-deserved reputation of Señor Montes de Oca in his profess on.

I trust that your illness will not assume a serious character. . . .[128]

In viewing the court question from Lerdo's standpoint, it was the fatal stab in the back to the stability of his government, coming from the most unexpected quarter—from an old friend who had

---

[125]Iglesias, *Autobiografía*, 63.

[126]See Hannay, *Díaz*, 152–153.

[127]See *Diario Oficial*, June 4, September 6, 1874.

[128]Lerdo to Iglesias, November 21, 1875, Archivo de Fernando Iglesias Calderón, Legajo 14, A.G.N. Lerdo publicized his "concern" for Iglesias' health and the favor that he had extended, probably to demonstrate the good feeling existing between them.—*Diario Oficial*, November 22, 1875.

When requesting biographical data from Iglesias, an agent of the H. H. Bancroft Company made a special inquiry about the estrangement between him and Lerdo: "Your relations seem to have been intimate and friendly with Lerdo until 1875. What was the cause of the difference in views?"—Ora Oak to José María Iglesias, October 1, 1885, Archivo de Fernando Iglesias Calderón, Legajo 15, A.G.N.

gained his court position undoubtedly through Lerdo's patronage. From the court, then, where he should have found the strongest brace for his administration, Lerdo encountered an internal earthquake which was to crack the foundation in 1876.

In regard to Iglesias, his conduct and attitude appeared unjustified, hypocritical, and a complete departure from his past character and career. Intelligent, respected, standing for moderation, peace, and order, he sacrificed his fine record in exchange for the unbecoming garb of a revolutionary. His reputation was deserving of something better than his conduct in promoting the court conflict and, later, the revolt in 1876.

Formal diplomatic relations, or the lack of them, during the presidency of Lerdo de Tejada were a continuance of the events and policies which Lerdo inherited from himself as foreign minister under Juárez, presenting not one colorful incident to enliven the monotony: in regard to the United States, the story was composed of a series of border frictions, mitigated by the moderate personalities conducting affairs; while in regard to Europe, the result was negative in that no relations were established with Britain and France, the principal countries of diplomatic and economic importance to Mexico. Except for the indirect and adverse effect which international relations had upon the introduction of capital, serving only to whet Mexico's zeal to partake in the material advances of the world industrial revolution, it would be possible to eliminate foreign policy altogether from a study of Lerdo's presidency.

At the beginning and throughout his term, Lerdo insisted on maintaining his old attitude toward Britain and France. That attitude, attuned to the national dignity and invulnerable to direct attack of the opposition, was a mere restatement that Mexico would never "take the first step" in order to broaden European relations, especially since her line of conduct had been drawn so positively in 1867 and "she had no motives or reasons for changing it."[129]

While Mexican legations were established in Italy, Spain, and the German Empire and relations with those countries were friendly enough,[130] the impasse between Mexico, on the one hand, and France and Britain, on the other, was frozen in the old *status quo*. Only

---

[129]*Diario Oficial*, July 3, 1874. See also *ibid.*, February 4, 1874. Both references contained good restatements of Mexico's European policy. The few sentences with which Lerdo always dispatched foreign affairs in his messages to congress, particularly those items pertaining to Europe, were a good index of the insignificance of foreign affairs. See Genaro Estrada (ed.), *Un Siglo de Relaciones Internacionales de México*, 113–119.

[130]Estrada (ed.), *Un Siglo de Relaciones Internacionales de México*, 113; *Diario de los Debates*, April 1, 1875, 7th Congress, IV, 5; *Diario Oficial*, January 21, 1874; *U. S. Foreign Relations, 1873*, I, 641.

once did the British Secretary of Foreign Affairs break the silence. He forwarded an importunate note to Lafragua, the Mexican secretary, complaining about the Indian incursions from Yucatán into British Honduras and stating that Britain would take matters into her own hands if Mexico failed to give immediate satisfaction.[131] Lafragua's reply, a detailed piece of research on Mexican-Honduran border history, pointed out cleverly that the British had sold firearms to the Indians of Yucatán and added a suave counter-stroke by mentioning that Britain had "no complaints" to lodge on border conditions in the area before she had recognized the Emperor Maximilian.[132] Even Lerdo's enemies were smug about Lafragua's conduct in handling the isolated incident; and the inimical Cosmes declared that the note in reply was the "only work of true merit" during the long public career of Lafragua.[133] Pleased with itself for having upheld the national decorum by twisting the British Lion's tail, the government sought to augment its domestic popularity by publishing the notes and reprinting, in the *Diario Oficial*, all favorable comments in the papers throughout the nation over a period of several weeks.[134] The exaggerated stress placed on such an insignificant matter demonstrated the general sterility of Mexico's European relations. Soon thereafter the mantle of silence and stagnation settled back on affairs, remaining undisturbed during the rest of Lerdo's term.

The dignified strait jacket which was Lerdo's policy toward Britain and France conflicted with his obvious preference for European over American capital for Mexican enterprises and for government loans. It was impossible to separate the existing breach of diplomatic relations from the hostile attitude of Mexico's European creditors, official and private. Thus, the irate members of the potent London Corporation of Foreign Bondholders blacklisted Lerdo's régime: "After consultation with the powerful bourses of the Continent, the Council notified the Mexican government that it would not be allowed to avail itself, directly or indirectly, of European markets for the purpose of raising capital."[135]

If Lerdo's enemies acceded to the proper stance he took toward Europe, there was a spirit of discontent about the narrowness of the international links which Mexico maintained. "Today the spirit of material enterprise looks for an advantageous alignment of foreign capital in our soil and for a higher rate of interest than

[131]Granville to the [Mexican] Minister of Foreign Affairs, December 2, 1872, *Diario Oficial*, March 1, 1873.

[132]Lafragua to the [British] Minister of Foreign Affairs, February 12, 1873, *ibid.*, March 1, 1873. English translations of the two notes may be found in *U. S. Foreign Relations, 1873*, I, 656–661.

[133]Cosmes, *Historia de Méjico*, XXII, 549.

[134]See *Diario Oficial*, March-April, 1873.

[135]Edgar Turlington, *Mexico and Her Foreign Creditors*, 188.

that which the market of Europe produces," announced a publicist of the time, adding that the necessity for diplomatic ties with the Old World was "more palpable" than ever before.[136] José María Vigil, a noted journalist and literary figure, while reflecting the same feeling of impatience, manifested indirectly that Lerdo was correct in placing national prestige above immediate economic advantage: "Our foreign affairs continue in the same state, that is, peace with friendly powers, without those [relations] which were interrupted on account of the foreign intervention being reunited." That protracted breach was the explanation of why Mexico had not felt a flood of immigration, capital, and enterprise, explained Vigil, "indispensable elements to complete the work of regeneration. Isolation is death in every sense: Mexico, in her own interests, ought to contract relationships with all the peoples of the earth. . . ."[137] But continuing in the same vein, Vigil named national prestige as the *sine qua non* of such renewed relations, which Lerdo defended as his own point of departure:

If neither the spirit of the century in which we live nor the special circumstances in which the Republic finds herself can constitute us into a species of Chinese Empire, isolated in the middle of the world, it appears to us that it is already time to multiply our foreign relations, provided always that this does not signify any sacrifice of the dignity or the well-intentioned interests of the country.[138]

Disgusted because he realized that British and other foreign creditors of Mexico had frustrated the attempt of Mexican individuals to obtain capital in Europe, Lerdo stated, through the usual medium of the *Diario Oficial*, that the crux of the diplomatic problem was not so lowly a matter as money, "but of more lofty things, like those of right, honor, and dignity." In her most difficult hour of trial, during the intervention, Mexico had demonstrated "that she did not need the English markets to give her lessons in decorum and dignity in complying with her promises." "It is not, as we have stated, a question of money for Mexico: it is something more than can be quoted in the mercantile exchanges of the world, because it treats of the honor, dignity, and the rights of the nation."[139] Pride and dignity, the outstanding personal characteristics of Lerdo, thus became the outstanding traits of his foreign policy.

Turning to the United States, the conduct of affairs ran smoothly under Lerdo, despite the discouraging number of border incidents which composed most of the diplomatic history of the period.

---

[136]*El Siglo*, October 28, 1873.
[137]*Ibid.*, September 23, 1873.
[138]*Ibid.*, September 23, 1873.
[139]*Diario Oficial*, July 28, 1874.

Cattle raids, Indian depredations, and smuggling were the three categories into which Americans divided their complaints against Mexico and the disorder prevailing on the right bank of the Rio Grande.[140] Although the grievances were not strictly unilateral, certainly the balance weighed heavily in favor of the Americans residing along the border.[141] Perhaps because of the moderation and understanding of the persons in charge of diplomatic affairs— Thomas H. Nelson and John W. Foster, the two United States ministers to Mexico during Lerdo's administration, Lerdo himself and his polished foreign minister, Lafragua[142]—the smouldering resentment in the Rio Grande Valley was held in check and did not flare into a dangerous international problem. Fortunately, too, there were men of reason in both countries who tried to mitigate the inflammatory articles printed in the American and Mexican press.[143] It should be noted, however, that Lerdo's successor, Porfirio Díaz, who planned his revolution in part from the Texas side of the Rio Grande, reaped the harvest of a "decade of frontier troubles"; for the United States government, provoked by the frictions accumulated along the border over a period of several

---

[140]The present writer acknowledges the use he has made for these general remarks of two unpublished monographs on United States-Mexican relations from 1867 to 1876, both of which deal in detail with the border episodes: Flora Register Arrowood, *United States-Mexican Relations from 1867–1872* (M.A. thesis, The University of Texas, August, 1934); Mary Marguerite Roy, *Relations between the United States and Mexico during the Administration of Lerdo de Tejada, 1872–1876* (M.A. thesis, The University of Texas, July, 1933). Chapter X of Callahan's *American Foreign Policy in Mexican Relations* also should be mentioned.

[141]William Roy Lewis, "The Hayes Administration and Mexico," *The Southwestern Historical Quarterly*, XXIV (October, 1920), 141–144.

[142]Foster described Lafragua as follows: ". . . a lawyer by profession, of high literary attainments, an historian, and a statesman of much experience. He was a fine type of the old Spanish *hidalgo*, courtly in his manners, always dressed in a black broadcloth suit, with a stiff stock about the neck, and wore colored spectacles."—*Diplomatic Memoirs*, I, 17. Foster made himself popular in Mexico by traveling extensively, learning Spanish, and mixing socially with the Mexicans.—Samuel Flagg Bemis (ed.), *The American Secretaries of State and Their Diplomacy*, VIII, 189.

[143]See *U. S. Foreign Relations, 1876*, 400–402 (trans. of an article by Matías Romero); "Our Mexican Troubles," *The Nation*, XXV (December 27, 1877), 391–392.

Edward Lee Plumb advised the American company which he represented in Mexico as follows: "Most of what you see in the newspapers of the United States regarding events here is the veriest trash and utterly unreliable, and is not worthy of a moment's consideration. The accounts that go to the State Department and my own to you, which are in entire accord, are all that can be depended upon from here. . . ."—Plumb to Thomas W. Pearsall, January 29, 1872, *Plumb Papers*, VIII. (Punctuation supplied by the present writer.)

years, used nonrecognition as a means of obtaining a semblance of order on the Mexican side of the river.[144]

The tangible contribution which Lerdo's administration made to Mexican-United States relations was the termination of the work of the Mixed Claims Commission, which had been established under the convention of 1868. It had been necessary on several occasions to extend the time limit to allow for completion of the decisions on all cases pending; but in 1876 the final settlement was made, although the exact adjustment was not available until a few days after Lerdo had fled from Mexico City.[145] In his last opening address to congress (September, 1876), Lerdo proudly announced that the total of the American claims, originally amounting to some 550,000,000 pesos, had been so reduced by the Commission that "not one-hundredth part will remain recognized of that enormous sum."[146]

The point most repeated about Lerdo's attitude on foreign affairs, either in regard to American or European relations, was his alleged fear of the United States, which "he himself expressed in these words: 'between strength and weakness, the desert,' that is, isolation."[147] Just when Lerdo voiced the maxim apparently has never been determined, but it is generally accepted as fact. Lerdo's apprehension, granting its existence, was probably less a fear of military aggression on the part of the Northern Neighbor than of the pacific and indirect influence resulting from large-scale incursions of American capital. While Lerdo did not exclude American impresarios from sharing in railroad concessions in Mexico, one having been granted to Edward Lee Plumb in the final months of the presidency,[148] his record proved that American entrepreneurs stood at the bottom of his list. Though perhaps exaggerated, there was probably much truth in Alfonso Teja Zabre's statement that "Lerdo feared the expansive force of American capital, as though he foresaw danger in railroad tracks."[149] It was certainly a notable coincidence that two Americans who held diplomatic

[144]Charles W. Hackett, "The Recognition of the Díaz Government by the United States," *The Southwestern Historical Quarterly*, XXVIII (July, 1924), 41–55; Valadés, *El Porfirismo, Nacimiento*, 304–305.

[145]Hackett, "The Recognition of the Díaz Government by the United States," *The Southwestern Historical Quarterly*, XXVIII, 36–37, 37n.

[146]*Diario de los Debates*, September 16, 1876, 8th Congress, III, 7.

[147]Genaro Estrada (ed.), *Un Siglo de Relaciones Internacionales de México*, p. xxi. See also Sierra (ed.), *México Su Evolución Social*, II, 430; García Granados, *Historia de México*, I, 117–118; Macedo, *Tres Monografías Que Dan Idea de una Parte de la Evolución Económica de México*, 200; Rosecrans to Seward, March 3, 1869; Rosecrans to the Secretary of State, March 22, 1869, *Mexico, Dispatches*, XXXV, A.U.S.

[148]*Diario Oficial*, December 18, 1874; Powell, *The Railroads of Mexico*, 108.

[149]Alfonso Teja Zabre, *Guide to the History of Mexico, A Modern Interpretation*, 322. But compare Valadés, *El Porfirismo, Nacimiento*, 340.

assignments in Mexico while Lerdo was minister of Foreign Relations—General William S. Rosecrans and Edward Lee Plumb—converted themselves, after leaving their official capacities, into aggressive lobbyists for American railroad projects in Mexico. The association of the two employments would not have dissipated Lerdo's strong patriotic apprehensions.

Whatever may have been the nature or degree of his fear of the United States, there were some historical precedents to justify his viewpoint, which was undoubtedly sincere and patriotic.[150] Even Edward Lee Plumb did not find the Mexican desire for isolation at all "strange," considering the fate of Texas, California, New Mexico, and Arizona. He also noted with understanding that "a large portion of the governing class in Mexico really, in their hearts, do not desire to promote but rather to delay and prevent the opening of communication and establishment of closer relations with the United States."[151] In the light of subsequent developments, most historians would probably agree that the Mexican people would not have suffered had Díaz's exaggerated recipe for the introduction of American capital been diluted with a dash of Lerdo's caution.

In concluding this brief survey of Lerdo's foreign policy, it should be remembered that his influence on Mexican foreign relations extended over a period of some thirteen years, interrupted only by the short interval after January, 1871, when he left the cabinet of Juárez. Cautious, consistent, nationalistic, and at times chauvinistic, Lerdo and his ideas left a deep impress on Mexican diplomatic history, his concepts reflecting admirably the pride of the Mexican people during and after the foreign intervention.

The governmental policy toward economic developments during Lerdo's administration was one of the most important aspects of the period. Closely tied with his foreign policy and centering on the problem of defining the basis on which foreign capital would enter Mexico, Lerdo's economic guidance was characterized by nationalism and *laissez faire*.[152] Judging by his actions and his consistently nationalistic outlook on foreign relations, Lerdo's ambitions for Mexico were: first, to smoke native capital from the

---

[150]See Cosmes, *Historia de Méjico*, XIX, 381–382; García Granados, *Historia de México*, I, 117–118; Macedo, *Tres Monografías Que Dan Idea de una Parte de la Evolución Económica de México*, 199–200.

[151]Plumb to J. Sanford Barnes, Mexico, July 31, 1871, *Plumb Papers*, VII.

[152]". . . it appears to us that one of the principal benefits which can be given to the nation is to convince the ranchers and merchants of the necessity of raising the spirit of enterprise among individuals and of not desiring to make of the government a species of tutor or proxy of the personal funds of citizens."—*Diario Oficial*, March 11, 1875.

traditional ruts of land investment, mortgages, and short-term, usurious loans into the new enterprises, especially railroad construction; and, second, to blend foreign capital with Mexican capital whenever necessary, placing all corporations formed, native, foreign, or mixed, under the fiction of a Mexican origin, completely subject to Mexican law, domiciled in Mexico, and severed from possible diplomatic redress against the Mexican government, thus avoiding international complications.

The oft-repeated and perhaps the most common accusation against Lerdo was that his government was indolent and decadent in regard to ecomomic promotion; and that he failed to heed the materialistic desires of "the people" who saw with anguish and envy the advances taking place in the great Northern Colossus, with its hundreds of miles of iron track, noisy locomotives, booming factories, telegraph lines, and other forms of machinery. If Lerdo's messages to congress were a fair index, if his concentration on railroad and telegraph promotion were analyzed impartially, it could be seen that he was neither unconscious of, nor negligent toward, the national longing for signs of practical progress. In truth, there was nothing sensational about his policy or accomplishments, statistically speaking, and there were no startling figures to quote when he left office, just as there were none after Díaz had been in the presidency four years.

Lerdo's policy was slow but promising and one which might have developed a Mexico for the Mexicans. Yet his impatient enemies misconstrued caution and farsightedness for stagnation. Had they pondered the economic issues more carefully, they would have understood that the only healthy modernization for an improverished Mexico was a slow one, dependent upon the coöperation and patience of the Mexicans and the amount of funds in the federal treasury. The Mexico of Lerdo's day was amazingly short on all three elements. As Lerdo once declared:

The executive has taken special care to continue investing, as much as the condition of the Treasury permits, in means of communication and various branches of material improvements so necessary for the promotion and development of the public wealth.[153]

Beyond that point, the Mexicans as individuals would have to display a little initiative themselves. While no contemporary ever had the perspective to see the stirrings of economic advance and the earnestness of Lerdo's government to provide the necessary conditions for business prosperity, a noted American financial historian has summarized those efforts as follows:

President Lerdo de Tejada was an able man—and one of the best qualified thus far called to the helm of state. Indeed, his progressiveness accounted in

---

[153]*Diario de los Debates*, September 16, 1874, 7th Congress, III, 13.

large part for the rapid economic advance of the country. The establishment
of banks had begun under Maximilian, and now the building of railroads under
the stimulus of government protection was begun, and in every department
of human activity there was progress.[154]

Railroads! Wealth! Progress! They were equivalents in the
Mexico of the 1870's. No other topic absorbed so much attention
or elicited so much interest during Lerdo's administration. Congress was engrossed constantly in discussion of railroad projects;
the press reflected a similar concentration; while a wave of American impresarios invaded Mexico, stirring the general enthusiasm
by fabricating grandiose illusions of a network of tracks crossing
the nation and converting it miraculously into the promised land
which men from Cortés to Napoleon III had surmised was latent in
Mexico.

"Mexico, which in its ideas has been elevated to the height of the
nations which are in the vanguard of Europe and America, lacks
only the railroad to acquire that well-being," wrote Vicente Riva
Palacio, reflecting the general importance of the railroad in the
scheme of Mexican ideology.[155] The question which had occupied
most prominently "the Mexican Congress, the President and his
cabinet, and the public press . . . for more than two years," observed
United States Minister Foster, had been that of government railroad concessions.[156] When Francisco Bulnes traveled across the
eastern United States in late 1874, his mind and eyes opened to
little but the romance of the American rails: the powerful locomotives, the number of lines converging upon Chicago, and the
"frightful velocity" at which persons moved in "a civilization
which corresponds to the fantásies of the rarest dreams."[157]

At the time Lerdo entered the presidency, facing a bubble of effervescence for railroads, Mexico had only one operable line of importance, the railroad from Mexico to Vera Cruz, which he himself
had inaugurated in January, 1873. Built primarily with British
capital at tremendous cost and hardship by the Mexican Railway
Company, it was bolstered by long-term government commitments
in the form of subsidies—subsidies which made a serious dent in
Mexico's always meager national revenues. That alone should
have served as a safety valve against railroad mania and as a source
of understanding for the official caution on further rail construction.

One of the first of many struggles involving railroads arose in
1873, when the Minister of Fomento revised the contract with the

[154]McCaleb, *The Public Finances of Mexico*, 144.
[155]Riva Palacio, *Historia de la Administración de Lerdo*, 336. See also González Navarro, *Vallarta*, 55.
[156]Foster to Fish, January 24, 1874, *U. S. Foreign Relations, 1874*, 723.
[157]*Diario Oficial*, January 8, 1875.

Mexican Railway Company, permitting (1) an increase in rates; (2) the right to build a wharf at Vera Cruz; and (3) the right to purchase the concession for a railroad from Vera Cruz to Puebla via Jalapa, already partially constructed.[158] The opposition raised a blatant protest on grounds that Lerdo was sacrificing national interest for the benefit of the British company, which, among other so-called fraudulent advantages, had gained a monopoly of the Gulf Coast traffic through the new concession on the Vera Cruz-to-Puebla line.[159] "The English company invades our territory, it is the arbitrator of our destinies, it is the soul of our public and private affairs," mourned Vicente Riva Palacio, a leader of the systematic opposition, who had revolutionary reason in his madness, and, he added, behind the arrangement was Lerdo's "mastery in the management of intrigue. . . ."[160] Although there were numberless charges against Lerdo for collusion with the British firm, even inimical writers have agreed that the implications were of an "absurd and calumnious species, because Don Sebastián Lerdo de Tejada was profoundly honorable," while his immeasurable pride made him look with disdain on such attacks and to scorn, as beneath his dignity, any attempt to refute them.[161]

Judging the question reasonably, Francisco Bulnes answered the opponents of the new contract that the Mexican Railway Company had overcome seemingly insuperable engineering obstacles and as a result found itself in a precarious financial position. Bulnes also pointed out, in defense of the government, that the old rates were suicidal to the company whose bankruptcy would signify a tremendous psychological handicap to further railroad development in Mexico. In regard to the monopoly charge, no other concessionaire had sought the Vera Cruz-to-Puebla contract, nor was the government in any way impeded from granting additional franchises for coastal transportation links.[162] At any rate, the executive eventually had its way on the renegotiation and could then turn its attention to the standard type of railroad problem, the granting of new concessions.

In general, the executive drafted contracts for two categories of concessions: those considered as trunk lines of national interest and those of a local nature, usually intrastate.

---

[158]*Ibid.*, May 3, 1873; Foster to Fish, December 31, 1873, *U. S. Foreign Relations, 1874,* 720.

[159]Riva Palacio chose the contract as the theme of one of his stereotyped attacks against Lerdo; but he did bring out every conceivable argument of the opposition.—*Historia de la Administración de Lerdo,* 354–363, 369–372, 379, 381–382.

[160]*Ibid.*, 379. Bancroft consistently parroted the conclusions of Riva Palacio.—Bancroft, *History of Mexico*, VI, 407.

[161]Cosmes, *Historia de Méjico*, XIX, 381; García Granados, *Historia de México*, I, 117.

[162]*El Domingo*, May 18, 1873.

The two projected trunk lines which commanded the focus of attention ran between Mexico City and some point on the Pacific Coast, a westward extension of the line from Vera Cruz to the capital, and between Mexico City and a point on the Rio Bravo, wherever the first American line was to terminate at the Texas-Mexican border. The competition for the contract to build the two trunk lines was severe, continuing through a large part of 1873. In the spring of that year, it appeared that Edward Lee Plumb, representing the International Railroad of Texas, had carried away the prize, since the Minister of Fomento had signed an agreement with him. Although the Plumb contract was rescinded subsequently by congress,[163] undoubtedly at Lerdo's signal, certain of the clauses should be noted as illustrative of Lerdo's apprehensions toward American capital: (1) No work was to begin on the Rio Bravo-to-Mexico City line until the International Railroad of Texas had built its line from San Antonio to the border, but construction on the Mexico City-to-Pacific line was to commence within nine months; and (2) the company was to be called "The Mexican International Railway Company," was to be "considered Mexican," and was to have no rights other than "those which the laws of the republic concede to Mexicans," even on alleging a denial of justice.[164]

Meanwhile, two other competitors had entered the field, presenting substantially the same offers as Plumb: James Sullivan, who had replaced General William S. Rosecrans on behalf of the Union Contract Company of Pennsylvania, and the Mexican Company Limited (generally styled the "Company of the Fourteen" after the number of directors), which in fiction was a native enterprise.[165] The congressional investigating committee then "ordered" the executive to reopen the negotiations and to draft a more favorable agreement with any one of the competitors, or on the basis of a joint undertaking of any two or all three of them.[166]

---

[163]*Diario Oficial*, November 9, 1873.

[164]Dublán y Lozano, *Legislación Mexicana*, XII, 451. A translation of the Plumb contract and other pertinent documents may be found in *U. S. Foreign Relations, 1873*, I, 673–690.

Plumb's letters (*Plumb Papers*, especially VIII–IX) give the fascinating inside story of his negotiations with important Mexican officials to align personal influence on the side of the company he represented. He was particularly anxious to obtain Lerdo's support for the railroad project and kept him fully informed at all times.—Plumb to J. Sanford Barnes, Mexico, September 9, and 29, 1871, *Plumb Papers*, VIII; *idem.* to *idem.*, July 27, August 24, 1872, *ibid.*, IX.

[165]A list of the fourteen directors appeared in *Diario Oficial*, October 8, 1873, March 12, 1874. All were residents of Mexico, although a part were of foreign nationality. See also García Granados, *Historia de México*, I, 118.

[166]Dublán y Lozano, *Legislación Mexicana*, XII, 513; *Diario Oficial*, November 9, 14, 1873; Riva Palacio, *Historia de la Administración de Lerdo*, 315.

Although the executive determined to concede the project to the Mexican Company Limited, it flatly denied the charge that the decision in any way involved the American nationality of the corporations which Plumb and Sullivan represented, pointing out that the new Mexican Company Limited's contract specifically allowed for fusion with one or both of the rejected American firms.[167] The favoritism to the "Company of the Fourteen" was probably less important for signifying Lerdo's fear of the commercial expansion of the United States, as his enemies claimed, than for reflecting his desire "for the formation of a national capitalism. . . ."[168]

Being primarily a company organized on paper and inseparable from the Mexican Railway Company (Vera Cruz-to-Mexico City line), the "Company of the Fourteen" directed its agents to Europe —significantly—in pursuit of the capital necessary to launch the enterprise. But the doors of the European financial marts were slammed bluntly in the faces of the Mexicans on account of the rancors of the foreign bondholders of the Mexican debt, still unliquidated. United States Minister Foster wrote:

The Mexican railroad company allege that the agents sent by them to Europe encountered the persistent opposition of the council of foreign bondholders in London, Paris, Frankfort, and other cities, and to its influence is attributed the complete failure to effect any financial arrangement, and the consequent inability to comply with the terms of the concession.[169]

Because of the attitude of Mexico's European creditors, the "Company of the Fourteen" was unable to comply with the stipulations of the contract which was declared defunct in 1874, thus returning the railroad problem to its original status.[170]

Undaunted by the failure and not indifferent to public aspirations for more railroad trackage,[171] the executive, under the direction of the Minister of Fomento, pursued the drafting of new contracts. At the time Lerdo was ousted by revolution, three concessions of national or international importance had been approved by congress, and on one of them some progress had been made in actual construction. The first was a contract for a line from the capital

[167]*Diario Oficial*, November 21, 1873, January 11, 1874; Foster to Fish, November 22, 1873, *U. S. Foreign Relations, 1874*, 718.

[168]Valadés, *El Porfirismo, Nacimiento*, 340. Riva Palacio favored the Sullivan offer, or so he feigned, and went through his routine to attack the administration for its decision in favor of the Mexican Company Limited.— Riva Palacio, *Historia de la Administración de Lerdo*, 277–283, 300–304, 310–313, 315.

[169]Foster to Fish, May 29, 1874, *U. S. Foreign Relations, 1874*, 752.

[170]*Diario Oficial*, May 12, 1874; Riva Palacio, *Historia de la Administración de Lerdo*, 412.

[171]See Blas Balcárcel (Minister of Fomento) to the Deputy Secretaries of the Congress of the Union, November 16, 1874, *Diario Oficial*, November 23, 1874.

to León (Guanajuato), via Querétaro, Salamanca, Celaya, and Guanajuato, granted to Sebastián Camacho and Antonio Mendizábal under the name of the Mexican Central Railroad, again a poor disguise for the Mexican Railway Company.[172] Under the terms of the arrangement, the government was to be one of the principal investors; the incorporation of United States as well as European capital was permitted; the company obtained an exclusive lottery privilege, the proceeds from which were to meet in part the subvention of 9,500 pesos per kilometer constructed; and the government required a bond of 150,000 pesos from the company to insure "the realization of the work and so that the concession may not be entirely illusory like the others have been. . . ."[173] Congress approved the contract, but not until the opposition had made the most of the "immorality" connected with the unique feature of the lottery,[174] and the deputies of the Pacific Coast states had complained about the failure of the government to consider their interests by not extending the line to the coast.[175] One deputy also demonstrated the prevailing belief in Lerdo's hostility toward United States capital when he commented on the provision in the contract which allowed the incorporation of American resources: "I am surprised only that the authorization comprehends the United States, when the tendencies of the circle who defend the proposal are to exclude from everything the influences of United States capital."[176]

The cartoonists also found a rich opportunity in the negotiation, especially by implying Lerdo's collusion with Ramón Guzmán and the Mexican Railway Company, for which the Mexican Central Company was erected as a screen. *El Padre Cobos* ran a series of pictures entitled "A Fable," satirizing the Mexican Central Company, its contracts, and the procedure through which it had passed:

(1) Lerdo (dressed as a child) held an egg marked "Lottery and Railroad": "This child laid the egg."

---

[172]Cosmes, *Historia de Méjico*, XXII, 704–705; Riva Palacio, *Historia de la Administración de Lerdo*, 448.

[173]Balcárcel to the Secretaries of congress, November 16, 1874, *Diario Oficial*, November 23, 1874. See also Riva Palacio, *Historia de la Administración de Lerdo*, 442–446. Cosmes echoed the adverse opinions of Riva Palacio. —Cosmes, *Historia de Méjico*, XXII, 701–706.

[174]Lerdo had opposed a lottery privilege for the construction of the Toluca-to-Mexico City railroad several years earlier.—Lerdo to Mariano Riva Palacio, February 13, 1871, Mariano Riva Palacio Papers, Folder 172, UT. When his opponents pointed out the inconsistency of the government's grant of such a privilege to the Mexican Central Railroad, Lerdo replied that since congress had seen fit to validate lotteries, it was reasonable to establish a monopoly, when it was intended for a beneficent purpose.—*Diario Oficial*, December 3, 1874.

[175]*Diario de los Debates*, December 4, 1874, 7th Congress, III, 839–844.

[176]*Ibid.*, December 4, 1874, 7th Congress, III, 839.

(2) Balcárcel (the Minister of Fomento) stood by a pot containing the egg: "This child cooked it."

(3) Camacho and Mendizábal (the concessionaires) stood by the egg, holding money bags: "These children take out the salt."

(4) Ramón Guzmán (Lerdo's congressional leader) stood with a long stick in front of the egg which had been placed in a bowl marked "Congress": "This child stirred it."[177]

The stepsister contract tied with the León-to-Mexico project was the concession granted to Edward Lee Plumb, the American still representing the International Railroad of Texas, for a line from León to an undetermined point on the Rio Bravo, via Lagos, Aguascalientes, Zacatecas, Durango, San Luis Potosí, Saltillo, and Monterrey. It was a stepsister because it was granted to one of the theretofore hapless American impresarios.[178] Although a serious venture on the part of the Mexican government, considering the 200,000-peso bond required of the company to insure faithful compliance, the terms were so stated as to make it a project of the future which would allow for sufficient time to complete and partly absorb the cost of the Mexico-to-León route.[179]

The grant of the contract to Plumb probably demonstrated that Lerdo was not opposed adamantly to American enterprise in Mexico; and that the legendary statement attributed to him—"between strength and weakness, the desert"—must be qualified considerably. It was obvious that he preferred native, or native and European capital to American; yet he was willing to modify his preference to the demands of the country and the international situation. Certainly, when it came to a choice of either sacrificing the national dignity by making diplomatic or other advances to Mexico's European creditors or turning toward United States capital, he never hesitated to take the second alternative.

The third important railroad grant, effective at the time of the revolution in 1876, went to David Boyle Blair for a line from Guaymas, Sonora, to a northern terminus on the international border within the limits of the area opposite the state of Arizona. Except that the subsidy was to be in unimproved national lands within Sonora, the agreement had no unusual features. However, Blair's company was not to alienate any of the lands acquired to citizens of

---

[177]*El Padre Cobos*, December 13, 1874.

[178]Plumb had informed the editor of the *Diario Oficial* that he was optimistic about the approval of his scheme and "that the railroad of Señores Camacho, Mendizábal, and Company [Mexico-to-León], far from prejudicing his project, will facilitate its realization."—*Diario Oficial*, November 27, 1874.

[179]Dublán y Lozano, *Legislación Mexicana*, XII, 749–758. The Plumb contract along with the executive's explanation may also be found in *Diario Oficial*, December 18, 1874. Congress passed on the agreement for the railroad and "corresponding telegraph line" on May 29, 1875.—*Ibid.*, June 7, 1875.

"the northern countries" without the express permission of the federal government.[180]

The second category of railroad concession was of local interest and granted to governors as a state project, to private companies, or to individuals. Among the more important concessions of this class which were subsidized by the federal government were: (1) from Pachuca to "any point" intersecting the Mexico City-to-Vera Cruz railroad, conceded to Governor Justino Fernández in 1873;[181] (2) from Puebla to Izúcar de Matamoros, Puebla, conceded to private individuals in 1873;[182] and (3) from Mérida to Progreso, Yucatán, conceded to private individuals in 1874.[183] In addition, there were a number of other small roads under construction or projected, especially in Jalisco, Zacatecas, and Vera Cruz.[184] Meanwhile, a segment of the Mexico-to-Toluca line, a concession antedating Lerdo's administration, had been completed from Mexico as far as Tlanepantla, and Lerdo attended the inaugural celebration in the spring of 1874.[185] Later in the same year two "very handsome" locomotives arrived for the Toluca line to replace the mule power being used, so that the trip from Tlanepantla to Mexico could be made at the fabulous rate of "half an hour more or less."[186]

However feeble some of the state projects may have appeared, the federal government was aiding them directly in some instances and always voicing praise for any actual progress realized. It was further evidence of Lerdo's hope to breed a "native capitalism" and his desire to prod Mexicans into sharing responsibility for effecting the national dream of modernizing Mexico.

In 1876, there were only about 416 miles of track in Mexico,[187] but progress was being shown on the Mexico-to-León route as well as on various state concessions, while the Vera Cruz-to-Jalapa railroad had been finished in 1875 after considerable effort and cost.[188] It seemed, then, that construction was on the verge of more substantial results when the Díaz revolution broke, interrupted the various works, and destroyed parts of the routes then in

---

[180]Dublán y Lozano, *Legislación Mexicana*, XII, 758–767; *Diario de los Debates*, April 24, 1875, 7th Congress, IV, 109; *Diario Oficial*, June 21, 1875.

[181]Dublán y Lozano, *Legislación Mexicana*, XII, 448–449; *Diario de los Debates*, May 25, 28, 1873, 6th Congress, IV, 609–613, 644–645.

[182]*Diario Oficial*, June 9, 1873.

[183]*Diario de los Debates*, April 22, 1874, 7th Congress, II, 165–167; *Diario Oficial*, December 11, 1874.

[184]*Diario Oficial*, December 16, 27, 1874; February 8, 1875.

[185]*Ibid.*, March 27, 1874.

[186]*Ibid.*, August 29, November 4, 1874.

[187]Powell, *The Railroads of Mexico*, 1. Luis Pombo calculated a total of 666 kilometers.—Luis Pombo, *México: 1876–1892*, 75.

[188]The Jalapa railroad was animal traction. See *Diario Oficial*, June 17, 1875; Valadés, *El Porfirismo, Nacimiento*, 344–345.

operation.[189] Porfirist historians have taken great pride in comparing the puny figure of 1876 to that of a much later period, without accounting for the essential experimentation performed by Juárez and Lerdo during the years 1867 to 1876 and without mentioning that after Díaz's first term, equivalent in time to Lerdo's administration, railroad mileage totalled but 674.[190] Sensational advance was not a part of Lerdo's railroad policy, but it is only fair to recognize in it the elements of sanity and patriotism.

While the interest in development of railroads virtually submerged other economic efforts of the government, consistently monopolizing the center of the stage, other efforts did exist, almost all of which were connected with the improvement of transportation and communication. Perhaps a poor second, but second only to the railroad schemes, was the extension of telegraph lines. One of Lerdo's cherished goals was to unite by telegraph every state capital with Mexico City;[191] and he always summarized telegraphic construction in some detail in his messages to congress. While many of the more ambitious states like Mexico, Jalisco, and Michoacán pushed ahead with their own resources in the building of local lines, the federal régime was shouldering the burden. Of course, the telegraph was no innovation with Lerdo's administration, much progress having been made in extending the network since the first line was installed in 1851.[192] But Lerdo was proud to inform congress in April, 1875, that his government had added 2,600 kilometers of telegraph lines since mid-1872.[193]

Though it is not the purpose here to present a statistical compilation of either state or federal telegraph lines, it should be noted that the government press carried complete reports on the arrival of equipment, the inaugural ceremonies for new lines, and other items pertinent to maintenance, repair, and construction. Since the government was constantly calling attention to telegraph developments, attempting to derive all possible credit for advances, it did seem that Lerdo hoped that an alternate sign of material progress would remove some of the impatience resulting from his cautious railroad policy. Perhaps exasperated by the frequent wail

[189]Vicente Riva Palacio, the Porfirst revolutionary leader and chief complainant against the alleged decadence of Lerdo's railroad policy, summarized the status of the railroads, the effect of the revolution, and the fate of the contracts outstanding when Lerdo was ousted from office in his *Memoria de Fomento, 1877*, 252–264.

[190]The figure, not the comment, is from Powell, *The Railroads of Mexico*, 1.

[191]*Diario de los Debates*, April 1, 1874, 7th Congress, II, 6.

[192]Two essays on the history of the Mexican telegraph and its founder, Juan de la Granja, may be found in *La Sociedad*, October 28, 1858; *Diario Oficial*, January 15, 1873.

[193]*Diario de los Debates*, April 1, 1875, 7th Congress, IV, 6.

of the opposition about the government's decadence on economic matters, the *Diario Oficial* wrote:

In the flowering republic of Chile there are 3,000 kilometers of telegraph lines; in Mexico there are more than 9,000. Those who speak of the *inertia of the government* should keep this fact in mind, considering also that in no American country, with the exception of the United States, is there a greater extension of this class than in the Republic of Mexico.[194]

After the priority expenditures on the railroads and telegraphs, the government distributed the remainder of its scant funds among subsidies for Pacific and Gulf Coast steamship lines, diligence routes, and road improvements. In addition, Lerdo garnered the funds to purchase four coast guard vessels, the real origin of the Mexican naval service.[195]

If Lerdo accomplished nothing spectacular, economically speaking, it was due to the lack of funds and the more pressing demands of governmental security and stability, not to negligence or his personal attitude, as generally concluded. That is one of the most distorted of many injustices which history has generously allotted him. Lerdo had made an honest statement when he informed congress that the executive had done the best "the condition of the treasury would permit" to give impulse to the various branches of material improvements.[196]

The years 1872 to 1876 saw a recrudescence of the ancient conflict between church and state which had been interred, supposedly, with Maximilian in 1867. Although Juárez's policy toward the church after the intervention has been praised for its moderation and astuteness,[197] it probably would be characterized more accurately as one of neglect and oversight. In 1867, while the conservative party was completely discredited and the church lay humble and supine, there was a perfect moment for constitutionalizing and enforcing the Reforms with a maximum of ease and a minimum of opposition. Time, the greatest of all healers, had replaced a bit of the old spirit of defiance into the empty political veins of the church, a spirit ready to reveal itself when friction with the state should arise. It was, then, a somewhat rejuvenated church which

[194]*Diario Oficial*, March 23, 1874.

[195]Dublán y Lozano, *Legislación Mexicana*, XII, 521–523; *Diario Oficial*, March 30, September 21, 1875.

[196]*Diario de los Debates*, September 16, 1874, 7th Congress, III, 13. See also Lesley Byrd Simpson's penetrat ng review of José C. Valadés, *El Porfirismo, Historia de un Régimen: El Nacimiento*, in *The Hispanic American Historical Review*, XXII (February, 1942), 119–120.

[197]Cosmes, *Historia de Méjico*, XXII, 523.

Lerdo faced on assuming the presidency in 1872; and what aggravated the four-year relationship from the outset was the church's disappointment in not discovering in Lerdo a sympathizer, as it erroneously had conjectured.[198] Overlooking the consistent endorsement of the liberal program in Lerdo's political career and implying clerical favoritism from his duties as rector of San Ildefonso, the political rights he had attempted to grant the clergy in the *convocatoria* of 1867,[199] and the number of times the opposition press had styled him "the Jesuit," the church fell under the temporary hallucination that Lerdo would inaugurate a pro-clerical government or one which would look upon the church with a kindly eye. Although Lerdo attempted to destroy the misconception, first by word and then by deed, the clerical resentment was in no manner mitigated.

The religious conflict under Lerdo was a continuous battle, but it revolved about three main issues, all of which have been relatively exhausted, in a factual sense, by previous historians: (1) the constitutionalizing of the Laws of Reform (1873) and the subsequent enabling act (1874); (2) the expulsion of the Jesuits (1873) and the *exclaustración* of the Sisters of Charity (1874–1875), as religious orders living in Mexico contrary to the Laws of Reform; and (3) the protection and favoritism which Lerdo allegedly granted to Protestants in Mexico.

The Laws of Reform, already discussed, were presumably a *fait accompli* when Lerdo came to office in 1872, and the constitutionalizing of them should not have been source of rancor to the clergy. Speaking before the senate in 1889, at the time of Lerdo's death, Alfredo Chavero pointed out that during the last days of Juárez "his constant preoccupation, the theme of his conversations, was his inflexible desire that the laws of the Reform would become a part of the Constitution." "The unexpected death of Señor Juárez did not permit him to realize his desire. Señor Lerdo rose to the presidency and it was his first concern to see it effected." In a short time, Chavero added, Lerdo promulgated the additions to the organic law, "and thus he had the glory of completing the work of Juárez."[200]

Why, then, did the church defy the government with vehemence if the constitutionalizing of the laws was a technical change, merely giving them a status loftier than the ordinary statute? Because Lerdo chose to enforce the laws to the letter, as they had not been enforced under a more careless policy during Juárez's last years.

[198]See Toro, *La Iglesia y el Estado*, 443.
[199]Dublán y Lozano, *Legislación Mexicana*, X, 50–51.
[200]*Diario de los Debates de la Cámara de Senadores*, April 23, 1889, 14th Congress, 2nd per., 188.

Just as an irritated church was determined to resent laws which
had teeth, so Lerdo was equally obstinate in his zeal to apply them,
for the struggle soon involved, in his way of thinking, something
completely divorced from religious issues: compliance with the
laws, one of the keystones of his entire program of government.
Once the opposing forces had joined, Lerdo realized that the prestige of his régime was at stake, and, far from being conciliatory,
he seemed to relish the conflict as offering a perfect example to
demonstrate to the nation that the federal government was not to be
sidestepped with impunity.

Edition after edition of the *Diario Oficial* carried items regarding disrespect of the Laws of Reform. If they were violated, the
government demanded a report on who was guilty, who was responsible for laxness, and what corrective measures were being
taken;[201] and the executive always incorporated the monotonous
moral about the necessary "respect for the laws." "No one is
empowered not to support the laws," insisted the concealed voice of
Lerdo, "and the priests by the right of the independence of the
church, cannot do so either."[202] In denouncing a presbyter who had
denied religious rites to a dying man because he would not sign a
protest against the Laws of Reform, the oracle of the administration warned: "The priest, be he Catholic or not, is a citizen of
Mexico, and as such he must support the existing laws and abstain
from procuring that they be disobeyed."[203]

With the promulgation of the detailed enabling act (1874), restricting public manifestations of religion and eliminating religious
instruction from the curricula of the public schools,[204] more fuel
was added to a blaze which had passed the limits of reconciliation
because of other events which had transpired in the interim. Of
course, the enabling act applied to all cults, but since Mexico was
overwhelmingly Catholic, it was virtually impossible to sell the idea
that such legislation was anything but patent hostility of the state
toward the Catholic Church. Actually, the enabling law, coinciding with the secular trend, was intended to put all religious expression off the streets, out of the public sight, and back into the
temples; nevertheless, the Catholic Church was bound to resent
the denial of its ancient ceremonials such as open-air festivals and
processions.

To carry on a desultory strife with the state, the church used the
media of the press, the pulpit, and its strong control over women,
and it was that last-named method, "a sordid war of salons and

[201]For a few examples, see *Diario Oficial*, April 3, 4, 5, 1874; January 4,
August 6, 1875.
[202]*Ibid.*, February 6, 1875.
[203]*Ibid.*, February 22, 1873.
[204]Dublán y Lozano, *Legislación Mexicana*, XII, 683–688.

kitchens,"[205] against which the government protested fiercely, reflecting Lerdo's increasing personal bitterness toward the clergy. "To gain ground for propaganda through the use of women and the ignorant always has been the tactics of the Roman clergy, confessing flatly their inability to open the road by means of explanation and clarity."[206] In addition, during the whole period of the administration, the government carried on a "running battle" with the three Catholic papers—*La Voz de México*, *El Pájaro Verde*, and *La Idea Católica*. The Catholic press "was cruelly sarcastic and passionately resisting" to Lerdo's presidential program,[207] and the *Diario Oficial* once indicated how weary it had become of upholding its part in the contest: ". . . we see [*El Pájaro Verde*] constantly occupied in the sterile work of combatting" the enforcement of the Laws of Reform.[208]

Meanwhile, a second issue developed which made the widening rift between Lerdo and the church irreparable: the expulsion in 1873 of several Jesuits of foreign extraction as "pernicious," and the *exclaustración* of a number of nuns in the order of the Sisters of Charity who were engaged in social work, primarily in hospitals. Long before the executive took action, the liberal press had prodded the government on account of its failure to proceed against the two religious orders, which, it was asserted, were functioning as monastic communities and openly flouting the laws.[209] Since the Jesuits and the nuns were given ample warning of an impending investigation into their activities,[210] it appeared that the church conspired to make a test case of the question. If so, the rejoinder of the government came quickly, for in sequence the Jesuits and the Sisters were hustled off to Vera Cruz for embarkation. To be consistent, less in his church policy than on his principle of respect for the law, Lerdo could not have acted otherwise; but he attempted to make clear that:

Señor Lerdo, as a sincere and just republican, could not expel the Jesuits from the nation by the fact that they are foreigners and disciples of Loyola,

---

[205]Sierra, *Evolución Política del Pueblo Mexicano*, 433.

[206]*Diario Oficial*, February 6, 1875. See also *ibid.*, February 11, 13, 1875; Toro, *La Iglesia y el Estado*, 446.

[207]Sierra, *Evolución Política del Pueblo Mexicano*, 432.

[208]*Diario Oficial*, January 4, 1875. Yet the government "welcomed" the establishment of a Protestant press, *La Verdad*, in 1873.—*Ibid.*, November 15, 1873.

[209]*Diario Oficial*, April 8, 1873. United States Minister Nelson noted that several European Jesuits in Mexico had provoked a violent opposition in the press, but that the government had announced it would take no action provided the Jesuits did not "render it necessary by systematic disregard of the laws. . . ."—Nelson to Fish, May 1, 1873, *U. S. Foreign Relations, 1873*, I, 668.

[210]The *Diario Oficial* (February 12, 1873) had called attention to the Jesuits, who were wearing their "ancient habits" on the streets of Mexico City, Acapulco, Vera Cruz, and Morelia.

since it is well known that men of all parts of the world may live here tranquilly, provided they do not declare themselves contumacious opposers of the legit.mate authorities.[211]

And much earlier the *Diario Oficial* had tried to explain to the Catholic *La Voz de México* that:

The President does not persecute Catholicism, or any other religion or sect, solely because it is such: if, tomorrow, some foreign priest, Protestant, Turkish, or Buddhist, comes to the country and practices the illegitimate methods which the expelled Jesuits practiced, he will be considered like the latter, without regard to his beliefs or religious doctrines, whatever they may be.[212].

Justo Sierra, writing for *El Siglo* and supporting the government in words which almost appeared to be those of Lerdo himself, pointed out that laws were laws and must be obeyed: ". . . the laws of exception are the bankruptcy of justice in a country, because they enclose a confession of impotency. . . ." And he continued:

It is necessary to keep in mind that this method [*i.e.,* expulsion of the Jesuits] has not been taken through fear, nor because the government might have been faced with the dangerous possibilities of this or that religious tendency; this, however serious it m'ght be, was completely outside [the government's] competency; nor because it believes that the truth of liberal principles needs its protection; on the contrary, it has desired simply to record that [the Jesuits] inhabit a country of efficacious laws and that they ought to be respected.[213]

The *exclaustración* of the Sisters of Charity offered little variation in the pattern followed against the Jesuits, except that femininity and the recognized social services which the nuns were performing swung much sympathy in their favor.[214] "Consistency" required that they cease their communal life,[215] but the government permitted them the option of remaining in Mexico as individuals, not continuing as a monastic order, or departing.[216] They chose the route of the Jesuits.

The final source of church-state conflict was Lerdo's favorable disposition toward the Protestant clergymen who were enter-

---

[211]*Ibid.,* April 7, 1875.

[212]*Ibid.,* August 7, 1873.

[213]*El Siglo,* August 16, 1873. *El Monitor,* the other outstanding liberal paper of Mexico City, though generally hostile toward Lerdo, also supported the expulsion of the Jesuits. See *El Monitor,* May 27, 31, 1873.

[214]Bancroft, *History of Mexico,* VI, 405; Pérez Verdía, *Historia de Jalisco,* III, 429; James A. Magner, *Men of Mexico,* 456, 457.

[215]John W. Foster, "The Contest for the Laws of Reform in Mexico," *The American Historical Review,* XV (October, 1909, to July, 1910), 526. The Sisters sought Foster's aid to ease the difficulties of their departure from Mexico.

[216]*Diario Oficial,* December 16, 1874; García Granados, *Historia de México,* I, 124.

ing Mexico in small numbers in the early 1870's. That attitude was the proverbial red flag before the bull, since the typical view of the Mexican clergy toward Protestants was anything but mild and probably well expressed in a pastoral letter, written in 1867, by the Bishop of Vera Cruz. Protestantism, expounded the Bishop, was a force of "heresy, error, schism, and rebellion," all Protestants being "wolves in sheeps' clothing."[217]

The generally accepted opinion that Lerdo consciously tried to cultivate a puny Protestant plant in Mexico's deep Catholic soil sprang principally from one episode. In April, 1873, Thomas H. Nelson, the United States minister to Mexico, introduced six Protestant missionaries to the President. One of them made a short address at the interview, and, in turn, "the President made an earnest and energetic reply, which was completely satisfactory to the gentlemen in question."[218] Indeed, one can understand why the speech was reassuring to the newcomers, but no great imagination was required to perceive why it was less "satisfactory" to the Catholic clergy. Lerdo's reply was as follows:

The Constitution of Mexico guarantees tolerance and protection to all religious opinions in the most absolute and unquestionable manner. Although the fanaticism of other forms of religion can at times arouse popular disturbances against the Protestants, I am certain that the opinion of all the enlightened classes of our society is ardently in favor of complete tolerance, and I shall answer for the conduct of all authorities who depend directly upon the Federal Government.

Besides the obligation of protecting religious liberty, I have the pleasure of saying that the preachers of Protestant doctrine in Mexico *have distinguished themselves by their conduct as citizens who obey the laws,* without one case to the contrary having come to my attention.[219]

Of course, each word was a handful of salt on the open wound between Lerdo and the Catholic Church, but when *El Pájaro Verde* protested bitterly against Lerdo's partiality, the *Diario Oficial* replied blandly that the President would praise "other cults" for similar merits provided "the priests of other religions or sects observe the same conduct."[220]

To criticize Lerdo for providing police protection to Protestants was not legitimate evidence of his favoritism. He merely attempted, as the law required, to extend security against the violence of aroused Catholic mobs. Since such incidents usually

---

[217]Reprinted in *El Siglo*, February 3, 1868.

[218]Nelson to Fish, April 26, 1873, *U. S. Foreign Relations, 1873*, I, 667–668.

[219]*Diario Oficial*, August 9, 1873. The italics are the present writer's. Also quoted by Cosmes, *Historia de Méjico*, XXII, 535. The second paragraph of Lerdo's speech undoubtedly was aimed at the Catholic clergy for their obstinacy toward the Laws of Reform and for denouncing the government on the expulsion of the Jesuits.

[220]*Diario Oficial*, August 9, 1873.

elicited diplomatic protests, the government was obliged to show some vigor in prosecuting the guilty leaders. The outstanding instance of that kind during Lerdo's term was the assassination of an American missionary in Jalisco in 1874 by a mob incited by Catholic priests.[221] Five persons were sentenced and executed for the atrocity, none of whom was a priest, however.[222]

Regardless of religious convictions, no thinking Mexican would have countenanced personal violence against non-Catholics. As Ignacio Altamirano, the great liberal author-statesman declared, when seeking aid for the Protestants against molestation:

I am a radical partisan of the tolerance of cults, and consequently I take to heart whatever is done by the fanatical enemies of that great political reform. The Protestants in the district of Chalco [state of Mexico] have accepted Protestantism with enthusiasm; but they fight with the priests. . . .

You may be sure that if this were England and the Catholics were oppressed, I would place myself on their side against the Lutherans [i.e., Protestants], because I defend not this or that religion, but the liberty of conscience which has cost us so much to attain.[223]

Other aspects of Lerdo's policy did show Protestant partiality, but not in any religious sense. For one thing, the *Diario Oficial* occasionally printed Protestant news in a tone invariably favorable. For example, it commented on a letter of a young Protestant minister, José María González, as follows:

[González] toils to conciliate religion with the sciences, with the advances of the century, and with republican institutions; he propagates *respect for the law* and love for the country; he counsels tolerance; he defends the dogmas of equality and liberty; and, for all this, he must have our poor sympathies. . . .

It is pleasing to us that liberty of cults may be a reality in Mexico. . . . [224]

On the other hand, the *Diario Oficial* knifed the Catholic Church frequently, partly a reflection of vengeance against the Catholic journals and partly in ridicule of certain social and educational concepts which the government considered antiquated, but never on any fundamental religious beliefs.[225] Lerdo was supposed to have favored Protestantism

not because its dogma is more profound than the Catholic, nor its philosophy more lofty, nor its morality more pure; it is because our masses have been taught neither the morality nor the philosophy nor the doctrines of Catholicism;

---

[221]Foster to Fish, April 15, 1874, *U. S. Foreign Relations, 1874*, 744.

[222]Foster to Fish, October 19, 1875, *ibid., 1876*, 386; *Diario Oficial*, March 6, 8, April 6, 12, 19, 25, 1874; October 18, 1875.

[223]Ignacio M. Altamirano to Mariano Riva Palacio, January 10, 1871, Mariano Riva Palacio Papers, Folder 172, UT.

[224]*Diario Oficial*, January 29, 1875. The italics are the present writer's. For additional examples, see *ibid.*, November 15, 1873; July 2, August 21, 1874.

[225]See an article entitled "How the Roman Priests Understand Progress," *ibid.*, August 28, 1875.

It is because . . . religion . . . has been taught only in its forms, which, however grandiose they may be, will serve only to dominate those who may be influenced by a species of religious materialism, but not to satisfy the aspirations of intelligence. . . .[226]

The evidence seemed rather clear that Lerdo favored the Protestants for educational reasons and more probably to advertise to the world that a devoutly Catholic Mexico was absolutely tolerant. But it is difficult to separate the complicated question from his increasing personal acrimony toward the Catholic clergy. It is interesting to note, however, that Juárez once told Justo Sierra: "He [Juárez] desired to Mexicanize Protestantism in order to conquer the Indians; these Indians need a religion which obliges them to read and does not force them to spend their savings on candles for the saints."[227] Was the Protestant policy another illustration of the unity of those two inseparable quantities, Juárez and Lerdo?

In attempting a hazardous conclusion about Lerdo's religious policy, it should be noted that historians partial to the Catholic Church could not be expected to view his career under any but the dimmest light.[228] To them he was a bitter enemy of the church and all the worse because he had stepped out of character—out of his religious past—to promote a concerted attack on Catholicism, solely for popularity and vanity. The church's attitude toward Lerdo was well summarized at the time of his death in 1889 by the Catholic *La Voz de México*, when it explained to a liberal journal why it had not eulogized the deceased ex-President:

Well, and what more should we have done [*i.e.*, written about Lerdo], foolish brother [*El Monitor*]? Perhaps we are obligated to mention the nocturnal assault on the domicile of the nuns in order to fling them into the street at midnight without protection? The Reforms and additions to the Constitution? The expulsion of the Sisters of Charity, and so many things worthy of eulogy and remembrance for the Catholics?[229]

The explanation of the harshness against Lerdo's religious policies, discharged by certain liberal historians writing under the Díaz régime, is less obvious; but one need only recall: first, that any attack against Lerdo was legitimate, since the Díaz epoch was open hunting season on Lerdismo; and second, that Lerdo's church policy

---

[226]*El Siglo* quoted by Cosmes, *Historia de Méjico*, XXII, 529. Because of the political orientation of *El Siglo* at the time, Cosmes believed that the article reflected Lerdo's personal views.

[227]Juárez quoted by Sierra, *Juárez*, 480. See also Leopoldo Zea, *El Positivismo en México*, 64–65.

[228]See P. Mariano Cuevas, S.J., *Historia de la Iglesia en México*, V, 384–386, 394, 405–406; Regis Planchet, *La Cuestión Religiosa en México*, 132; Bravo Ugarte, *Historia de México*, III, 360–361.

[229]*La Voz de México*, April 25, 1889.

had to be placed in a gloomy light in order to justify Díaz's reversal to conciliation and relaxation of the Laws of Reform.[230]

Actually, there was little anti-Catholic in Lerdo's religious policy. In a Mexico where the masses were devoutly Catholic, he was attempting to apply to the letter of the law the separation of church and state, the complete tolerance of all religions, and the advanced tenets written into the organic law. The consistency with which he applied that policy was admirable. But by using the Laws of Reform as his greatest national lesson in "respect for the law," he tread on clerical toes and threw that element of society into the willing arms of the Díaz revolutionists who were collectors of all forms of discontent against the government. It can be said with certainty, however, that had any other group of the population obstinately defied "the law," as did the clergy under Lerdo, he would have turned upon it with an equivalent zeal.

The administration of Sebastián Lerdo was probably the most tolerant and liberal régime which Mexico had ever known, because Lerdo placed individual guarantees on a par with peace, order, and respect for the law and because of the tranquil conditions prevailing during most of the four-year period. He seemed to believe, with the ardor of a religious faith, that "the rights of man" and effective national government were compatible goals for the Mexico of his day. Men said what they pleased, as was reflected in the opposition speeches in congress; wrote what they pleased, as shown in the opposition press; and chose a faith according to their own consciences, knowing that the government would not molest them in their form of worship and would protect them from violence to the extent possible.[231]

To determine the exact amount of credit which should go to Lerdo for the varied cultural awakening of the era as a return on his investment in liberties would be precarious; but the liberal soil he tried to cultivate appeared to yield a fertile harvest from the efforts of private initiative. Certainly, the government displayed interest in the promotion of education and literature and the development of a national theater;[232] and it gave a stamp of approval

[230]Cosmes was perhaps the most inconsistent of the "liberal" writers who attacked Lerdo's religious policy.—*Historia de Méjico*, XXII, 523–524, 532–539, 574–591. See also Bulnes, *El Verdadero Díaz*, 93.

[231]It was significant that Lerdo liked to style his own régime "the tolerant, patriotic, and progressive administration which Señor Lerdo directs. . . ."— *Diario Oficial*, January 1, 1875.

[232]On education, see Callcott, *Liberalism in Mexico 1857–1929*, 95–97. Armando de María y Campos had only the highest praise for the "magnificent gesture of the Lerdist administration in protecting national authors. . . ."— María y Campos, *La Dramática Mexicana durante el Gobierno del Presidente Lerdo de Tejada*, 38. See also *ibid.*, 11, 29.

to the numerous private organizations, political, economic, scientific, and literary, which were established and flourished.

By far the most important political aspect of Lerdo's program of liberalism was the freedom he promised the press which he honored with a blind zeal during his years in office. It seemed that Lerdo was willing to sacrifice anything before reneging on that commitment, even when he was justified in so doing. Ironically, the freedom of the press, by his standards one of the brightest jewels of his presidency, transformed itself into a monster which turned upon its patron. In time the press became a potent instrument of revolution and another of the principal causes of Lerdo's eventual downfall.

In his Manifesto of 1872, Lerdo vowed respect for the sanctity of the constitutional guarantees, adding that:

the most precious of them, the freedom of the press, which protects and defends the others, will be inviolable for me, as it was, without exception, in the protracted period during which I functioned as a minister for the illustrious President [Juárez] whose loss we lament. . . . Of the excesses which the press may commit, the best corrective is the press itself, enlightened, free, the echo of all opinions and all parties.[233]

Lerdo's consistent attitude toward the publishing world of his time—"absolute freedom of the press," not just in words but in practice—was a Magna Carta confirmed time and again in the *Diario Oficial*:

We have presented our opinion, specifically, on diverse occasions in the following manner: the press should only be combatted by the press itself; if it complies with its mission, it will prosper, if it does not comply with it, it will encounter discredit and ruin where it should find popularity and prestige.[234]

In fact, Lerdo was magnanimous to the point of overlooking almost every calumny about his government as conjured by a diabolically imaginative opposition press, "except those which have as their object to present it as an adversary of the free manifestation of ideas."[235] For, explained the *Diario Oficial* on behalf of the President, "we have always upheld and we shall never cease to uphold" the liberty of the press, since "it is better to tolerate the abuses of the press or attempt to avoid them: thus thought Señor Juárez and thus thinks Señor Lerdo. . . ."[236] Pursuing to the letter his famous maxim, "the press will correct the press," Lerdo never failed to refute the implication that he had interfered with publications or sought to suppress an opposition journal: "[the gov-

---

[233]*Diario Oficial*, July 28, 1872.

[234]*Ibid.*, May 21, 1873.

[235]*Ibid.*, March 3, 1875.

[236]*Ibid.*, October 23, 1873. Note again the continuity in the policies of Juárez and Lerdo.

ernment] has demonstrated that in place of fearing, it prefers the battle of the press."[237]

It was odd that the guarantee of liberty for the press did not evoke unconditional praise from all factions, regardless of political alignment. No doubt Lerdo hoped that tolerance would act as the cement of his popularity and tried to extract all possible credit from his policy. Mexico had not yet learned to appreciate its freedom of the press, once reminded the *Diario Oficial,* which pointed by way of comparison to a speech of Domingo Sarmiento, the famous schoolmaster president of Argentina, in which that "illustrious" statesman had recommended "certain obstacles to the liberty of printing." "Happy Mexico . . . that it has managed already to assure forever the most absolute independence of writing!"[238]

No, Mexico did not appreciate its freedoms and was not to appreciate them as long as Lerdo was president. The opposition was able to twist and distort so skillfully that the policy itself became a boomerang. On the one hand, the conservative Catholic press scolded Lerdo severely for granting "freedom of writing without limitation." "The disdain into which President Juárez fell," warned *La Voz de México,* "was due to the violent irresponsibility of the opposition press which accosted and ridiculed him in the most abject manner."[239] If, as *La Voz de México* claimed, absolute liberty of the press would cause "society to become unhinged," eventually retorted the *Diario Oficial,*

why does the circumspect *La Voz de México* use that liberty, when it pretends to insult the liberal party and the government of the Republic? If tomorrow our society is unhinged, it will be said of *La Voz de México* with excessive justice: here is one of the guilty parties![240]

On the other hand, the stereotyped method which the opposition employed to undermine Lerdo's policy was by indirection. Since none could deny effectively that the press was not free, with the existence of so many polemical organs, he was charged with garroting the press "by closing his ears to its clamors," its warnings, its interpellations of governmental action, and, above all, his refusal to heed its advice and carry out its dictates. Lerdo denied those accusations futilely, declaring that he was not "irritated" by the printed manifestations of the opposition and that he was conscious of all of them; but "being responsible for his acts as chief of the nation, he has the indisputable right to resolve the questions of his incumbency according to his individual criterion."[241] Oddly, Lerdo

---

[237]*Ibid.,* March 3, 1874.
[238]*Ibid.,* July 24, 1874.
[239]*La Voz de México,* July 30, 1872.
[240]*Diario Oficial,* June 13, 1874.
[241]*Ibid.,* January 3, 1874. See also *ibid.,* February 7, 1875.

is more remembered for his failure to bow to "public opinion," as expressed in a violent enemy press, than for the freedom he allowed to the journalists of all factions.

While the "battle of the press" as it was waged under Lerdo would form a detailed study in itself, only some of the salient general features can be pointed out here to demonstrate the significance of the issue, particularly as a major cause of his defeat in 1876.[242] In Mexico City alone during the year 1873, there were some fifty-seven periodicals of all types,[243] indicating the fertility of Lerdo's policy. The titles of various papers often revealed the nature or political orientation: *La Iberia* and *La Colonia Española* were primarily for the reading consumption of Spanish residents in Mexico, while *Trait d'Union* and *The Two Republics* served a similar purpose for the French and Americans, respectively. *El Rey Don Sebastián (King Don Sebastián)* was obviously an opposition organ whose banner was a play upon Lerdo's so-called despotic tendencies. Whenever a new contestant entered the journalistic arena, the government bade it welcome and success, regardless of political outlook. Thus, when *El Látigo (The Lash)* popped into the publications circle, the *Diario Oficial,* in sarcastic fashion, announced that "we should say with frankness that, in our way of seeing, the title appears adequate for its principal object [*i.e.,* "to lash" the administration]. Nevertheless, from the present we give *El Látigo* the most cordial welcome, wishing it many subscribers."[244]

To understand the importance of the press and to make use of it for historical purposes is to realize two things: first, that the press of Lerdo's day was the sole medium of importance for the political education of the literate and interested people; and, second, that the editors themselves were among the outstanding literary and political figures of the time with their pronounced personal interests and prejudices. There was no such rarity as an "independent" press, though many papers laid claim to impartiality. To mention a few of the famous names of the journalistic world during Lerdo's presidency will serve to prove how important the press was as a political instrument and how dangerous it remains as an historical document unless carefully evaluated: Vicente Riva Palacio, Ireneo Paz, Juan N. Mirafuentes, Emilio Velasco, Justo and Santiago Sierra, Francisco G. Cosmes, José María Vigil, Guillermo Prieto,

---

[242]The generalizations which follow are based principally on a study of *Diario Oficial, El Monitor, El Siglo, El Ahuizote,* and *El Padre Cobos.* Also of great value for understanding the methods of a revolutionary press are the memoirs of Ireneo Paz, editor of *El Padre Cobos (Algunas Campañas,* III).

[243]*Diario Oficial,* January 1, 1874. A listing by title may be found in this issue. See also José de J. Nuñez y Domínguez, *Martí en México,* 26–27.

[244]*Diario Oficial,* June 26, 1875.

Francisco Bulnes, Rafael de Zayas Enríquez, Isidro Montiel y Duarte, Manuel Rivera Cambas, Alfredo Bablot, Alfredo Chavero, Vicente García Torres, Eduardo Ruíz, Francisco Sosa, Darío Balandrano, Anselmo de la Portilla, José Martí, Gustavo Baz, and Andrés Clemente Vázquez.

The press contestants under Lerdo may be divided into two classes: the pro-administration group, led by the *Diario Oficial* and supported by papers which were subsidized with government funds, like *El Federalista, El Eco de Ambos Mundos*, and *La Revista Universal;* and the opposition group headed by such papers as *El Monitor, El Ahuizote, El Padre Cobos, El Radical*, and many others.[245]

In a sense, the *Diario Oficial* was like the fox at bay surrounded by a pack of yelping hounds—the opposition press. It was expected to answer all rumors, lies, charges, and interpellations about the actions and intentions of the executive. Obviously, its purpose was to canonize the President—to present his policies and acts in the most favorable light possible; but with the hounds at bay, it could not afford to be caught in a lie or inconsistency. Consequently, the *Diario Oficial* either told the truth or remained silent, disavowing responsibility for a particular matter, or generalized and fabricated in cases where no positive evidence could be brought to bear against it. Moderate in tone, straightforward in style, accurate in factual material, and appealing to reason and an understanding of the government's position, the *Diario Oficial* made an admirable effort to meet the heavy responsibilities imposed upon it, even with the physical limitation of only about two pages per day available for editorials.[246]

As frequently noted, the *Diario Oficial* was Lerdo's voice transcribed in print, and it openly admitted that its opinions "are those of the persons who direct the administration."[247] In fact, the phraseology appeared to possess some of the peculiarities of Lerdo's style of writing, which once provoked a word in praise of Darío Balandrano, the editor in chief, "for interpreting with so much fidelity the patriotic sentiments of Señor Lerdo . . . which appear written by the very hand of that Gentleman."[248] Moreover, the assistant editor of the *Diario Oficial*, Andrés Clemente Vázquez,

---

[245]*El Padre Cobos* frequently satirized the subsidized press. In one cartoon, Lerdo was depicted as leering lustfully at a group of harlots representing the "purchased" government papers.—*El Padre Cobos*, December 20, 1874. See also the cartoon in *ibid.*, January 11, 1874.

[246]Each edition of the *Diario Oficial* was four pages, made up approximately as follows: about two pages for foreign and domestic news, reprints, and editorial comments; about one page for advertising; and one or more pages for official decrees and documents.

[247]*Diario Oficial*, October 5, 1873.

[248]*Ibid.*, January 13, 1875.

revealed that "Señor Balandrano was the one who daily gave account to him [Lerdo] of what the press said, and the one who, at the same time, transmitted the private answers of the Chief of the Nation."[249]

If the fox at bay had to be cautious, that was not so in the case of the hounds. Their purpose was to discredit, ridicule, and, later, to destroy the government by whatever means, fair or foul, were the most efficacious. Unfortunately for Lerdo, the hounds used more of the foul than otherwise. Since the opposition press was irresponsible, it chose its methods without any sense of political fair play. Once reassured of Lerdo's zeal for freedom of the press, it propagated scorn and ridicule, inconsistent interpretations of his policies, and malicious lies and rumors. And it should be noted that after Lerdo had effected his reëlection in 1876, the opposition press threw all restraint overboard and launched forth on a campaign for "the right of revolution" and the destruction of the government by violence.

In attempting to judge the attack of the opposition press fairly, one can perceive that it was based on inconsequential details and trivialities which were often unverified. There were some three or four themes, played over and over in humdrum fashion with increasing hyperbole: (1) Lerdo was a despot and a destroyer of state sovereignty; (2) the administration was lax, venal, decadent, corrupt, and negligent, having sold the interests of the nation to the Mexican Railway Company and having turned its back on her economic aspirations; and (3) Lerdo had failed to take into his confidence, as councilors, the "representatives of all factions," governing paternalistically, personally, and domineeringly—as he had ruled over his students as rector of San Ildefonso—and leaving the cabinet posts in the possession of a group of resurrected political mummies, the blind instruments of his will.[250] While playing

---

[249]*El Monitor*, January 17, 1877.

[250]The above points were brought out clearly in the first editorial of Juan N. Mirafuentes for *El Ahuizote*, February 5, 1874. Mirafuentes concluded his blast of the trumpet in representative fashion: "Don Sebastián has concentrated in his person all the powers and all the liberties. Seated on the chest of the treasury, he smiles ironically at the nation, satisfied with his omnipotence."

Miguel Trejo y Lerdo de Tejada, a great-grandson of Sebastián's brother Miguel, informed the present writer that he had inherited a portion of Sebastián's library through his father. Unfortunately, only four volumes are extant, most of the books having been lost through decomposition under bad storage conditions. These four volumes, ironically, are bound editions of the satirical *El Ahuizote*, in which Lerdo played the principal target.—Interview, Mexico, D.F., July 23, 1947. According to the apocryphal memoirs, Vicente Riva Palacio, one of the editors of *El Ahuizote*, visited Lerdo during his exile in New York and apologized: "Ah! Don Sebastián! I would give my right arm if I had not written the terrible crudities of 'El Ahuizote.' "—*Memorias Inéditas del Lic. Don Sebastián Lerdo de Tejada*, Segunda Parte, 78.

repeatedly the record of its unpleasant- melody, the opposition was not hindered by moderation or blessed with a very large stock of synonyms for such words as despot and tyrant. But its attack was as effective as a long column of soldiers marching across a strong bridge in precise cadence, setting in motion an ever-increasing vibration until the foundations eventually were loosened.

The matting on which to attach the decorations was essentially personal, just as Mexican parties were the groupings around personalities. Lerdo, his appearance and habits, and those of his ministers, parliamentary leaders, and other confidants made a perpetual target for the cartoonists, poets, and editorialists. The governmental functionaries appeared in the cartoons in various shapes, from Biblical characters to animals, and usually in a form more crude or obscene than clever.[251]

Since Lerdo's personal life while president was one of the fertile fields of the opposition press, it is necessary to pause and outline it briefly. He obviously enjoyed his position as chief magistrate and made no effort to conceal the fact; and he so handled affairs of state as to leave ample leisure time for many public formalities as well as private pleasures. Even his bitter political enemy, Ireneo Paz, admitted that Lerdo had a marvelous memory, wrote little, and because of his "colossal talent," could dispatch public business with aplomb: "he had everything at his fingertips."[252] And Ramón Prida added: "His clear intelligence permitted him to dispatch the serious affairs which were brought to him in a short time; for which reason he dedicated less time each day to business."[253]

Lerdo spent his leisure hours in afternoon drives in an open carriage along Bucareli Avenue, where all the fashionable world could see that he was not engaged during every waking moment in affairs of the cabinet; or he sat up in all-night vigils, and, being a chain smoker, filled the air with "continuous spirals of smoke"; or (so his enemies claimed) "the old celibate" disturbed his peaceful ways with an occasional "affair of gallantry." At any rate, the nocturnal diversions resulted in his arising "at eleven or twelve in the morning . . . and to govern," which was the origin of the charge that: "It was the government of a man who arose late."[254]

The longest handle which the opposition press grasped was Lerdo's frequent dining with his ministers or friends at the elegant

[251]*El Ahuizote* and *El Padre Cobos* were the chief illustrated papers of the opposition.
[252]Paz, *Díaz*, I, 181.
[253]Prida, *De la Dictadura a la Anarquía*, I, 46.
[254]Quevedo y Zubieta, *El Caudillo* . . . , 225.

restaurant, the Tívoli de San Cosme.[255] Whether Lerdo was more gourmand than *gourmet* cannot be determined because of the mangled reports of the press. He obviously enjoyed delicate foods and fine wines, particularly the sumptuous banquets served at the Tívoli by the French chef, Monsieur Porraz, who was reported to have amassed a fortune from the bills of the "official gastronomy" alone.[256] Thus, Lerdo, the man who was reputed to have "a sun for a brain," also obtained a reputation as "the most toasting president" Mexico ever had, because of his penchant for Bacchus and the epicurian delights.[257]

Despite the patent abuse made of the freedom of the press, particularly in regard to the President's private life, Lerdo refused to retract his promise, even though his prized personal dignity had to be sacrificed: ". . . we are among the first to condemn the waywardness of the press," explained the *Diario Oficial*,

of whose abuse the President of the republic is the first victim; from satire and insult to caricature, all is wielded against him, in the name of freedom of the press. Nevertheless, Señor Lerdo has never thought that he may proceed to *punish officially* any public writer: certain institutions must be allowed with all their consequences, although among these may figure defamation and calumny which have their corrective in good public sense or in their own exaggerations.[258]

The only stains which Lerdo ever had on his record for violating freedom of the press occurred in the last stages of his presidency, most of the cases being imprisonments carried out under other pretexts than press criticisms and when the country was in the throes of revolution. The opposition press raised a tremendous lament about the President's arbitrariness, however, which was totally unwarranted.[259]

---

[255]After enjoying the sights of Paris, Vicente Riva Palacio boasted that the finest French restaurants were "inferior one hundred times to our Tívoli. . . ." —Vicente Riva Palacio to José, August 14, 1870, Vicente Riva Palacio Papers, Folder 183, UT. For a good description of the cultured atmosphere of the Tívoli and the "cuisine" of its famous chef, Monsieur Porraz, see *El Mensajero*, January 17, 1871.

[256]Quevedo y Zubieta, *El Caudillo* . . . , 224. Lerdo even took Porraz with him on the inaugural trip of the Mexico-to-Vera Cruz railroad.—Cosmes, *Historia de Méjico*, XXII, 468.

[257]Quevedo y Zubieta, *El Caudillo* . . . , 220n, 224.
When Lerdo entertained "in the Palace," he did so in conformity with his Chesterfieldian manners, with elegance, correctness, and luxury. See *Diario Oficial*, January 15, 1875. José F. Vérgez, a Cuban journalist, left an interesting description of one of Lerdo's presidential dinners given in the apartments of the National Palace.—Vérgez, *Recuerdos de México*, 150–151.

[258]*Diario Oficial*, June 1, 1874.

[259]C. Edwards Lester, a propagandist for Díaz, made the ridiculous statement that under Lerdo the "liberty of the Press was subverted by bribery, or overthrown by force, or as a last resort editors and proprietors were seized in their beds, and cast into prison with highwaymen and murderers."—*The Mexican Republic, An Historic Study*, 60.

The first of the cases was "the exile" of General Vicente Riva Palacio to San Juan del Río. The opposition protested that the government had assigned Riva Palacio to the new command in order to quash his polemical attacks in *El Ahuizote,* the satirical paper which was replete with gross cartoons and broadsides against the administration. Meanwhile, Riva Palacio resigned his commission and continued his revolutionary machinations unmolested, in the press and otherwise. The *Diario Oficial* explained that Señor (not General) Riva Palacio had for some time employed a "systematic opposition" against the government, despite the fact that he was under military discipline and receiving his salary as a general with regularity. Also, the President had overlooked his written diatribes with "benevolence or disdain," until his conduct involved military discipline:

> Señor Riva Palac'o, as a journalist, was and is very certain of the disdain . . . of the government in regard to whatever he has written or writes aga'nst it; but treating of the conservation of good military discipline, now this was a different matter, and the conduct, not of the writer, but of the military officer depending on the government could not be passed over unobserved.[260]

In addition, stated the *Diario Oficial,* a thinking public would not accuse Lerdo of having acted against Riva Palacio "because he fears his pen," since "the said writer may continue combating the government as he has done to the present time."[261] If Riva Palacio was ridiculed by the deputies in congress when he filed charges against Lerdo for the violation of constitutional guarantees, if he was styled caustically "ex-General" by the pro-administration press,[262] it was a mild punishment for what he deserved. Perhaps out of deference for Vicente's father, Mariano Riva Palacio, but more probably because of his policy toward the press, Lerdo failed to make a much-needed example of a man whose political career was devoid of principle and who had been guided by impulse, impetuosity, and the desire for glory and office. At any rate, Riva Palacio published a long polemic against Lerdo, the classic

---

[260]*Diario Oficial,* March 3, 1875.

[261]*Ibid.,* March 3, 1875. Riva Palacio's florid resignation from his command read as follows: "But however great may be that honor [*i.e.,* to hold a commission of general], I do not desire because of it to see myself prevented from manifesting my opinions freely. For that reason, I return to you my cited commission, requesting that you be kind enough to concede my absolute separation from the army. . . ."—Vicente Riva Palacio to the Minister of War, March 1, 1875, Vicente Riva Palacio Papers, Folder 185, UT.

[262]*El Padre Cobos,* April 4, 8, July 25, 1875; Prida, *De la Dictadura a la Anarquía,* I, 45; Secretary of Congress to Vicente Riva Palacio, April 7, 1875, Vicente Riva Palacio Papers, Folder 185, UT.

account of the administration, unfortunately,[263] and then revealed his true color by dashing off to support the revolution of Díaz. The *Diario Oficial* commented:

Vicente Riva Palacio has published a sufficiently lengthy manifesto. In order to prove the tyranny and despotism of the government, it will suffice to say that [the government] knew perfectly well all the machinations of that gentleman in favor of the revolution, and, far from molesting him . . . it left him with the most absolute liberty until he launched himself into the revolutionary arena.[264]

The other notable cases were imprisonments, involving Ireneo Paz, editor of *El Padre Cobos,* Juan N. Mirafuentes, editor of *El Ahuizote,* and Alberto Bianchi, an editor of *El Monitor,* all of the opposition. Neither Paz nor Mirafuentes was imprisoned for his writings, but for involvement in revolutionary plots, although both tried to leave the impression that the government had acted against their self-styled powerful pens. Bianchi, however, had written and produced an inflammatory play against the government which had been judged a breach of the peace in a time of revolutionary upheaval. In none of the incidents did the government act harshly against the persons concerned, and none of the presses with which they were connected was suppressed.[265] Incidentally, Paz, an incorrigible revolutionist backing Díaz since 1869, after brazenly describing his activities in promotion of the revolt of 1876, clamored about the arbitrariness of the government on account of his imprisonment, because "the government knew that I was not mixing, that I did not think of mixing myself . . . in the revolution. . . ."[266] After he was sentenced to exile, Paz was permitted to remain at his home in Mexico City while awaiting transportation to Vera Cruz, and during that period he continued his writings for *El Padre Cobos.*[267] Such was the despotism of Lerdo.

Meanwhile, after some complicated legerdemain, Lerdo bowed to an order of the Supreme Court and released Bianchi. "It is gratifying to note in this occurrence," commented United States Minister

[263]*Historia de la Administración de Lerdo.* The work was published toward the close of Lerdo's administration and evoked the following comment from the *Diario Oficial:* "We have let pass unnoticed the evaluations which the so-called history contain, because the motives which inspire the author are well known."—*Diario Oficial,* June 12, 1875.

[264]*Ibid.,* May 27, 1876.

[265]On the imprisonment of Mirafuentes, see *ibid.,* December 15, 1875; Paz, *Algunas Campañas,* III, 349; *El Padre Cobos,* September 30, 1875. On Bianchi, see María y Campos, *La Dramática Mexicana durante el Gobierno del Presidente Lerdo de Tejada,* 43–46. Paz described his imprisonment in *Algunas Campañas,* III, 367–369, 373–374, 386, 390–400.

[266]Paz, *Algunas Campañas,* III, 350–353, 373.

[267]*Ibid.,* III, 412.

Foster, "the progress in this country of respect for law and of recognition of constitutional guarantees."[268]

By mid-1876 the opposition press was openly an engine of revolution, either backing the Porfirists or denouncing the government as illegal and calling upon José María Iglesias, the president of the court, to assume the presidency on December 1, 1876, the end of Lerdo's first term in office.[269] The so-called illegal reëlection of Lerdo in the summer of 1876 was an excellent new theme for the press to seize as a means of fomenting unrest. Why Lerdo permitted such license until the midnight hour of his presidency was inexplicable except that he was bitterly reluctant to sacrifice his principle on freedom of the press: "The press will correct itself."

With his back to the wall and when it was too late, Lerdo suspended the constitutional guarantee on freedom of the press, about one month before he fled from the capital in the face of the triumphant Díaz revolution. The Minister of Government issued an explanatory circular on the suspension, a circular which was absolutely true and also admitted how dismally Lerdo's theory had miscarried:

The opposition press overflowed in a scandalous manner, abusing the liberty which Article 7 of the Constitution concedes and the unlimited tolerance of the Executive of the Union.

Said press was serving as an organ of the revolution, publishing the plans of pronouncement of the enemies and their illegal decrees. . . . This press disseminated the real or feigned information of the military operations of the enemy, it revealed to the enemy the movements of our troops, their numbers, and their equipment, and daily it was publishing false triumphs of the revolutionists and false defeats of the loyal troops; it was exaggerating the numbers of the enemy and diminishing those of the government.

Said press, attributing to the President, the ministers, and other public functionaries, ineptitude, vices, and depraved passions, attempted to quit them of all respectability. Alleging that the government did not recognize the English debt, affirming that it wasted the public funds, that it made ruinous contracts, and that it had compromised the major part of the products of the maritime custom houses, [said press] spread a lack of confidence among merchants and capitalists, preventing the government from practicing financial operations which would produce what was necessary to cover its pressing needs. Finally, this press, declaring itself openly revolutionary and subversive, has preached that the present government will be legitimate only until November 30 next, and that if the chamber of deputies should declare that there has been an election, it is lawful for the public to revolt.[270]

That circular was a sad synthesis of how a Mexican opposition press took advantage of the tolerance of a president and of a presi-

---

[268]Foster to Fish, July 15, 1876, *U. S. Foreign Relations, 1876*, 408.

[269]*El Monitor, El Ahuizote*, and *El Padre Cobos* backed the revolt of Porfirio Díaz; while *El Siglo* was the rallying point for the cause of Iglesias, who counted upon many of the old Lerdists. The revolution will be discussed in the following chapter.

[270]Dublán y Lozano, *Legislación Mexicana*, XIII, 86–87.

dent who was unwilling to adapt a principle to a set of practical circumstances. As Zayas Enríquez explained—and he should have known, being the editor of a paper making "a systematic opposition to the federal executive"[271]—Díaz found his strongest ally in the opposition press

which completely robbed the government of its prestige, introduced lack of confidence and depression into the ranks of the army, and fired the public mind against what we then called "the most disgraceful tyranny." What a tyranny! It not only sanctioned liberty, but even permitted license in the press! The more exhaustively one studies this period [i.e., Lerdo's administration], the more he is confirmed in the conviction that defeat was due not so much to the Revolutionaries as the Government, which literally wrought its own downfall.[272]

Thus it came about that Lerdo's policy of freedom of the press not only contributed substantially to his downfall but indirectly assured him a warped and insignificant place in history, by breeding hostile writers and bequeathing a stack of hostile materials drafted under the heated passions of the moment. Many years after he had passed from the scene, a strange incident occurred in Mexico City, which, in an ironical sort of way, avenged him for the abuses of the journalists. A group of editors who had obtained an interview with the Minister of Government was pleading for a little freedom of the press, then in a strait jacket knitted by the Díaz régime. The minister was Romero Rubio, although he was no longer identified as Lerdo's old parliamentary leader but as Díaz's father-in-law (times had changed!). Rubio replied elusively to the editors humbly gathered before him who were ever fearful of additional government reprisals: ". . . here it has not been understood how to practice that wise maxim of Don Sebastián that *the press corrects itself with the press,* and whose principle one must set aside. . . ."[273]

The administration of Sebastián Lerdo de Tejada was far from faultless, far from democratic, far from spectacular. It was, however, a concerted effort to place in practical operation the theories conquered through years of revolution. Cautious economically, promising politically, patriotic, tolerant, and liberal, it held out the hope of an evolutionary politico-social progress. There was a strict compliance with the forms and routine of republicanism, freedom to exercise party activities, and perhaps too strong a dose of liberalism. Since it was too healthy a régime for anyone to appreciate,

---

[271]*Diario Oficial,* October 31, 1874.
[272]Zayas Enríquez, *Porfirio Díaz,* 127.
[273]Rubio quoted by Paz, *Díaz,* II, 71.

it succumbed to the principle of revolution. Despite his vanity, pride, and abundance of self-confidence, qualities which saved him from pity, one must admire the cultured man who stated his aims lucidly and attempted sincerely to comply with them. He was a creature of principles with many of the attributes of a great statesman. That he was a patriot, none could deny.

Chapter X

The Fatal Year 1876: Revolution, Defection, and Defeat

The final year of Lerdo's presidency, which marked the termination of a varied political career, was composed of the inadequate expedients of his government to cope with the unusual conditions always surrounding revolution. Of necessity, normal constitutional-administrative procedures and further efforts toward reform and advancement were paralyzed. Basically, the brief period of some eleven months revolved about three inseparable events: the revolution of Porfirio Díaz, initiated at the beginning of 1876; the reëlection of Lerdo in the summer of that year; and the defection and revolution of José María Iglesias, president of the Supreme Court, which began in October.

Order cannot be expected of a period of civil strife, especially one so bisected by interior currents and interconnected events. Perhaps it would be unsound historically to depict the year as other than turbulence and confusion. Not only was the strength of the government sapped by the defection of key members of the administration, but the uprising of Iglesias was actually a major revolution within the official circle, timed to crush Lerdo's cause and to rescue Díaz from probable defeat and permanent oblivion. Moreover, the two revolts, while they remained isolated, were linked by unsavory negotiations between their two leaders. Each tried to outlie the other as to the patriotism of his ultimate intentions and therefore his right to dominate the cause against Lerdo. Both Díaz and Iglesias were wise enough to realize, however, that there was no honor among the thieves of governmental machinery, and consequently the attempted fusion of their two movements failed miserably.

To those complicating features and the explosiveness which was ever an accompanist to a Mexican presidential election were added the fascinating factors of personality. What were the true motives of the principals and their followers in the revolutions of 1876? One word would suffice to answer for Díaz and Iglesias: ambition. Nor was that impetus absent from Lerdo's intentions to retain the presidential chair; but judging by his innate pride and the circumstances in which he found himself, the desire for power did not dominate his actions. His ego must have dictated, on the other hand, that to step down from office in the midst of revolutionary turmoil would have been a brand of cowardice and the desertion of his platform of peace, order, and obedience to republican *forms* of government. Never had he blemished his career by meddling in revolutionary activities, though the opportunities had been numerous. His stainless personal record in that regard placed right and justice in his favor. There were few outstanding statesmen of nineteenth-century Mexico to whom the same comment would have applied.

In that connection, it becomes necessary to orient a viewpoint to history and not to historical perspective—that is, to judge the men and events as they were in 1876, not decades later. When the eulogists of Díaz rationalized his personal revolution and the absurd ideology under which it was launched, they were rather chagrined that he had violated patently every one of his promises and that his program of government appeared in many ways like an extreme version of Lerdo's which he had denounced in obstreperous tones in 1876. The convenient detour around the embarrassment was to cite a list of figures on railroads, telegraphs, foreign trade, national revenue, etc., all of which were the exclusive product of the genius Porfirio and which justified his leading "the people" in their right of revolution against the tyrant Lerdo.

However that may be, it threw little light on the true situation in 1876, when Díaz and his so-called accomplishments were unknown quantities. "Cincinnatus" had openly joined the ranks of the professional revolutionists in 1871–1872 (revolt of La Noria), and his resounding defeat had almost been the coffin of his career; but he and his heterogeneous group had scavenged all discontent under Lerdo, effecting a unique resuscitation during a period of some four years. When Díaz began "pronouncing" against Lerdo, none with any degree of enlightenment should have been deceived that he was other than a typical barracks leader, without the slightest variation in the usual Mexican motif. Hence, it can be asserted that the men who backed Don Porfirio were composed of the "outs" of the political milieu who hoped for tangible reward; but of principle they knew not the definition.

Despite the obvious, some strange legends surround the "victory" of Díaz in 1876 which should be dispelled at the outset. First, Díaz himself had little if any personal credit to glean from the result, since it was the fortuitous shifting of events which spelled his triumph. One of Díaz's flattering biographers reluctantly admitted, in an understatement, that the various factors of the revolution "make one suspect that it was not General Díaz exclusively but Providence which determined his victory."[1] Still another more critical publicist has declared that Don Porfirio's success was born of defection, most dramatically illustrated by Iglesias' action and

---

[1] García Naranjo, *Porfirio Díaz*, 199.

"the facility" with which Mexican politicians deserted "from their natural obligations or from the fidelity which they owe to their nation and to their government."[2]

Leaving Díaz's personal rôle aside, the most misleading mirage surrounding the year 1876 was that the Porfirist movement had the aspects of a "popular" uprising. Quite to the contrary, it was a complicated revolt among the militarists and politicians. One writer, typical of those who fell victim to Porfirist revolutionary propaganda, has stated: "The whole truth was that the eyes of the country were dazzled by the dashing figure of young Porfirio Díaz and that the timeservers were by no means willing to intrust their fortunes to Iglesias."[3]

That comment was valid only as applied to the period after Díaz's decisive victory (Battle of Tecoac), when the hesitants no longer vacillated in regard to who would win the ultimate decision. Writing just before he had learned of the results of Díaz's triumph at Tecoac, United States Minister Foster observed:

The movement of General Porfirio Díaz, in its inception and progress, has not met with the hearty approval of any very large or respectable body of the public men of the country, as it was generally recorded by them as unwarranted at the time of its inauguration, and as a political enterprise of professional revolutionists.[4]

Furthermore, Zayas Enríquez, a Porfirist himself it will be recalled, stated that unless Díaz could "electrify" Mexican society with sensational achievements, "he would remain in the category of a common revolutionist, actuated by criminal ambition."[5]

That Lerdo was discredited completely by 1876 and that "public opinion" hailed the arrival of Díaz were *ex post facto* rationalizations of Porfirists and other deluded publicists. "Public opinion" and "popular support" were terms used loosely and indiscriminately by Mexican writers and in fact defied any workable definitions. Of course, all the Porfirist editors represented themselves as the oracles of "public opinion," just as Iglesias prated that he was the personification of that ephemeral force; hence, public opinion was the biased sentiment of the man expressing himself and to give it a broader interpretation would be altogether erroneous. Díaz, with a motley of professional military discontents, won the revolution through opportunism, the strange operation of events,

---

[2]Pcdan, *Porfirio Díaz Debe y Haber*, 261.
[3]Callcott, *Liberalism in Mexico 1857–1929*, 100.
[4]Foster to Fish, November 11, 1876, *U. S. Foreign Relations, 1877*, 378. It is interesting to note that Foster forgot this dispatch when compiling the glories of the Porfirist dictatorship years later as "abundant justification for the conduct of Díaz."—John W. Foster, "Porfirio Díaz: Soldier and Statesman," *The International Quarterly*, VIII (December-March, 1903), 351.
[5]Zayas Enríquez, *Porfirio Díaz*, 129. See also Magner, *Men of Mexico*, 454.

and military might, the substance of which was composed of recruits "who for the most part do not even know whether it is a Viceroy or a President who governs Mexico. . . ."[6] Consequently, any remarks to the effect that Díaz was a popular hero, that his victory came about through "public opinion," or that Lerdo was rejected completely by that nebulous force are most safely eliminated from any discussion of the fall of Lerdo from Mexican politics.

Similar to the Porfirist party, the Iglesistas were propelled by the hunger for spoils. Being old Lerdists for the most part, they had shared in the lesser offices of government but never in the policy-making positions. Once their hopes were dissipated for obtaining those positions, they became fertile seed for revolution. As frequently pointed out, Iglesias was the cultivator of the crop of discontents who were mostly civilians, unskilled in the practical art of the *cuartelazo*. Although he failed ignominiously— his defeat by Díaz in 1876 was one of the famous comedies in Mexican history— he spent his life explaining that he had no personal ambition in revolting against Lerdo, but his books and his acts only inflated him as a hypocrite. It was not that Iglesias abhorred Lerdo's reëlection and the usual methods employed to effect it, although the President of the court suddenly became hypersensitive to matters with which he had long been familiar and acquiesced in. Nor was it that he protested the reëlection. But to slink off surreptitiously, to raise armies, to dispatch a network of spies for the purpose of provoking defection in the federal army or to align Díaz's "right of revolution" to his "principle of legality"[7] were not the most pristine actions for the highest judicial magistrate of the nation to prove that patriotism and self-sacrifice were the guiding lights of his conduct. A man who had to write so much to explain his lack of ambition must have had a great deal of ambition on his conscience.[8]

On the other hand, Lerdo and his partisans certainly had personal interests in the survival of the existing government, although they were less obvious due to Lerdo's policy of freezing the old Juárez bureaucracy in öffice. Nevertheless, the hypothetical, disinterested man of 1876—there was no such creature, of course— who believed in peace, order, evolution, and the acceptance of the the forms of the Constitution, however fraudulent, as preferable to violence and "the right of revolution," would not have hesitated

---

[6]Ignacio Mañon y Valle to Mariano Riva Palacio, May 3, 1876, Mariano Riva Palacio Papers, Folder 174, UT. The statement applied to the soldiers serving under two Porfirist revolutionary leaders in the state of Mexico.

[7]The quoted phrases were extracted from a letter of one of Iglesias' revolutionary agents who was attempting to entice Díaz to subordinate his revolution to that of the President of the court.—Juan Rosas to Porfirio Díaz, October 10, 1876, Archivo de Fernando Iglesias Calderón, Legajo 14, A.G.N.

[8]Iglesias' well-known and lengthy apology is *La Cuestión Presidencial en 1876*.

to choose Lerdo over his two insurrectionary competitors. Lerdo's administration and program were liberal, progressive, and in tune with national aspirations and *capabilities;* and there were few statesmen in Mexico's past who had attempted more sincerely to live up to their promises. His words and actions during four years seemed more substantial than the familiar subterfuges which always accompanied revolution in the form of manifestoes and other worthless literature.

Yet the individual's choice among the three rivals was determined by practical considerations. When the revolutions broke in 1876, factional lines remained fluid, even among the principals. The "important people" could not afford to be on the losing side because that might compromise their political, economic, and social futures. Lerdo's government, down to the outbreak of Iglesias' plot, seemed stable and capable of crushing the Díaz uprising, but the new explosion cleft the government supporters and its military power, setting in motion a chain of disastrous defection which made Díaz's victory possible. With Lerdo eliminated and Díaz in possession of Mexico City, the "mugwumps" no longer hesitated in regard to the convenient side to choose, for Iglesias had been totally inept as a political strategist making use of revolutionary tactics. Under ordinary circumstances, then, Lerdo's government, despite many signs of internal weakness, probably would have routed the Porfirist faction and was doing so in late 1876. If any one man directly erected the dictatorship of Porfirio Díaz, it was José María Iglesias.

Though Iglesias may have been the immediate cause of Lerdo's downfall, the basic causes lay rooted in Lerdo's administration and even date back to the restoration of the republic in 1867. As already mentioned, the Porfirist party had intrigued systematically to seize power from that time. Díaz's Plan of La Noria and its aftermath were an abortive dress rehearsal for the one of 1876, except for two factors: the Porfirists in 1876 made no preliminary attempt to gain control of the government through a campaign and balloting, as they had done in 1871; and the Lerdist party of 1871—Lerdo, like Iglesias, was president of the court—had scorned the proposals of the Porfirists to join in the revolution against Juárez after defeat at the polls. Iglesias, however, was made of different stuff and launched his own revolt in 1876.

Other major causes of the fall of Lerdo may be discovered in his presidency. The previous chapter was an attempt to isolate the main fibers which composed his administration and to indicate how most of his policies contributed to undermining his power. His adamance in retaining the old Juárez cabinet directly led to the formation of the party of Iglesias, welded by the executive-judiciary conflict, while his legally impregnable church policy had alienated the clergy and devout Catholics, a force in politics which Díaz later found strong enough to merit conciliation. Moreover, the delay on railroad development gave the opposition the only meaty propaganda with which to fabricate the idea that a radical change was essential. Finally, the opposition press, entwined with all other factors, served as the engine to undermine the prestige of the government, to advocate violence, and to disseminate the idea that revolution was ineluctible, or, to borrow a phrase from a vivisectionist of revolution, that it was "in the air."[9]

Nor can it be denied that Lerdo largely wrought his own downfall. His career had demonstrated that among his strongest characteristics were will, determination, and the strength of convictions in the face of disheartening criticism which would have bent an ordinary man. Yet his will had galvanized into something like inflexibility, and his effort to prove that he was master of himself apparently had insulated him from sound suggestions for change. Thus his attitude toward factions worked well to a certain point and probably could have been modified successfully until late 1875, so as to conciliate the dissidents gathering around Iglesias before they had crystallized into a hardened core of opposition. So, too, he could have adapted his policies toward the church and press to practical conditions. He refused to bend his principles, however, and it is axiomatic that those who wield power constantly face adjustment to the demands of ever-changing political situations. While Lerdo's platform represented a balanced assortment of securities, he became complacent and failed to watch for fluctuations in the political market, as any skilled investor will do, and the crash was upon him before he could redistribute his funds.

Furthermore, Lerdo failed to nip the revolutionary leaders when they were within his grasp. Conditions in 1876 demanded the use of the iron fist and some resounding examples, for which Lerdo held the necessary legal excuse in the grant of "extraordinary faculties" to the executive by congress. Underestimating the ability of his enemies, he permitted men like Ireneo Paz, José María Iglesias, and Vicente Riva Palacio to continue breeding their embryonic plans for revolution under the passive gaze of the government, while the opposition press accelerated to an unprecedented pitch its appeal to violence. As a consequence, leaders of the revolutions escaped, and Lerdo's reluctance to use harshness was interpreted as a sign of the weakness of the government.

The above considerations form the pattern of basic and immediate causation of Lerdo's fiasco and the prefacing guide for any detached interpretation of the events of the fatal year 1876.

---

[9]Crane Brinton, *The Anatomy of Revolution*, 80–81.

The revolution of Porfirio Díaz was initiated at the village of Tuxtepec in the state of Oaxaca, January, 1876, with the promulgation of a plan signed by an obscure colonel named Sarmiento. Though typical of the sterile class of literature upon which so much Mexican paper had been squandered, it must be noted that the document incorporated a preamble, which ran the gamut of Lerdo's tyrannical inclinations, a provision for "no reëlection" of the president, and something vague about free suffrage. Retrospect has determined that the only fact worthy of historical remembrance in the Plan of Tuxtepec was that Porfirio Díaz was invested with leading the "regenerative army" in the reconquest of Mexico's popular liberties.[10]

Díaz himself was not in Mexico at the time of the pronouncement of Tuxtepec. After conferring with his accomplices in Mexico City in October, 1875,[11] he wrote to Riva Palacio from Vera Cruz, in December, that the government compassed his arrest "without more reason" than the preservation of the public peace, and hence his exit was necessary. Considering the revolutionary instructions which Porfirio gave to Riva Palacio in the remainder of his letter, he had little cause for indignation about the official intent toward his person. At any rate, since "circumstances" did not permit him "to be a passive hero,"[12] he embarked at Vera Cruz for the United States, eventually reaching Brownsville, Texas, where he and Manuel González raised a force with which they captured Matamoros in March, 1876, thanks to the defection of the federal troops garrisoned at the port.[13]

Another of Díaz's early revolutionary steps, occurring about the same time, was the revision of the Plan of Tuxtepec at Palo Blanco, a small settlement near the northern frontier. The amended document completed the formal propaganda of his movement. It was the same pork with scarcely a change of sauce, except that under "article 6" the Tuxtepecanos posed an offer to José María Iglesias (open for one month) to join them as the provisional revolutionary president, which proposal, if accepted, would limit the President

---

[10]*Diario Oficial*, December 4, 1876; *Diario de los Debates*, 8th Congress (1877), I, 3–4; Quevedo y Zubieta, *El Caudillo* . . . , 254–255.

[11]Paz, *Algunas Campañas*, III, 350–353.

[12]Porfirio Díaz to Vicente Riva Palacio, Vera Cruz, December 2, 1875 Vicente Riva Palacio Papers, Folder 185, UT. The *Diario Oficial* denied the rumors that the government plotted violence against Díaz.—*Diario Oficial* December 25, 1875.

[13]Walter Prescott Webb, *The Texas Rangers, A Century of Frontier Defense* 284–285; Valadés, *El Porfirismo, Nacimiento*, 15; García Granados, *Historia de México*, I, 130–131; Foster to Fish, February 2, 1876, *U. S. Foreign Relations, 1876*, 392.

of the court to "administrative" functions.[14] Iglesias rejected Díaz's clever strategy, since he had grander visions of his part in the scheme of Mexican affairs and was not yet ready to play the puppet for the practical Porfirio. In "complying with my duty," he wrote, ever drawing from his storehouse of self-adulatory phrases, "I do not accept nor can I accept, any revolutionary plan; and the strict observance of the Constitution will continue to be my invariable rule of conduct."[15] Praising Iglesias for his spurious expression of loyalty, the. *Diario Oficial* commented accurately that Díaz's pronouncement was "a pale reflection of the ambition which dominates the signatory of that plan." "Palo Blanco and La Noria [Díaz's pronouncement against Juárez in 1871] are the same thing. It is useless to say more."[16]

After issuing the Plan of Palo Blanco, Díaz's campaign in the north continued in a state of suspended animation until late May, when General Escobedo pacified Tamaulipas and General Carlos Fuero, governor and military commandant of Nuevo León, routed the rebels and their invincible hero in the Battle of Icamole near Monterrey.[17] Facing that miscarriage with its concomitant loss of face, Díaz hastily retreated back to Texas and New Orleans, leaving Manuel González, his chief lieutenant, in charge of the rebel remnants.[18] He made his way by ship back to the coast of Vera Cruz and then to Oaxaca, assuming command of the rebel forces in the south which had met with greater success in contending with the government troops in the interim.[19]

It is humorous to note in passing that Porfirist historians elaborate Díaz's hegira from New Orleans to Vera Cruz in some detail and with novelistic furbish, obviously to offset the nullity which he was personally in winning the revolution. Dark glasses, an assumed name, a leap into shark-infested waters, the collusion of a

---

[14]*Diario Oficial*, December 4, 1876; *Diario de los Debates*, 8th Congress (1877), I, 4–5; Quevedo y Zubieta, *El Caudillo* . . . , 255–256; García Granados, *Historia de México*, I, 139. Tuxtepecano was a synonym for the Porfirist rebels of 1876.

[15]Iglesias to the editors of the *Diario Oficial*, April 8, 1876, *Diario Oficial*, April 8, 1876.

[16]*Ibid.*, April 8, 1876.

[17]General Fuero's report of the battle was published with a tactical map in *ibid.*, June 9, 1876.

[18]Cosmes, *Historia de Méjico*, XXII, 781–782. González later made a famous march from Tamaulipas to Oaxaca, arriving in the nick of time at the battlefield of Tecoac to save the day for Díaz.

[19]García Granados, *Historia de México*, I, 140–141.

Vera Cruz maritime official, and constant exposure to capture were among the Romanesque trappings of his voyage, "which contributed in a grand way to invest General Díaz before the eyes of the people with the aureole of a hero of a fantastic novel."[20]

While Díaz's antics in the north had been checkmated, the original *cuartelazo* at Tuxtepec had expanded to place the rebels in control of a large part of Oaxaca as well as a part of Puebla, where terrain and the difficulties of maintaining lines of communication—the geographical factor—had been major obstacles to the federal army. In a series of battles which General Ignacio Alatorre had fought against the insurrectionists during the first five months of 1876, the government had checked the movement but had engineered no decisive victory. That was a psychological advantage for the brigands who were aroused to continue their efforts. On the other hand, the outcropping of other sporadic uprisings, especially in Vera Cruz, Jalisco, Morelos, and Aguascalientes, led by various military agents of Díaz, were suppressed successfully by the date of the presidential election in June and July.[21]

Despite United States Minister Foster's optimistic reports that the success of federal troops against the rebels had "encouraged the government and strengthened its adherents,"[22] Lerdo's régime had not shown the energetic persecution of insurrection characteristic of Juárez's last administration under more pressing circumstances. Since the revolution had broken out as a rash of minor, isolated uprisings, the government may not have been able to discern immediately that the heart of the Porfirist strength lay in Oaxaca. Moreover, protracted fighting in Michoacán against guerrilla bands throughout the year 1875 had drained the resources of the treasury, as Lerdo admitted to congress,[23] and the initial fighting with Díaz had aggravated the financial condition. Nor was the government able to count upon one of the most skillful and consistently successful of its revolt-quashing generals, Sóstenes Rocha, who had been removed from his responsible command for implication in a projected *coup d'état* against Lerdo in February,

[20]Cosmes, *Historia de Méjico*, XXII, 783. For full details, see *ibid.*, 783–790; Bancroft, *Vida de Porfirio Díaz*, 501–505; García Granados, *Historia de México*, I, 139–141.

[21]*Diario Oficial*, May 29, 1876; Cosmes, *Historia de Méjico*, XXII, 751–752; Bravo Ugarte, *Historia de México*, III, 364–365; Foster to Fish, April 22, 1876, *U. S. Foreign Relations, 1876*, 397.

[22]Foster to Fish, May 27, 1876, *U. S. Foreign Relations, 1876*, 403; *idem.* to *idem.*, May 15, 1876, *Mexico, Dispatches*, LVI, A.U.S.

[23]*Diario de los Debates*, April 1, 1876, 8th Congress, II, 14.

1875.[24] All of those factors helped to explain the government's seeming tardiness in blotting the unrest, particularly in Oaxaca.

But the major cause and the one which never has been explained satisfactorily was the alleged willful negligence of Minister of War Ignacio Mejía, a man of national reputation in high favor among many of the army officers who had a preternatural nose for scenting defection, an iron fist for crushing it, and an excellent record in the War Department under Juárez. From the outset of Lerdo's administration, the systematic opposition had tried to drive a wedge of suspicion between the President and the outstanding Minister in his cabinet; so, perhaps it was not of great significance that the revolutionary press emphasized Mejía's presidential ambitions as the cause of his treason toward Lerdo in permitting the revolt to live in Oaxaca, that is, through failure to take energetic action. Although the *Diario Oficial* defended Mejía against the charges,[25] he was swept from the cabinet in the surprise shuffle of August, 1876; he did consider himself of presidential caliber, competing in the campaign of 1880; and he was a native of Oaxaca, where he apparently found his chief political support.[26] Finally, after Lerdo was ousted in November and before Díaz had consolidated his position, Ignacio Altamirano learned about two agents who were en route to Guerrero to influence the governor of the state "to pronounce, but in behalf of Mejía. . . ."[27]

Perhaps it will never be determined whether Mejía purposely postponed decisive action in Oaxaca and blocked the dispatch of adequate reinforcements to General Alatorre, who was conducting the field campaign there. Yet none knew better than the Minister of War that Mexican insurrection had to be pursued ruthlessly and

---

[24]United States Minister Foster wrote that Rocha "voluntarily acknowledged his complicity and alleged that he had unwittingly been made the dupe of conspirators."—Foster to Fish, March 2, 1875, *Mexico, Dispatches*, LIII, A.U.S. The plot has remained unsolved, however. Rocha probably was the military aspect of a revolution planned by others whose names were never revealed. Ireneo Paz, who was connected closely with the pre-revolutionary activities of Díaz, believed that the purpose was to elevate Iglesias to the presidency.—Paz, *Algunas Campañas*, III, 341. However that may have been, Iglesias made use of Rocha in his revolt of 1876.—Iglesias, *La Cuestión Presidencial en 1876*, 41–42, 118. See also *Diario Oficial*, February 26, 28, March 3, 1875; Paz, *Díaz*, I, 189–191; Cosmes, *Historia de Méjico*, XXII, 692; Riva Palacio, *Historia de la Administración de Lerdo*, 457–459; *El Padre Cobos*, March 4, 7 (cartoon), 1875.

[25]*Diario Oficial*, May 4, 1876. For illustrations of Mejía's presidential appetite and his purported treason against Lerdo, see the cartoons in *El Padre Cobos*, March 12, April 13, 20, 27, June 1, 1876.

[26]Valadés, *El Porfirismo, Nacimiento*, 39; García Granados, *Historia de México*, I, 229–231, 243.

[27]Ignacio [Altamirano] to Vicente [Riva Palacio], November 25, [1876], Vicente Riva Palacio Papers, Folder 185, UT.

nipped in the bud, if possible; and none had a more able record to prove his peculiar genius for tackling that type of politico-military problem. If General Mejía were guilty, as indicated by the weight of evidence, his passive defection was a major blow to Lerdo, second in importance only to that of Iglesias. It was significant, too, that a few days before Lerdo changed his cabinet, the Secretary of the American legation made the following comment about Mejía's importance: "It is presumed that his action either way [*i.e.*, for or against Lerdo] will decide the fate of the administration."[28]

With a semblance of order reëstablished by mid-1876, though the state of siege was ruling in many states,[29] Lerdo effected his reëlection, as was to have been anticipated. Far different from his unanimous selection in 1872, the balloting was conducted under extraordinary circumstances with the use of the normal procedures. Of fraud, force, and violence there was probably neither more nor less than had been an integral part of previous elections. Conforming to routine, the opposition set up a resounding protest against Lerdo's victory, pretending that such practices were of unprecedented corruption, which was nothing more than the fabrication of the requisite pretext for revolution or the justification of the one already in progress.[30]

Actually, the complaints were ridiculously shallow, at least in comparison with the election of Juárez in 1871, for then the Indian President had held office for thirteen years, while Lerdo was seeking his first reëlection in 1876. In addition, the opposition of 1871 had gone through the motions of using the legal forms before resorting to violence, but in 1876 it determined to employ the bizarre tactics of passivism, as pointed out by the United States Minister:

No other candidate for the Presidency than Mr. Lerdo has been regularly presented to the popular suffrage, although the name of General Mejía, present minister of war, has been informally mentioned; and there is no doubt but that Mr. Lerdo will receive the majority of the votes cast.[31]

Since the Iglesista faction remained in clandestine form, it did not propose its leader as a candidate, while Díaz "went to search for power by another road, that of revolution."[32] Consequently, the opposition placed a peculiar twist on its clamors, to the effect that

---

[28]Richardson to Fish, August 26, 1876, *U. S. Foreign Relations, 1876*, 409. Zayas Enríquez doubted that Mejía had been disloyal to Lerdo.—Zayas Enríquez, *Porfirio Díaz*, 123.

[29]Dublán y Lozano, *Legislación Mexicana*, XIII, 7–8, 11–13.

[30]Iglesias' comments about the electoral methods used in 1876 were representative of a multitude of others: "Frauds, erasures, corruption, and abuses of every kind reached a height of notorious scandal."—Iglesias, *La Cuestión Presidencial en 1876*, 23.

[31]Foster to Fish, June 22, 1876, *U. S. Foreign Relations, 1876*, 405.

[32]Paz, *Algunas Campañas*, III, 365.

there had been no legal election because of the operation of martial law, the abstinence of the anti-Lerdists, and the failure to obtain returns from the required majority of electoral districts.[33]

Still, the presidential election was not valid until verified by congress, which may have seemed a formality in 1876, but actually became the occasion determining the fate of all factions involved, since that congressional decree was the indispensable pretext which Iglesias needed to launch his revolt of "legality."

That Lerdo was fully aware of the probability of Iglesias' revolt was revealed by the astuteness with which he delayed the congressional verification of his second term in office and wrapped his intentions in a cloud of mystery.[34] El Siglo, headquarters of the Iglesista complot, began to show signs of strain, which sprang from suspense after the electoral count. It related a story of several deputies who had approached Lerdo to inquire about "his intention on the reëlection." Lerdo replied, purportedly, that "he had very little interest in the reëlection, that he was leaving his friends in entire liberty to decide in truth what they believed most adequate, and that if, in their judgment, there had been no elections, thus they might decide it."[35]

Unfortunately, moaned El Siglo, "when Señor Lerdo says something, it is difficult to know his true meaning, because his deception is notable." Having made the opening, the Iglesista paper continued to belabor the President in accordance with the fashion of the moment:

Señor Lerdo is a man, to whom, as much for weakness of character as for self-love, it is never pleasing to request; furthermore, this [personal trait] has for its object to excuse him from gratitude; he desires, then, that his thought be divined, and that what he wishes be done, without his expressing his desires; the secret of the influence which some near to Lerdo have is due to the fact that they divine and anticipate his desires, removing the mortification of his enunciating them. . . .[36]

Yet Lerdo had one more partial surprise for his Iglesista opponents: a change in the cabinet. On August 31, with scarcely a hint of warning, Lerdo thanked Ministers Ignacio Mejía (War) and Blas Balcárcel (Fomento) for their kindly services to his administration and appointed Romero Rubio (Foreign Affairs), Antonio

---

[33]". . . we shall abstain from the vote as a useless thing," advised El Padre Cobos, "and because, furthermore, it would make us appear accomplices of the promoters of the approaching electoral farce."—El Padre Cobos, June 8, 1876. El Padre Cobos failed to mention that its candidate, Porfirio Díaz, could not compete in the election and revolt against the government simultaneously. See also the editorials of Emilio Velasco, the former Lerdist turned Iglesista, denying the validity of Lerdo's reëlection.—El Siglo, August 5, 7, 1876.

[34]See Cosmes, Historia de Méjico, XXII, 773–774.

[35]El Siglo, August 17, 1876.

[36]Ibid., August 17, 1876.

Tagle (Fomento), Juan José Baz (Government), and Mariano Escobedo (War), thus constituting a new, full-blown ministry.[37] Except for Baz, all were old and loyal Lerdists who had waited and worked patiently for an opportunity which they perhaps had long since renounced as outside the realm of feasibility. One man, however, was conspicuous for his absence in Lerdo's belated cabinet reform—the astute Ramón Guzmán. Scenting the sinking of the ship, he had deserted in May for a convenient foreign respite, probably to chasten himself in the eyes of the new régime which he obviously believed imminent.[38]

Among the plausible reasons for Lerdo's unprecedented cabinet change was suspicion of Mejía's treachery, or perhaps his realization, at the strike of midnight, that his party policy had failed. But the practical reason no doubt was his unavoidable compromise with the deputies, through which he obtained, in exchange for forming the new ministry, the assurance that they would verify his reëlection. El Siglo fathomed the maneuver before it transpired, and, in bitterly partisan fashion, explained Lerdo's attitude toward his old ministers and the raison d'être for the new ones: "It is certain Lerdo could not tell his true motives; [but] he could say: 'I accept the resignation [i.e., of Mejía and Balcárcel] because I am afraid that my partisans will not help me in the cámara to consummate the electoral fraud.' "[39]

From August 31, when the cabinet change occurred, until October 26, when Lerdo's reëlection was verified by the congress which had convened in Mexico City, there was an ominous lull in the maze of revolutionary events. It was the disarming calm before the climax of the storm. As the second division of the federal army under General Alatorre lay astride the path to Mexico City of the dormant Porfirist rebels in Oaxaca, the President of the Supreme Court lay in hiding at his home in the capital, absenting himself from official duties under the pretense of an illness which already had

---

[37] Richardson to Fish, September 7, 1876, U. S. Foreign Relations, 1876, 411–412; García Granados, Historia de México, I, 142–143; Bancroft, History of Mexico, VI, 424–425.

[38] Guzmán personally informed Ireneo Paz—the two men happened to be aboard the same vessel bound for New Orleans—that he had been unable to overcome Lerdo's "obstinacy" for reëlection, and hence he chose to avoid being submerged in the President's "inevitable" downfall.—Paz, Algunas Campañas, III, 415. Paz later wrote to El Padre Cobos, while in exile at New Orleans, where Guzmán was residing temporarily, that: "All who hear Ramón Guzmán speak . . . comprehend that he has good nostrils, which smell the fall of Don Sebastián, and that he does not want to sink with him, so that he may place his sumptuous fortune outside risk."—El Padre Cobos, June 8, 1876. When Guzmán departed from the capital, however, the Diario Oficial printed only a factual notice without further comment.—Diario Oficial, May 21, 1876.

[39] El Siglo, September 1, 1876. See also ibid., August 21, 22, September 2, 1876; Iglesias, Autobiografía, 65–66.

passed.[40] Strange and suspected visitors came to his door, while federal agents kept his residence under surveillance.

José María Iglesias was a nervous man in those late days of September, an exceedingly nervous man. What was making him so nervous? He wanted to save the country's sovereign rights, so he said, from the transgressions which Lerdo was about to commit against them; he wanted to rescue the Constitution from a tragic doom. Yet he was afraid that Lerdo would not commit those transgressions. Unfortunately, none of Iglesias' heroic deeds as Sir Galahad of the organic law could be initiated until congress, then in session, had promulgated the formal verification of Lerdo's reëlection, the date from which, according to Iglesias, the national code would be shattered into fragments. Each day with increasing anxiety he prayed that congress would shatter the national sovereignty so that he could pick up the pieces, and each day he was disappointed. His plans—all hinging on one technicality beyond his control—and his followers were prepared to act the farce of "legality," but the signal had to emerge from congress. State governors had been approached in an effort to win their support to the cause, and Governor Antillón of Guanajuato had consented to convert his state fief into the rallying point; Iglesias' flight from Mexico City and from the talons of Lerdo was arranged; and his manifesto to the nation was drafted in protest of the reëlection, composed of those admirably vacuous phrases for the writing of which Iglesias had no rival. "Over the Constitution, nothing, over the Constitution, no one!" was the worthy platitude with which he had concluded his treatise. Only the date remained to be entered on the manifesto, contingent upon the action of the deputies.

History will never know how many fingernails Iglesias chewed, how many hairs he pulled from the fringe on his head, how many miles he paced the floor, or how many times he glanced furtively from the windows of his home to count the government agents watching his activities. Still, one can be assured that he was an anxious man during those last days in September, since the passing of each day made his position more precarious.

It never occurred to the "Representative of Legality" to stand firm, to resign from the court if he were opposed sincerely to reëlection (it was not unconstitutional), or simply to protest Lerdo's conduct as contrary to good precedent. Nor did it occur to him to seek Lerdo directly, "to whom I had given, from whom I had received, constant proofs of gracious friendship,"[41] and beseech him to call new elections and step down from office. The sole idea

---

[40]The facts for the following summary are based upon Iglesias' *La Cuestión Presidencial en 1876*, especially 49–52. See also García Granados, *Historia de México*, I, 144–148.

[41]Iglesias, *La Cuestión Presidencial en 1876*, 78.

which engrossed Iglesias was his fear that Lerdo would not give him a pretext for launching a revolt. Therefore, Iglesias must have been sickened when Lerdo delayed the vital pretext in September, 1876.

At last the President of the court could hesitate no longer. Through the aid of friends, he slipped by the federal police and took the road to Toluca, where he lay in hiding for several days. By the time he had advanced to Salamanca, completed negotiations with Governor Antillón, and had established his "capital" at Guanajuato, congress had decreed Lerdo's reëlection;[42] hence Iglesias, the *pronunciamiento* sheep in legal clothing, could at last launch himself into the rôle of constitutional savior.[43]

The details of Iglesias' subsequent activities, while playing president at Guanajuato, were of little concern and may be traced in his lengthy apology in which every line strangely resembled a self-condemnatory alibi: "I made my purpose a mystery to no one, because I was not dealing in a gloomy conspiracy, but in compliance with a sacred obligation, so pure and open that I could proclaim it in the middle of the plaza that the sun might bathe it in publicity."[44]

The undeniable result of Iglesias' revolt was that it gave the mortal blow to Lerdo's government. United States Minister Foster saw clearly that the political and military aftermath had been "very marked" and that it "had the effect to greatly strengthen the revolutionary spirit in all parts of the country," making Lerdo's task "in suppressing the revolution . . . twofold." The necessary shift of federal troops to counteract the threat of state forces which General Antillón had placed at the disposition of Iglesias had drained the federal garrison in Mexico City as well as the federal troops in the Valley of Mexico.[45] And Justo Sierra, one of those who supported the movement of Iglesias, admitted that: "The attitude of the president of the court produced an immense confusion from which arose the triumph of the revolution [of Díaz]."[46]

Although Lerdo did not abandon hope, even after the staggering blow dealt by Iglesias, the rapidly-moving events which took place

[42]Dublán y Lozano, *Legislación Mexicana*, XIII, 88.

[43]Iglesias, *La Cuestión Presidencial en 1876*, 51–59.

[44]Iglesias, *ibid.*, 25. Compare Podan, *Porfirio Díaz Debe y Haber*, 251; García Granados, *Historia de México*, I, 144–145.

[45]Foster to Fish, November 11, 1876, *U. S. Foreign Relations, 1877*, 378–379.

[46]Sierra, *Evolución Política del Pueblo Mexicano*, 438. For comments on the nature of Iglesias' conduct and its. effects, see also Hilarión Frías y Soto, *Juárez Glorificado* . . . , 437; Arosemena, *Estudios Constitucionales sobre los Gobiernos de la América Latina*, II, 274; Ordaz, *La Cuestión Presidencial*, 25; Bancroft, *History of Mexico*, VI, 425–426;. García Naranjo, *Porfirio Díaz*, 199; Bravo Ugarte, *Historia de México*, III, 366; Magner, *Men of Mexico*, 456.

in the subsequent three weeks probably were academic in so far as he was concerned. The outcome of the decisive battle of Tecoac, fought between the federal troops and Díaz's rebels, seemed to be significant for Díaz's career but not Lerdo's.

With its military resources split against two revolutions and the public thrown into new ferment and hesitancy about which actor of the three-ringed circus would emerge victorious, the government determined to strike Díaz with its best-equipped division, the second, still commanded by General Alatorre. Perhaps "enlightened" of his own significance by the movement of Iglesias, Alatorre decided that he, too, could interpret the Constitution. It was not enough that Lerdo faced a Sir Edward Coke on the court, but he must deal with one in the army as well. Even that difficulty might have been obviated by the simple expedient of relieving Alatorre of his command; but according to a captain of the second division, the officers were devoted to their General and would not have permitted the tyrant Lerdo to remove him.[47]

After Lerdo learned that Iglesias' agents had approached Alatorre in early November to obtain his defection to the "cause of legality,"[48] he recalled his General to the capital for a conference. Perhaps conscious of the solid intrenchment of Alatorre with his officers, Lerdo patched together some makeshift agreement with the General, the details of which remained unknown, and he returned to his division, loyal to Lerdo at least until November 30, 1876, when the President's first term ended.[49]

Beyond that point? Alatorre had remarked to one of the agents of Iglesias

that with no one did he conclude promises on political questions, leaving himself the most complete liberty in order to work in the field of events according to his sentiments, which would always be for the good of the country.[50]

One wonders, on carrying Alatorre's attitude to the logical conclusion, whether he did not reason that it would be "for the good of the country" to have General Alatorre renamed President

---

[47]Enrique A. Turnbull, *El Ejército Federal y la Reelección* . . . , 8–9, 17–18.

[48]Iglesias, *La Cuestión Presidencial en 1876*, 119, 153, 160. Although Iglesias was somewhat contradictory in regard to the answers which Alatorre made to the coaxing of his agents, it was obvious that Alatorre (1) recognized Lerdo as the rightful president through November 30, 1876, and (2) would in no manner commit himself to the cause of Iglesias. Alatorre's attitude toward the Porfirists was demonstrated by the bloody battle he fought against them at Tecoac.

[49]Turnbull, *El Ejército Federal y la Reelección* . . . , 17–18; Quevedo y Zubieta, *El Caudillo* . . . , 277–278; Iglesias, *La Cuestión Presidencial en 1876*, 159–163.

[50]Iglesias, *La Cuestión Presidencial en 1876*, 160.

Alatorre. Why limit his prospects after the defeat of the Díaz rebels, with a devoted, well-equipped division at his back? The plot had thickened: the fierce battle which Alatorre waged against Díaz a few days later was probably not for Lerdo, but under the inspiring vision of a presidential chair in which one General Alatorre was to be seated. That was why the Battle of Tecoac, generally conceded as the defeat of Lerdo, seemed to make no difference to his fate.[51]

Within a short time after he returned to his troops, Alatorre placed the column on the march to join in a decisive engagement with the rebels. The battle took place on November 16, in the rugged mountains of Oaxaca, near the ranch of Tecoac.[52] Although Don Porfirio's rebels, led by himself, Vicente Riva Palacio, Tiburcio Montiel, and Juan Méndez, considerably outnumbered the force of the government, Alatorre's division had superiority in training, discipline, and equipment, especially artillery. Not at all the typical insurrectionary engagement in which a few harmless shots are fired and the losing side either ran or defected en masse to the winner, the Battle of Tecoac was a stiff and bloody contest, beginning in the early morning and lasting until mid-afternoon.[53] Both Díaz's eulogists and his enemies have agreed that Alatorre had pounded the rebels to the stage of bewilderment and was in the act of launching the final assault, which would have been the *coup de grâce* to the Porfirist party and Díaz's future as well, when a cloud of dust appeared on the near horizon of the battlefield. Alatorre assumed

---

[51]Enrique Turnbull, speaking for the officers of the second division, proved that: (1) they were first of all devoted to Alatorre; (2) the Tuxtepecanos should be defeated as "illegal and subversive of the constitutional order"; and (3) Lerdo, after November 30, should be treated "as a usurper and subjected to trial. . . ." In regard to the Battle of Tecoac, Turnbull added that had Alatorre won, "certainly we would not have supported the reëlection [of Lerdo], but neither would the Plan of Tuxtepec have ruled."—Turnbull, *El Ejército Federal y la Reelección* . . . , 16, 19.

Confirming the above conclusion on Alatorre's secret plans, which is not the orthodox historical viewpoint, was a statement made by the noted historian, Pérez Verdía. Licenciado Curiel, at one time the secretary of General Díaz, personally informed Pérez Verdía of a letter from Lerdo to Alatorre, recovered after the Battle of Tecoac. In the letter, Lerdo allegedly had urged Alatorre to press his campaign to a successful conclusion, promising the militarist to resign and promote his (Alatorre's) presidential election.—Pérez Verdía, *Historia de Jalisco*, III, 449, 449n.

[52]Quevedo y Zubieta, who knew both Alatorre and Díaz, presented a detailed study of the battle in *El Caudillo* . . . , 229–300.

[53]United States Minister Foster learned that the losses ranged from 250 to 2,000, "but the former number is probably not far from the facts," he observed skeptically.—Foster to Fish, November 28, 1876, *U. S. Foreign Relations, 1877*, 381. Years later he wrote that an estimated 4,200 had been killed or wounded at Tecoac.—Foster, "Porfirio Díaz: Soldier and Statesman," *The International Quarterly*, VIII, 351.

that it was one of the units which he had posted as a rear guard. But he was taken by surprise, the unpardonable military sin, for the dust was produced by the forces of Manuel González, enhanced by the soldiers of General Francisco Tolentino, a federal officer who had defected with his unit a few days prior. González cut into the left and rear flank of Alatorre's division, turned apparent defeat of the Porfirists into a complete rout of the federal forces, and emerged as the rescuer of Díaz and the savior of the day for the Tuxtepecanos.[54]

Historically, Tecoac determined Díaz's career, for he could not have survived another major setback. What if Alatorre had been the conqueror of the day? What ambitions and intentions he truthfully held for "after November 30" remained locked within the recesses of his own brain. It was certain, however, that they augured no good for Lerdo.

Back in Mexico City a temporary consternation reigned over Lerdo and his followers after receipt of the news of the disastrous defeat. It was probably the indecision which falls upon men during that brief interval required to accept facts as they are and not as they are desired to be. Further defections of federal units and the loss of another battle in Tamaulipas apparently dispelled all doubts surrounding reality, and the only questions which had to be resolved were when and in what manner to depart Mexico City.

Though Lerdo at that moment was eliminated definitely as a force in Mexican politics, he became the balance of power, the arbitrator between Díaz's revolution in the south and Iglesias' revolution in the north. First, Lerdo did not resign his *de jure* right to the presidency but secured it by an overwhelming vote of confidence from congress in a secret session of November 18, two days after Tecoac.[55] Then, after some undoubtedly heated secret discussions with his divided councilors, Lerdo determined to deliver the federal garrison in Mexico City (about 1,000 troops) to General Luis Mier y Terán, a key Porfirist captured in an earlier battle.[56] As Iglesias later mourned, Lerdo had handed the loyal federal troops and the nerve center of the nation to the Porfirists, thus crushing his "cause of legality."[57] Indeed, those final arrangements

[54]Quevedo y Zubieta, *El Caudillo* . . . , 295–296; Fortunato Hernández, *Un Pueblo, un Siglo y un Hombre (1810–1910)*, 336; Podan, *Porfirio Díaz Debe y Haber*, 247–248; Paz, *Díaz*, I, 216; García Granados, *Historia de México*, I, 151–152. On Tolentino's defection, see *El Monitor*, November 8, 1876.

[55]*Diario de los Debates*, November 18, 1876, 8th Congress, III, 407; *El Monitor*, November 19, 1876.

[56]Unsigned to Iglesias, November 19, 1876; "T" to Iglesias, November 21, 1876, Archivo de Fernando Iglesias Calderón, Legajo 15, A.G.N. Both letters were written by agents of Iglesias in Mexico City. See also Foster to Fish, November 28, 1876, *U. S. Foreign Relations, 1877*, 381–382.

[57]Iglesias, *La Cuestión Presidencial en 1876*, 180, 186–187.

for preserving order recognized the practical force in Mexican politics, secured a quick victory for Díaz, and saved Mexico from further bloodshed and destruction which would have accompanied a decision in favor of Iglesias. At the same time, Lerdo must have derived a personal vengeance, amid the bitterness of defeat, by thus silencing the revolutionary parrot of constitutional phrases. To state that there was no vindictiveness in Lerdo's ultimate decision would be a falsehood and contrary to human nature, for, as he told American reporters after reaching New York: "I believe that the triumph of the revolutionaries is due to the attitude assumed by the vice-president, Señor Don José María Iglesias. It undermined my supporters."[58]

About 2:00 A.M. on the morning of November 21, Lerdo, his cabinet, a few devoted followers, and a cavalry escort departed Mexico City via the road to Toluca, destination unknown. With them were 50,000 pesos extracted from the funds of the federal treasury, which indicated not so much Lerdo's dishonesty as his firm belief in the legality of his position and his probable intent to make a second stand, perhaps in Jalisco, where General José Ceballos still commanded a large force of federal troops.[59] Since Ceballos had announced his intent to support Iglesias, after learning of Lerdo's flight from the capital,[60] that scheme had to be discarded. Lerdo and his constantly diminishing coterie stopped briefly at Toluca, passed through Morelia, and turned south, traversing the state of Guerrero to a terminus at the port of Acapulco. According to Lerdo's own narration of his flight, there were no difficulties, hardships, or "rebels" encountered during the journey;[61] therefore, the story that he was captured by one of Díaz's lieutenants and owed his release and escape to the magnanimity of the conquering Hero was another misconception which wormed its way into history.[62] Of course, the opposition press of the capital, still not glutted with its excesses against the President, spread the wildest tales of his cowardice, his capture, and even his disguise as a woman, since the popular thing at the moment was to kick the defeated.[63]

---

[58]Quoted by *El Siglo*, March 9, 1877.

[59]*Veredicto del Gran Jurado Nacional . . . en el Juicio Instruido contra el Ciudadano Francisco Mejía . . .*, 4, 7–14. Francisco Mejía, Lerdo's minister of Finance, was tried subsequently by congress for having signed the warrants on the treasury for delivering the money, but was acquitted. See also *El Siglo*, June 13, 1877; García Granados, *Historia de México*, I, 169. It was difficult to understand why Díaz had any claim on the funds removed.

[60]*El Estado de Jalisco* (Guadalajara), November 28, December 2, 1876.

[61]Lerdo quoted by *El Siglo*, March 9, 1877.

[62]See Prida, *De la Dictadura a la Anarquía*, I, 60.

[63]See especially *El Monitor* during late November, 1876, and the months of December, 1876, and January, 1877. Some wild and usually distorted rumor about Lerdo's whereabouts appeared in almost every issue.

While Lerdo and his chief followers, Baz, Escobedo, and Rubio,[64] waited at Acapulco to embark for the United States via Panamá and the Atlantic Ocean route, they probably discovered with grim satisfaction that a certain José María Iglesias, despite his pseudo-legal phrases, had been unable to cope with the practical force which was the ultimate determinant of the revolution. After some complicated bickering with Díaz, during which most of his followers defected to the other side, Iglesias made a wild and undignified dash from Guanajuato to the port of Manzanillo, hotly pursued by Porfirist forces for much of the distance. He managed to escape, however, taking passage aboard a steamer bound for San Francisco, where he arrived in late January, 1877.[65]

Shortly after Iglesias had vanished, Lerdo boarded a vessel at Acapulco.[66] The vanishing shore was the last view he was to have of Mexico. The true emotions and thoughts which circulated in his mind in those days after defeat were never recorded, although the author of the apocryphal memoirs attempted to recapture them.[67] Perhaps his innate skepticism was an antidote to any remorse, disillusionment, or bitterness which might have clouded his sentiments. One wonders if, during his ruminations while awaiting the ship at Acapulco, he recalled the optimistic words which he had spoken to the deputies of congress when he had assumed the constitutional presidency at the peak of his popularity and career:

All my hopes and all my efforts will be directed so that when I end the period of my administration, I may contemplate the Republic enjoying, in full peace, the benefits which liberty procures, which the law guarantees, which enlightenment develops, and which the patriotism of the people conserves.[68]

---

[64]Francisco Mejía, the minister of Finance, and Darío Balandrano, editor in chief of the *Diario Oficial*, apparently had intended to accompany the President but later deserted and returned to Mexico City.—*El Siglo*, February 1, 1877; *El Monitor*, February 7, 1877.

[65]Iglesias, *Autobiografía*, 69–70; García Granados, *Historia de México*, I, 156–160; Paz, *Díaz*, I, 217; Guillermo Prieto, *San Francisco in the Seventies: The City as Viewed by a Mexican Political Exile* (trans. and ed. by Edwin S. Morby), pp. v–viii.

[66]*El Monitor*, February 10, 1877; Foster to Fish, February 12, 1877, *Mexico, Dispatches*, LVIII, A.U.S.

[67]*Memorias Inéditas del Lic. Don Sebastián Lerdo de Tejada*, Primera Parte, 68–73.

[68]*Diario de los Debates*, December 1, 1872, 6th Congress, III, 682.

Chapter XI

Exile: Thirteen Years of Pride and Principle

In the second week of February, 1877, the steamship *Colon* docked at the harbor of New York carrying a passenger list with at least four persons of Mexican nationality: Sebastián Lerdo de Tejada, Mariano Escobedo, Manuel Romero Rubio, and Juan José Baz. Although prominent political refugees of a recent revolution which had taken place in the Southern Republic, they seemed to be under no financial distress, for they lodged in a sumptuous suite of rooms at the fashionable Hotel Windsor.

For the moment, New York reporters were attracted to the Windsor to ferret out the latest news from Mexico, to scrutinize the person of the man who had been president of that country for more than four years, to wheedle what plans, if any, he had to convert his *de jure* position back into a *de facto* one, and to extract any interesting comments which he was willing to release about his downfall:

President Lerdo is a man of small stature, and with a rather slight figure. His resemblance to ex-Gov. Tilden is most remarkable in almost every particular, except the slight peculiarity in the eyes. He wears no beard, his face is round, his complexion light, and his grayish thin hair is carefully brushed over his head. His eyes, which were dark and bright, and his exceedingly small and finely-shaped feet, were the only Spanish characteristics to be noticed. He was plainly dressed in black. His manners were very courteous and suave, and his voice very pleasant and gentle. During the conversation he shrugged his shoulders and gesticulated with his hands in the vivacious style óf his race. He rolled and smoked a cigarette, and laughed as if he enjoyed himself whenever the reporter put a question which he did not intend to answer.[1]

Apparently with some reluctance, Lerdo spoke to the reporters in a cursory manner about the events of the revolution, the fatal effect of Iglesias' attitude, his pleasant ocean voyage from Panamá, and his conviction that constitutional government would triumph in Mexico over military dictatorship, even though "the Mexicans were in a state of great uncertainty. . . ."[2] In regard to his own inten-

---

[1]*The New-York Daily Tribune*, February 12, 1877, p. 8. See also *The New York Herald*, February 12, 1877, p. 3; *El Siglo*, March 9, 1877. *The Daily Graphic* (New York) stated with telegraphic terseness: "Another Mexican President, Lerdo, in town. Mexico is now largely exporting presidents. Lerdo strongly resembles Samuel J. Tilden."—*The Daily Graphic*, February 12, 1877, p. 707. The sarcasm in part referred to Iglesias, who also had migrated to the United States. An excellent sketch of Lerdo appeared in *ibid.*, February 13, 1877, p. 717.

[2]*The New-York Daily Tribune*, February 12, 1877, p. 2.

tions, Lerdo hesitated to commit himself, stating that all would depend on "future events": "The President then remarked that his party would be in New York for several days at least, but that they did not know at present what their next movement would be."[3]

Although Lerdo settled down to spend the last thirteen years of his life as a voluntary exile, scarcely leaving the environs of New York City, the party which bore his name spent almost three years in death throes. And it did not die exactly: it was kneaded astutely by Díaz into the variegated ingredients of his own régime. As far as any overt activity was concerned, however, Lerdo completed his formal political career with the promulgation in New York of two manifestoes, both dated 1877. The first, published soon after his arrival in the United States, reiterated his claim as *de jure* president of Mexico, enumerated the benefits of his administration, and rightfully accused Iglesias of fomenting the revolt which permitted the victory of Díaz and the principle of bullets over ballots.[4] The second document was a mere patriotic protest against an executive decree of the United States government which ordered American troops in Texas to pursue marauders across the Rio Grande if necessary to check the raiding rampant in that area.[5]

Meanwhile, in Mexico, General Díaz was facing the practical problems of government, particularly the consolidation of his revolutionary régime amid the clamors of military and other place seekers with whom he was compromised. In addition, there were two national figures in exile, Iglesias and Lerdo, both claiming the constitutional presidency and backed by a large number of the more respectable civilian elements in politics as well as a small portion of the outstanding military figures. Though Díaz was supported by the practical forces of local chieftains, men trained in revolutionary methods, his tenure was somewhat precarious until the United States granted recognition, a diplomatic victory which was not achieved until April, 1878.

During the period when American recognition was withheld, General Escobedo, Lerdo's close friend and last minister of War and a Mexican soldier of French intervention fame, attempted to organize a counterrevolution on the northern frontier of Mexico

[3]*Ibid.*, February 12, 1877, p. 2.

[4]"Sebastián Lerdo de Tejada, El Presidente Constitucional de México a Sus Conciudadanos," New York, February 24, 1877, Archivo de Fernando Iglesias Calderón, Legajo 15, A.G.N. General Escobedo, who accompanied Lerdo into exile and then migrated to Texas, gave a copy of the document to a Galveston reporter. It was translated and printed in *The Galveston Daily News*, April 12, 1877.

[5]"Sebastián Lerdo de Tejada, El Presidente Constitucional de México a Sus Conciudadanos," New York, June 2, 1877, Archivo de Fernando Iglesias Calderón, Legajo 15, A.G.N.; *El Monitor*, June 30, 1877; Iglesias, *La Cuestión Presidencial en 1876*, 332–335.

to effect the restoration of Sebastián. Choosing the comforting safety of southern Texas as a base for his machinations, Escobedo arrived at Galveston from New York in April, 1877. Dapper, suave, and discreet, he was the type of man one might expect Lerdo to entrust with such a difficult and delicate mission. A Galveston reporter described him as follows:

> General Escobedo's personal appearance betrays the man of mark. He is quite tall and commanding in figure; he has black hair and full beard and moustaches—the beard considerably mixed with gray—and anything but tawny, almost fair complexion. From his physiognomy it is evident that he is of pure Castilian stock. His forehead is high and pallid almost to whiteness; his eyes dark and slightly languid. He is about forty-nine years old. He was dressed in a black fatigue suit with brass buttons and wore a silk hat.[6]

Mimicking the precedent of Lerdo, Escobedo dealt in vague generalities when questioned by the reporter about the nature of his visit: "He was here on a trip of pleasure, but at the same time in the capacity of a spectator of affairs of the Rio Grande." "This was his general answer," remarked the undeceived journalist, "to a question whether he was not on a mission from President Lerdo looking to measures for the restoration of the latter to power."[7] Passing on to San Antonio, where he erected his revolutionary headquarters in one of the local hotels, Escobedo retained his tight-lipped policy, which ruse concealed nothing and confused no one regarding his objectives. Disheartened news correspondents, however, continued to find him not only "studiously polite, never pausing to prepare an answer, charming you with the most engaging smile," but also "more than a match for even the experienced terriers of the New York press."[8]

It would be possible to embellish with numberless minor details the efforts of the Lerdists to provoke a restorative revolution along the Rio Grande, most of which centered around the plottings of Escobedo in southern Texas, from the spring of 1877 until the summer of 1878. Escobedo's brief internment by the United States troops in July, 1877, temporarily interrupted the disorganized movement, which had accomplished nothing more substantial than a few abortive thrusts across the river;[9] but the formal end of those ineffective military schemes came with the capture of Escobedo in northern Mexico at Cuatro Ciénegas, Coahuila, in July, 1878, and the disintegration of the straggling column of recruits

---

[6]*The Galveston Daily News*, April 11, 1877.
[7]*Ibid.*, April 11, 1877.
[8]*Ibid.*, April 15, 1877.
[9]*Ibid.*, July 22, 25, 1877. See also the issues of May 16, June 13, 17, 21, 1877.

which he had managed to assemble.[10] Although the Lerdist movement along the Rio Grande elicited no small amount of Texan interest, especially in promoting the belief that "a great rebellion" would spread against Díaz as a result,[11] it terminated in a dismal military fiasco predicated upon puny resources, poorly managed, timed, and applied.[12] If Escobedo's plotting was a serious irritant when combined with other troubles which swamped the early months of Porfirismo, it certainly never advanced to be reckoned as a major threat to the stability of the newly-founded administration.[13]

Beyond the activities in Texas, one last abortive complot was hatched in Mexico which was connected generally with the resuscitation of Lerdismo, though the association was never proved. Díaz's response was the notorious massacre of nine alleged revolutionists at Vera Cruz in June, 1879. The barbarous incident properly belongs to the Díaz period as an example of the disciplinary methods which the new Chief of State would apply to those who sought to undermine his position. Though Lerdo, a recluse in distant New York, could have had only the vaguest knowledge of the immediate plans of the insurrection,[14] it was believed that Rubio, Escobedo, Carlos Fuero, and other key Lerdists, then residing in Mexico City, had been the engineers of a scheme to oust Díaz and restore his exiled opponent.[15] At any rate, the finale was the brutal slaughter of June, 1879, at Vera Cruz, none of the nine victims being implicated except by suspicion and highly circumstantial evidence and none of them being principals of the

---

[10]*La Libertad* (Mexico), August 20, 1878; *El Monitor*, July 27, 1878; Prida, *De la Dictadura a la Anarquía*, I, 61; García Granados, *Historia de México*, I, 190.

[11]*The Dallas Daily Herald*, April 26, 1878. Escobedo's movement "has been well and deeply laid," noted the *Daily Herald* erroneously, "the utmost secrecy having been observed."—*Ibid.*, May 8, 1878.

[12]Valadés, *El Porfirismo, Nacimiento*, 126–128.

[13]A letter which Lerdo wrote to General Escobedo in May, 1878, revealed that he was watching the border revolutionary activities carefully, even from his detached point of observation in New York, and that he was hopeful of their ultimate success.—Lerdo to M. Escobedo, New York, May 25, 1878, Archivo de Fernando Iglesias Calderón, Legajo 15, A.G.N.

[14]A typical, unverified charge, written by a eulogist of Díaz, placed the responsibility for the execution of the nine on Lerdo.—García Naranjo, *Porfirio Díaz*, 209. It is humorous to note that Porfirist historians were uniformly indignant about the use by the Lerdists of ugly, revolutionary methods.

[15]Hector Ribot, *Las Últimas Revoluciones*, 17; García Granados, *Historia de México*, I, 209; Zayas Enríquez, *Porfirio Díaz*, 146–147; Paz, *Díaz*, II, 17–18.

old Lerdist party. On such a lugubrious note sounded the political death knell of the man and his party—Lerdo and Lerdismo.[16]

After his first months in New York, Lerdo was isolated in a strange city and country, in the midst of a people speaking a quaint tongue, and far from everything he had known and lived throughout his life. To a more flexible man, to one who had less of the "principle" about him—or call it pride and obstinacy, for all three words are closely allied—that protracted twilight of twelve years would have been an intolerable self-martyrdom; but to Lerdo it was the essential termination of his consistent personality and career. Undoubtedly, he longed for the familiar scenes and friends with a depth difficult to describe, though it can be surmised with certainty that he never would have confessed the sentiment to anyone. Nor did he ever seem to waver in his purpose to stand as the unique symbol of protest to the Díaz régime and the principle of revolution. Had he returned supplicant for admission into the conciliating embrace of Porfirismo, as did Iglesias and his faction and the main partisans of Lerdo himself, he would have suffered disastrously in self-esteem. No other recourse to exile would have seemed logical for a man with his character and determination. He had first of all to live with himself, and it was possible to do so only outside his beloved Mexico.

The minutiae which composed his daily routine over a period of many years are virtually nonextant, the natural result of his retirement into the shell of a recluse. According to Gonzalo A. Esteva, who "had the fortune of visiting him frequently in New York,"[17] Lerdo enslaved himself to a rigid routine which consisted of arising at a specified hour, taking an hourly walk in downtown New York each evening along an exact route, and receiving his guests at night between the hours of nine and ten, or in the afternoons on Sundays. Soon tiring of the hubbub and expense of the Hotel Windsor, he moved to a fashionable boarding establishment known as Lenox House, where he lodged with his inflexible schedule until death. Like his black suit and spotless white linen, his study was always immaculate, each pen, pencil, and sheaf of papers having its precise locus.

In addition to occasional visitors and summer excursions to the nearby beach to escape the oppressive heat of New York,[18] Lerdo occupied his time with reading, particularly on American geography

[16]José C. Valadés has made the finest study of the Vera Cruz episode, although he presented his materials so as to place the brunt of responsibility upon the erratic Luis Mier y Terán, the governor of the state who actually carried out the executions.—*El Porfirismo, Nacimiento*, 143–158.

[17]*Sebastián Lerdo de Tejada, 1823–1889: In Memoriam*, 33 (hereafter cited *In Memoriam*). The following summary is based on the brief description written by Esteva in *ibid.*, 33–35.

[18]Valenciano de Rhodo, D. *Sebastián Lerdo de Tejada y la Misión de la América Española*, 1.

and politics and on international affairs; and though he never left New York City, at least for any distance, he appeared to know in detail about the scenic excursions for tourists in all parts of the United States. Then, he became proficient in speaking and writing English, which proved the nimbleness of his mind at age fifty-three, for he knew nothing of the language when he arrived in New York in 1877. Perhaps the acquisition of the language combined with his profound knowledge of Mexican law enabled him to carry on a modest though apparently lucrative legal practice through which he served both Americans and his own countrymen.[19]

It would be fascinating to have a list of the men who visited Lerdo in exile and even more fascinating to have a record of the conversations which took place. As the author of the apocryphal memoirs of Sebastián has pointed out, Juan N. Navarro, the consul general of New York and an ancient acquaintance of Sebastián, was perhaps his most regular caller,[20] while Gonzalo A. Esteva claimed to have been a frequent visitor, as previously mentioned. Also, John W. Foster, United States minister to Mexico during most of Lerdo's presidency, spoke in the plural of "visits which I made to him in his retirement in New York," for which Lerdo seemed very grateful.[21] Of course, there were probably many Mexicans, known and unknown, who left their calling cards at Lenox House during the course of more than a decade, but such matters being of little moment have escaped documentation.[22]

---

[19]*In Memoriam*, 34. *El Monitor* once printed an undoubtedly exaggerated report that Lerdo had received 200,000 pesos for acting as legal counsel in some "intricate mercantile transactions" in New York.—*El Monitor*, December 2, 1882. See also Higinio Vázquez Santa Ana, *Bosquejos Biográficos de Hombres Ilustres Nacionales*, 141.

Juan Antonio Lerdo de Tejada, great-nephew of Sebastián, informed the present writer that Sebastián received retainer fees from two United States corporations during his exile, but he was unable to recall further details.— Interview, Mexico, D.F., August 2, 1947.

[20]Juan Navarro was frequently mentioned in the second part of the *Memorias Inéditas del Lic. Don Sebastián Lerdo de Tejada*, especially 16, 50, 70–71. As early as 1864, about the time Navarro became consul-general, Lerdo mentioned him in a diplomatic dispatch as "friend Navarro."—Lerdo to Romero, Chihuahua, October 16, 1864, Romero (ed.), *Correspondencia de la Legación Mexicana*, IV, 547. Navarro was probably the most secure bureaucrat Mexico ever had. In a magazine article which he wrote in 1901, to advertize Díaz in the United States, Navarro declared: "I have lived in your powerful and interesting country for more than thirty-seven years. . . ."— Juan N. Navarro, "Mexico of Today," *The National Geographic Magazine*, XII (June, 1901), 238. See also Salado Álvarez, *Memorias*, I, 377.

[21]Foster, *Diplomatic Memoirs*, I, 85.

[22]Again, the author of the apocryphal memoirs wrote of many persons who visited or corresponded with Lerdo. The second part of the spurious polemic dealt almost exclusively with Lerdo's life and reflections in exile; however, the document is replete with gross errors and bias and therefore is almost too treacherous for any historical purpose.

Perhaps the most significant social call ever paid Lerdo was attempted but not consummated. In the spring of 1883, while Manuel González was serving as president of Mexico during the only interregnum which broke the long dictatorship of Porfirio Díaz, the "Hero" of Tuxtepec made a grand tour of the United States. With him were his young bride, Carmen Romero Rubio, and his new father-in-law, Manuel Romero Rubio, whose name had the familiar ring of a man who had once stood as a mainstay of Lerdismo and as one of Lerdo's trusted confidants. Rubio had abandoned Lerdo and the rigors of exile about a year and a half after his arrival in New York,[23] and his return to Mexico was accompanied by a spectacular rise in political prominence under the aegis of the Tuxtepec régime. To the romanticists it might seem cynical to connect Rubio's sudden transformation and success with the joining of his daughter in holy wedlock with Don Porfirio himself; but historically it is too gross a coincidence to overlook. The author of the apocryphal memoirs probably made his closest guess to reality when he placed the following words in Sebastián's mouth: "And I do not know in truth which of those two men was more despicable, the one who sold his daughter or the one who bought her."[24]

However that may be, the celebrated travelers stopped at the Hotel Windsor, Lerdo's old residence, during more than two weeks of a lavish round of entertainment in New York.[25] At some lull in the social activities, Rubio and Díaz, father-in-law and son-in-law, respectively, paid their respects to Lerdo, perhaps in hopes of conciliating the staunchest enemy of Porfirismo. As the story goes —and it is confirmed by reliable sources which vary only in detail —Lerdo glanced at the two calling cards and agreed to receive the man who had fought against him openly as a revolutionist. But glancing at the card of the man who had betrayed him in order to ingratiate himself with the Hero of Tuxtepec, he replied with five crisp words which spoke volumes: "I do not recognize it." Thus was shattered the personal assault on his retirement and the chief attempt to add the leader of Lerdismo to the multitude of Lerdist trophies which Don Porfirio already had appended to the glory of his régime.[26]

---

[23]A notice of Rubio's return to Mexico was printed in *El Monitor*, June 16, 1878.

[24]*Memorias Inéditas del Lic. Don Sebastián Lerdo de Tejada*, Segunda Parte, 66.

[25]Díaz and his party arrived in New York in late March and departed on April 25, 1883. His activities were carried in *The Daily Graphic* on a day-to-day basis, but no mention was ever made of the exiled ex-President Lerdo.

[26]The above story was told personally by the son of Porfirio Díaz to Juan Antonio Lerdo de Tejada, great-nephew of Sebastián.—Interview, Mexico, D.F., July 11, 1947. See García Granados, *Historia de México*, II, 57; *Memorias Inéditas del Lic. Don Sebastián Lerdo de Tejada*, Segunda Parte, 64–66.

That there was a dearth of material on Sebastián's life as an exile was a product of his isolation and was of small historical loss. Yet what he thought and might have written would have been invaluable. One of his greatest sins of omission, from the historical standpoint, was his failure to write his experiences and impressions of over two decades of turbulent Mexican history. It would have been possible for his pen alone to have resolved many of the controversial subjects which emerged from the events of that epoch. No contemporary Mexican, after Juárez's death, had played a more important rôle in national politics; none had maintained a more varied and intimate association with the great figures of his time; and none had been more continuously connected with Juárez. Seldom, too, had a prominent political ghost discovered himself in more detached surroundings with the necessary leisure and the calm of reflection for writing. The environment was perfect for Lerdo to place on paper his personal opinions of his own administration, the mistakes he had committed, his observations on the statecraft of Díaz, and so many intimate secrets of politics and personality which ever escape the official document. By failing to explain his own position when he possessed the ideal opportunity, Lerdo inadvertently assured his own historical neglect and perhaps cheated himself from the honor of making one of the great contemporary contributions to the history of nineteenth-century Mexico. The frequency with which secondary writers cite the spurious polemic known as the *Memorias Inéditas* is proof enough that a substantial work coming from Sebastián's pen would have held transcendental historical importance.

On April 21, 1889, Juan Navarro, Mexican consul general at New York, filed the following telegram to Matías Romero, minister of Mexico at Washington: "Señor Lerdo died today at 1:45 [P.M.]."[27] The cause was capillary bronchitis and death had come quickly. The news was forwarded to Mexico immediately,[28] and

The present writer also interviewed an elderly gentleman in Mexico City who happened to be present at a Mexican dinner party given in New York on the evening of the day in which the incident had occurred. Though the person was a small boy at the time and did not comprehend the significance of the remarks made at the table, he did recall that both Rubio and Díaz were present and that Sebastián's attitude was a topic of discussion. The person interviewed supplied the information only on condition that his name would not be revealed.

[27]Navarro to Romero (telegram), New York, April 21, 1889, *Correspondencia de la Legación Mexicana en Washington*, Legajo 125, Archivo de Relaciones Exteriores. See also *The New York Times*, April 23, 1889, p. 5; *The New York Herald Tribune*, April 23, 1889, p. 1.

[28]Romero to the Minister of Foreign Relations (telegram), Washington, April 21, 1889, *Correspondencia de la Legación Mexicana en Washington*, Legajo 125, Archivo de Relaciones Exteriores.

filled the columns of the press in the capital on the following day. Thus a man whose name had long since vanished from the Mexican political horizon came back to life through death.

Meanwhile, the government of Díaz set in motion the machinery for transforming the rather embarrassing anomaly into a grand fête, not to pay tribute to a deceased and discredited statesman, although that was the patent purpose, but to demonstrate the magnanimity of Don Porfirio toward his most recalcitrant enemy. The two chambers of congress, whose composition appeared in 1889 more Lerdista than Porfirista,[29] suspended their sessions for several days. and decreed special honors,[30] including the payment for burial expenses and transference of the body by rail from New York.[31] In addition, General Mariano Escobedo was dispatched to New York to accompany the body back to Mexico City; consequently, it appeared that the man who had attempted to restore Lerdo in 1877–1878, by military action, was allowed that pleasure in 1889, under rather cynical circumstances. Whether the selection of Escobedo for the mission was a touch of Díaz's sarcasm cannot be proved, but the choice seemed inappropriate and the implications undeniable. If true, then, it was merely another manifestation of the hypocrisy which surrounded the entire funeral arrangement.[32]

After the United States government had rendered the body appropriate military honors in New York, it was brought by rail to El Paso and thence along a route very similar to one which Lerdo had traveled with Juárez and Iglesias for the triumphal return to the capital after the departure of the French in 1867.[33] The special train arrived at Mexico City on May 13, the event serving to reopen the graves of events long buried, and there was a suppressed excitement in the city, perhaps because of the interesting implications which would develop around the funeral ceremony. Most of the papers managed to compile eulogies about Lerdo's career, carefully avoiding the treacherous ground around his presidency and the revolution of Díaz in 1876. The veneer was sham and artificiality, as Francisco Sosa pointed out in a letter to Lerdo's

[29]"Lerdo, without leaving his exile, conquered without firing a shot. The present administration is altogether the Lerdist administration. There is nothing more than one change and one addition: the change is the person of the Executive; the addition is the country placed under North American enterprises. . . ."—*Diario del Hogar*, April 28, 1889.

[30]*Diario de los Debates, Cámara de Diputados*, April 22, 1889, 14th Congress, II, 120–125; *ibid., Cámara de Senadores*, April 22, 1889, 14th Congress, 2nd per., 184–186.

[31]Dublán y Lozano, *Legislación Mexicana*, XIX, 370; *El Tiempo* (Mexico), May 11, 1889.

[32]See García Granados, *Historia de México*, II, 173.

[33]Details of the route and the honors arranged for the body of Lerdo at various stops along the way were given in *In Memoriam*, 55–65.

old enemy, Vicente Riva Palacio: "Today the corpse of Señor Lerdo arrived. You will see in the periodicals the narration of the sumptuous funeral services, and of how much has been done. Things of the world!"[34]

Though the policy of suppression of the Díaz government was reflected in the caution of the press, *El Tiempo,* with unusual courage, stripped the flattery written to Lerdo of its hypocrisy: All the liberal press was making "truly stupendous eulogies" to the deceased, but why was so capable a patriot not called back so that his services might have been used for the benefit of Mexico and so that "he would not have died in bitter ostracism, a thing which is very sad and painful for those who love their country"? Why, too, was there a glaring silence in regard to Lerdo's cautious policy toward American capital and the freedom he had so generously granted to the press? "The deceased ex-President of Mexico never persecuted the journalists in a manner which has been witnessed here subsequently." Perhaps recalling the healthfulness of discretion, *El Tiempo* concluded: "We do not wish to say it, nor to make more commentaries. It is a task which we leave to our readers, because they are in a better aptitude and situation than we for stating *truths.*"[35]

The funeral service, lasting several hours, took place on May 14, the day after the body had arrived in Mexico City.[36] The notables of the Mexican social and political world appeared en masse to attend the display in the Chamber of Deputies. One by one the puppet orators performed in the presence of the master of Mexico, Porfirio Díaz, and each perorated on prosaic metaphors. It was glaringly conspicuous that the speakers traced Lerdo's career only to the end of the intervention, stopping abruptly as if he had never been president or ousted from his position by a revolution led by the paragon of peace and order who sat in the audience.

But it was Francisco Bulnes, with his erupting delivery and pungent expressions, who held the primary interest of the listeners, as indicated by the inappropriate applause which interrupted his oration from time to time.[37] Unlike the other speakers, Bulnes touched upon the fatal year 1876: "Why did [Lerdo] fall? I cannot, gentlemen, remain silent on this point. . . ." Lerdo, "the great man," did not understand that bread and liberty were essential complements, and consequently "the cannon shots of Tecoac audaciously called . . . 200,000 laborers to fasten together 10,000 kilo-

---

[34]F[rancisco] Sosa to Vicente Riva Palacio, Mexico, May 13, 1889, Vicente Riva Palacio Papers, Folder 190, UT.

[35]*El Tiempo,* April 26, 1889.

[36]The funeral speeches were reprinted in *In Memoriam,* 69–100. A detailed description of all the honors and services was printed in *Diario del Hogar,* May 15, 1889.

[37]*La Voz de México,* May 15, 1889.

meters of rails. Bread began to be the inseparable companion of peace."[38] Then Bulnes finished by converting his speech into a subjective eulogy to Díaz for railroad expansion and a taunt at Lerdo as an exile:

[Lerdo] saw the flowers of Jalapa in the immense market of New York, and the fruits of Veracruz fell over his table. Everything arrived from *la patria,* except the voice which would tell him *come back!!*[39]

When the flow of poor taste had run its course, they buried Lerdo's body at the cemetery of Dolores in the rotunda of the "Illustrious Men" of Mexico, an honor which he richly deserved. Grand nationalist and patriot, the forgotten little man of Mexican history seemed like a giant of character, pride, and principle by the side of the living sycophants who had gathered to gossip at his funeral. It remained the task of history, noted *El Tiempo,* to judge the true eminence of Lerdo, as a statesman, politician, jurisconsult, and orator "by the light of truth and without the clouds of passion."[40] And the task remained untouched through the decades, though the foregoing chapters were a belated effort in that direction.

---

[38]*In Memoriam,* 78, 80.
[39]*Ibid.,* 81.
[40]*El Tiempo,* May 16, 1889.

EPILOGUE

The Man in History

The man in history? Sebastián Lerdo lives not in history: he survives in the marginal twilight of fable and error, in that distorted zone which arises from prejudices and hatreds oft-repeated. Submerged in the shadows of Juárez and Díaz, his consistent personality has never been displayed as an entity, and it grows dimmer with the weathering of time.

Yet the failure to account for Lerdo's position has left a gaping hole in the interpretation of Mexican history for the years 1861 to 1876; for it is impossible to single out an individual, excepting perhaps Juárez, who had a more prominent and continuous rôle in the political events of that period. Nor is it certain that even Juárez should be excepted. Despite the existence of an obvious fact, Lerdo's influence has remained unexplored and unperceived, though it is striking, whether one investigates national politics, diplomatic history, liberalism, administrative methods, constitutional reform, or church-state relationship.

How has it been possible for the ever-enlarging circle of Juárez's biographers to neglect Lerdo's connection almost entirely? How have the publicists of the history of the Reform been able to overlook that Lerdo's presidential administration was the practical blossoming, the climax, and abortive failure of liberalism? Why have Porfirist historians refused to recognize that many of the truly efficient administrative methods employed by Díaz had their birth or incubation under Lerdo before him?

But the familiar paths of Mexican history have been worn into deep ruts by the easy repetition of unevaluated statements. It is too late and too much to expect the major reshuffling of interpretation to make room for the place which Lerdo should occupy. Countless future biographers of Juárez, or historians of his epoch, will rescramble the familiar materials, shifting the emphasis here and there, but always apprehensive that someone like Lerdo might detract from the glory of their hero; and hence they will discard him in the prosaic manner. Countless future biographers of Díaz will cite the figures on economic advances in the 1900's to rationalize the importunate necessity of overthrowing the decadent President of 1876.

Thus, Lerdo, perhaps the most outstanding example among many, many forgotten statesmen submerged in the patina surrounding Juárez and Díaz, will survive in history as an inconvenient fact to be dispensed with glibly as a hindrance to something more important.

Lerdo lives not in history and he probably never will. Of course, it is unfortunate that he has been maltreated by the printed page, but there is never any great loss through the absence of biographical eulogy. The real penalty must be charged to the completeness and accuracy of the general history of Mexico.

Bibliography[1]

I. Sources

A. Manuscripts and Typescripts[2]

The Archives of the United States, Washington, D.C.
Dispatches from Mexico, Department of State, 1867–1877.
Archivo del Colegio Nacional de Abogados, Mexico, D. F.
Libro Donde se Asientan las Matrículas de los Individuos de Este Ilustre Nacional Colegio de Abogados.
Colegio de Abogados (Books of account for dues and fees).
Archivo General de la Nación, Mexico, D. F.
Archivo de Fernando Iglesias Calderón.
Ynstrucción Pública. Vols. XLI–XLIII, LI, LX–LXIII, LXXIII–LXXVI, LXXXI.
Archivo del Museo Nacional de México, Mexico, D. F.
Legajo 50–L–14–I (Miscellaneous letters).
Archivo de Relaciones Exteriores, Mexico, D. F.
Correspondencia de la Legación Mexicana en Washington, Legajo 125.
José María Lafragua, Su Expediente Personal.
Miguel Lerdo de Tejada, Su Expediente Personal.
Sebastián Lerdo de Tejada, Su Expediente Personal.
Archivo de la Suprema Corte de Justicia, Mexico, D. F.
Decretos de la Suprema Corte de Justicia, Año de 1856.
Biblioteca Nacional de México, Mexico, D. F.
Archivo de Benito Juárez.
The Latin-American Collection, The University of Texas, Austin, Texas.
Correspondence of Jesús González Ortega, 1851–1860. Vol. I (Typescripts).
Correspondence of Manuel Doblado, 1861 (Typescripts).
Mejía, F., *Épocas, Hechos y Acontecimientos de Mi Vida, y de los Que Fui Actor y Testigo.* Mexico, November, 1878.
Secretarios de Estado del Gobierno Mexicano (No date).
The Library of Congress, Washington, D.C. (Division of Manuscripts).
The Papers of Edward L. Plumb. 14 vols.
Miscellaneous papers in the possession of Juan Antonio Lerdo de Tejada y Sanz and Antonio Lerdo de Tejada, Mexico, D. F.
The University of Texas Archives, Austin, Texas.
Ignacio Comonfort Papers.
Mariano Riva Palacio Papers.
Vicente Riva Palacio Papers.

B. Printed Documents and Correspondence

Andrade, Vicente de P., *Partidas de Bautismo de Gobernantes de México.* Mexico (Tip. Sucesores de Francisco Díaz de León), 1904.

---

[1]The writer has included only the works cited in the text and acknowledges the direct and indirect use he has made of other studies not incorporated in this bibliography.
[2]MSS. except as indicated.

Boletín Oficial del Consejo Superior de Gobierno del Distrito Federal, III, September 27, 1904 (Record of baptism).

British and Foreign State Papers. Vols. LII, LVIII, LXVII. London (William Ridgway), 1868–1883.

Buenrostro, Felipe, *Historia del Primero y Segundo Congresos Constitucionales de la República Mexicana.* 9 vols. Mexico (Tipografía Literaria de Filomeno Mata), 1874–1882.

Castañeda, Carlos E. (ed.), *La Guerra de Reforma según el Archivo del General D. Manuel Doblado, 1857–1860.* Vol. III of *Nuevos Documentos Inéditos ó Muy Raros para la Historia de México.* San Antonio (Casa Editorial Lozano), 1930.

Castillo Negrete, Emilio del, *Galería de Oradores de México en el Siglo XIX.* Vol. III. Mexico (Imprenta de J. Guzmán y Hermanos), 1880.

Catálago de las Obras Que Forman la Biblioteca Pública de la Escuela N. Preparatoria Fundado el Año de 1879. Mexico (Imprenta Horcasitas, ᵀermanos), 1881.

Colección de Artículos y Documentos Relativos a los Atentados Cometidos en Jalisco por D. Sebastián Lerdo de Tejada y D. José Ceballos desde Junio de 1875 hasta 6 de Enero de 1877. 2 vols. Guadalajara (Tip. de S. Banda), 1877.

Colección de los Decretos y Órdenes de Interés Común Que Dicto el Gobierno Provisional en Virtud de las Bases de Tacubaya. Vol. III. Mexico (Imprenta de J. M. Lara), 1852.

Colección de Leyes, Decretos y Circulares Expedidas por el Supremo Gobierno de la República, 1863–1867. 3 vols. Mexico (Imprenta del Gobierno en Palacio), 1867.

Colección de las Leyes, Decretos, Circulares y Providencias Relativas á la Desamortización Eclesiástica, á la Nacionalización de los Bienes de Corporaciones, y á la Reforma de la Legislación Civil Que Tenía Relación con el Culto y con la Iglesia. 2 vols. Mexico (Imp. de J. Abadiano), 1861.

Colección de las Leyes, Decretos y Órdenes Espedidas por S.A.S. el Presidente de la República D. Antonio López de Santa Anna desde 1° de Enero de 1855. Vol. VIII. Mexico (Imprenta de J. M. Fernández de Lara), 1855.

Correspondence Relative to the Present Condition of Mexico Communicated to the House of Representatives by the Department of State. Washington (Government Printing Office), 1862.

Derecho Internacional Mexicano. 2 vols. Mexico (Imprenta de Gonzalo A. Esteva), 1878–1879.

Diario de los Debates, 1869–1876. Mexico (Tipografía de Filomeno Mata), 1871–1880.

Diario de los Debates, 1877. Vol. I. Mexico (Imprenta de Ireneo Paz), 1877.

Diario de los Debates de la Cámara de Diputados, 1889. Mexico (Imp. de "El Partido Liberal"), 1891.

Diario de los Debates de la Cámara de Senadores, 1888–1889. Mexico (Imp. del Gobierno Federal), 1889.

Diputación Permanente del 3ᵉʳ Congreso de la Unión, Actas del 13 de Junio al 14 de Diciembre de 1863. Mexico (Tipografía Literaria de F. Mata), 1883.

Distribución Anual de Premios en el Colegio Nacional y Más Antiguo de San Ildefonso el 16 de Noviembre de 1855. Mexico (Imprenta de C. Lara), 1855 (In the Biblioteca Lafragua, Puebla, Mexico).

Dublán, Manuel, and Lozano, José María (eds.), *Legislación Mexicana ó Colección Completa de las Disposiciones Legislativas Expedidas desde la Independencia de la República.* Vols. VII–XIX. Mexico (Imprenta del Comercio de Dublán y Chávez, et al.), 1877–1890.

Estrada, Genaro (ed.), *Un Siglo de Relaciones Internacionales de México (á Través de los Mensajes Presidenciales)*. Number 39 of Archivo Histórico Diplomático Mexicano. Mexico (Publicaciones de la Secretaría de Relaciones Exteriores), 1935.

García, Genaro (ed.), *La Intervención Francesa en México según el Archivo del Mariscal Bazaine*. Vol. XVII of *Documentos Inéditos ó Muy Raros para la Historia de México*. Mexico (Librería de la Vda. de Ch. Bouret), 1908.

————————, *La Revolución de Ayutla según el Archivo del General Doblado*. Vol. XXVI of *Documentos Inéditos ó Muy Raros para la Historia de México*. Mexico (Librería de la Vda. de Ch. Bouret), 1909.

Gutiérrez, Blas José, and Alatorre, Flores (eds.), *Leyes de Reforma, Colección de las Disposiciones Que se Conocen con Este Nombre Publicadas desde el Año de 1855 al de 1870*. Vol. II, Parte ii. Mexico (Miguel Zornoza, Impresor), 1870.

Lafragua, José María, *Memorandum de los Negocios Pendientes entre México y España Presentado al Exmo. Sr. Ministro de Estado por el Representante de la República el Día 28 de Julio de 1857*. Poissy (Tipografía de Arbieu), 1857.

Legislación Mejicana ó Sea Colección Completa de las Leyes, Decretos y Circulares Que se Han Expedido desde la Consumación de la Independencia: Tomo Que Comprende de Enero a Diciembre de 1855. Mexico (Imprenta de Juan R. Navarro), 1855.

Manning, William R. (ed.), *Diplomatic Correspondence of the United States, 1831–1860*. Vol. IX. Washington (Carnegie Endowment for International Peace), 1937.

Memoria Presentada al Congreso de la Unión por el Secretario de Estado y del Despacho de Fomento, Colonización, Industria y Comercio de la República Mexicana Vicente Riva Palacio. Mexico (Imprenta de Francisco Díaz de León), 1877.

Memoria Presentada al Exmo. Sr. Presidente Sustituto de la República por el C. Miguel Lerdo de Tejada Dando Cuenta de la Marcha Que Han Seguido los Negocios de la Hacienda Pública en el Tiempo Que Tuvo á Su Cargo la Secretaría de Este Ramo. Mexico (Imprenta de Vicente García Torres), 1857.

Papers Relating to the Foreign Relations of the United States, 1873–1877. Washington (Government Printing Office), 1873–1877.

Payno, Manuel, *Cuentas, Gastos, Acreedores y Otros Asuntos del Tiempo de la Intervención Francesa y del Imperio*. Mexico (Imprenta de Ignacio Cumplido), 1868.

————————, *México y sus Cuestiones Financieras con la Inglaterra, la España y la Francia*. Mexico (Imprenta de Ignacio Cumplido), 1862.

Peña y Reyes, Antonio de la (ed.), *La Labor Diplomática de D. Manuel María de Zamacona como Secretario de Relaciones Exteriores*. Number 28 of Archivo Histórico Diplomático Mexicano. Mexico (Publicaciones de la Secretaría de Relaciones Exteriores), 1928.

Pérez Lugo, J., *La Cuestión Religiosa en México, Recopilación de Leyes, Disposiciones Legales y Documentos para el Estudio de Este Problema Político*. Mexico (Publicaciones del Centro Cultural "Cuauhtemoc"), 1926.

Personas Que Han Tenido á su Cargo la Secretaría de Relaciones Exteriores desde 1821 hasta 1924. Number 6 of Archivo Histórico Diplomático Mexicano. Mexico (Publicaciones de la Secretaría de Relaciones Exteriores), 1924.

Puig Casauranc, J. M., *Archivos Privados de D. Benito Juárez y D. Pedro Santacilia*. Vol. I. Mexico (Publicaciones de la Secretaría de Educación Pública, Biblioteca Nacional), 1928.

Riva Palacio, Mariano, and Martínez de la Torre, Rafael, *Memorandum sobre el Proceso del Archiduque Fernando Maximiliano de Austria.* Mexico (Imprenta de F. Díaz de León y S. White), 1867.

Roel, Santiago (ed.), *Correspondencia Particular de D. Santiago Vidaurri, Gobernador de Nuevo León, 1855–1864.* Vol. I, Juárez-Vidaurri. Monterrey (no publisher named), 1946.

Romero, Matías (ed.), *Correspondencia de la Legación Mexicana en Washington durante la Intervención Extranjera, Colección de Documentos para Formar la Historia de la Intervención.* 10 vols. Mexico (Imprenta del Gobierno en Palacio), 1870–1892.

Ruíz, Manuel, *Exposición Que el C. Lic. Manuel Ruíz, Ministro Constitucional de la Suprema Corte de Justicia de la Nación Presenta al Soberano Congreso de la Unión Pidiendo el Cumplimiento de las Disposiciones Contenidas en los Artículos del 103 al 105 de la Constitución General.* Mexico (Imprenta de Nabor Chávez), 1868.

Saldívar, Gabriel (ed.), *La Misión Confidencial de Don Jesús Terán en Europa, 1863–1866.* Second Series, Number 1 of Archivo Histórico Diplomático Mexicano. Mexico (Publicaciones de la Secretaría de Relaciones Exteriores), 1943.

Sebastián Lerdo de Tejada, 1823–1889: In Memoriam. Mexico (Tip. de "El Partido Liberal"), 1889.

Suplemento al Primer Cuaderno de Documentos Publicados por el General González Ortega para Esplorar la Opinión de Sus Conciudadanos en Favor de una Rebelión contra el Gobierno Nacional de México (Title page missing).

Veredicto del Gran Jurado Nacional, Dictamen de la Sección y Defensas Pronunciadas en el Juicio Instruido contra el Ciudadano Francisco Mejía por las Responsabilidades Oficiales de Que se le Acusó como Ministro de Hacienda Que Fué de la Administración Pasada. Mexico (Vicente S. Reyes, Impresor), 1877.

Zarco, Francisco (ed.), *Historia del Congreso Estraordinario Constituyente de 1856 y 1857.* 2 vols. Mexico (Imprenta de Ignacio Cumplido), 1857.

C. Newspapers[3]

El Ahuizote (Mexico).
The Daily Graphic (New York).
The Dallas Daily Herald (Dallas, Texas).
Diario de Avisos (Mexico).
El Diario del Hogar (Mexico).
El Diario del Imperio (Mexicó).
Diario Oficial del Gobierno Supremo de la República (Mexico).
Diario Oficial de la República Mejicana (San Luis Potosí).
El Domingo (Mexico).
El Eco Nacional (Mexico).
El Estado de Jalisco (Guadalajara).
El Estandarte Nacional (Mexico).
Gaceta del Gobierno de México (Mexico).
The Galveston Daily News (Galveston, Texas).
El Globo (Mexico).
La Libertad (Mexico).
El Mensajero (Mexico).
El Monitor Republicano (Mexico).
El Nacional (Mexico).

---

[3]Includes only original newspaper sources cited.

The New-York Daily Tribune (New York).
The New York Herald (New York).
The New York Times (New York).
The New York World (New York).
El Omnibus (Mexico).
La Orquesta (Mexico).
El Padre Cobos (Mexico).
Los Padres del Agua Fría (Mexico).
El Palo de Ciego (Mexico).
Periódico Oficial del Gobierno Constitucional de la República Mexicana (Chihuahua, Paso del Norte).
El Siglo XIX (Mexico).
La Sociedad (Mexico).
El Tiempo (Mexico).
The Two Republics (Mexico).
El Universal (Mexico).
La Voz de México (Mexico).

D. Accounts by Contemporaries, Special and General

Bartlett, I. S., "President Juárez at Old El Paso," *Bulletin of the Pan American Union*, XLI (November, 1915), 641–658.
Basch, Samuel, *Recuerdos de México, Memorias del Médico Ordinario del Emperador Maximiliano (1866 á 1867)*. Trans. from the Italian by Doctor D. Manuel Peredo. Mexico (Imp. del Comercio de N. Chávez), 1870.
Baz, Gustavo, *Vida de Benito Juárez*. Mexico (Casa Editorial y Agencia de Publicaciones de Enrique Capdevielle y Cª), 1874.
Baz, Gustavo, and Gallo, E. L., *History of the Mexican Railway*. Trans. by George F. Henderson. Mexico (Gallo & Co.), 1876.
Blanchot, Colonel Ch., *Memoires L'Intervention Française au Mexique*. 3 vols. Paris (Libraire Emile Nourry), 1911.
Blanco, Miguel, *Rectificaciones Históricas, Colección de Artículos Escritos por el C. Miguel Blanco*. Mexico (J. S. Ponce de León), 1871.
Bulnes, Francisco, *El Verdadero Díaz y la Revolución*. Mexico (Eusebio Gómez de la Puente), 1920.
————————, *El Verdadero Juárez y la Verdad sobre la Intervención y el Imperio*. Paris, Mexico (Librería de la Vda. de Ch. Bouret), 1904.
Cosmes, Francisco G., *Historia General de Méjico, Continuación á la de Don Niceto Zamacois*. Vols. XIX–XXII. Barcelona, Méjico (Ramón de S. N. Araluce), 1901–1902.
Foster, John W., *Diplomatic Memoirs*. 2 vols. Boston, New York (Houghton Mifflin Company), 1909.
————————, "Porfirio Díaz: Soldier and Statesman," *The International Quarterly*, VIII (December-March, 1902–1903), 342–353.
Frías y Soto, Hilarión, *Juárez Glorificado y la Intervención y el Imperio ante la Verdad Histórica*. Mexico (Imprenta Central), 1905.
Hall, Frederic, *Life of Maximilian I., Late Emperor of Mexico, with a Sketch of the Empress Carlota*. New York (Published by James Miller), 1868.
Iglesias, José María, *Autobiografía del Sr. Lic. D. José M. Iglesias*. Mexico (Antigua Imprenta de E. Murguía), 1893.
————————, *La Cuestión Presidencial en 1876*. Mexico (Tipografía Literaria de Filomeno Mata), 1892.
————————, *Revistas Históricas sobre la Intervención Francesa en México*. 3 vols. Mexico (Imprenta del Gobierno en Palacio), 1867–1869.
Lerdo de Tejada, Miguel M., *Apuntes Históricos de la Heróica Ciudad de Vera-Cruz*. 3 vols. Mexico (Imprenta de Ignacio Cumplido, Imprenta de Vicente García Torres), 1850–1858.

——————, Comercio Esterior de México desde la Conquista hasta Hoy. Mexico (Impreso por Rafael Rafael), 1853.

——————, Cuadro Sinóptico de la República Mexicana en 1856 Formado en Vista de los Últimos Datos Oficiales y Otras Noticias Fidedignas. Mexico (Imprenta de Ignacio Cumplido), 1856.

Moctezuma, Francisco Guerrero, "El Colegio de San Ildefonso en 1847, según un Coleg·al de Entonces," Boletín de la Escuela N. Preparatoria, Número Estraordinario (1909), 22–24.

Munguía, Jesús, Defensa Eclesiástica en el Obispado de Michoacán desde Fines de 1855 hasta Principios de 1858. Vol. I. Mexico (Imprenta de Vicente Segura), 1858.

Navarro, Juan N., "Mexico of Today," The National Geographic Magazine, XII (June, 1901), 235–238.

Ordaz, Emilio, La Cuestión Presidencial. Mexico (Imprenta de Francisco Díaz de León), 1876.

Paradinas, Nicolás, Relación de Méritos y Exercicios Literarios del Doctor Don Ignacio Lerdo de Texada y Matute, Presbítero Domiciliario de México y Capellán Rector del Real Seminario de Minería de la Misma Ciudad. Mexico, November, 1813.

Payno, Manuel, Memoria sobre la Revolución de Diciembre de 1857 y Enero de 1858. Mexico (Imprenta de I. Cumplido), 1860.

Paz, Ireneo. Algunas Campañas, Memorias. 3 vols. Mexico (Imprenta de Ireneo Paz), 2nd ed., 1884–1885.

——————, Porfirio Díaz, 12ª Leyenda Histórica. 2 vols. Mexico (Imprenta y Encuadernación de Ireneo Paz), 1911.

Pérez, Juan E., Almanaque de las Oficinas: Guía de Forasteros para el Año de 1871. Mexico (Imprenta del Gobierno en Palacio), 1871.

Peza, Juan de Dios, Epopeyas de Mi Patria, Memorias. Mexico (J. Ballescá y Cª, Sucesores), 1904.

Pombo, Luis, México: 1876–1892. Mexico (Imprenta de "El Siglo Diez y Nueve"), 1893.

Portilla, Anselmo de la, Méjico en 1856 y 1857, Gobierno del General Comonfort. New York (Imprenta de S. Hallet), 1858.

Prieto, Guillermo, Lecciones de Historia Patria Escritas para los Alumnos del Colegio Militar. Mexico (Oficina Tip. de la Secretaría de Fomento), 3rd ed., 1891.

——————, Memorias de Mis Tiempos 1840 á 1853. Paris, Mexico (Librería de la Vda. de C. Bouret), 1906.

——————, San Francisco in the Seventies: The City as Viewed by a Mexican Political Exile. Trans. and ed. by Edwin S. Morby. San Francisco (Printed by John Henry Nash), 1938.

Pruneda, Pedro, Historia de la Guerra de Méjico desde 1861 á 1867. Madrid (Elizalde y Compañía), 1868.

Quevedo y Zubieta, Salvador, El Caudillo, Continuación de "Porfirio Díaz Ensayo de Psicología Histórica." Paris, Mexico (Librería de la Vda. de C. Bouret), 1909.

[——————], Porfirio Díaz (Septiembre 1830–Septiembre 1865), Ensayo de Psicología Histórica. Paris, Mexico (Librería de la Vda. de C. Bouret), 1906.

Ríos, Enrique M. de los (ed.), Liberales Ilustres Mexicanos de la Reforma y la Intervención. Mexico (Imprenta del "Hijo del Ahuizote"), 1890.

Riva Palacio, Vicente, Historia de la Administración de D. Sebastián Lerdo de Tejada. Mexico (Imprenta y Litografía del Padre Cobos), 1875.

Rivera, Manuel, Historia Antigua y Moderna de Jalapa y de las Revoluciones del Estado de Veracruz. 5 vols. Mexico (Imprenta de I. Cumplido), 1869–1871.

Rivera Cambas, Manuel, *Historia de la Intervención Europea y Norte-Americana en México y del Imperio de Maximiliano de Hapsburgo*. 3 vols. Mexico (Tipografía de Aguilar e Hijos), 1888–1895.

Romero, Matías, *Biografía del Ciudadano Benito Juárez*. Puebla (Imprenta del Gobierno en el Hospicio), 1867.

————————, "The Philosophy of the Mexican Revolutions," *The North American Review*, CLXII (January, 1896), 33–47.

Salm-Salm, Princesa de, *La Princesse Agnes de Salm-Salm au Mexique en 1867, Ses Souvenirs sur la Chute et la Fin de Maximilien 1er*. Ed. by Philippe de Toulza. Paris (Victor Palmé), 1874.

Schofield, Lieutenant-General John M., "The Withdrawal of the French from Mexico," *The Century Illustrated Magazine*, N. S., XXXII (May–October, 1897), 128–137.

Sheridan, P. H., *Personal Memoirs*. 2 vols. New York (Charles L. Webster & Company), 1888.

Sierra, Justo, *Evolución Política del Pueblo Mexicano*. Mexico (Fondo de Cultura Económica), 2nd ed., 1940.

————————, *Juárez Su Obra y Su Tiempo*. Mexico (J. Ballescá y Compañia), 1905–1906.

Stevenson, Sara Yorke, *Maximilian in Mexico: A Woman's Reminiscences of the French Intervention, 1862–1867*. New York (The Century Co.), 1899.

Suárez y Navarro, Juan, *Historia de México y del General Antonio López de Santa-Anna, Comprende los Acontecimientos Políticos Que Han Tenido Lugar en la Nación desde el Año de 1821 hasta 1848*. 2 vols. Mexico (Imprenta de Ignacio Cumplido), 1850–1851.

Turnbull, Enrique A., *El Ejército Federal y la Reelección, Defensa del C. General Alatorre y la Segunda División*. Mexico (Imprento Poliglota de Carlos Ramiro), 1877.

Valenciano de Rhodo, R. G., *D. Sebastián Lerdo de Tejada y la Misión de la América Española*. New York, 1897 (In the Biblioteca de la Secretaría de Hacienda, Mexico, D.F.).

Vérgez, José F., *Recuerdos de Méjico*. Barcelona (Imp. de Henrich y Cª), 1902.

Zamacois, Niceto de, *Historia de Méjico desde Sus Tiempos Más Remotos hasta Nuestros Días*. Vols. XIV–XVIII. Barcelona, Mexico (J. F. Parres y Comp.ª), 1880–1882.

Zayas Enríquez, Rafael de. *Benito Juárez Su Vida—Su Obra*. Mexico (Tipografía de la Viuda de F. Díaz de León), 1906.

————————, *Porfirio Díaz*. Trans. by T. Quincy Browne, Jr. New York (D. Appleton and Company), 1908.

II. SECONDARY WORKS

A. Interviews

Interview of the writer with Juan Antonio Lerdo de Tejada y Sanz, great-nephew of Sebastián Lerdo de Tejada, Mexico, D. F., July 11, August 2, 1947.

Interview of the writer with Miguel Trejo y Lerdo de Tejada, great-grandson of Miguel Lerdo de Tejada, Mexico, D. F., July 23, 1947.

Interview of the writer with Antonio Lerdo de Tejada, great-nephew of Sebastián Lerdo de Tejada, Mexico, D. F., July 9, 1947.

Interview of the writer with the late Father Mariano Cuevas, S.J., Mexican church historian, Mexico, D. F., June 16, 1947.

B. Unpublished Studies

Arrowood, Flora Register, *United States-Mexican Foreign Relations from 1867–1872* (M.A. thesis, The University of Texas Library), 1934.

Caldwell, Maurice Elward, *The War of "La Reforma" in Mexico, 1858–1861* (Ph.D. thesis, The University of Texas Library), 1935.

Roy, Mary Marguerite, *Relations between the United States and Mexico during the Administration of Lerdo de Tejada, 1872–1876* (M.A. thesis, The University of Texas Library), 1933.

Sepúlveda, César, *Breves Notas Biográficas sobre D. Sebastián Lerdo de Tejada* (paper of 21 pp., a copy of which is in the writer's possession). Mexico, October, 1942.

C. General and Special Studies

Acevedo, Javier de P., *Europa y México, 1861–1862.* Habana (Imp. Rambla, Bauza y Ca.), 1935.

Acton, John Emerich Edward Dalberg, First Baron Acton, *Historical Essays & Studies.* Ed. by John Neville Figgis and Reginald Vere Laurence. London (Macmillan and Co., Ltd.), 1908.

Alconedo, Ernesto, *et al., Diez Civiles Notables de la Historia Patria.* Mexico (Secretaría de Instrucción Pública y Bellas Artes), 1914.

"Algunos Gregorianos Ilustres," *Boletín Oficial* (Mexico), XIV, April 29, 1910.

Arosemena, Justo, *Estudios Constitucionales sobre los Gobiernos de la América Latina.* Vol. II. Paris (A. Roger y F. Chernoviz), new ed., 1888.

Bancroft, Hubert Howe, *History of Mexico.* Vols. V–VI. San Francisco (The History Company), 1885–1888.

—————, *Vida de Porfirio Díaz, Reseña Histórica y Social del Pasado y Presente de México.* San Francisco (The History Company), 1887.

Bannon, John Francis, S. J., and Dunne, Peter Masten, S. J., *Latin America, An Historical Survey.* Milwaukee (The Bruce Publishing Company), 1947.

Bemis, Samuel Flagg (ed.), *The American Secretaries of State and Their Diplomacy.* Vol. VIII. New York (Alfred A. Knopf), 1928.

Bravo Ugarte, José, *Historia de México.* Vol. III. Mexico (Jus, Revista de Derecho y Ciencias Sociales), 1944.

Brinton, Crane, *The Anatomy of Revolution.* New York (W. W. Norton & Company), 1938.

Burke, Ulick Ralph, *A Life of Benito Juárez, Constitutional President of Mexico.* London (Remington and Co., Ltd.), 1894.

Bustos, José M., *Biografía del R. P. José Soler de la Compañía de Jesús.* Mexico (Antigua Imprenta de Murguía), 1910.

Calderón, Fernando Yglesias, *Rectificaciones Históricas, El Egoismo Norte-Americano durante la Intervención Francesa.* Mexico ("Imprenta Económica"), 1905.

→Callahan, James Morton, *American Foreign Policy in Mexican Relations.* New York (The Macmillan Company), 1932.

—————, "The Mexican Policy of Southern Leaders under Buchanan's Administration," *Annual Report of the American Historical Association for the Year 1910,* 135–151.

Callcott, Wilfrid Hardy, *Liberalism in Mexico 1857–1929.* Stanford University, California (Stanford University Press), 1931.

—————, *Santa Anna, The Story of an Enigma Who Once was Mexico.* Norman (University of Oklahoma Press), 1936.

Ceballos, Ciro B., *Aurora y Ocaso.* Mexico (Imprenta Central), 1907.

Chynoweth, W. Harris, *The Fall of Maximilian, Late Emperor of Mexico.* London (Published by the author), 1872.

Corti, Count Egon Caesar, *Maximilian and Charlotte of Mexico.* Trans. from the German by Catherine Alison Phillips. 2 vols. New York, London (Alfred A. Knopf), 1928.

Cuevas, P. Mariano, S. J., *Historia de la Iglesia en México*. Vol. V. El Paso (Editorial "Revista Católica"), 1928.

Decorme, P. Gerardo, S. J., *Historia de la Compañía de Jesús en la República Mexicana durante el Siglo XIX*. Vol. I. Guadalajara (Tip. "El Regional"), 1914.

Denhardt, Robert, "Mexican Demography," *The Pacific Historical Review*, VII (March, 1938), 147–159.

Divulgación Histórica, IV (April 15, 1943). (Frontispiece cited.)

Dumke, Glenn S., "Across Mexico in '49," *The Pacific Historical Review*, XVIII (February, 1944), 33–44.

Duniway, Clyde Augustus, "Reasons for the Withdrawal of the French from Mexico," *Annual Report of the American Historical Association for the Year 1902*, I, 315–328.

Fernández·Ledesma, Enrique, *Galería de Fantasmas, Años y Sombras del Siglo XIX*. Mexico (Editorial México Nuevo), 1939.

Fitzgibbon, Russell H., "Glossary of Latin-American Constitutional Terms," *The Hispanic American Historical Review*, XXVII (August, 1947), 574–590.

Foix, Pere, *Juárez*. Mexico (Ediciones Ibero Americanas), 1949.

Foster, John W., "The Contest for the Laws of Reform in Mexico," *The American Historical Review*, XV (October, 1909–July, 1910), 526–546.

Frazer, Robert W., "The Ochoa Bond Negotiations of 1865–1867," *The Pacific Historical Review*, XI (December, 1942), 397–414.

————, "The United States, European, and West Virginia Land Company," *The Pacific Historical Review*, XIII (March, 1944), 28–40.

Galindo y Galindo, Miguel, *La Gran Década Nacional, ó Relación Histórica de la Guerra de Reforma, Intervención Extranjera y Gobierno del Archiduque Maximiliano, 1857–1867*. 3 vols. Mexico (Imprenta y Fototipia de la Secretaría de Fomento), 1904–1906.

García Granados, Ricardo, *La Constitución de 1857 y las Leyes de Reforma en México, Estudio Histórico-Sociológico*. Mexico (Tipografía Económica), 1906.

————, *Historia de México desde la Restauración de la República en 1867 hasta la Caída de Porfirio Díaz*. 4 vols. Mexico (Librería Editorial de Andrés Botas e Hijo), ?—1928.

————, *Por Qué y Como Cayó Porfirio Díaz*. Mexico (Andrés Botas e Hijo, Sucr.), 1928.

García Naranjo, Nemesio, *Porfirio Díaz*. San Antonio (Casa Editorial Lozano), 1930.

Gómez Haro, Enrique, "¿Qué Frutas Ha Dado el Seminario Palafoxiano de Puebla?" *Palafoxianum* (Puebla, February-March, 1944).

González Navarro, Moisés, *Vallarta y Su Ambiente Político Jurídico*. Mexico (Junta Mexicana de Investigaciones Históricas), 1949.

Gualot, Paul, *La Vérité sur L'Expédition du Mexique d'après les Documents Inédits de Ernest Louet, Payeur en Chef du Corps Expéditionnaire*. Vol. II, *L'Empire de Maximilien*. Vol. III, *Fin d'Empire*. Paris (Paul Ollendorff), 2nd ed., 1890.

Hackett, Charles W., "The Recognition of the Díaz Government by the United States," *The Southwestern Historical Quarterly*, XXVIII (July, 1924), 34–55.

Hannay, David, *Díaz*. London (Constable & Company, Ltd.), 1917.

Harding, Bertita, *Phantom Crown: The Story of Maximilian & Carlota of Mexico*. New York (The Bobbs-Merrill Company), 1934.

Hernández, Fortunato, *Un Pueblo, un Siglo y un Hombre (1810–1910), Ensayo Histórico*. Mexico (Imprenta de Ignacio Escalante), 1909.

Hyde, Montgomery, *Mexican Empire: The History of Maximilian and Carlota of Mexico*. London (Macmillan & Co., Ltd.), 1946.
Johnson, Richard A., "Spanish-Mexican Diplomatic Relat ons, 1853–1855," *The Hispanic American Historical Review*, XXI (November, 1941), 559–576.
Leal, José Román, *México Constitucional*. Mexico (Imprenta de M na y Vilaseca), 1886.
Lester, C. Edwards, *The Mexican Republic, An Historic Study*. New York (The American News Company), 1878.
Lewis, William Roy, "The Hayes Administrat on and Mexico," *The Southwestern Historical Quarterly*, XXIV (October, 1920), 140–153.
McCaleb, Walter Flavius, *The Public Finances of Mexico*. New York, London (Harper and Brothers), 1921.
Macedo, Pablo, *La Evolución Mercantil, Communicaciones y Obras Públicas, la Hacienda Pública: Tres Monografías Que Dan Idea de una Parte de la Evolución Económica de México*. Mexico (J. Ballescá y Cª, Sucesores), 1905.
Magner, James A., *Men of Mexico*. Milwaukee (The Bruce Publishing Company), 1942.
María y Campos, Armando de, *La Dramática Mexicana durante el Gobierno del Presidente Lerdo de Tejada*. Mexico (Compañía de Ediciones Populares, S.A.), 1946.
Masseras, E., *Un Essai d'Empire au Mexique*. Paris (G. Charpentier), 1879.
Mecham, J. Lloyd, *Church and State in Latin America: A History of Politico-Ecclesiastical Relations*. Chapel Hill (University of North Carolina Press), 1934.
————————, "The Origins of Federalism in Mexico," *The Hispanic American Historical Review*, XVIII (May, 1938), 164–182.
Memorias Inéditas del Lic. Don Sebastián Lerdo de Tejada. Brownsville (Imp. de "El Porvenir"), Novísima Edición, 1910–1912 (Apocryphal).
Miranda y Marrón, M., "El Colegio de San Ildefonso de 1848 á 1867," *Boletín de la Escuela Nacional Preparatoria*, II (December, 1909–January, 1910), 116–132.
Molina Enríquez, Andrés, *Los Grandes Problemas Nacionales*. Mexico (Imprenta de A. Carranza e Hijos), 1909.
Musser, John, *The Establishment of Maximilian's Empire in Mexico*. Un versity of Pennsylvania (The Collegiate Press, George Banta Publishing Company), 1918.
Negrete, Doroteo, *La Verdad ante la Figura Militar de Don Miguel Negrete*. Puebla ("La Enseñanza," S.A.), 1935.
Nuñez y Domínguez, José de J., *Martí en México*. Mexico (Imprenta de la Secretaría de Relaciones Exteriores), 1934.
Olivo Lara, Margarita, "Biografías de Veracruzanos Distinguidos," *Anales del Museo Nacional de Arqueología, Historia y Etnografía*, VI, Cuarta Época (1929), 68–400.
Ollivier, Emile, *L'Empire Libéral, Études, Récits, Souvenirs*. Vol. IX. Paris (Garnier Frères), 2nd ed., 1904.
Ortega y Pérez Gallardo, Ricardo, *Historia Genealógica de las Familias Más Antiguas de México*. Vol. III. Mexico (Imprenta de A. Carranza e Hijos), 1910.
Osores, Félix, *Noticias Bio Bibliográficas de Alumnos Distinguidos del Colegio de San Pedro, San Pablo y San Ildefonso de México*. Vol. XIX of Genaro García (ed.), *Documentos Inéditos ó Muy Raros para la Historia de México*. Mexico (Librería de la Vda. de Ch. Bouret), 1908.

"Our Diplomacy during the Rebellion," *The North American Review*, CII (April, 1866), 446–472.

"Our Mexican Troubles," *The Nation*, XXV (December 27, 1877), 391–392.

Owsley, Frank Lawrence, *King Cotton Diplomacy: Foreign Relations of the Confederate States of America.* Chicago (The University of Chicago Press), 1931.

Parada Gay, Francisco, *Breve Reseña de la Suprema Corte de Justicia de la Nación.* Mexico (Antigua Imprenta de Murguía), 1929.

Parra, Porfirio, *Estudio Histórico-Sociológico sobre la Reforma en México.* Guadalajara (Imp. de "La Gaceta de Guadalajara"), 1906.

Paz, Ireneo (ed.), *Los Hombres Prominentes de México.* Mexico (Imprenta y Litografía de "La Patria"), 1888.

Paz, Octavo (ed.), *Album a Juárez.* Mexico (Imprenta Mundial), 1931.

Pereyra, Carlos, *México Falsificado.* 2 vols. Mexico (Editorial Polis), 1949.

Pérez Verdía, Luis, *Compendio de la Historia de México desde sus Primeros Tiempos hasta los Últimos Años del Gobierno del General Díaz.* Guadalajara (Librería y Casa Editorial Font, S.A.), 8th ed., 1942.

——————, *Historia Particular del Estado de Jalisco desde los Primeros Tiempos de Que Hay Noticia hasta Nuestros Días.* Vol. III. Guadalajara (Tip. de la Escuela de Artes y Oficios del Estado), 1911.

Perkins, Dexter, *The Monroe Doctrine, 1826–1867.* Baltimore (The Johns Hopkins Press), 1933.

Phipps, Helen, *Some Aspects of the Agrarian Question in Mexico: A Historical Study.* University of Texas Bulletin, No. 2515 (Studies in History, No. 2). Austin (The University of Texas Press), 1925.

Planchet, Regis, *La Cuestión Religiosa en México.* El Paso (Editorial Revista Católica), 3rd ed., 1927.

Podan, Mateo, *Porfirio Díaz Debe y Haber, Estado del Activo y del Pasivo Históricos del Famoso Estadista y Caudillo Mexicano.* Mexico (Andrés Botas, Ediciones Botas), 1944.

Powell, Fred Wilbur, *The Railroads of Mexico.* Boston (The Stratford Co.), 1921.

"The President of Mexico," *The Eclectic Magazine of Foreign Literature*, LX (November, 1863), 369–373.

Prida, Ramón, *De la Dictadura a la Anarquía, Apuntes para la Historia Política de México durante los Últimos Cuarenta y Tres Años.* 2 vols. El Paso (Imprenta de "El Paso del Norte"), 1914.

Prida Santacilia, Pablo, *Siguiendo la Vida de Juárez.* Mexico (Ediciones Palafox), 1945.

Priestley, Herbert Ingram, *The Mexican Nation, A History.* New York (The Macmillan Company), 1938.

Quiroz y Gutiérrez, Nicanor, *Historia del Seminario Palafoxiano de Puebla, 1644–1944.* Puebla (Ediciones "Palafox"), 1947.

Rabasa, Emilio, *La Organización Política de México, la Constitución y la Dictadura.* Madrid (Editorial-America, Sociedad Española de Librería), 1917(?).

Reyes, Rodolfo, *Benito Juárez, Ensayo sobre un Carácter.* .Madrid (Ediciones Nuestra Raza), 1935.

Ribot, Hector, *Las Últimas Revoluciones.* Mexico (Imprenta 1a de Humboldt), 2nd ed., 1910–1911.

Rippy, James Fred, *The United States and Mexico.* New York (F. S. Crofts and Co.), rev. ed., 1931.

Riva Palacio, Vicente (ed.), *México á Través de los Siglos.* Vols. IV, V. Mexico, Barcelona (Ballescá y Comp.a, Espasa y Comp.a), no date.

Robertson, William Spence, "The Tripartite Treaty of London," *The Hispanic American Historical Review*, XX (May, 1940), 167–189.

Rocha, José, *Galería de los Hombres Ilustres del Estado de Guanajuato*. Vol. I. León (Imprenta de E. Randolph), 1899.

Roeder, Ralph, *Juárez and His Mexico, A Biographical History*. New York (The Viking Press), 1947.

Ruíz, Eduardo, *Biografía del Ciudadano Melchor Ocampo*. Mexico (Tip., Lit. y Encuadernación de I. Paz), 1893.

Salado Álvarez, Victoriano, *Memorias*. Vol. I, *Tiempo Viejo*. Mexico (Edición y Distribución Ibero Americano de Publicaciones), 1946.

Scholes, Walter V., "*El Mensajero* and the Election of 1871 in Mexico," *The Americas*, V (July, 1948), 61–67.

Sierra, Justo (ed.), *México Su Evolución Social*. 2 vols. Mexico (J. Ballescá y Compañía, Sucesor), 1900–1901.

Silva Herzog, Jesús, *El Pensamiento Económico en México*. Mexico (Fondo de Cultura Económica), 1947.

Simpson, Lesley Byrd, Review of José C. Valadés, *El Porfirismo, Historia de un Régimen: El Nacimiento*, in *The Hispanic American Historical Review*, XXII (February, 1942), 116–122.

Sonolet, Louis, "L'Agonie de L'Empire du Mexique d'après des Lettres et des Notes Inédites du Général Castelnau," *La Revue de Paris*, IV (July-August, 1927), 590–625, 862–898.

Teja Zabre, Alfonso, *Guide to the History of Mexico, A Modern Interpretation*. Mexico (Press of the Ministry of Foreign Affairs), 1935.

Toro, Alfonso, *La Iglesia y el Estado en México, Estudio sobre los Conflictos entre el Clero Católico y los Gobiernos Mexicanos desde la Independencia hasta Nuestros Días*. Mexico (Publicaciones del Archivo General de la Nación), 1931.

Torrea, Juan Manuel, "Sebastián Lerdo de Tejada," *Memoria de la Academia Nacional de Historia y Geografía*, No. 2 (Mexico, 1946), 28–50.

Turlington, Edgar, *Mexico and Her Foreign Creditors*. New York (Columbia University Press), 1930.

Valadés, José C., *El Porfirismo, Historia de un Régimen: El Nacimiento*. Mexico (Antigua Librería Robredo de José Porrua e Hijos), 1941.

Valle-Arizpe, Artemio de, *Historia de la Ciudad de México según los Relatos de Sus Cronistas*. Mexico (Editorial Pedro Robredo), 1939.

Vázquez Santa Ana, Higinio, *Bosquejos Biográficos de Hombres Illustres Nacionales*. Mexico (Secretaría de Gobernación), 1920.

Villaseñor y Villaseñor, Alejandro, *Obras del Lic. Alejandro Villaseñor y Villaseñor*. 2 vols. Mexico (Imp. de V. Agüeros), 1897–1906.

Viramontes, Leonardo S., *Biografía Popular del Benemérito de América Benito Juárez*. Mexico (Tipografía de la Viuda de F. Díaz de León), 1906.

Webb, Walter Prescott, *The Texas Rangers, A Century of Frontier Defense*. Boston, New York (Houghton, Mifflin Company), 1935.

Zea, Leopoldo, *El Positivismo en México*. Mexico (Fondo de Cultura Económica), 1943.

INDEX